# Understanding Global Security

Fully revised to incorporate recent developments, this third edition of *Understanding Global Security* analyses the variety of ways in which people's lives are threatened and/or secured in contemporary global politics. The traditional focus of Security Studies texts: war, deterrence and terrorism, are analysed alongside non-military security issues such as famine, crime, disease, disasters, environmental degradation and human rights abuses to provide a comprehensive survey of how and why people are killed in the contemporary world.

New to this edition:

- Greater coverage of the evolving theoretical literature on security, including more analysis of critical theory perspectives and emerging schools of thought.
- A revamp of the sections examining the causes of inter-state war and counter-terrorism strategies.
- Analysis of key recent developments including the global economic recession, Haiti earthquake of 2010 and Fukushima nuclear disaster of 2011.
- New quantitative analysis of the impact of global crime and environmental change.
- Greater evaluation of the divergences in how human security is interpreted and the future prospects for this way of thinking and acting in international relations.

User-friendly and easy to follow, this textbook is designed to make a complex subject accessible to all. Key features include:

- **'Top ten' tables** highlighting the most destructive events or forms of death in those areas throughout history.
- **Boxed descriptions** elaborating key concepts in the fields of security and International Relations.

- **'Biographical boxes'** of key individuals who have shaped security politics.
- **Further reading and websites** at the end of each chapter guiding you towards classic texts and the most up-to-date information on the various topics.
- **Glossary** of political terminology.

This highly acclaimed and popular academic text will continue to be essential reading for everyone interested in security.

**Peter Hough** lectures in International Relations and heads up this subject at Middlesex University, UK.

# Understanding Global Security

## 3rd edition

**Peter Hough**

Routledge
Taylor & Francis Group

LONDON AND NEW YORK

First published 2004
Second edition, 2008
Third edition, 2013
by Routledge
2 Park Square, Milton Park, Abingdon, Oxon, OX14 4RN

Simultaneously published in the USA and Canada
by Routledge
711 Third Avenue, New York, NY 10017

Routledge is an imprint of the Taylor and Francis Group, an informa
business

British Library Cataloguing in Publication Data
A catalogue record for this book is available from the British Library

*Library of Congress Cataloging in Publication Data*
Hough, Peter, 1967–
Understanding global security / Peter Hough. — Third edition.
pages cm
Includes bibliographical references and index.
1. Security, International. I. Title.
JZ5595.H68 2013
355'.033—dc23
2012048393

ISBN: 978-0-415-68839-0 (hbk)
ISBN: 978-0-415-68840-6 (pbk)
ISBN: 978-0-203-79821-8 (ebk)

Typeset in Century Old Style
by Florence Production Ltd, Stoodleigh, Devon, UK

Printed and bound in the United States of America by Publishers Graphics,
LLC on sustainably sourced paper.

Printed and bound in Great Britain by
TJ International Ltd, Padstow, Cornwall

For Daisy and Rosie

# Contents

CONTENTS

# CONTENTS

# Figures, boxes and tables

## Figures

## Boxes

## Tables

# Acknowledgements

The idea for the first edition of this book arose out of a general discussion with editorial staff from Routledge and I must thank them, and in particular Craig Fowlie, for putting their faith in me and for marketing the book so well that it has now gone to a third edition.

Many people have helped in the process of developing this work through three editions over the past ten years by offering advice and/or support, including the following: Mohammed Al-Amin; Tunç Aybak; June Burnham; Heather Deegan; Paula Dunbar from the National Oceanic and Atmospheric Administration of the US government; Andy Frary; Roy and Sandra Hough; Dave Humphreys; Angela and Paul Lambillion; Kate McGee of the World Health Organization's Department of Injuries and Violence Prevention; Lloyd Pettiford; Norman and Frances Say; Jeroen Warner; Lindsey Wright; and Peter Willetts.

Numerous seminar discussions with students (too many to name) have also informed my thinking on many of the topics covered in the book. Finally, I must thank Lisa, Daisy and Rosie for their patience, support and inspiration.

# Acronyms

| | |
|---|---|
| AAA | American Anthropological Association |
| AIDS | acquired immune deficiency syndrome |
| ANC | African National Congress |
| ARN | Armed Revolutionary Nuclei |
| ASEAN | Association of South East Asian Nations |
| AU | African Union |
| CAFOD | Catholic Agency for Overseas Development |
| CCPCJ | Commission on Crime Prevention and Criminal Justice (UN) |
| CEDAW | Convention on the Elimination of all forms of Discrimination Against Women |
| CERD | Convention on the Elimination of all forms of Racial Discrimination |
| CFCs | chloro-fluoro-carbons |
| CIA | Central Intelligence Agency (USA) |
| CICP | Centre for International Crime Prevention (UN) |
| CJD | Creutzfeld-Jakob disease |
| CND | Commission on Narcotic Drugs (UN) |
| CTBT | Comprehensive Test Ban Treaty |
| DDT | dichloro-diphenyl-trichloroethane |
| EADRCC | Euro-Atlantic Disaster Response Coordination Centre (NATO) |
| EAPC | Euro-Atlantic Partnership Council |
| EC | European Community |
| ECA | Earth Crossing Asteroid |
| ECOSOC | Economic and Social Council (UN) |
| ECOWAS | Economic Community of West African States |
| EEZ | Exclusive Economic Zone |
| EFTA | European Free Trade Association |

| | |
|---|---|
| ETA | Basque Fatherland and Liberty |
| EU | European Union |
| FAO | Food and Agricultural Organization |
| FARC | Revolutionary Armed Forces of Colombia |
| FIFA | International Federation of Association Football |
| GAVI | Global Alliance for Vaccines and Immunization |
| GDP | gross domestic product |
| GHS | Globally Harmonized System of Classification and Labelling of Chemicals |
| GOARN | Global Outlook and Alert Response Network |
| GPEF | Global Programme to Eliminate Filariasis |
| GPHIN | Global Public Health Intelligence Network |
| GPPPs | global public–private partnerships |
| HDI | Human Development Index |
| HIV | human immunodeficiency virus |
| HNP | Health, Nutrition and Population Division (World Bank) |
| HOLN | Health Organization of the League of Nations |
| ICC | International Criminal Court |
| ICFTU | International Confederation of Free Trade Unions |
| ICIDI | Independent Commission on International Development Issues |
| ICJ | International Court of Justice |
| IDNDR | International Decade for Natural Disaster Reduction |
| IGO | intergovernmental organization |
| IHR | International Health Regulation (WHO) |
| ILC | International Labour Conference |
| ILC | International Law Commission (UN) |
| IMF | International Monetary Fund |
| INCB | International Narcotics Control Board |
| INGO | international non-governmental organization |
| IO | international organization |
| IPE | International Political Economy |
| IR | International Relations |
| IRA | Irish Republican Army |
| ISDR | International Strategy for Disaster Reduction |
| LDC | less developed country |
| LIEO | Liberal International Economic Order |
| LRA | Lord's Resistance Army |
| MAD | Mutually Assured Destruction |
| MARS | Major Accident Reporting System (EU) |
| MDG | Millennium Development Goal |
| MIC | methyl-isocyanate |
| MNC | multi-national corporation |
| MRTA | Tupac Amaru Revolutionary Movement |
| MSF | Médecins Sans Frontières |
| NAALC | North American Agreement on Labor Cooperation |
| NAFTA | North American Free Trade Agreement |
| NAM | Non-aligned Movement |

| | |
|---|---|
| NATO | North Atlantic Treaty Organization |
| NCB | National Crime Bureau |
| NEO | Near Earth Object |
| NIC | National Intelligence Council (USA) |
| NIEO | New International Economic Order |
| NPT | Non-Proliferation Treaty (nuclear weapons) |
| OAS | Organization of American States |
| OECD | Organisation for Economic Co-operation and Development |
| OIHP | L'Office Internationale d'Hygiene Publique |
| OPEC | Organization of Petroleum Exporting Countries |
| OSCE | Organization for Security and Co-operation in Europe |
| PCIJ | Permanent Court of International Justice |
| PHARE | Poland and Hungary Aid for Economic Reconstruction |
| PKK | Kurdish Workers Party |
| PLO | Palestinian Liberation Organization |
| POPs | persistent organic pollutants |
| PSC | private security company |
| SALT | Strategic Arms Limitation Talks |
| SARS | severe acute respiratory syndrome |
| SAS | Special Air Service |
| SDI | Space Defence Initiative |
| SIPRI | Stockholm International Peace Research Institute |
| SORT | Strategic Offensive Reduction Talks |
| START | Strategic Arms Reduction Talks |
| TCP | trichlorophenol |
| TEEB | The Economics of Ecosystems and Biodiversity |
| UN | United Nations |
| UNCED | United Nations Conference on the Environment and Development |
| UNCHE | United Nations Conference on the Human Environment |
| UNCLOS | United Nations Conference on the Law of the Sea |
| UNDCP | United Nations International Drug Control Programme |
| UNDP | United Nations Development Programme |
| UNEP | United Nations Environment Programme |
| UNESCO | United Nations Educational, Scientific and Cultural Organization |
| UNFPA | United Nations Population Fund |
| UNICEF | United Nations Children's Fund |
| UNITA | National Union for the Total Independence of Angola |
| UN-OCHA | United Nations Office for the Coordination of Humanitarian Affairs |
| UNODC | United Nations Office on Drugs and Crime |
| UNRRA | United Nations Relief and Rehabilitation Administration |
| WFP | World Food Programme |
| WHO | World Health Organization |
| WMD | weapons of mass destruction |
| WSSD | World Summit on Sustainable Development |

# Security and securitization

> . . . only freedom can make security secure.
>
> Karl Popper (Popper 1966: 130)

## Defining security

### Security Studies

The study of security in the global context is a sub-discipline of the wider subject usually still referred to as *International Relations*. International Relations is the study of all political interactions between international 'actors', which include: states (represented by governments), international organizations (either inter-governmental or non-governmental[1]) and, to a lesser extent, some wealthy, private individuals. Security Studies concerns itself with a sub-set of those political interactions marked by their particular importance in terms of maintaining the security of the actors and people. Where the line demarking International Relations' sub-discipline is to be drawn is increasingly contentious, as indeed is the demarcation of International Relations in relation to the wider realm of Political Science. Increased political interaction between actors, other than through the traditional state-to-state route, has served to blur the distinction between domestic and foreign policy and widened the scope of International Relations. The process commonly referred to as globalization has led to internal political issues becoming increasingly externalized and external political issues increasingly internalized. Traditionally domestic policy concerns, like health and rights, are more prominent than ever on the global political agenda and events occurring in other states, such as disasters or massacres, are more often than ever deemed to be of political significance for people not personally affected. In light of these changes, and the reduced prevalence of inter-state war, it has become a matter of contention amongst theorists of International Relations whether Security Studies should maintain its traditional emphasis on military threats to the security of states or widen its focus. Alternative perspectives have argued increasingly that the discipline should either: (1) extend its reach to include non-military threats to states and, perhaps, other actors; or (2) go further and bring within its remit the security of all actors in relation to a range of threats, both military and non-military.

The main *paradigms* of International Relations offer alternative conceptual frameworks for comprehending the complexity that emerges from attempting to study the huge volume of interactions between actors that makes up the contemporary global system. These different 'lenses' for making sense of this political complexity focus in very different ways when it comes to thinking about issues of security in International Relations.

### Realism

Realists are the traditionalists in International Relations and Security Studies and still the dominant paradigm, both academically and in terms of the 'real world' as the approach favoured by governments in conducting their foreign policies. Classical Realism emerged in the 1940s and dominated the young discipline of International Relations with a straightforward and almost unchallenged view of how and why politics on the world stage was conducted. The 'actors' were states. Intergovernmental organizations (IGOs) were merely alliances of convenience between states whilst international non-governmental organizations (INGOs) were considered irrelevant (and indeed, by comparison with today, were so at the time). Hence the world, in political terms, was a state system. The interactions between the states in the system could be characterized as 'power politics'. A pessimistic view of human nature permeates Realism meaning that, on the world stage, it is assumed that states should not trust other states and therefore seek to 'look after number one' by extending their own power wherever possible in order to secure themselves.

This promotion of the self-interest of states is captured in the term 'national interest' (see Box 1.1). For Realists, governments making a clear distinction between 'high' and 'low' politics in their policy-making best serve the national interest. Individual concerns with health, welfare and other 'low politics' issues are the stuff of domestic politics and need to be kept separate from the 'high politics' of state security. This approach was justified on the premise that failing to deter or losing a war would undermine the satisfaction of low politics aspirations. Individual interests were inextricably tied up in the national interest. Hence in the UK in the late 1940s society tolerated food rationing whilst the government poured the country's shrunken exchequer into developing atomic weapons. Individual hardship was considered a price worth paying to avert the potentially catastrophic hardship of failing to deter invasion from the Soviet Union.

The conundrum that emerges from assuming that a state's security is achieved by its pursuing the maximization of its own power is that all states cannot simultaneously follow this prescription. The security of one's own state is likely to be enhanced at the expense of another state in what has been termed the *security dilemma*. For Realists the security dilemma is averted by their faith in the *balance of power*. The balance of power keeps a sense of order to the 'anarchy' of the state system as there is a mutual interest for the most powerful amongst them to work together and preserve the status quo. The security of the most powerful states rests on not allowing any one of them tipping the balance by becoming too powerful. For classical Realists, then, Security Studies was pretty much synonymous with International Relations.

The rise in significance of economic interactions between states in the 1960s and 1970s broadened the focus of International Relations beyond military power politics to incorporate economic power issues. Realist thought metamorphosized into 'Neo-Realism', which maintained the focus on states and the pursuit of power but accepted that not everything that happens in the world is determined by military might. States could become powerful by concentrating on their economies (such as West Germany and Japan), being lucky enough to possess a key economic resource (such as the oil-producing states) or by exerting diplomatic influence in the world without the resort to arms or threat of armed action. In light of this a new sub-discipline of International Relations emerged considering such matters, *International Political Economy (IPE)*. For (Neo-)Realists then, Security Studies became the military arm of International Relations and IPE its economic sister.

> ## Box 1.1 The national interest
>
> The idea of the national interest being pursued in foreign policy was central to the development of Realism in the post-Second World War years and continues to be very influential in both academic circles and in governments. The term seeks to encapsulate the point that governments need to act according to the interests of their own people even if this conflicts with the interests of other states and peoples. Hence the term tends to be employed by politicians when seeking to offer a justification for a policy considered by some to be immoral, such as a lucrative arms deal with a government known to oppress its population. Morgenthau brought the concept to prominence, stating that the fundamental aim of foreign policy must be to ensure: 'the integrity of the nation's territory, of its political institutions and of its culture' (Morgenthau 1982: 973). In a world of self-serving states this was best pursued by policies which seek to maintain or increase the power of the state.
>
> The amorality of national interest is criticized by those who consider that morality can and should inform foreign policy just as it does in domestic policy. Additionally, the concept presupposes that sovereignty is the ultimate of all political goals which does not accord with the European experience, where it has been concluded by a number of governments that the voluntary 'pooling of sovereignty' is in the best interest of their administrations and their peoples. Defining what is and is not the best interests of a state is also far from straightforward given the range of options open to governments in conducting their foreign affairs. Morgenthau and fellow arch-Realist the US Foreign Minister Henry Kissinger famously argued over whether the war in Vietnam was in the US national interest.
>
> In defence of the concept of national interest, for all its analytical shortcomings, it cannot be denied that many governments today do continue to use it as a basis for the conduct of their foreign policy. The Foreign Minister of Australia, in a 2002 speech in advance of the publication of a government paper 'Advancing the National Interest' states that: 'The Government has ensured that Australia's national interest is advanced in an ambitious yet pragmatic and clear-minded fashion. Because if we don't . . . no one else will' (Downer 2002).

## Pluralism

Pluralism emerged as a paradigm of International Relations from the 1960s, made up of scholars unconvinced that Neo-Realism had evolved far enough from Realism to take account of the changes that had occurred in the world since the 1940s. It began to be argued that adding the pursuit of economic power to the pursuit of military power by states was still too simplistic an understanding of world politics. Pluralists, as the term implies, consider that a plurality of actors, rather than just states, exert influence on the world stage. State dominance of international relations was being eroded from above and below, the Pluralists contended. IGOs (such as the European Community and organizations of the United Nations) had become more than expedient alliances and come to mould state policies together into common interests which sometimes redefined or contradicted 'national' interests. INGOs, such as pressure groups and multi-national corporations (MNCs), were becoming significant players on the world stage in their own right and were not necessarily acting in accord with their 'home' government. In addition, Pluralists built on the political philosophy of Liberalism to argue that the amorality of the national interest was not an appropriate guide to foreign policy. Individual people prosper from the mutual benefits inherent in cooperation and would find their interests better served in a world in which states and their interests, as defined by their governments, ceased to dictate their lives.

For Pluralists these developments were making the interactions of politics in the world more complex and varied. 'Low' politics issues, such as environmental change or economic development, were becoming international as well as domestic political issues. International Relations could no longer assume all that happens in the world was related to a military – or even an economic – balance of power between states. This aspect of international affairs was important but not all-subsuming and an issue-based approach was necessary. This approach accepts that many non-military issues are legitimate concerns of International Relations and that they might be contended over without reference to military power on an increasingly busy world stage.

For Pluralists then, Security Studies was but a small sub-set of the broad subject that is International Relations.

## Marxism

The Marxist paradigm of International Relations is related to but not synonymous with Marxist political thought. Proponents of the Marxist paradigm of International Relations are usually also *ideological* Marxists, but not necessarily so and, in political practice, Marxist governments have usually pursued foreign policies broadly Realist in character. For such Marxist, or *Structuralist*, thinkers the Neo-Realist and Pluralist conversion to appreciating the importance of economic factors in the conduct of politics in the world was both belated and insufficient. Economic concerns, rather than military or issue-specific power, determine the fate of the world's peoples and always have done. In this view globalization is nothing new; it is merely the latest phase of the world's 'haves' exploiting the 'have nots'. Imperialism is not a relic of a bygone age but a persistent feature of a global system built on the capitalist logic of ever-increasing profit. From a Marxist perspective inter-state competition is a side show to the 'competition' between the wealthy peoples of the world (most of the developed world and a small fraction of elites in the less-developed world) and the poor, in which there is consistently only one winner.

Marxists thus see International Relations as largely synonymous with IPE. Security Studies, as it has evolved, is superfluous since human and global security can only ever come through global, structural change. Military strategy serves global economic interests rather than national security interests. Wars are fought to preserve or maintain exploitative economic systems (i.e. over colonies or over the economic mastery of the whole system, like the Cold War). In this view the fates of individuals are determined not so much by their states but by the wider global system and only world Socialist revolution could improve their prospects.

## 'Reflective theories' and Social Constructivism

In the 1990s dissatisfaction with the three main paradigms of International Relations (IR), and their myriad offshoots and hybrid theories, produced a range of theoretical challenges influenced by a new wave of postmodernist thinking on *methodology* (how you study a subject). The 'scientific method' – seeking to understand the behaviour of states by the objective testing of theories and concepts – came to be questioned by a new breed of IR scholars. *Critical Theorists*, such as Booth and Wyn Jones, questioned the premise that studying human behaviour can ever be objective and scientific and that the study of IR inevitably reflected a Western bias (Booth 1991; Wyn Jones 1999). In a similar vein feminist scholars, such as Tickner and Enloe, came to argue that IR had an inherent male bias and that concepts like sovereignty and power were in need of re-appraisal in order to achieve an understanding of the political world based on all of its people (Tickner 1992; Enloe 1990). From these 'reflective theories' a fourth paradigm of International Relations known as Social Constructivism emerged. Changes in the 'real world' of international relations as well as in thinking on how to study it also stimulated the new theories. The way in which the Cold War ended and the panning out of the 'New World Order' which followed, prompted a number of scholars to challenge many of the assumptions of the discipline across the paradigms. In particular, Social Constructivism argued that understanding political events in the world necessitated more introspection and less grand abstract theorizing. The paradigm favours a more sociological approach and advocates a greater appreciation of the cultural dimension of policy-making. It began to be argued that maybe the actors on the world stage do not really follow any kind of rational script, be it written in the language of self-interest, mutual interest or dictated by economic circumstance. Perhaps, at least some of the time, foreign policy reflects parochial ideological or moral guidelines rather than objective gains. By the 1990s Ruggie, a lifelong Pluralist, contended that that paradigm and Neo-Realism had come to share so much common ground, in assuming states to be rational gain-driven actors (only differing in **how** they gain), that they should henceforth be considered as a single paradigm of 'neo-utilitarianism' (Ruggie 1998: 1–39).

The USSR's voluntary 'defeat' in the Cold War, when Gorbachev negotiated a 'surrender' with the enemy for what he considered to be the good of his country, appeared to defy the logic of Realism and the national interest.[2] In the proceeding years the reluctance of the newly reunified Germany to use its enhanced physique to exert greater power in Europe, favouring instead throwing their weight behind European integration, appeared to offer greater evidence of a government acting according to ideas rather than interests. Constructivists consider that the three established paradigms all downplay the normative element of politics in attempting to build 'value-free' 'scientific' models to explain the actions of international actors. Thinking purely about 'who gets what' in reference to particular actors ignores the role that can be played by human agency. The 1989 anti-communist revolutions in

Eastern Europe had demonstrated that ideas and people power could overcome the interests of states and mould events.

Whereas Pluralists and Marxists tended to focus on other aspects of International Relations, leaving Security Studies to the Realists, Social Constructivists mounted the first concerted attack on the logic of Security Studies as it had developed during the Cold War years. Ontological questions largely ignored between 1940 and 1990 began to be asked. Who are being secured? Who are doing the securing? What is it to be secure?

## Wide and narrow conceptions of security

This book adopts a broad and deep interpretation of security encompassing a varied range of perceived threats to humankind, which takes the subject area well beyond the framework of traditional treatments of international security politics which have tended to focus on military threats emanating from other states. This broader approach to conceptualizing global security gained ground in the 1990s when the ending of the Cold War seemed, to many statesmen, academics and members of the general public, to herald a new era of international politics. In this 'New World Order' the threat of global nuclear Armageddon had subsided allowing previously marginalized issues to emerge from the shadow of superpower rivalry and register on the international political agenda. Such an approach to the subject was, however, articulated as far back as 1983 when Ullman defined a threat to security as:

> an action or sequence of events that (1) threatens drastically and over a relatively brief span of time to degrade the quality of life for the inhabitants of a state or (2) threatens significantly to narrow the range of policy choices available to a government of a state, or to private, nongovernmental entities (persons, groups, corporations) within the state.
>
> (Ullman 1983: 133)

Such an expansive interpretation of security found many critics amongst Realists, who were not shaken from their belief in maintaining a narrower focus on what constitutes Security Studies by the ending of the Cold War. Walt has forcefully argued this case: 'security studies may be defined as the study of the threat, use and control of military force' (Walt 1991: 212). Walt and the traditionalists fear that widening the definition of security risks rendering the concept redundant by making it too all-encompassing and diluting the important task of analysing military threats and inter-state conflict. Underlying this fear is the belief of many Realists that military threats are actually more apparent in a post-Cold War world devoid of that traditional guarantor of state security, the military balance of power. This 'anti-New World Order' thesis was epitomized by Mearsheimer's lament in 1990 that 'we will soon miss' the Cold War (Mearsheimer 1990). Some traditionalists consider the demise of the Cold War to signal a need for Security Studies to go 'back to basics' rather than broaden its base, since international politics shorn of the nuclear balance of power imposed by the two superpowers would find the need to rediscover lost arts of multilateral diplomacy, conflict resolution, fighting limited wars and conventional defence (Chapman 1992).

Although there is a case to be made that military threats in the twenty-first century are as apparent as ever, and maybe even greater than during the Cold War, wideners and deepeners of security contend that they are not the only threats that face states, people and the world as a whole. Indeed, they never have been. Throughout history people have been killed by things other than soldiers and weapons, and states have been weakened or destroyed by things other than military conflict. Ullman argued that the security implications for states of demographic pressures and resource depletion needed to be taken on board alongside military threats from other states (Ullman 1983). This logic was developed further in a seminal article by Mathews towards the end of the Cold War which highlighted the need for states to give proper concern to the newly apparent threats posed by environmental problems such as ozone depletion and global warming (Mathews 1989). With the shadow of the Cold War lifted many other 'wideners' emerged in Security Studies literature in the 1990s. Ayoob highlighted that internal rather than external threats were the principal security concern of most less developed countries (LDCs) (Ayoob 1997). Peterson and Sebenius made the same point with reference to that most developed and powerful state, the USA, positing that a crisis in education and a growing economic 'underclass' should be understood as security threats (Peterson and Sebenius 1992). Lynn-Jones and Miller addressed the need to give attention to a range of previously neglected internal and external threats such as virulent nationalism and the social impact of migration (Lynn-Jones and Miller 1995). Although viewed as unwelcome by traditionalists, such as Walt and Mearsheimer, this widening of security did not undermine the Realist logic of conventional Security Studies. The focus was still on the state system and seeing relationships between states as governed by power. Widening was simply a case of extending the range of factors which affect state power beyond the confines of military and trade affairs.

An argument for a more profound widening of security than tacking on some non-military issues to the range of threats to states emerged through the 1990s in a new approach that came to be characterized as the 'Copenhagen School', after the Copenhagen Peace Research Institute. Buzan trailblazed this approach in the early 1990s (Buzan 1991) but it crystallized later in the decade, when he teamed up with Waever and de Wilde in producing the groundbreaking work, *Security*.

> Threats and vulnerabilities can arise in many different areas, military and non-military, but to count as security issues they have to meet strictly defined criteria that distinguish them from the normal run of the merely political. They have to be staged as existential threats to a referent object by a securitizing actor who thereby generates endorsement of emergency measures beyond rules that would otherwise bind.
>
> (Buzan, Waever and de Wilde 1998: 5)

Hence the Copenhagen School went further than the 'wideners' in two ways. First, they facilitated the consideration of non-military issues, even if they had no military dimension, so long as they represented 'existential threats'. Second, the approach also partially deepened the meaning of security by arguing that issues can be considered matters of security even if they are not threatening states (see Table 1.2). A key influence on this was the largely unforseen revival in nationalism in Europe being played out in the post-Cold War landscape of Eastern Europe, particularly in Yugoslavia. The fact that conflict and the disintegration of a state occurred not as a result of a state security dilemma but because of internal 'societal security' dilemmas (competition between different nationalities within the state) prompted an attempt to incorporate sub-state groups into security analysis.

## *The deepening of security*

Going beyond the Copenhagen School in extending the domain of Security Studies is the 'deepening' approach led by Pluralists, Reflective Theorists and Social Constructivists. Deepeners embrace the concept of 'human security' and argue that the chief *referent object* of security should not be the state or certain sub-state groups, such as stateless nations, but the individual people of which these institutions/ groups are comprised. The Pluralist Falk, for example, considers that security ought to be defined as: 'the negation of insecurity as it is *specifically* experienced by individuals and groups in concrete situations' (Falk 1995: 147). This is a significant leap from widening which, as Falk describes: 'still conceives of security largely from the heights of elite assessment, at best allowing the select advisor to deliver a more enlightened message to the ear of the prince' (Falk 1995: 146). Ken Booth, a self-styled 'fallen Realist' led this challenge arguing in contradiction to the assumptions he once shared that: 'Security and emancipation are in fact two sides of the same coin. It is emancipation, not power and order, in both theory and practice, that leads to stable security' (Booth 1991: 539).

The root of the problem with the traditional approaches to security politics is what Wyn Jones, like Booth a Critical Theorist, describes as the 'fetishization of the state' (Wyn Jones 1999: ch. 4). This tendency in International Relations is not resolved by the Copenhagen School approach. The Copenhagen School approach accepts the idea that non-military issues can be securitized and that the referent object of this can be something other than a state but maintains the logic that only the state can be the *securitizing actor* (i.e. decide whether the issue is acted upon as a matter of urgency). Hence statecentricism is maintained, if in a subtler form. The practical limitation with this is that not only are the traditional security agents of the state (i.e. the army, externally, and police, internally) often inadequate for dealing with security problems affecting the people of that state, they are often a chief cause of those problems. Buzan accepts that states can be the source of threats rather than protection for individual people but considers that this is a property of only certain types of states. 'Strong states' coexisting in 'mature anarchy', which have increasingly become the norm through democratization and the development of international human rights law, can be relied upon to secure individuals (Buzan 1991: 98–111). Hence Buzan and Waever are Neo-Realist wideners, albeit of a much more refined form than those who had preceded them.

Whilst the practical concern that widening the focus of Security Studies should not distract attention from military threats has some validity, the intellectual rationale for maintaining a narrower focus is weak. In a book taking a wider approach to security (though not as wide as the Copenhagen School), Wirtz contends that: 'if the threat of force, the use of force or even the logistical or technical assistance that can be supplied by military units does little to respond to a given problem, it probably is best not to treat the specific issue as a security threat' (Wirtz 2002: 312). He also scoffs at the idea that global warming should be construed as a security issue stating: 'It is not exactly clear. . . . how military forces can help reduce the build-up of greenhouse gases in the atmosphere' (Wirtz 2002: 311). This view gives an indication of how blinkered the mainstream study of security can be. Defining an issue as one of security on the basis of whether or not it involves military forces strips the term of any real meaning. Security is a human condition. To define it purely in terms of state bodies whose aim it is to help secure their state and people in a certain dimension, rather than the people whose security is at stake, is both odd and nonsensical. This way of framing what is and what is not a security issue is akin to saying that children being taught to read by their parents are not being educated or that happiness does not exist unless it is induced by the performances of state-sponsored clowns. A security issue, surely, is an issue which threatens (or appears to threaten) one's security. Defining a security issue in behavioural terms rather than excluding certain categories of threats because they do not fit conventional notions of what defines the subject area gives the term some objective meaning. If people, be they government ministers or private individuals, perceive an issue to threaten their lives in some way and respond politically to this then that issue should be deemed to be a *security* issue.

It should be noted, though, that human security itself is a contested concept with more and less expansive versions having come to be employed in both academic and political discourse. Wider human security is often characterized as combining 'freedom from want' and 'freedom from fear' (from the UNDP description of the concept) in that it considers any issues with direct or indirect life-threatening consequences for individuals to be matters of security. Concerns among some advocates of an individual-focused approach to security that 'existing definitions of human security tend to be extraordinarily expansive and vague' (Paris 2001: 88) led them to favour a more restricted version based purely on 'freedom from fear'. This narrow version of human security concentrates on direct and deliberate violent threats, excluding less directly human-caused forms of insecurity like diseases and disasters. The Canadian government have generally been supportive of such an approach in their advocacy of human security as a pragmatic determinant of when specific, concrete foreign policy actions – such as taking part in a humanitarian intervention or developing international human rights conventions – should be undertaken. In contrast, the Japanese government's endorsement of human security has tended to be more in line with the expansive version as favoured by the UNDP and employed in this volume. There is a fatal fatalism in assuming that only direct and deliberate threats to life can be deemed worthy of security status. Such a restriction might make the concept easier to deal with but does so by simply choosing to ignore the insecurities of most of the world's people even when the means of securing them are apparent.

Hence, by adopting the wide human security framework, the notion of security is recast as a social construct stripping away the need for the analyst to speculate on what *they think* is the most threatening of the myriad issues on the contemporary international political agenda and concentrate instead on analysing how and why certain issues actually are perceived of as vital and responded to in an extraordinary way by decision-makers. This approach is appropriate since it is demonstrable, through opinion polls, that people do think of their security in different terms today than they did during the Cold War (see Table 1.1). It is also observable in various ways that the international political agenda has become far more diverse since 1990 with governments giving greater priority to issues such as environmental change, drugs and public health. Even explicitly military organizations, like NATO, are increasingly focusing on non-military activities such as disaster relief.

## Who's securing whom?

The preoccupation of Security Studies with the state is very much a relic of the Cold War. In some ways this is understandable since the discipline of International Relations, and its sub-discipline Security Studies, only emerged in the 1930s and was thus very much forged in an era of unprecedented military threats. Realism was in the ascendancy at the close of the Second World War since the application of force had proved its worth in curbing aggression and restoring order in Europe and Asia. Pre-Second World War international cooperation, in the form of the League of Nations, and 'softly softly' appeasement diplomacy *vis-à-vis* aggressors comprehensively failed to keep the peace. In addition, the total war of the Second World War and the 'total phoney war' of the Cold War, whereby whole populations were threatened by state quarrels in ways not seen before, bound individuals to the fates of their governments like never before.

Hence in the 1940s the twin concepts of 'national interest' and 'national security' took centre stage in International Relations and Security Studies. Walter Lippmann, an American journalist who popularized the term 'Cold War' also defined the nature of security that would characterize that era. 'A nation has security when it does not have to sacrifice its legitimate interests to avoid war and is able, if challenged, to maintain them by war' (Lippmann 1943: 32). The USA's new pre-eminence and preparedness to act on the world stage in 1945 was an additional key factor in promoting this approach. The government of the USA found itself in a position of unprecedented dominance and compelled to utilize its power in a way that it had shown little inclination to do in the past. Using the precursor 'national' in a government's political rhetoric is always a device to convince society to rally behind the government and garner legitimacy for a potentially controversial policy. The US government was embarking on a radical new direction in its foreign policy and needed its society united and on board for the journey (McSweeney 1999: 20–1). US academic, and godfather of Realism in the 1940s and 1950s, Hans Morgenthau summarized this new dynamic.

> The nation state is to a higher degree than ever before the predominant source of the individual's moral and legal valuations and the ultimate point of reference for his secular loyalties. Consequently, its power among the other

**Table 1.1(a)** Single biggest fears in the world (%)[a]

| | | |
|---|---|---|
| 1 | Crime | 27[b] |
| 2 | Terrorism | 15 |
| 3 | Health/economic insecurity | 13 |
| 4 | Accidents/natural disasters | 12 |
| 5 | War | 8 |

Notes

[a] Based on a survey of 6,043 people in 11 countries: Brazil, Canada, France, India, Japan, Russia, South Africa, Thailand, Turkey, USA, UK. They were asked to name the single greatest threat to their life.

[b] Some respondents gave no answer.

Source: Human Security Centre (2005: 52–2).

**Table 1.1(b)** Single biggest fears for Africans (%)[a]

| | | |
|---|---|---|
| 1 | Economic insecurity[b] | 37[d] |
| 2 | Disease[c] | 21 |
| 3 | Corruption | 7 |
| 4 | Illiteracy | 6 |
| 5 | War | 6 |
| 6 | Political conflict | 5 |
| 7 | Environmental destruction | 3 |

Notes

[a] BBC World Service poll of 7,671 people from Kenya, Tanzania, Mozambique, Ghana, Nigeria, Cameroon, Malawi, Zambia, Rwanda and Ivory Coast.

[b] 'Economic Insecurity' conflated from the poll's categories of 'poverty' (24%), 'unemployment' (10%) and 'poor economic development' (3%).

[c] This category collates 'HIV/AIDS' (14%) and 'poor health' (7%).

[d] Some respondents gave no answer.

Source: BBC (2004).

**Table 1.1(c)** Biggest fears for EU citizens (%)[a]

| | | |
|---|---|---|
| 1 | Crime | 76 |
| 2 | Economic | 52 |
| 3 | Terrorism | 33 |
| 4 | Environment | 12 |
| 5 | Natural disaster | 11 |
| 6 | Accidents | 10 |
| 7 | War | 7 |
| 8 | Human rights | 6 |

Note

[a] 28,640 asked to choose up to three most important challenges to security of EU citizens. The responses are collated into the categories used here by the author.

Source: Eurobarometer (2011).

nations and the preservation of its sovereignty are the individual's foremost concerns in international affairs.

(Morgenthau 1972: 32)

The scale of the threat posed by nuclear war in the second half of the twentieth century served to weld the security of individual people in the USA and elsewhere to that of their governments. The state would assume the responsibility for protecting its citizens and demand their loyalty in return in a strengthened version of the 'Social Contract' relationship articulated by political philosophers such as Hobbes and Locke from the seventeenth century. Hobbes's advocacy of the need for the *Leviathan* (meaning a strong state) to save individuals from the dangerous anarchy that would otherwise result from the pursuit of their own selfish interests was a major influence on Morgenthau and the Realists. In the late twentieth century the anarchy was the international state system and the dangers came, to a greater extent than ever before, from other states.

Hence the Realist approach to International Relations represented a revival of the understanding that the state was crucial to securing the lives of its citizens in a different guise. In between Hobbes and Morgenthau, however, political philosophy and state governance in Europe and North America was more influenced by Liberalism and a very different notion of security. Eighteenth-century Liberal philosophers were alarmed that the social contract had become overbalanced and that the Leviathan was endangering rather than protecting its individuals. Paine, Montesquieu, Mill and Smith all referred to 'security' in their notable works and Bentham saw security and liberty as synonymous declaring that, 'without security equality could not last a day' (Bentham 1876: 96).

McSweeney observes that security over time had come to be defined in International Relations solely as an adjective rather than a noun or, as 'a commodity rather than a relationship' (McSweeney 1999: 15). The human part of a human condition had been lost and the term become synonymous with *realpolitik*, the interest of the state. Military might and the application of the 'national interest' can secure lives but it can also, of course, imperil them. Additionally, human lives can be imperilled by a range of issues other than military ones (Table 1.3). A thorough application of security in the study of global politics must, surely, recognize this or else admit that it is a more limited field of inquiry: 'War Studies' or 'Strategic

**Table 1.2** Narrow, wide and deep conceptions of security

| Referent object of security | Types of issues | | |
|---|---|---|---|
| | Military | Non-military | |
| | | Using military means | Unsolvable by military |
| State | Narrow | Wide | |
| Non-state actor | | | Copenhagen School |
| Individual | | | Human Security |

Studies', for example. The conceptualization of International Relations, like the conduct of International Relations, was very much frozen in time between 1945 and 1990.

## The international political agenda

The meaning of 'security' is not just an arcane matter of academic semantics. The term carries significant weight in 'real world' political affairs since threats to the security of states have to be a priority for governments and threats to the lives of people are increasingly accepted as more important than other matters of contention. The need to widen the meaning of security in global politics was recognized by prominent statesmen long before it achieved a certain fashionability following the end of the Cold War. In the late 1970s the Independent Commission on International Development Issues (ICIDI), chaired by former West German chancellor Willy Brandt and including the former premiers of the UK and Sweden, Heath and Palme, concluded in their influential report that:

> An important task of constructive international policy will have to consist in [sic] providing a new, more comprehensive understanding of 'security' which would be less restricted to the purely military aspects. . . .
> Our survival depends not only on military balance, but on global cooperation to ensure a sustainable biological environment based on equitably shared resources.
>
> (ICIDI 1980: 124)

The Brandt Report helped raise the profile of poverty as an international issue (see Chapter 4) but global security politics continued to be focused on military matters in general, and the Cold War in particular, until the passing into history of that conflict at the end of the 1980s. As with the academic treatment of security, however, it is important to remember that the notion that the conduct of international security politics should be about non-military as well as military issues was not born of the 1990 peace dividend. Rather, it first emerged in those two previous eras of Liberal optimism which followed the twentieth century's other two global conflicts. Though its chief historical legacy is a failure to keep the peace, the League of Nations first implemented the idea that some lateral thinking was required to avert war by incorporating within its system of organizations, alongside conflict resolution mechanisms, 'specialized agencies' focusing on health and welfare. The Second World War, which prompted the dissolution of the League, led the United Nations to change the military approach to security of its predecessor, more in line with Realist logic, but it still persisted with the lateral approach. The specialized agencies were retained and the UN Charter openly declares as an aim: 'the creation of conditions of stability and well-being which are necessary for peaceful and friendly relations among nations' (Article 55). In addition the Constitution of the World Health Organization (WHO), the largest in the widened roster of specialized agencies taken under the UN's wing, explicitly states that human well-being is a precondition for world peace (see Chapter 7). The UN also went further than the

League of Nations in for the first time giving international expression to the idea of keeping the peace for individual people as well as states through the enshrinement of human rights, thus moving towards a deepened understanding of security.

In the 1990s the UN was able to revive and further develop this line of thinking within the concept of human security.

> The concept of security must change – from an exclusive stress on national security to a much greater stress on people's security, from security through armaments to security through human development, from territorial to food, employment and environmental security.
>
> (UNDP 1993)

Probably the first articulation of human security in international politics came two years earlier at a Pan-African conference co-sponsored by the UN and the Organization for African Unity.

> The concept of security goes beyond military considerations. [It] must be construed in terms of the security of the individual citizen to live in peace with access to basic necessities of life while fully participating in the affairs of his/her society in freedom and enjoying all fundamental human rights.
>
> (African Leadership Forum 1991)

The UNDP line has been endorsed by other UN agencies, in the General Assembly and by former Secretary-General Kofi Annan. The more 'Realist' element of the UN system, the Security Council, has been less radical but has become a 'widener', if not a 'deepener'. In 2000 the Security Council passed a resolution on a non-military issue for the first time when it debated the global HIV/AIDS pandemic (see Chapter 7).

Many states have come to take a widened approach to security since the 1990s. The US Clinton administration made extensive use of academic advisers and a burgeoning literature on the 'national security' imperative of taking on board non-military concerns now that the Soviet threat had receded. The impact of this was made explicit in the 1994 'National Security Strategy', an annual foreign policy manifesto. 'Not all security risks are military in nature. Transnational phenomena such as terrorism, narcotics trafficking, environmental degradation, rapid population growth and refugee flows also have security implications for both present and long term American policy' (White House 1994: 1). Clinton's widening approach to security owed much to his special adviser, Strobe Talbot, who, in turn, was inspired by Joseph Nye's concept of 'soft power' (Nye 1990). Soft power for Nye denotes the non-military dimension of state power, particularly rooted in the world of information. For the US government being 'on top' of information on global issues was useful not only for better comprehending problems like AIDS and transnational crime but for advancing the USA's standing in the world. Explicit recognition that the protection of US citizens was a domestic as well as foreign policy matter came in the aftermath of the September 11th 2001 terrorist strikes on New York and Washington with the launch of a new government department for 'Homeland Security'.

Fewer countries have taken the more radical step of deepening as well as widening in embracing human security. The Canadian government like their southern neighbour were influenced by Nye but have gone further and repeatedly expressed their support for human security in their foreign policy statements. Canada's Foreign Minister from 1996 to 2000, Lloyd Axworthy, advanced the concept rhetorically in the UN General Assembly and other global forums and practically, by being a leading advocate for the creation of the International Criminal Court (ICC). Cynics have suggested that this strategy was just a tactical move by the Canadian government to raise the diplomatic profile of a middle ranking power in an exercise of populism (McDonald 2002: 282). Axworthy's advocacy of 'soft power' gives some credence to this since Nye's concept ultimately is concerned with the advancement of state interests rather than altruism or the global interest, but the Canadian government has done much to further global political responses for the common good. The Canadians, for example, have been at the forefront of campaigns to ban the use of land mines and reform the UN Security Council so that it is less constrained by power politics.

Perhaps most significantly for the advancement of deepened security, the Canadian government signed a declaration with their Norwegian counterparts at the 1998 Lysøen Conference launching the Human Security Network. This network advocates the development of global policies focused on the human interest, whether or not these happen to coincide with state interests. By 2012 the network had expanded to include eleven other states, both geographically and politically diverse (Austria, Chile, Costa Rica, Greece, Republic of Ireland, Jordan, Mali, Netherlands, Slovenia, Switzerland and Thailand).

> Human security has become both a new measure of global security and a new agenda for global action. Safety is the hallmark of freedom from fear, while well-being is the target of freedom from want. Human security and human development are thus two sides of the same coin, mutually reinforcing and leading to a conducive environment for each other.
>
> (Human Security Network 1999)

## The securitization of issues

It is clear that designating an issue as a matter of security is not just a theoretical question but carries 'real world' significance. The traditional, Realist way of framing security presupposes that military issues (and certain economic issues for Neo-realists) are security issues and as such must be prioritized by governments above other 'low politics' issues, important though these might be.

As stated earlier, governments do tend to be somewhat Realist in their foreign policies and this high-politics/low-politics distinction is evident in the level of state expenditure typically allocated to the achievement of military security as opposed to other issue areas. The government of South Africa trebled its allocation of the state exchequer for fighting AIDS for 2002–3 to $1 billion from the previous financial year. This was a significant response by the government to criticism that they had not done enough to tackle this massive threat to life. However, the increased expenditure needs to be set in context. For the same financial year the slice of the budget set aside for military defence was $21 billion. However, there seems little doubt that few South African citizens would consider the prospect of armed invasion from Mozambique, Zimbabwe or any other state more of a threat to their lives than AIDS.[3] Around 5 million people in South Africa (11 per cent of the population) are infected with HIV, and AIDS is the country's biggest killer, claiming an estimated 40 per cent of all deaths in 2002 (Dorrington, Bradshaw and Budlender 2002). In comparison, South Africa has no obvious external military threat. Straight comparisons between government expenditure on different areas are problematic since different policy goals cost different amounts of money. Similarly, you could posit that South Africa's lack of military adversaries is a measure of the success of its defence policy. Even if this were to be accepted, however, the threat of AIDS remains acute in South Africa and there is little doubt that more could be done to alleviate the problem. The government of poorer Uganda, for instance, cut HIV prevalence by half in the late 1990s through a concerted public information campaign (Ammann and Nogueira 2002).

South Africa is by no means unusual in such a disparity of priorities and, indeed, has done more than most countries to shift priorities away from military defence if you bear in mind that, in the early 1990s, it became the only state in history to unilaterally disarm itself of nuclear weapons. Military threats are, of course, more apparent to some countries than others, and so global figures give a better insight into the balance between health and defence expenditure. The scale of threats to the world as a whole are quantifiable and, as a result, the misprioritizing of expenditure becomes obvious. World military expenditure accounts for 2.6 per cent of global GDP (SIPRI 2011), whilst world health expenditure makes up 8.2 per cent of global GDP (WHO 2012a; 2012b). Over a third of the world's health expenditure is private and so cannot be considered as government prioritizing of health (except in so far as it is considered as an alternative to public health). Overall, then, governments allocate about twice as much money to health as to military security. Consider this in relation to the relative threat to people's lives posed by military and health threats (Table 1.3).

In considering the figures in Table 1.3 a few qualifications need to be taken into account. It is entirely natural to die of ill-health since we all die in the end and 'old age' or 'natural causes' make up a proportion of the deaths by 'disease'. However, a third of all deaths are from communicable diseases which cannot be thought of as inevitable and many of the people who die from non-communicable diseases die 'prematurely' from diseases like cancer which are, at least partially,

**Table 1.3** Global causes of death, 2008 (million)

| Disease/ill-health | 52.25 |
| Disasters/accidents | 3.63 |
| Suicide | 0.78 |
| Criminal violence | 0.54 |
| War/political violence | 0.18 |

Source: WHO (2011).

avoidable. Additionally, 'disease' incorporates deaths from malnutrition which most certainly are politically avoidable (see Chapter 4). Also, while some accidents may be unavoidable and, to a certain extent, 'natural', this is, in fact, a pretty small proportion even for 'natural disasters' (see Chapter 9).

It is an indication of how the study of security in International Relations has become skewed over time that the issue most associated with the discipline is a comparatively minor threat to most people in the world. Of all of the security threats considered in this book the average citizen of the world is least threatened by military action from another state or a foreign non-state actor. Threats are invariably close to home and familiar. This is exemplified by the fact that more people kill themselves each year than are killed in both homicides and 'political killings' combined. Suicide is not considered in this study since this is a voluntary death but this is an area the WHO have recently increased research into since there are clearly underlying reasons why people, in increased numbers, take their own lives.

Security 'wideners', including some Realists, accept that non-military issues can become 'securitized' and hence be privileged with 'national security' status. The issues securitized in this way, however, are arbitrarily defined. The tendency has been, on the one hand, to select non-military issues which military forces can help deal with, such as fighting drugs barons abroad or assisting in civil emergency operations. On the other hand, 'securitization' has sometimes been granted to external non-military problems on the basis that they have domestic military repercussions. Issues such as AIDS or environmental degradation in distant countries may de-stabilize regional balances of power and trigger military conflict which the onlooking government may be drawn into or affected in some capacity. Hence, with widening, the logic of national interest and prioritizing high politics is not really challenged. It is more of a refinement of the way in which external threats are calculated and a case of allowing 'low politics' to rise to prominence in the absence of major 'high politics' threats. Military defence is still being prioritized and security is still being defined as a very specific noun rather than as an adjective.

The political practice of widening security has sometimes proved counter to the interests of the people affected by the issue due to a clumsy militarization of tasks previously performed by more appropriate personnel. Recent post-conflict 'nation-building' exercises in Afghanistan and Iraq have been notable for a militarization of development projects, with remaining armed forces being redeployed to reconstruction tasks and 'winning the hearts and minds' of the locals. Such 'humanitarian' roles may have some beneficial results for local populations but are, of course, ultimately driven by military expediency rather than human security. The disillusionment of pressure groups with this phenomenon was made clear in 2004 when Médecins Sans Frontières pulled out of Afghanistan with its President Dr Rowan Gillies, declaring: 'we refuse to accept a vision of a future where civilians trapped in the hell of war can only receive life-saving aid from the armies that wage it' (Gillies 2004). One consequence of this phenomenon has been a backlash against the concept of human security by development theorists as merely representing the militarization of development. Many academic applications of the concept have, indeed, taken the approach that it is a 'merging of development and [military] security' (Duffield 2001) but, for the concept to have real meaning, it is important not to conflate it with 'widened security' and recognize that the human securitization of development puts the security of the vulnerable centre-stage, not the geopolitical interests of states.

The Copenhagen School approach takes a step forward from widening in using the methodology of the 'speech act' to define when an issue becomes a security issue. In this approach security issues can be military or non-military but are distinguishable by the urgency that is attached to them in political discourse. 'If by means of an argument about the priority and urgency of an existential threat the securitizing actor has managed to break free of procedures or rules he or she would otherwise be bound by, we are witnessing an act of securitization' (Buzan, Waever and de Wilde 1998: 25). This methodology allows for a more behavioural definition of security than 'conventional widening' since issues given priority by people other than the government are included in the framework. However, this approach still leaves the act of securing threatened people to the state. This can result in life-threatening issues being excluded from consideration because the government still chooses not to prioritize them or because the voices speaking for securitization are insufficiently loud. Security threats particular to women, for example, tend to be marginalized because of difficulties in 'being heard' amongst the 'speakers of security' in society (see Chapter 5). Non-military issues are more easily accommodated by the speech act approach but there is still a large measure of subjectivity and relativism in leaving the demarcation to governments rather than objective analysis.

Security **is** subjective in that individual fears do not necessarily tally with the reality of threats but individual needs are a better guide to the issues that matter than the priorities of governments. The security of governments does not equate with the security of the people they are meant to represent. This has already been acknowledged by governments in sanctioning the development of global human rights law and is still evident in the existence of global systemic failings such as the widespread persistence of hunger and treatable diseases in a world with sufficient food and medicine to counter them (see Table 1.4).

**Table 1.4** Security threats

| Threats | The threatened | | | |
| --- | --- | --- | --- | --- |
| | Individuals | Societal groups | Government | The world |
| Individuals | Crime, 'hate crimes' | | | |
| Societal groups | 'Hate crimes' | Genocide | Civil war | |
| Government | Human rights abuses | Genocide, politicide | War, economic sanctions | Nuclear war |
| Global | Poverty, industrial accidents, pollution | Global warming | Global warming | |
| Non-human | Disease, natural disasters | | | Asteroid/comet collision |

## Conclusions

If politics is about the 'authoritative allocation of values' (Easton 1965: 96) issues arise over contention over certain values. In International Relations the traditional assumption has been that the core value is the preservation of state sovereignty and that this automatically commands pride of place at the top of the domestic and international political agendas. However, it has become increasingly evident over the years that values other than this are becoming prioritized and that the pursuit of state security can often undermine human security. Political issues are myriad but can ulitmately be distilled down to contention over the allocation of certain core values such as security, economic gain and altruism.

It is perfectly natural to give priority to security over the other values since it is a precondition for realizing their allocation. If security is considered from the perspective of individual people, however, issues are less easily compartmentalized. Most issues of state altruism, such as the granting of emergency foreign aid, are matters of life and death to the people affected. Many issues of state economic gain, such as altering the terms of international trade, are security matters for people in other states affected by the change. State altruism exists in the world, as do some limitations to the pursuit of economic gain, but not to the same prominence as in the domestic politics of states where individual people are empowered with votes and/or rights of citizenship. Individual security is recognized in democratic states as overriding other values (at least most of the time) as is evidenced by health and safety laws restricting business activities and 'social security' laws. In global politics issues of life and death frequently are not treated as priorities because they do not coincide with state gain or security. The blinkered pursuit of profit can enrich some but imperil others. If saving others from abuse or disaster is seen as an act of charity, rather than political duty, it will only happen infrequently and selectively. Perceived threats (Table 1.1) and actual threats to people (Table 1.3) are so far removed from the way in which issues are conventionally ordered on the political agenda by states that International Relations theory and international political practice needs to find ways of accommodating them, or cease to be connected in any meaningful way with human behaviour and needs.

Human rights policies have developed significantly in recent decades but this has not yet come close to securing **all** humans. Governments tend to prioritize the rights and lesser interests of their own citizens over the fundamental rights of others, and human rights are still routinely treated as secondary to 'national security' issues where the two are perceived to clash. The tightening up of migration laws and the increased surveillance of foreign citizens in the present 'war against terror' in the USA and Western Europe represent cases in point. The lives of far more people in today's world, however, are imperilled by human rights abuses than by terrorist and conventional military attacks. Throughout the total war era of the twentieth century a case could be made that the security of individuals was inextricably tied up with that of their states, but that era has now passed into history. Today the issues that threaten people's lives bear such little relation to those issues that dominate the international political agenda that statecentricism is impeding both the study and the practice of that most fundamental of political concerns:

securing people. The word security derives from the Latin *sine cura*, meaning 'without care'. As such it is a fairly elastic term since the 'cares' may be major fears or minor frustrations. Complete freedom from care is both impractical and undesirable. Human life that does not have any everyday concerns is unimaginable and a complete absence of risk-taking in society would eliminate much beneficial scientific progress and entertainment from life. As such this inquiry into security in global politics focuses on the most meaningful fears there are: threats to the lives of people.

## Key points

- The study of global security is a sub-set of the discipline of International Relations.
- The Realist paradigm of International Relations traditionally has dominated the study of security and focused inquiry on military security in inter-state relations.
- The end of the Cold War brought about a re-appraisal of the Realist orthodoxy in Security Studies since the scale of military threats had receded and the logic of the balance of power as a necessary condition for peace had been undermined.
- Some Neo-Realists contend that Security Studies should still be preoccupied with state security and military issues or risk becoming too diverse a subject to give proper treatment to these still vital concerns.
- 'Wideners' in Security Studies (including some Neo-Realists) favour extending the subject to incorporate non-military issues which affect the security of the state.
- A 'deepening' approach to Security Studies, favoured by the Pluralists and Social Constructivists in International Relations, widens the range of issues to be considered but also shifts the focus of the discipline to the security of people rather than of states: that is human security.

## Notes

1. Non-governmental actors are taken to include all private organizations with political influence. Hence, alongside those groups conventionally thought of as 'NGOs', pressure groups, the term also covers multi-national corporations (MNCs), non-state 'terrorist' groups, organized crime groups and religions.
2. Although it can be argued that, unusual though this 'surrender' was, it was essentially a victory for the power politics approach of the USA in the 1980s which compelled the USSR to capitulate.
3. Four per cent of South Africans identified war as their biggest security threat in a 2005 opinion poll (Human Security Centre 2005).

## Recommended reading

Buzan, B. Waever, O. and de Wilde, J. (1998) *Security: A New Framework for Analysis*, Boulder and London: Lynne Rienner.

Collins, A. (ed.) (2006) *Contemporary Security Studies*, Oxford: Oxford University Press.

Falk, R. (1995) *On Humane Governance: Toward a New Global Politics*, Cambridge: Polity.

Mathews, J. (1989) 'Redefining Security', *Foreign Affairs*, 68(2): 162–77.

McSweeney, B. (1999) *Security, Identity and Interests: A Sociology of International Relations*, Cambridge: Cambridge University Press.

Morgenthau, H. (1972) *Politics Among Nations*, 5th edn, New York: A. Knopf.

Ullman, R. (1983) 'Redefining Security', *International Security*, 8(1): 129–53.

Wyn Jones, R. (1999) *Security, Strategy and Critical Theory*, Boulder: Lynne Rienner.

## Useful web links

Human Security Network: http://www.humansecuritynetwork.net/
Stockholm International Peace Research Institute (SIPRI): http://www.sipri.se/
United Nations Development Programme: http://www.undp.org/
World Health Organization's *World Health Report*: http://www.who.int/whr/en/

# Military threats to security from states

Once the expenditure of effort [in war] exceeds the value of the political object the object must be renounced and peace must follow.

Carl von Clausewitz in *On War*
(Clausewitz 1976: 92; see Box 2.1).

War between states has always been central to the study of International Relations and widely accepted as an inevitable feature of state-to-state relations. This is understandable given that this form of conflict, historically, has been so prominent and so costly in lives. The Realist model of powerful states vying for supremacy, restrained only by the countervailing power of other states, seems to be borne out by considering the scale and nature of the major wars in history. Most of the conflicts listed in Table 2.1 were 'clashes of the Titans' involving the world's premier military powers. The four biggest clashes had a catalytic effect on international relations

---

### Box 2.1 Carl von Clausewitz

Clausewitz's *On War* remains the most revered book on military strategy ever written and a standard text on contemporary reading lists for Security Studies students and military officer trainees, despite being written in the 1830s and never finished by the author. Clausewitz wrote the book whilst serving as the head of a Prussian military academy in Berlin. He had previously served as an officer in the Prussian army after joining as a cadet at the age of twelve and had seen action from a young age in the Napoleonic War. Clausewitz died in the cholera epidemic that swept Europe in 1831 before completing the book, but it was published posthumously by his widow in 1832.

As a result of this, *On War* contains a number of gaps and has frequently been misinterpreted. In particular, Clausewitz's insistence on seeing war as a facet of politics has often wrongly been understood as the glorification of war. Clausewitz shared Machiavelli's pessimism about human cynicism in politics but, as the quote which opens this chapter indicates, advocated war only when absolutely necessary and justifiable. The uncertainties inherent in battle, or the 'fog of war', make any decision to initiate conflict a gamble which should only be undertaken when the odds are stacked in your favour.

Over a hundred years after his death Clausewitz's rational approach saw him lauded by International Relations Realists as 'one of their own' but, such is his insight, other approaches have come to claim inspiration from his work. Wyn Jones, a Constructivist critic of Realism, comments: 'I doubt very much that Clausewitz, with his speculative bent and his interest in Hegelian dialectics, would have ever made the grade in traditional security studies' (Wyn Jones 1999: ch. 5).

**Table 2.1** The ten bloodiest inter-state wars in history

| War | Years | Deaths |
|---|---|---|
| 1  Second World War | 1939–45 | 20,000,000 |
| 2  First World War | 1914–18 | 8,500,000 |
| 3  Thirty Years War | 1618–48 | 2,071,000 |
| 4  Napoleonic War | 1803–15 | 1,869,000 |
| 5  War of the Spanish Succession | 1701–13 | 1,324,300 |
| 6  Korean War | 1950–53 | 1,200,000 |
| 7  Vietnam War | 1965–73 | 1,200,000 |
| 8  The Crusades | 1095–1272 | 1,000,000 |
| 9  Iran–Iraq War | 1980–8 | 850,000 |
| 10  Seven Years War | 1755–63 | 500,000 |

Source: White (2001).

beyond their direct human and governmental impact in the states directly involved. These wars were infernos in which new international orders, normatively altering state relations, were forged. The Korean and Vietnamese wars, however, were only indirect clashes of the Titans and, in fact, great power collisions have not been seen since the ultimate of such clashes in 1939–45. That the potential 'mother' of all clashes of the Titans, the Cold War, should end with a peaceful transition to a new order, rather than military victory, served to challenge the ascendancy of Realism in the study of military security. Incidences of inter-state war, in general, have also receded over recent decades (Human Security Centre 2005). The spectre of this sort of war, however, still looms large over much of the conduct of government foreign policies. There can be little doubt that the Afghan and Iraq wars have been the most high-profile international political events since 2001, when the normal order of security prioritization was briefly overturned by the September 11th strikes.

## Prelude to the present order

Two issues, very much global in their scope, dominated international relations in the latter part of the twentieth century: the Cold War and the process of decolonization. Both issues were largely resolved by the early 1990s, but their legacy lives on in many aspects of the contemporary global political system and in the conceptualizing of their military security by states. The biggest Cold War alliance still exists, some Cold War conflicts still persist and the extraordinarily deadly means of prosecuting wars devised in this period continues to threaten the security of the whole world. Decolonization extended the state system to the whole world for the first time, transforming the make-up of that once exclusive club of sovereign states into the diverse membership that characterizes it today whilst legitimizing independence struggles, many of which continue to resonate.

## The Cold War

The term 'Cold War' entered popular parlance in the USA in 1946–7 to describe the tense hostility that had set in in relations with their recent wartime allies the USSR. The politician Bernard Baruch, writer Walter Lipman and journalist H.B. Swope have each been credited with coining the phrase but its origins are, in fact, far older. The Spanish writer Don Juan Manuel first used the expression in the fourteenth century to describe a state of relations between countries that is not characterized by actual war but which is, nonetheless, extremely hostile. Manuel was describing relations between Spain and the Moslem world but the ideological confrontation between the Communist world, led by the USSR and the USA-led capitalist world, which was being played out in the late 1940s fitted the description well.

The period of hostility and rivalry between the two coalitions of states, from the end of the Second World War in 1945 to 1990, was unlike any other phase of history. The two sides avoided outright military conflict with each other but fought out many *proxy* wars, whereby one side would fight an enemy sponsored by the other side (such as with the US war in Vietnam or the USSR's invasion of Afghanistan) or both sides would sponsor rivals in a conflict whilst cheering on from the sidelines (as for example with the Arab–Israeli dispute). Whilst this era cannot be said to be one of peace when it contained two of the bloodiest wars in history, in Korea and Vietnam, direct war between the major protagonists was avoided by the maintenance of a *balance of terror,* whereby both sides were deterred from such action by the massive scale of each other's military capabilities. The key variable that made this such a distinct phase of history was, of course, the advent of atomic/nuclear weapons, which served to make war something that threatens not only hostile states but the entire population of the Earth.

Why the wartime allies came to divide into two such antagonistic opponents so shortly after the Second World War is hotly disputed by historians of the period. Three broad schools of thought have emerged: the Traditionalists, the Revisionists and the Post-Revisionists.

*Traditionalists* lay the blame for the Cold War with the USSR. Writers such as Feis and Schlesinger argue that the confrontation occurred because, shortly after the ending of the Second World War, the USSR behaved in a manner which suggested they wanted to expand their influence over Europe and, at the same time, rebuffed American gestures of support and cooperation (Feis 1970; Schlesinger 1967). The USSR was slow to withdraw troops from East Europe and Northern Iran after victory had been achieved in the Second World War, turned down the offer of American economic aid (the Marshall Plan) and also rejected their offer to scrap their own arsenal of atomic weapons in exchange for a UN inspection system to prevent any state procuring such weapons (the Baruch Plan). From this perspective the USA were entitled to interpret Soviet intentions as being hostile and respond accordingly.

*Revisionists* take the opposite viewpoint with writers, such as the Kolkos and LaFeber, pinning the blame for the Cold War on US aggression towards the USSR (Kolko 1972; LaFeber 1991). The hostility of Western capitalist states to Communism can be dated back as far as the Russian Civil War when a number of states, including the USA, actively supported the Monarchists against the Bolsheviks, who had assumed power following the 1917 revolution. In light of this, cooperation in the Second World War was merely a marriage of convenience and the decision of the USA to detonate atomic weapons in Japan in 1945 was as much a show of strength towards the USSR as a means of ending Japanese resistance, it is claimed. Revisionists argue that the USSR's dominance of the 'Eastern Bloc' after 1945 was merely a defensive measure to create a buffer against American dominance of Europe and ideological hostility to Communism. Hence the revisionist view is that US rather than Soviet hostility prompted the Cold War.

*Post-Revisionists* emerged in the 1970s and 1980s with a different take on the causes of the Cold War. Writers such as John Lewis Gaddis, instead of blaming either side for initiating hostilities, take a more detached, Realist view which argues that both sides acted expansively in an inevitable process of filling the power vacuum that had been created in Europe (Gaddis 1997). The decline in power of Germany, France and the UK after the Second World War transformed the political landscape of the world with two superpowers outside of the European heartland now ruling the roost. Those two superpowers, acting in accord with the logic of power politics, competed for the mastery of Europe. The USSR did so in a traditional manner, by colonizing neighbouring countries in Eastern Europe. The USA did so in a more subtle manner, by linking themselves to the countries of Western and Southeastern Europe, militarily through NATO and economically through the Marshall Plan and other agreements. Hence, from this perspective, the Cold War was a classic balance of power struggle like many others throughout history, only this time conducted on a bilateral rather than multilateral basis.

Whichever perspective on the Cold War is taken, it is clear that American foreign policy underwent a profound shift in the late 1940s. The isolationist stance that had characterized US policy from the 1920s, entering the Second World War only after being invaded, was swept aside by a new approach to become known as the *Truman Doctrine*. President Harry Truman announced in 1947 that 'it must be the policy of The United States to support free peoples who are resisting subjugation by armed minorities or outside pressures'. The 'armed minorities' referred to were Marxist revolutionaries and the 'outside pressures' was code for the USSR. This represented a shift from the previous president Franklin Roosevelt (who died in 1945), who had been more tolerant of the USSR and consented to the principle of a Soviet sphere of influence in East Europe at the Moscow Conference of 1944 (although he was not present at the meeting). The Moscow Conference confirmed an earlier, unofficial agreement made over dinner in London between UK Prime Minister Churchill and USSR leader Stalin when the two famously carved up Eastern Europe on a map sketched on a napkin.

The change in US strategy can be explained in part by a change in president, but also by the coming to light of apparent evidence of Soviet expansionist intentions. Truman's declaration was greatly influenced by the so-called 'long telegram' of 1946 sent to the White House from Moscow by the US deputy-ambassador to the USSR, George Kennan. Kennan had closely analysed speeches of Stalin and concluded that Communist expansion was more than the Marxist rhetoric others assumed it to be and was a real threat to the capitalist world. Kennan was switched to a job as head of a State Department policy-planning unit and elaborated on his views for the future direction of US foreign policy: 'the main element of any United States policy towards the Soviet Union must be that of a long-term patient but firm and vigilant containment of Russian expansive tendencies' (Kennan 1947: 575).

Most now consider that talk of Communist world revolution was more Soviet rhetoric than reality but the threat was taken seriously and the USA's response was certainly more than rhetorical. American containment was put into practice with the signing of a series of bilateral and multilateral military alliances in the late 1940s and 1950s between the USA and countries of Asia and Europe located close to the USSR. The support for 'free peoples' heralded by Truman was put into practice in 1950 with the armed intervention by the USA and a number of allies in South Korea to aid their resistance struggle against invasion by Communist North Korea.

The Cold War went through distinct phases where hostility between East and West became more or less intense. Writers differ in the precise dating of these periods of a thawing or freezing in Cold War relations but there is broad agreement on three main phases (see Table 2.2).

## Decolonization

At around the same time as the Cold War was coming to an end another prolonged global struggle, erupting in periodic bursts of violence, was receiving its curtain call on the world stage. In 1990 Namibia finally achieved independence from a colonial power, South Africa, in the throes of democratic revolution. Although this was not the world's last colonial struggle, the end of the 24-year armed campaign was important symbolically because it left the African continent free of European and European settler rule. In 1945 there were only three independent states in Africa: South Africa (independent from the UK since 1910), Ethiopia (liberated from Italian rule in 1941) and Liberia (the only African state never to be colonized). Revolutions rarely happen in isolation and the process whereby Africa and large swathes of Asia threw off colonial rule can be viewed as a global phenomenon.

That this wave of decolonization (a previous wave had swept Latin America in the nineteenth century) should occur at the same time as the Cold War is not merely a quirk of history. The same balance of power shift which saw Western European powers fall behind the USA and USSR in the global pecking order and contributed to the Cold War, gave the colonies of France, the UK and other states the opportunity to turn the pre-1945 order on its head. This was most explicitly demonstrated in Vietnam, where anti-colonial war against France was directly succeeded by Communist war against a new external foe, the USA. In addition, Marxist ideology saw colonialism as a symptom of capitalism and hence the struggle against colonizers as something to be encouraged. This appeared to be confirmed in 1961 when Soviet President Khruschev announced that the USSR would support 'wars of national liberation' throughout the world. This perception of Soviet and Chinese influence prompted US involvement in Vietnam. In general, however, it was post-colonial power struggles rather than the overthrow of European rule, which tended to be transformed into Cold War conflict. In Angola the USSR, along with Cuba, gave backing to leftist guerillas, whilst the USA supported the anti-Communist

**Table 2.2** Phases of the Cold War

---

### *First Cold War, 1945–69*

---

### 1 Confrontation, 1945–62

The Cold War could be said to have begun with the declaration of the Truman Doctrine in 1947 but hostilities in US–USSR relations can be traced back to the closing stages of the Second World War and even before. In 1949 the USSR developed the atom bomb and NATO was formed, setting the parameters for two armed camps and a massive arms build-up. The Berlin blockade brought the two sides near to war that year when the USSR challenged the US–UK–French control of West Berlin. That year also saw China undergo Communist revolution and then, in the following year, fight with the North Koreans against the USA and her allies.

The Warsaw Pact was formed in 1955 by the USSR as an East European military alliance to rival NATO, and the USA and USSR came as close as they ever did to war in 1962 with the Cuban missile crisis when the USSR attempted to station warheads on the island.

---

### 2 Coexistence, 1963–9

The Cuban missile crisis was resolved with a deal whereby the USA removed missiles from Turkey in exchange for the USSR not stationing weapons on Cuba. The very real possibility of nuclear war in 1962 prompted improved dialogue between the two superpowers. Arms control agreements were initiated and the logic of deterrence set in to US–Soviet relations with both sides recognizing the other's right to parity in military terms as a means of guaranteeing peace through the *balance of terror*. There was still military conflict in the Cold War, however, as evidenced by the US role in the Vietnam War from 1961 to 1975 supporting South Vietnam against Communist North Vietnam.

---

### *Détente, 1969–79*

---

A major improvement in relations between the USA and USSR occurred after the accession of Nixon as US president. Extensive bilateral arms control deals were agreed and the 1975 Helsinki Accords saw the East and West blocs agree on various forms of political cooperation. The USA recognized Communist China for the first time in 1979. Some tensions remained, such as in the support for opposing sides in the Arab–Israeli disputes from 1973, but there was optimism that the Cold War might be coming to an end.

---

### *Second Cold War, 1979–90*

---

### 1 Confrontation, 1979–85

The USSR's invasion of Afghanistan in 1979 ended détente. The USA did not consider this a tolerable incursion into a country in the Soviet sphere of influence and a period of renewed intense antagonism between East and West occurred. President Reagan increased military expenditure, abandoned arms control agreements and cut many economic links with what he termed 'the evil empire'.

---

### 2 End of the Cold War, 1985–90

Reagan's aggression succeeded in upping the ante to a point the USSR could not match, particularly with the 'Star Wars' Space Defense Initiative (SDI). Gorbachev came to power in the USSR in 1985 and, in order to save his country from economic ruin, embarked on a policy of rapprochement with the West, pulling out of Afghanistan and signalling a withdrawal from East Europe. Gorbachev and US President Bush declared the Cold War to be over at the 1989 Malta Summit as Communist governments fell in the six countries of the Eastern Bloc. A 1990 Paris Treaty officially ended the 45-year power struggle.

---

faction. That China should find themselves on the same side as the Americans in this conflict, however, gives some credence to the post-revisionist assessment of the Cold war as more of a plain power struggle than an ideological confrontation.

Indeed, decolonization was applauded not only by governments of the left. The USA used its position of mastery over the old powers of Europe to assert its moral support for the principle of self-rule for colonies. One of the few things the two new superpowers could agree upon in the late 1940s and early 1950s was that the age of colonialism was a part of the old European order which should be swept away. This was, of course, a somewhat hypocritical view given the USSR's recent acquisition of six satellite states in Eastern Europe and the USA's colonial rule of Puerto Rico and indirect control over South Korea, South Vietnam, Taiwan and the Philippines, but it was clear that the world had entered a new phase of international relations in 1945 in more ways than one.

## A New World Order?

President George Bush (senior) is generally credited with having popularized contemporary usage of the term New World Order in a series of speeches in 1990 and 1991 to signify that the UN-backed and US-led allied force sent to Kuwait to drive out invading Iraqi forces was indicative of a very different world than that seen up until the end of the Cold War. 'What is at stake is more than one small country, it is a big idea – a New World Order, where diverse nations are drawn together in common cause to achieve the universal aspirations of mankind: peace and security, freedom, and the rule of law' (Bush 1991). With the dark shadow of Cold War lifted there was optimism that the USA, Russia, China and other great military powers could free the UN Security Council from its Cold War straitjacket and cooperate to punish aggression, such as that exerted by Iraq, in a way not seen in the twentieth century or, to any real extent, at any previous time in history.

Such optimism for a brighter future whilst basking in the afterglow of a triumphant victory is nothing new in international relations. The defeat of Napoleon Bonaparte in 1815 at Waterloo was achieved by a coalition of European powers ending twelve years of conflict and followed up by the Congress of Vienna which heralded a period of great power cooperation known as the 'Concert of Europe'. For a period of nearly forty years there was peace in Europe assisted by a loose system of diplomatic co-management of the Continent between five countries: Britain, Prussia, Russia, Austria-Hungary and, novelly, their defeated but not estranged enemy France. The outbreak of the Crimean War of 1854, when Britain and France fought together with Turkey against Russia, ended the Concert and Europe eschewed any attempt at collective policing until after the next epoch-making conflict, the First World War.

The 1919–20 Paris Peace Settlement following the First World War ushered in a new attempt to construct a better world order, led by the *Idealists*, most clearly articulated with the creation of the League of Nations. Idealist is a term that came to be applied to statesmen of the age, such as US President Woodrow Wilson, and academics, such as the UK's first professor of International Relations Alfred Zimmern, who advocated that states should forgo the selfish pursuit of national interest and conduct their foreign affairs with a greater stress on international cooperation, morality and diplomatic openness. The world had been plunged into a war far more devastating than anything seen previously because states had aggressively pursued their own interests to the disregard of other states, bar those they had aligned themselves with in secretive military alliances. Hence the League of Nations sought to provide an arena whereby states could resolve disputes openly in conference or through the rulings of an international court (the Permanent Court of International Justice) and where protection for states could come from a global guarantee (collective security) rather than through constructing covert military pacts.

As with the Concert of Europe, the League of Nations ultimately collapsed amidst a new great power collision. Idealism came to be derided by a new generation of statesmen and scholars, the *Realists*, as being dangerously naive and utopian. The Realists advocated a return to the order of the Concert of Europe on a global scale, with peace maintained by the great powers whilst respecting a balance of power between them. In this view the Crimean War had only occurred because Russia had upset the balance and the Concert should have been restored after they had been defeated. Balance had been noticeably lacking in international relations for the first half of the twentieth century, with the great powers generally divided into two armed camps and their expansions of power left unchecked. Idealism was not destroyed by the Realist backlash, however, and the construction of a new world following the Second World War did not abandon its ideas so much as temper them with a heavy dose of Realism.

The 1945–90 world order, in character, in many ways can be said to have been a hybrid of both the Concert and the League systems. The League of Nations was revamped in the guise of the United Nations and open diplomacy and international cooperation again encouraged. At the same time, however, a Realist version of collective security was devised to be at the heart of the UN with a 'concert' of five great powers entrusted to manage the system. The five great powers, the USA, UK, USSR, China and France, enjoyed the spoils of being on the winning side in the Second World War but the new system learned the lesson of the Concert that was ignored by the League and sought to keep the vanquished on board. Germany and Japan thus became key players in the new system (albeit economically rather than militarily) rather than dangerously ostracized. Japan had been on the winning side in the First World War but felt excluded by the other victors at the Paris Peace Settlement when the spoils were shared out, whilst Germany's harsh treatment is widely acknowledged as a factor behind the rise of Nazism.

The optimism of 1945 was shorter lived than in either 1815 or 1920, however, as a new conflict cast its shadow over the world almost immediately as the worst conflict in human history came to an end. The year 1990 saw reawakened optimism, particularly since the Cold War had ended with the leading protagonists on good terms and seeming to share a common vision for the future of the world.

## *Democratization*

The most profound suggestion of what the ending of the Cold War meant for international affairs and global security was the widely cited view of US academic

Fukuyama that the West's victory marked the 'end of history' (Fukuyama 1992). Fukuyama reasoned that the ideological triumph of Liberalism over Communism was an ultimate victory that had set the world on a course for a new future, in which like-minded capitalist and Liberal democratic states conducted their relations in peace. This thesis reversed the Hegelian dialectic of Marxist theory and married it to the long-established Liberal principle that 'democracies don't go to war with each other'. Kant proposed this as far back as 1795 in his magnum opus 'Perpetual Peace' (Kant 1970) and it has been a consistent normative and empirical claim of Pluralist International Relations scholars since the mid-twentieth century. Most notably, Deutsch in the 1950s developed the idea of regional 'security communities' which develop as a result of greater cross-border social communication as people discover their common interests (Deutsch *et al.* 1957).

It is important to remember that the Cold War was more of a struggle between Communism and 'non-communism' than totalitarianism and democracy. The Western alliance were happy to prop up numerous dictatorships in the cause of deterring Communism and the USA even assisted in snuffing out democracy in Chile (1973) and Guatemala (1954) when elections delivered leftist governments on their doorstep. The West's victory over the Soviet Union and its 'allies' did, though, serve to accelerate the progress of democratization on both sides of the Iron Curtain. Although power politics can be seen to have played a significant part in 'breaking' the Soviet empire, the West's victory undoubtedly had an ideational dimension. The 1989 revolutions which swept through the six 'Eastern bloc' Soviet satellite states, and effectively brought to an end the Cold War, occurred because ordinary East Europeans wanted to live like West Europeans. The USSR's subsequent transformation has been less complete but all but one of its fifteen successor states (Belarus) have, at least partially, embraced democracy. Western democracies have assisted the new states through the painful process of social, economic and political transition and, freed from Cold War constraints, their tolerance of intolerance has receded. The USA in the 1990s switched from the Truman Doctrine to the 'Clinton Doctrine' in which promoting the spread of democracy became an explicit foreign policy aim. NATO has followed suit in insisting to the lengthy queue of prospective new members to its victors' club, that only states with impeccable democratic and human rights credentials be allowed in. This had not been a precondition in earlier times when Greece, Turkey and Portugal had been recruited without such stipulations.

The proposition that democracies do not go to war with each other is well supported empirically, so the fact that more and more states in the world have embraced democracy in recent years has given scope for optimism in the realization of Kant's vision. Kant, in fact, proposed that it was the trinity of democracy, trade and international cooperation which were the basis for a peaceful world and these three factors are all more prominent today than at any point previously in history. Over two centuries after its promulgation, the Kantian peace proposition has been rigorously tested by Pluralists for its applicability to the contemporary global political system. Russett and Oneal's 'Triangulating Peace', for example, drew on over a decade of statistical analysis with each of these three corners of the 'peace triangle' examined in turn to show how they mutually reinforce each other over time in 'virtuous circles' (Russett and Oneal 2001). Democracies trade with each other more and form common organizations more, both of which are phenomena also demonstrably contributing to pacific relations. Democracies in dealing with other democracies more easily find non-military means to resolve inevitable clashes of interest that arise in their relations and increasingly realize that their interests are not served by violent confrontations. Democratic peace is a political theory with uncharacteristically solid empirical foundations if we consider that: '[e]stablished democracies fought no wars against each other during the entire twentieth century' (Russett and Starr 1996: 173). If we also consider that the number of democratic states in the world has increased from 66 (out of 164) in 1987 to 147 (out of 194) by 2010[1] (Freedom House 2011) the future prospects for perpetual peace look good also. Both of these sets of figures are challengeable, but the overall trends they indicate are not.

> [T]hrough careful statistical analysis, the chance that any two countries will get into a serious military dispute can be estimated if one knows what kinds of governments they have, how economically interdependent they are, and how well connected by a web of international organizations.
>
> (Russett and Oneal 2001: 9)

## Collective security

As referred to earlier, the optimism generated by the end of the Cold War soon appeared to have some foundation when the two former chief protagonists were able to agree to sanction UN-sponsored military action against Iraq for the invasion of Kuwait in 1990. In reaching this agreement the world's two premier powers were activating a long-cherished Idealist dream which had not only seemed impossible during the Cold War but had never in history been realized. Pierre Dubois, writing in the early fourteenth century, advocated the idea of the international community cooperating to keep the peace and the Liberal philosophers Kant and Bentham revived the notion, as an alternative to the balance of power, in the nineteenth century. The idea is also mentioned in the Holy Qur'an (49:9). Under this system acts of aggression prompt collective responses against the aggressors by the whole international community, rather than just by the attacked state and its allies or other states who consider their interests to be affected by the action. It was not until the League of Nations, however, that a system was put in place to make this idea a reality. The League enshrined collective security in its covenant, stating in Article 16 that a state waging war declared unjust by its member-states would be, in effect, waging war against the organization itself. A fifteen-member Council of the League of Nations would make such judgements on behalf of the wider membership.

As already discussed, the League's peacekeeping mechanism failed and collective security was never activated. The outbreak of the Second World War was, of course, the clearest indication of this failure but by this time the League was an irrelevance anyway, having failed to act against blatant acts of aggression by its member-states on a number of occasions throughout the 1930s. The 1931 Japanese invasion of Manchuria, 1935 Italian invasion of Abyssinia (Ethiopia) and German military re-occupation of the Saar prompted some condemnations, but no military response. Soviet, German and Italian interventions in the 1936–9 Spanish Civil War were similarly ignored and although the USSR were expelled from the League in 1939 for the invasion of Finland, this was too little too late.

The League failed to implement collective security for two key reasons.

### It did not represent the whole international community

The League of Nations was handicapped from the start by not being a truly 'global' organization. The emerging superpower, the USA, never took up membership despite the fact that its President Woodrow Wilson had at the Paris Peace Settlement been its chief advocate. The USA, instead, retreated into its shell after the First World War not to emerge until 1940 when the world had become a very different place. The other emerging superpower, the USSR, only joined the League in 1934, whilst Germany, Japan and Italy withdrew their memberships in annoyance at the token criticism they had received for their military adventurism. Collective security rests upon a genuinely collective commitment to upholding the peace and this is unlikely to be found if militarily powerful states are unwilling to contribute to this process or act against it.

### Its decision-making procedure was unworkable

Shorn of any involvement by the USA and any real commitment to peace from Germany, Japan, Italy and the USSR, the League was left dominated by just two of the powerful states of the day, France and Great Britain. These two countries held permanent seats in the Council (as did the USSR during their membership) and represented the only serious military antidote to violations of the League's covenant. The French and British, however, having recently emerged from the bloodiest war in their histories and now embroiled in economic depression, did not have the stomach to become 'world policemen'. The two governments' policies towards aggression from other great powers was at the time one of 'appeasement' rather than confrontation, the hope that granting some concessions to their rivals may be the best means of averting another catastrophic war. Hence the British and French governments went out of their way to ensure that condemnations of Japan for the horrific Manchurian invasion were not too severe and that economic sanctions levied against Italy for the seemingly motiveless annexation of Abyssinia were cosmetic. The Council's voting system rested on unanimity which meant that Britain and France could always dictate the system, as could any of the other thirteen temporary member-states during their stay in the spotlight. Unanimity in an international organization, even amongst a sub-group of fifteen, is hard to find at the best of times and the 1930s was far from the best of times.

## *UN collective security*

The United Nations, in taking over the mantle of global peacekeeping from the League, did not abandon collective security but sought to learn from its predecessor in devising a new more realistic and Realistic system. The UN from the start set about ensuring that its membership was as universal as possible, in spite of a deep division in the international community from the global conflict just passing and the new one beginning to emerge. It maintained the idea of a fifteen-member sub-group to decide on peacekeeping strategy but was more explicit in granting privileges to the most powerful states. Unanimity was replaced with a voting system in which only five of the UN's Security Council would have the power to veto agreements (UK, France, USA, USSR and China). Those same five states would enjoy permanent membership of the Council with the other ten members periodically elected from the rest of the UN membership and denied the power of veto.[2] These five states from the winning side in the Second World War were considered the great powers of the future and would, therefore, be essential in the implementation of collective security since their would be no standing UN army for such operations.

For the Security Council to act against threats to peace, whether to implement collective security or a lesser joint response, nine 'yes' votes are needed from the fifteen government representatives present at its venue in New York. Those nine affirmative votes, however, must include the assent of the 'permanent five'. Hence even fourteen against one would not be enough to secure agreement for an action if the 'one' is a permanent member. Those five countries, in effect, represent a sub-system within a sub-system, since their agreement is a precondition for action on behalf of the near-universal UN membership. Security Council members can elect to abstain rather than vote for or against a resolution which, for the permanent five, does not represent a veto and would permit action if nine other votes are accrued. China chose this option in voting on the 1990 Resolution triggering the Gulf War (Resolution 678) to distance itself from military action against Iraq but not be seen to block the will of the other Security Council members and the international community at large.

The Gulf War stands as one of only three occasions when collective security has been enacted. The first occasion was during the 'hottest' of the Cold War proxy conflicts, the Korean War. In 1950 the UN Security Council authorized international military action against North Korea for the invasion of South Korea. This first ever realization of a centuries-old Liberal dream was, however, very much a fluke event never likely to be repeated during the Cold War. The Soviet Union and China did not use their vetoes to avert action against their Communist ally because neither of them were present in the Security Council when the vote was taken. Communist China had not been able to take up their seat in the UN, and with it their permanent place in the Security Council, because the USA had refused to grant diplomatic recognition to the new regime following the 1949 revolution. In protest at this the USSR boycotted a session of the Security Council allowing the USA to opportunistically push through a resolution that would otherwise certainly have been vetoed.

The USSR never repeated this form of protest and the Security Council remained paralysed until 1990 by the fact that the permanent five (including Communist China from 1979) were unable to find unanimity to sanction any full military action against acts of aggression violating the UN Charter. The veto had been envisaged as a rare option of last resort for the permanent five, necessary to keep them on board for the maintenance of international peace, but became a routinely used tactic to protect Cold War allies. In the first Cold War it was the USSR that made most use of the veto and in the second, when the changing UN membership began to deprive them of guaranteed support, it was the USA. This placed out of bounds any action against both countries' own military adventurism in Vietnam and Afghanistan or in response to the interventions of their 'client states' such as Israel (in the Lebanon) and Cuba (in Angola).

Collective security, covered by Chapter 7 of the UN Charter, is not the only peacekeeping option open to the Security Council and other, lesser, measures aiming to keep the peace were utilized during the Cold War. Chapter 6, which calls upon states to resolve disputes peacefully where possible, has been used as the basis for many Council resolutions sending in multilateral teams of UN monitoring troops to uphold ceasefire lines whilst diplomatic solutions are sought. Such UN forces were sent in to Kashmir and Palestine in 1948 to assist in resolving the Arab–Israeli and Indo-Pakistani territorial disputes. The fact that both these conflicts are still far from resolved today gives an indication of the limitations to this UN peacekeeping strategy.

The realization that UN-assisted mediation was a limited means of restoring peace and that collective security was hamstrung by Cold War politics, prompted efforts outside of the Security Council in the 1950s to try another approach to peacekeeping. UN Secretary-General of the time Dag Hammarskjöld and the General Assembly, in which all UN members are represented equally, were central to this process. The 1950 'Uniting for Peace' General Assembly resolution, sponsored by the USA, aimed to pre-empt the inevitable presence of a veto-wielding USSR in a future scenario similar to the Korean War. Uniting for Peace gave the General Assembly a role in security issues, previously considered the exclusive domain of the Council. A special session of the Assembly could be called and be able to recommend international action in the absence of a Security Council agreement. There are no vetoes to be wielded at the General Assembly and every UN member is present so the required two-thirds majority for a resolution is far more likely than at the Security Council. Hammarskjöld put this new power into practice when he became a far more active Secretary-General than his predecessor on taking over the job in 1953. A UN Emergency Force was sent in to supervise the withdrawal of British, French and Israeli troops from Egypt during the 1956 Suez Crisis, despite the fact that the UK and France had prevented the Security Council authorizing any response to their invasion. Hammarskjöld, as well as seeking to circumvent the Security Council, pioneered new approaches to peacekeeping beyond mediation. What Hammarskjöld referred to as 'preventive diplomacy' sought to initiate third-party involvement in disputes before they became militarized whilst what became known as 'peace enforcement' envisaged a more proactive deployment of UN peacekeeping forces than the manning of ceasefire lines. These ideas went beyond the 'pacific settlement of disputes' confines of

Chapter 6 but were less contentious, and hence less likely to invoke a veto, than the collective security of Chapter 7. Hence Hammarskjöld referred to such measures as 'Chapter six and a half' of the Charter.

Chapter six-and-a-half peace enforcement was first clearly put into practice in 1960 when a brutal civil war in the Congo, following its independence from Belgium, prompted a rare display of solidarity between the Cold War protagonists on the Security Council. A UN force, made up of troops from a number of impartial countries, was sent in to the Congo not just to keep warring factions apart but to create the conditions for peace, using force where necessary. Some temporary calm was achieved by the UN intervention but optimism was punctured by the public decapitation of some Irish soldiers and the USSR's loss of appetite for such an extended UN role as the conflict unfolded. Hammarskjöld died in an aeroplane crash over the Congo in 1961 (prompting numerous conspiracy theories) and the idea of peace enforcement appeared to have died with him. The USA from the 1960s became far less enthusiastic about finding ways to get around the problem of Security Council vetoes since it was an option they increasingly wished to utilize. Hence, UN forces that were dispatched to trouble spots over the next thirty years confined themselves more to forming 'thin blue lines' of largely inactive troops stationed between the protagonists.

Boutros Boutros-Ghali revived the spirit of Hammarskjöld in the 1990s when it became clear that even the post-Cold War world would feature a frequently immobilized Security Council. The increased number of civil wars was making both Chapters 6 and 7 insufficient for the job and prompting the threat of Chinese and Russian vetoes, not in support of ideological brothers in arms but the principle of sovereignty. Boutros-Ghali revamped preventive diplomacy and peace enforcement in his 'Agenda for Peace' initiative, paving the way for the Security Council sanctioning expansive operations in Bosnia-Herzegovina and Somalia in the early 1990s. As with the Congo, however, these operations were not major successes. The failure of UN troops to protect Bosnian Moslem citizens from Serb nationalist violence forced them, humiliatingly and symbolically, to hand over the mantle of peacekeeping to NATO. In Somalia there were strong echoes of the Congo, when a US force sent in to bring stability and humanitarian relief to a complex civil war pulled out amidst accusations of having exacerbated the conflict and with televised images of their dead troops being dragged thorough the streets being beamed around the world.

Such images were still fresh in the minds of public and political opinion when an even fiercer internal conflict in Rwanda erupted in 1994 and, this time, there was no preventive diplomacy. When, five years later, violence erupted again in Yugoslavia it appeared as though the Security Council was still operating in the 'old world order' when Russian and Chinese vetoes proscribed collective security in spite of the obvious lesson from up the road in Bosnia that preventive diplomacy was not enough. Again NATO stepped in to fill the global void but this time with a full-scale and successful military operation. Although UN collective security was invoked for a third time to legitimize the US war against Afghanistan in 2001–2 this was more of an act of symbolism since the world's most powerful state did not need military support to defeat one of the world's weakest. When the USA and UK then acted without either UN or NATO authorization in going to war with Iraq in 2003 collective security appeared to becoming, once again, a distant dream.

Collective security has not been enacted since 2001 but peace enforcement was given a new lease of life in 2011 when the Security Council sanctioned a military-backed 'no fly zone' over Libya to diminish the capacity of the Gadaffi regime to slaughter anti-government protestors growing up throughout the country, which ultimately led to his overthrow and assassination. NATO took on the enforcement role but in a more partial and expansive manner than the Russian, Chinese and some Arab governments sometimes found palatable, again illustrating the difficulties inherent in this approach to making peace.

## Just war

One of the chief sources of optimism that marked the onset of the 'New World Order' was that the ending of the Cold War might also bring to an end the era of total war, which had so characterized the twentieth century. The Gulf War, as well as recapturing the seemingly lost dream of collective security, witnessed a revival of another old doctrine of international affairs thought consigned to history during the three world wars, just war. Just war doctrine dates back as far as the fourth century when Christian theologians, led by St Augustine, sought to move away from absolute pacifism and accommodate the idea that war might be morally acceptable in certain circumstances. In the seventeenth century the undisputed 'father of international law', Dutch jurist Hugo Grotius, gave the doctrine a secular and legalistic footing amidst the backdrop of the Christian in-fighting of the Thirty Years War tearing Europe apart (Grotius 1853). Grotius set out to codify universally applicable principles by which it could be judged that going to war was morally acceptable, *Jus ad bellum*, and accompanying principles for judging the moral prosecution of a war, *Jus in bello*. The separate doctrines emphasize the key point that a war deemed just at the outset can become unjust if prosecuted in an immoral way. Precise interpretations of just war vary but, by the late twentieth century with writers such as Ramsey (1968) and Walzer (1978) repackaging Grotius's work, the key principles of the twin doctrines could be distilled down to the following:

### Jus ad bellum (justice in going to war)

(a) Must be waged by a sovereign authority.
(b) Must be a just cause for the war: self-defence or the enforcement of human rights.
(c) Peaceful means of resolving the dispute must have been exhausted.
(d) Must be likely to succeed.

### Jus in bello (justice in the conduct of war)

(i) Means used should be proportionate to the wrong being rectified.
(ii) Unavoidable killing of non-combatants should be avoided.
(iii) Wounded troops and prisoners of war should not be killed.

Aspects of *Jus in bello* became codified in the laws of war, particularly in the numerous Geneva and Hague Conventions, which evolved through the nineteenth and early twentieth centuries. *Jus ad bellum* during this period, however, tended not to amount to much more than principle (a) as the Westphalian notion of sovereignty crystallized into a form that legitimized whatever the state felt was necessary for its security or aggrandizement. Wars of colonial expansion presented perhaps the clearest departure from notion of justice but justifications for such campaigns were still made on the basis that the vanquished peoples would benefit from being 'civilized'. Perhaps the most extreme articulation of this came from Gentili, who declared the genocidal Spanish campaign against native Americans in the sixteenth century to be a just war since the victims were cannibals (Gentili 1933).

The concept of total war in the twentieth century did most to set back the just war tradition. The idea that the whole of society were directly involved during war, rather than just the professional apparatus of government, had developed from the nineteenth century, with the growth of military conscription and state-promoted nationalism, but became fully realized in the era of the world wars. From the perspective of any of its participants, the First World War exceeded any notion of proportionality and was entered into without much regard to diplomatic alternatives to fighting. The Second World War, from the perspective of the allied forces, satisfied the conditions of *Jus ad bellum* but possibly not principle (i) and most certainly not principle (ii) of *Jus in bello*. The arguments offered by the governments of the UK, USSR and USA in defence of ignoring non-combatant immunity in the war against Germany and Japan seemed to illustrate that the moral judgements facing governments in the twentieth century were far starker than in previous ages. The British blanket bombing of German cities brought criticism from some clerics in the Church of England, but was generally deemed acceptable, since the enemy had done the same thing, and necessary, since the just defeat of Germany required not only military victories but the diminution of their war-making capacity. Soviet violence against German invaders in driving them back to where they came from was horrific but generally viewed in the same way since it was not disproportionate to what they had suffered. The US atomic strikes on Japan were indiscriminate but maybe ultimately saved lives since they finally brought to its knees an enemy apparently determined to fight on well beyond any realistic hope of winning the war. In an age when the means of waging war were so much greater than before it appeared that moral niceties had become subsumed by necessity.

The Cold War institutionalized this amoral necessity into everyday international politics. Nuclear deterrence rested on the notion that whole societies were legitimate and realistic military targets which, in itself, must negate any notion of proportionality as well as non-combatant discrimination. The rectification of what sort of wrong could justify the annihilation of the whole population of a country, or even the world?

The recession of such a scale of nuclear threat in the 1990s saw a concerted effort to recapture all aspects of the just war tradition in the Western-led wars of the New World Order. During the Gulf War the US-led coalition limited itself to the realization of its UN-authorized aims and did not seek to topple the Iraqi regime, despite military and political pressure to do so. Saddam Hussein was forced out of

Kuwait but not out of office. The war was also conducted along lines which sought to minimize civilian casualties through the use of 'smart' weaponry better able to target military and official state sites than in bombing campaigns of earlier eras. Similar sorts of campaigns were waged by NATO against Yugoslavia in 1999 and by the USA and UK against Afghanistan in 2001–2 and Iraq in 2003. The 1999 Kosovan War, in particular, marked a revival of morality in military conduct since it was in aim, principally, a humanitarian intervention.

Grey areas still remain in terms of deeming when a war is 'just'. Cynics have contended that the 'smart' bombing-led wars of recent years are as much a device for sanitizing war for domestic public consumption as showing compassion for civilians. Bombing from afar saves the lives of the bombers more than it does the civilians living near targeted sites. Few would suggest that the USA and their allies deliberately and routinely struck civilian targets in any of the four above-mentioned wars but civilian deaths did occur in all conflicts, particularly in Iraq. Just war doctrine acknowledges that accidental 'collateral damage' does not de-legitimize a war, but were the civilian deaths in Iraq, Yugoslavia and Afghanistan avoidable? It has been suggested that a ground campaign against Yugoslavia, rather than an almost entirely aerial battle, would have endangered fewer Yugoslav civilians since ground troops are better equipped with their own eyes to discriminate between combatants and non-combatants than aircrew kitted out with even the 'smartest' of computerized sightings (Mandelbaum 1999; Robertson 2000: 414–17). This argument is believed to have been aired within NATO ranks but US reluctance to be embroiled in 'another Somalia' favoured the option eventually taken. It has proven to be extremely difficult to be discriminating in the ground campaign in Iraq, however, as prolonged, crude urban warfare has led to hundreds of thousands of non-combatant deaths.

Ambiguities arise in putting non-combatant discrimination into practice. The dilemma ignored in the Second World War and the Cold War, about who is and is not a legitimate target in the modern era, is still there. Large proportions of non-military personnel contribute to the war effort of a country in some way. Munitions workers might be an obvious extension from servicemen but what about other sections of society supporting a targeted government? The Kosovan and Iraq (2003) wars saw journalists supporting the enemy deliberately targeted. In both of these cases it was state-run television companies, which were government propagandist machines, that were openly struck but non-Iraqi journalists also died in the latter conflict. 'Al Jazeera', an influential Arab nationalist satellite television service based in Qatar, had their Baghdad offices bombed in a strike officially described as a mistake but which raised suspicions beyond the Arab world. Another 'mistake' which aroused great suspicion occurred in 2002 when an Israeli jet released a one-tonne bomb on a Palestinian residential block in Gaza killing fifteen civilians, including nine children. A Hamas leader and known Israeli target inhabited the block. This episode was a clear breach of the principle, but a wider question of intent can be raised which is more problematic. Given the fact that it appears civilians inevitably die in modern war does resorting to war itself, even if the means employed attempt to be discriminating, violate the notion of non-combatant immunity? The norm arose in a different era when battlefields were fields and civilian massacres a sideshow.

A revival of the concept of non-combatant immunity has not erased the moral ambiguities surrounding the legitimacy of war.

The New World Order wars also raised questions of proportionality. Did NATO air strikes against Yugoslavia prompt Serb nationalists to step up the campaign against Kosovar Albanians, leading to more suffering than would have occurred if no military action had been taken? Did more Afghani citizens die (albeit accidentally) in US strikes than the 3,000 New York and Washington residents killed in the 2001 al-Qa'ida strikes which prompted the response? An even more problematic moral quantification emerged in 2003. Was the 2003 Iraq war justified on the basis that it pre-empted future threats from that country? This dilemma divided Western opinion from the start but, a few years into the conflict, few backers could be found.

As with much of humanitarian international law and custom, just war is a grey area in which inconsistent interpretation and application is inevitable. Owing to what Clausewitz called the 'friction' of war it is impossible to be entirely accurate in predicting the outcome of a military campaign or to fight a perfect battle free of mistakes. Should, though, the response to an imperfect system of rules be to have none at all? The questions posed about the recent wars could also be countered by clearer international legal guidelines. Yugoslavia and NATO could simultaneously point to UN Charter articles to support their positions that the other side was at fault in the 1999 war. A retreat from total war and the strengthening of a legal and ethical framework for fighting future wars in the human interest is surely something to be welcomed. The International Criminal Court provides some evidence that this is the way the international community is evolving (see Chapter 5).

## Conflict resolution

A central feature of the New World Order was an increased commitment by the international community to work towards resolving violent conflicts. There was scope for optimism in the 1990s that the open sores that were the late twentieth century's 'proxy wars' could be allowed to heal now that the superpower interest in their maintenance was removed. Additionally, it was hoped that the 'peace dividend' of the East–West thaw could now be allocated to restoring order to militarized disputes unrelated to the Cold War. The results of this have been quite impressive. Research suggests that twice as many conflicts based on self-determination (both inter-state and civil) were resolved in the 1990s than in the whole Cold War era. Fourteen such conflicts were 'contained' and seventeen 'settled' in the New World Order era as opposed to six and nine, respectively, between 1945 and 1990 (Gurr, Marshall and Khosla 2001: 17). In the 1990s the determination of the USA to utilize their power in order to play the world policeman role in a diplomatic context was a significant factor. US presidents played pivotal roles in the negotiation of settlements for the resolution of the Yugoslav wars of secession (in 1995 at Dayton), Northern Ireland 'troubles' (in 1998 at Belfast) and the ultimately unsuccessful Oslo Accords (1993) aiming to resolve the Palestinian–Israeli conflict. Of more lasting significance, and frequently overlooked, is a major increase in UN peace work. Despite continued frustration with attempts to implement collective security and intervene on cases of genocide, the UN Security Council's use of preventive diplomacy missions increased sixfold and peacekeeping actions fourfold between 1990 and 2002 (Human Security Centre 2005: 152–4).

Post-1990 conflict resolution has not, however, been just about a revival of collective security and superpowers policing less powerful actors; more subtle techniques have been an additional feature. Less powerful states have played arbitration roles, such as the government of Norway, which has played a role in attempting to forge peace in the inter-state conflicts between Israel and the Arab states, India and Pakistan and civil wars in the Philippines and, most notably, Sri Lanka. Humanitarian pressure groups have become an increased factor in promoting negotiation and compromise. International Alert have been prominent in instigating peace processes in many conflict areas and the Norwegian government have developed partnerships with groups such as the Norwegian Institute of International Affairs to lend assistance to the resolution of persistent armed conflicts such as in the Congo. Pressure groups cannot bring force to resolve disputes but stand a better chance than governments of being considered as impartial by those embroiled in conflict and can use their expertise to suggest innovative solutions to complex disputes.

## New World Disorder?

Realist caution against optimism that the passing into history of the Cold War would herald a new, uniquely pacific era of international relations could be considered borne out by certain developments since 1990 which have not enhanced the military security of the world's states or people.

### *Is it really over? The persistence of Cold War disputes*

In a 1998 article in a Russian academic journal, the prominent foreign policy analyst Sergei Kortunov asked 'Is the Cold War Really Over?' (Kortunov 1998). Similarly British academic Prins has posited: 'Is the end of the Cold War, therefore, only the end of Part I, just as *Star Wars*, the movie, promises?'(Prins 2002: 46). That the Cold War has not ended might initially appear an absurd suggestion when we cast our minds back to the momentous changes that occurred at the end of the 1980s. The images of the Berlin Wall and Iron Curtain being dismantled whilst the leaders of the two Cold War superpowers publicly declared the conflict to be over portrayed peace in as explicit terms as ever seen in history, but, in fact, many of the same points of confrontation remain.

The Korean peninsula remains firmly frozen in the Cold War era, divided into two ideologically defined states precisely as it was at the point of East–West stalemate after the war in 1953. Communist North Korea's relations with the West remain practically non-existent whilst it maintains political links with its war ally, China. North Korea's confirmation as a nuclear power in 2006 has seen this trouble spot become more potentially dangerous than at any time since the 1950s.

Relations between the USA, and most other Western states, with their second major Cold War foe, China, have remained frosty in the years since 1990. Economic cooperation has blossomed through mutual interest but diplomatic and military tensions remain. It is worth remembering that no official end to this dimension of the Cold War ever occurred. No equivalent to the 1989 Malta Summit or 1990 Paris Treaty was signed by China and the USA and a number of issues remain wholly unresolved. Most prominently, the status of Taiwan remains a source of tension and the island remains in a non-sovereign limbo, being claimed by China but still assured by the USA of its independence.

Whilst undoubtedly more cordial than during the Cold War and smoother than with those countries who have not abandoned Communism, US–Russian relations since the 1991 collapse of the USSR have not been exactly harmonious. The Kosovan War of 1999 was a bitter humiliation for Russia since to them it appeared to demonstrate Western contempt for their long-cherished foreign policy goal of 'pan-Slavism', in which Eastern Europe was understood as part of their sphere of influence.[3] Having stopped the UN from taking action against Yugoslavia, the Russian government failed to dissuade NATO from acting in its place. A desperate attempt to claw out some role in Kosovo saw Russian troops unilaterally dispatched to Pristina, where NATO forces were gathering in a post-war peacekeeping force. A desperate scramble ensued as Russian troops secured Pristina airport in advance of the British in an incident which came close to producing a direct skirmish between the two sides not seen during the Cold War.[4] Russia secured a role in the peacekeeping process but, in a sign of how things had changed, were unable to maintain sole control of the airport since support troops were blocked from flying over the airspace of former allies Hungary or Romania due to Western pressure on **their** new allies. The encroachment of the USA and their allies into their backyard was confirmed, in Russian eyes, when in the same year as the Kosovan War, NATO expanded its membership to recruit three of their former Warsaw Pact allies: Poland, Hungary and the Czech Republic. The further 2004 expansion took this a stage further by bringing into the fold three former members of the USSR itself in Latvia, Lithuania and Estonia. Far from exiting the stage after 1990, a Cold War alliance had not only played on but extended its role and subsumed part of its original object of containment. NATO have repeatedly assured Russia that their containment is not its game any more and, while expanding eastwards, gave them a guarantee that no east-facing missiles would be sited in the territories of the new member-states. The fact remained, however, that this was an alliance set up to counter Russian (Soviet) power and it was still there.

The Cold War 'hangover' offers a vindication of the post-revisionist view that the conflict was, in essence, just another balance-of-power struggle. The balance has tilted but elements of the struggle remain. Clark, in 2001, argued that the Cold War had not yet been fully resolved because the **process** of peacemaking (as opposed to an event such as the Malta Summit or Paris Treaty) had not been completed (Clark 2001: 6–11). The lack of a systematic attempt to mould a genuinely New World Order in the 1990s can be explained in a number of ways, Clark posits. First, the fact that this was a cold rather than 'hot' war served as a disincentive to the protagonists to encourage a thaw. 'Since the Cold War was not a proper war it is fitting that it should be brought to an end by a peace that is not a proper peace'

(Clark 2001: 4). The originator of the term Cold War, Don Juan Manuel, noted this problematic phenomenon half a millennium earlier. 'War that is very strong and very hot ends either with death or peace, whereas cold war neither brings peace nor gives honour to the one who makes it' (Halliday 1986: 2). Second, the Cold War was also an unusual war in that it was resolved through negotiation and a voluntary, rather than imposed, climb down by one side. The fact that fruitful negotiations between warring parties preceded rather than proceeded the conflict served to make them appear superfluous later on. Third, even 'normal' multilateral wars are rarely ended at a stroke. Complete harmony is unlikely to succeed the hostility and certain unresolved issues are likely to live on. Prins's own answer to his question on whether the Cold War could be replayed is that a sequel is indeed possible, but is 'unlikely to be cast with the same team of actors'(Prins 2002: 48). Clark makes a convincing case that there is often a certain 'time lag' following major multilateral conflict before real peace is achieved but could it be that the Cold War will not so much fade away as metamorphosize into another global conflict?

This view was most notably articulated by the US Realist Huntington in his influential 'Clash of the Civilizations' thesis (Huntington 1993). Huntington contended that transnational cultural conflict was now where the logic of the security dilemma could best be applied, rather than inter-state rivalry. Major antagonism between democracy and Communism may be over but there is no 'end of history' and the 'civilization' of Liberal-democracy faces other challenges to its hegemony, particularly from the 'civilization' of Islam. The rise of anti-Western Islamic fundamentalism led by al-Qa'ida, Western-led wars in the Moslem states of Iraq and Afghanistan and the Islamophobic dimension of the Yugoslav wars seemed, to many, to bear out this prophecy. To others, however, this was more of a Cold War hangover than a new Cold War, with an exaggerated 'green peril' filling the void created by the demise of 'red peril' in the lazy analysis of 'fault line babble' (Halliday 2001: 114).

## Democratic war?

Whilst the idea of cultural conflict has risen in prominence, a corollary to this is that not everyone is convinced that democratization is the route to 'perpetual peace'. Whilst it may be true that democracies do not fight each other, they are equally prone to be embroiled in war as non-democracies and have a propensity to fight autocracies. The restraint shown by democracies in resolving disputes with states with similar political systems is frequently not exhibited in resolving disputes with non-democracies. Indeed evidence can be found to suggest that some democracies are predisposed towards violent resolutions of disputes when dealing with dictatorships. Supportive cases include: the 1956 Suez dispute, when France, Israel and the UK invaded Egypt, Israeli incursions into the Lebanon and the twenty-first-century US-led wars in Afghanistan and Iraq. Perhaps it is cultural affiliation rather than democracy that is the key to peace? Democratic peace proponents Russett and Oneal admit that two autocracies are more likely to have peaceful relations that one democracy and one autocracy (Oneal and Russett 1997: 283). In addition, democratizing states have been shown to be more prone to conflict than stable autocracies due to the nationalistic zeal which typically accompanies revolution (Snyder 2000; Zakaria 1997). Social Constructivists have highlighted the phenomenon of 'warlike democracies' to demonstrate how ideas and perception undermine the logic of democratic peace. '[D]emocracies to a large degree create their enemies and their friends – "them" and "us" – by inferring either aggressive or defensive motives from the domestic structures of their counterparts' (Risse 1995: 19–20). Risse does, however, concede that democracies are overwhelmingly peaceful in their relations with other democracies. In a similar vein, Brock, Geis and Mueller posit a 'dyadic democratic peace theory' since 'democracies are peaceful *towards each other* but *in general* they are as war prone as any other regime type' (Brock, Geis and Mueller 2006: 3). Perpetual peace, then, might only become a reality when there are only 'us' and no 'them' in the world. This 'end of history' is not yet with us.

## *From balance to an imbalance of power*

The chief cause of Realist caution or fear for the 'New World Order' was that it threatened a central tenet of their recipe for world order, the balance of power. The unipolar world that has emerged, according to orthodox Realist logic, should prove unsustainable and prompt other states to topple the USA's pole position. This has not happened, of course, but the fear persists among some statesmen and Realist commentators that American preponderance is bound to breed resentment and be a source of general global instability. Some Western governments have voiced concern over the implications of US freedom to manoeuvre on the world stage with French statesmen and commentators, in particular, making reference to the dangers inherent in there being a world 'hyperpower'. Kagan, an American academic with strong political connections to the State Department, has articulated the concern that a hyperpower is reflexively drawn to an aggressive foreign policy.

> A man armed only with a knife may decide that a bear prowling the forest is a tolerable danger, because hunting it with a knife is riskier than lying low and hoping it never attacks. The same man armed with a rifle, however, will likely make a different calculation.
>
> (Kagan 2003: 2)

This scenario becomes problematic when the man takes to shooting at targets just in case they turn out to be a bear. These concerns came to greatest prominence in 2003 when the USA sidestepped both the UN and NATO in prosecuting war against Iraq. Other states, in no way aligned to the USA, have been more vitriolic than the French in their criticism of their foreign policy. President Bush's assertion in the aftermath of the Afghanistan war in 2002, and lead-up to the Iraqi war, that Iran was part of an 'axis of evil' prompted Iranian Foreign Minister, Kamal Kharazi, to state that '[t]he world will not accept US hegemony'(Theodoulou 2002). US preponderance is such that their hegemony looks unchallengeable but there is little doubt that it has bred resentment in some parts of the world which threatens to puncture the idea of post-Cold War peace.

## *Back to the drawing board: arms control*

The clearest manifestation of the dangers considered by many to be inherent in the breakdown of the Cold War bipolar balance of power has been the strain put on global arms control agreements by the new alignment. The balance of power has been explicitly recognized in multilateral treaties amongst the great military powers going back to the 1920s[5] but was most institutionalized into the relations of the two Cold War nuclear superpowers, despite the level of hostility that existed between them. A combination of bilateral and multilateral arms control agreements involving much of the international community contributed to the bipolar 'balance of power' that marked the Cold War and has persisted since its declared end, despite the onset of unipolarity. The Cold War balance was only achieved from the 1960s when the USSR's nuclear arsenal began to match that of the USA and paved the way for agreements reminiscent of the Washington Conference, based on the cold logic of the nuclear 'balance of terror'. Nuclear weapons by then had come to serve a different role in superpower strategy and diplomacy than they had in the 1940s and 1950s. The fact that the USSR had caught up meant that the USA could no longer use its superiority for diplomatic 'compellance' and that these unprecedented power capabilities would be deployed in a more defensive manner, to deter the Soviet Union.

Deterrence, like arms control, was not new to the Cold War period but took on an added dimension to displays of 'gun boat diplomacy' in earlier ages, because of the sheer scale of the threat now being projected. Both superpowers had the capability to annihilate the other state and its people, necessitating the added ingredient of 'Mutually Assured Destruction' (MAD) to keep the balance. MAD, which did indeed appear mad to many at the time, nevertheless gave meaning to nuclear deterrence. For both superpowers to be deterred from attacking each other they needed to know that initiating war would be futile since they, as well as the their enemy, would face annihilation. For the logic of MAD to operate both the USA and USSR needed to have a 'second strike capability', to be able to respond to any attack by the other. In other words, both sides needed to be in a position where they could not only obliterate the other in a first strike but also do so in response to the other side initiating hostilities. Hence, in spite of improved Soviet–US relations in the aftermath of the 1962 Cuban missile crisis and the gradual acceptance of military parity by both sides, the development of nuclear weapons and delivery systems accelerated until the end of the decade. By the 1970s, however, the Strategic Arms Limitation Talks (SALT) of 1972 and 1979 established the first meaningful bilateral arms control agreements with ceilings placed on the production of a range of weaponry.

As well as maintaining an equilibrium between the superpowers, the balance of terror rested on keeping the balance bipolar since MAD logic would be lost in a multipolar system. Hence multilateral arms control agreements keeping the 'nuclear weapons club' an exclusive one formed an equally important dimension of Cold War military security diplomacy. The 1963 Limited Test Ban Treaty prohibited the overground testing of nuclear weapons by the then three nuclear powers, USA, USSR and UK. By the signing of the 1968 Non-Proliferation of Nuclear Weapons Treaty (NPT) two other nuclear powers, France and China, had joined the club and agreed to the NPT's key rule constraining its members, like magicians in the 'Magic Circle', from revealing their secrets to outsiders. The same five states that made up the disharmonious concert of permanent members in the Security Council found it far easier to reach accord in nuclear diplomacy since, like magicians, they may be in competition with each other but could all lose out from openly showing how anyone could pull a rabbit out of their hat.

The end of the Cold War permitted the two principal protagonists to greatly scale down their armaments in bilateral accords, the Strategic Arms Reduction Talks (START), a decade after SALT II had been abandoned by the USA in the final phase of the conflict. Both sides, persuaded that they no longer had the need for a second strike capability against the other, agreed to massive cuts in their arsenals safe in the knowledge that they would still have enough firepower to deter any other military threats that existed in the world.

Whilst bilateral arms control initially prospered in the post-Cold War afterglow, the multilateral regimes became strained by the new military power configurations of the 1990s. Non-proliferation had been one thing the five official nuclear powers could agree on during the Cold War but now, their commitment began to waver. Chinese state officials, by now focusing their concerns on the Asian rather than global balance of power, are widely suspected of having assisted the Pakistani government in developing nuclear weapons to counter India's unofficial though well-known nuclear capability. Throughout the 1990s the nuclear club became far less exclusive. Pakistan and India openly tested their new weapons and, in doing so, the latter denounced the 'nuclear apartheid' of the NPT in privileging the 'big five' (Singh 1998). The break-up of the USSR saw some of its nuclear arsenal apparently go missing when a recount was taken after fifteen new states had succeeded the superpower. A protocol to START tidied this up by giving incentives to get Belarus, Ukraine and Kazakhstan to agree not to be nuclear states but the nightmare scenario emerged that some Soviet nuclear material could have got onto the global black market (see Chapter 10).

By the 1990s it was also apparent that Israel and North Korea, too, were nuclear powers and that Iraq and Iran were on the way to following suit. The NPT offers the incentive to non-nuclear states of aid for peaceful nuclear power production in exchange for not developing military uses for this resource. This, however, was not an incentive for India or Pakistan to sign up and joining the nuclear club was widely greeted with jubilation amongst the peoples of the sub-continent. Not all Western military strategists were alarmed at this particular breach of the magicians' code. The cause for greater reflection in the recourse to nuclear rather than conventional weapons might bring some stability to Indo-Pakistani relations, many reasoned. More worryingly for the old order was that North Korea and Iraq, who were signatory to the NPT, had managed to evade detection and gone down the road of developing the weapons unbeknown to the world. The North Koreans trumpeted their achievement in an exercise of mini-coercion aimed at securing aid concessions from an alarmed West; Iraq's progress was stumbled across by invaders during the Gulf War.

These developments showed up a central problem of the NPT, and of arms control in general, that of implementing and verifying agreements. Counting naval destroyers in the 1920s was relatively straightforward but modern weapons of mass destruction (WMD) are more easily kept out of sight even in an age of satellite observation. The NPT limps on with some successes, such as South Africa's unilateral disarmament of 1991, but other contemporary multilateral regimes looked increasingly irrelevant. The Comprehensive Test Ban Treaty (CTBT), the successor to the Limited Test Ban Treaty, has yet to come into force since not all nuclear states (both military and non-military) have ratified – including the USA. Other non-nuclear WMD regimes are limited in their effectiveness. The Biological Weapons Convention came into force in 1975 but has no formal verification system and looks unlikely to ever achieve any effective verification since biological weapons are far harder to detect than the nuclear weapons which evaded detection in North Korea and Iraq. Chemical weaponry arms control dates back to the 1925 Geneva Protocol which, in the aftermath of its use in the First World War, prohibited the military application of poison gas. Today, international legal force is centred on the 1993 Chemical Weapons Convention which bans all forms of military chemical applications and commits ratifying countries who stockpile such weapons to destroy them. The regime does feature an inspection system but has been patchily implemented by the key parties and main chemical weapons holders, the USA and Russia, and not ratified at all by the potential chemical weapons states of North Korea, Israel, Egypt and Syria.

Under Bush (Jr) the world's sole superpower embarked upon a far more unilateralist WMD strategy, in line with its preponderance of military power. As well as snubbing the CTBT and showing limited interest in developing the biological and chemical weapons regimes, the USA also changed direction in bilateral agreements with its former Cold War foe. START II in 1993 was due to deepen the cuts of Russian and US nuclear weapons but was abandoned by the Americans and eventually replaced with a lesser agreement, the Strategic Offensive Reduction Talks (SORT), in 2002. A change in direction under the presidency of Obama, though, saw START revived with the ratification of the 2011 'new START' agreement which set new, lower ceilings on both sides' strategic nuclear warheads and introduced a more rigorous inspection regime. Whilst the moniker NewSTART is apt in terms of Russo-American relations the treaty maintains a pretence of bipolar equality since the Russians have come to accept the notion of US 'flexibility', in which bilateral ceilings can be exceeded by bringing weapons out of storage in an emergency (this power is also open to Russia but is of much more value to the US since they have far more and more sophisticated weapons in storage).

US nuclear strategy has also moved into a new era with hopes based on the potential for physical defence rather than psychological deterrence in the form of a missile shield. The idea of deploying satellite-based interceptors to protect the USA (and potentially its allies) from attack was first mooted in the 1980s with SDI and did much to break the USSR in the arms race, even though the capability was not really there at the time. US pursuance of missile defence has divided opinion across the world. Many statesmen and commentators are horrified at the prospect of effectively abandoning forty years of carefully constructed, if imperfect, agreements limiting the spread of deadly weapons. In a prescient lead article just days before the September 11th 2001 al-Qa'ida strikes on the USA, the normally pro-American *Economist* newspaper voiced its concerns over missile defence:

concentrating on the possibility of future missile threats seems to be blinding the Bush team to other dangers. There are plenty of other ways to deliver a nuclear, chemical or bug bomb. . . . What folly for America to spend billions on missile defences, while unravelling the rules which limit the weapons that may someday get through or around them.

(*Economist* 2001)

US proponents of missile defence have argued that the Cold War logic underpinning existing arms control agreements has no application in the contemporary system and thus offers little basis for enhancing international security. Enthusiasm for the US initiative does not come only from American unilateralists, the avowedly multilateral British Liberal politician, Paddy Ashdown, has added his support: 'the world is no longer bi-polar. It is a disobedient, fractured and splintering place. And it is the fractures and splinters, not the giants, who now threaten the peace' (Ashdown 2001).

Some are sceptical as to whether there really was a superpower consensus on MAD during the Cold War and others have suggested that, even if there was, it was as much by luck as design that a peace of sorts was maintained for forty-five years. The USSR, whilst talking in terms of parity and agreeing ceilings on established weaponry, developed new forms of missile in the late 1970s and continued to consider that superiority was possible through technological innovation. The fact that the Warsaw Pact countries put far more emphasis on conventional forces and central European battle preparations than NATO, implies that the Soviet government was less convinced than their US counterparts by the logic of deterrence. Within the USA too there were significant dissenting opinions on the applicability of MAD. The USSR's weapons developments of the late 1970s and invasion of Afghanistan prompted a new strand of thinking in military security circles which began to speak of 'Nuclear Utilization Theory', which envisaged pre-emptive limited nuclear strikes to stop inevitable Soviet aggression (Kennan 1984). Additionally, historical research on the Cold War has uncovered evidence that the world was brought closer than anyone even imagined to the brink of global nuclear war. In 2002 it emerged that a Soviet nuclear submarine sailing near Cuba during the 1962 missile crisis had a depth charge dropped on it by a US destroyer, which did not realize the vessel's capability. A decision on whether to launch a nuclear strike in response required the consensus of all commanders on a submarine and, in the vote which followed the American action, one of the three Soviet commanders on board vetoed such a strike (Rennie 2002). Did Commander Arkhipov save the world? Similarly, even in the absence of a 'real' crisis as a backdrop the 1983 NATO military exercise 'Able Archer' nearly provoked a nuclear response when it was initially interpreted by the Kremlin as a genuine attack (Prins 2002: 32–4).

People make mistakes and it is in this context that the rationality of deterrence maybe breaks down. With the proliferation of nuclear rivalries around the world (India v. Pakistan over Kashmir, Israel v. Iran or Syria over Palestine or the Lebanon, China v. USA over Taiwan, North Korea v. USA over South Korea) the possibility of accidental war has multiplied, even if one were to accept the logic of nuclear deterrence and posit that deliberate war is less likely. The logic of deterrence is shakier still if the potential threat of WMD held by non-state actors is taken into consideration. The suicide bombers who inflicted the gravest external military strike on mainland USA in its history in 2001 could not have been deterred nor stopped by a missile shield and they possessed only pocket knives and ingenuity.

## Where do you draw the line? The persistence of territorial disputes

In considering the optimism generated by the decline in number of conflicts since 1990, it is worth bearing in mind that this is a relative decline from an all-time high of over 150 conflicts a year at the end of the 1980s and beginning of the 1990s (Gurr, Marshall and Khosla 2001). Border disputes remain very much a feature of today's world. As already referred to, some explicitly Cold War disputes linger on more than a decade after the apparent end of that conflict, whilst other disputes subsumed by the global struggle persist in spite of change in the global political backdrop. Arab–Israeli peace remains far from certain and the conflict retains a one-sided proxy element to it with continued US support for Israel, even in the absence of a Cold War dimension.

Some conflicts have emerged or worsened **because of** rather than in spite of improved Russo-American relations. The rise since the 1990s of the phenomenon of 'failed states', where domestic sovereign control breaks down indefinitely, provide the clearest cases of this. In some parts of the world superpower competition for influence was succeeded from the end of the 1980s by disinterest. The fate of Afghanistan epitomized this with a 1980s proxy war transformed into an ignored 1990s civil war, only to be internationalized again in 2001 when superpower interest for non-Afghani reasons was re-ignited. War between Ethiopia and Eritrea and internal strife in Somalia and Sudan, although less explicitly post-Cold War conflicts, also bore the hallmarks of 'New World Order' global indifference.

The post-Cold War landscape also featured some new sources of international tension. The break-up of the Soviet Union was rapid and, as a result, 'messy' with large ethnic Russian populations left marooned in non-Russian successor states as a consequence of policies of 'Russification', through which Moscow had hoped to dilute national differences. A legacy of this is a continuing Russian military presence in Moldova and Georgia and ethnic tensions between the Russian and titular nationality. In the latter this flared up to the extent of international war in 2008 when the Georgian government attempted to reassert control over the Russian-controlled enclave of South Ossetia by launching a military attack on the capital city, Tskhinvali. The Georgians appeared to have gambled on the Kremlin being distracted by the Beijing Olympics but this strategy backfired when the Putin government responded quickly and aggressively to defeat them in a short 'classic' inter-state war of the sort rarely seen in recent decades.

A particular source of instability in the contemporary world is the seeming intractability of some conflicts. The longer a war persists the more difficult peacemaking becomes and 'perpetual war' seems a more apt description for some parts of the globe than the onset of perpetual peace. Indo-Pakistani rivalry over the status of Kashmir is as old as both countries and the conflict is now more insoluble than ever given that it has now taken the form of a 'Cold War-esque' nuclear rivalry. The internationalized civil war in the Congo shows no sign of abating over fifty years after the end of appalling colonial rule by Belgium and a brief but fruitless display of Cold War internationalism left behind, perhaps, the world's first 'failed state'.

Virulent nationalism has enjoyed something of a revival in Europe since 1990, prompting the view that the Cold War might actually have kept the lid on a number of conflicts now free to boil over. '[T]he Cold War period might be seen as an aberration from a story that is now, in some respects being resumed' (Clark 2001: 24). The Yugoslav secessionist wars of the 1990s in many ways did appear to be a revival of the Balkan Wars which preceded the First World War and the civil war, which occurred alongside the Second World War. Similarly, old scores left unsettled by their grandparents were taken up by nationalists as ethnic strife re-emerged in Chechenya, Moldova, Romania and Georgia and between Azerbaijan and Armenia. As Nye suggests, perhaps the end of the Cold War has heralded not so much the 'end of history' as the 'return to history' (Nye 2005: 247) (see Table 2.3).

## An end to 'high politics'?

Military threats to security have certainly not gone away in the years since the demise of East European Communism. However, although it persists in a number of forms, the Cold War's ultimate security threat of global nuclear Armageddon has receded and this has transformed defence policy in many states of the world. Whereas it could be said to be 'business as usual' in much of Asia and Latin America and 'a change for the worse' in much of Africa, military security policies have changed in the states most affected by the Cold War, those of Europe and North America. In East Europe the former Communist states have either switched to the winning side or become preoccupied with new internal threats from secessionists. The Western Cold War allies' response to the successful avoidance of that war has been to show a far greater preparedness to get embroiled in new wars essentially of their choosing. These 'New World Order Wars' and lesser military incursions have been prompted not by imminent threats to 'national security' but more by justice and the maintenance of regional order. At least for part of the world, the idea that war is an option of last resort and all-subsuming of other concerns is eroding. For many states the resort to force is not being eliminated from foreign policy; it is becoming a more pragmatic, mainstream part of it, in line with Clausewitzian thinking.

For many other states, though, war with another country has become a much less likely prospect since the 1990s. Between 2004 and 2006 there were no inter-state wars in the world but twenty-seven intra-state wars and five 'internationalized' intra-state wars (i.e. featuring an external intervention) (Uppsala/PRIO 2010). This trend prompted the 'New Wars Thesis' from the 1990s most associated with Mary Kaldor. '[P]olitical violence at the beginning of the twenty-first century is more omnipresent, more directed at civilians, involves a blurring of the distinctions between war and crime, and is based on and serves to foment divisive identity politics – these are the characteristics of "new wars"' (Kaldor 2007: ix).

**Table 2.3** Indicators of contemporary state military power

(a) Expenditure on defence, 2010

| | State | Amount (US $) | Proportion of GDP(%) |
|---|---|---|---|
| 1 | USA | 698 billion | 4.8 |
| 2 | China | 119 billion (estimate) | 2.1 |
| 3 | United Kingdom | 59.6 billion | 2.7 |
| 4 | France | 59.3 billion | 2.3 |
| 5 | Russia | 58.7 billion (estimate) | 4.0 |
| 6 | Japan | 54.5 billion | 1 |
| 7 | Saudi Arabia | 45.2 billion | 10.4 |
| 8 | Germany | 45.2 billion (estimate) | 1.3 |
| 9 | India | 41.3 billion | 2.7 |
| 10 | Italy | 37.0 billion (estimate) | 1.8 |
| | *World* | *1.63 trillion* | *2.6* |

Source: SIPRI (2011).

(b) Size of full-time armed forces (2006)

| | State | Number |
|---|---|---|
| 1 | China | 2,285,000 |
| 2 | USA | 1,468,364 |
| 3 | India | 1,325,000 |
| 4 | North Korea | 1,106,000 |
| 5 | Russia | 1,106,000 |
| 6 | South Korea | 687,000 |
| 7 | Pakistan | 617,000 |
| 8 | Iran | 523,000 |
| 9 | Turkey | 510,000 |
| 10 | Egypt | 468,000 |

Source: IISS (2010).

(c) Size of nuclear arsenal

| | State | No. of weapons |
|---|---|---|
| 1 | Russia | 11,000 |
| 2 | USA | 8,500 |
| 3 | France | 300 |
| 4 | China | 240 |
| 5 | UK | 225 |
| 6 | Pakistan | 90–100 |
| 7 | India | 80–100 |
| 8 | Israel | 80 |
| 9 | North Korea | 'a few' |

Source: SIPRI (2011).

## *From deterrence to the management of security?*

As Rasmussen has persuasively argued, the changing nature of military threats is resulting in the means–ends rationality of traditional state security policy in some countries being gradually replaced by a 'reflexive rationality'. 'Risk is becoming the operative concept of Western security' (Rasmussen 2001: 285). Deterring or being ready to respond to massive military threats is no longer a sufficient basis for the construction of many states' defence policy. As the Cold War has receded into history a more subtle strategy has been both necessary and possible for governments operating in relative peace. The management of security entails seeking to limit the risks likely to be encountered in the future as well as tackling imminent problems.

NATO's transformation since 1990 exemplifies this approach. As Forster and Wallace note: 'NATO is becoming more of a European-wide security organization, less of an alliance' (Forster and Wallace 2001: 107). The enlargement of NATO, and its wider extension through the Partnership for Peace programme with non-members, has not been inspired by the organization's desire to become even more powerful, it is about the 'management of the future' and stabilizing of Eastern Europe (Rasmussen 2001: 289). NATO has also become increasingly involved in non-military security activities such as facilitating relief in cases of natural disasters (see Chapter 8). It is, indeed, increasingly doubtful whether NATO is much of a military alliance at all. The first and only time the organization's collective defence 'trigger clause', Article 5, was enacted was in 2001 in response to the September 11th al-Qa'ida strikes in the USA. This was purely a symbolic act of solidarity as the USA made it clear that the organization was not needed in the subsequent war in Afghanistan. When NATO could not agree on a collective response against Iraq in 2003 it was sidestepped by the USA and UK in much the same way as NATO had sidestepped the UN in the 1999 Kosovan War. The Kosovan War stands as the only full military engagement by NATO but the solidarity was, again, more symbolic and diplomatic than a case of military necessity. The USA, and their key ally in the informal 'alliance of English speaking nations' the UK, do not need NATO in a military security sense but the organization still serves their interests as a means of institutionalizing a wider security community in Europe.

The invasion of Iraq by an 'alliance of English speaking nations' (including Australia) represented a dramatic attempt at managing the future, risking the antagonism of some of their partners in the European security community, and their own casualties, in order to pre-empt bigger future risks from arising. Iraq did not present a 'clear and present danger' to any of the three invading states but it was reasoned by them that, if military action was avoided, the country **could** pose a major security threat through the development of weapons of mass destruction. The overthrow of Saddam Hussein was also seen as a means to stabilize the Middle East and contribute long-term to the mitigation of risks associated with anti-Western sentiment in the region. The US missile shield project and the rise of non-military 'national security' initiatives from the State Department (for example tackling AIDS and transnational crime) in recent years, too, suggest that a longer game of state security is increasingly being played.

Not all states enjoy the luxury of being able to attempt to manage their and their people's security but it is an observable trend in some parts of the world. NATO, from the outset, sought to keep members like Greece and Turkey from fighting each other but this became more pressing once the Cold War was over and such countries were stripped of a common enemy. The Organization for Security and Co-operation in Europe (OSCE) sought to build bridges between NATO and the Warsaw Pact states in the era of détente and looked, briefly, as if it might take on the mantle of keeping order in Europe at the end of the Cold War, before NATO revamped itself. The European Union was forged by the need to manage the future of German relations with her European neighbours and its expansions have sought to stabilize the continent, though it too has been superseded in this regard by NATO.

The Association of South East Asian Nations (ASEAN) has cooperative peace-keeping mechanisms pre-dating the end of the Cold War but, like NATO, sought to both deepen and widen security cooperation in the 1990s. The ASEAN Regional Forum and Councils for Security Cooperation in the Asia Pacific were developed to build bridges with China, maintain US interest in the region and generally reduce future uncertainty in the region. US troops have taken part in the 'Cobra Gold' joint military exercises with Thailand and Singapore, with Chinese officials present as observers and cooperation on non-military security issues such as piracy and environmental pollution have been developed (Simon 2002). In Africa ECOWAS has sought to fill the void of Northern indifference prompted by the end of the Cold War by enhancing regional stability through the Mechanism for Conflict Prevention, Management and Resolution, Peacekeeping and Security established in 1999.

Military conflict should no longer automatically be seen as 'high politics' and something resorted to when 'national security' is threatened. Humanitarian interventions and missions to maintain general order without 'national interests' being obviously at stake, such as in Kosovo and East Timor, are becoming more common (see Chapter 5). Wars are increasingly fought for other, less fundamental foreign policy aims. This was most clearly illustrated by the 2003 Iraq war, prosecuted ostensibly on the war aim of better implementing an arms control agreement. The Iraq war also served to show how wars have become more 'routinized'. Despite months of diplomatic build-up to the conflict and in-depth media coverage, it was not clear when the war had actually started. Since the UK and USA had been bombing Iraq for 12 years, and attracting relatively little political interest in doing so, the boundaries between war and diplomacy were barely evident.

Other states have decided to spend the post-Cold War peace dividend on non-military concerns. Most European states' military expenditure has reduced and at such a rate in countries like Belgium and Germany that concerns have been raised within NATO about a 'free rider' problem developing, with countries enjoying the security provided by collective defence without contributing much to it themselves. Iceland has not possessed its own armed forces either during or since the Cold War, allowing the USA to simultaneously protect and utilize the island for its geopolitical value, until choosing to leave in 2006. Costa Rica abandoned its armed forces after a civil war in 1949 (save for some state paramilitaries used for border controls and internal security) and has managed to remain an oasis of peace in an otherwise volatile region.

Other states have resorted to calling up private, freelance military forces in time of emergency rather than incur the costs of building up and constantly modernizing their own armed forces. Governments of failed, unstable or weak states, such as Sierra Leone, Ivory Coast, Angola and Papua New Guinea, have recruited from specially designed private military companies such as 'Sandline international' and 'Executive Outcomes' to help them deal with civil insurgencies. In addition, though, powerful states have also increasingly sought private solutions to military security problems. The USA recruited around 30,000 guards and analysts from 50 private security companies (PSCs) between 2004 and 2011 to assist their occupation in Iraq. This development opens up a legal minefield since private operatives fall outside of the confines of public international law, a problem that became apparent in Iraq with several accusations of excessive force levelled against PSCs who had been granted certain immunities from prosecution in order to carry out their duties by the US government.

There are few states in the world where the military security agenda is dominated by a major, imminent threat posed by another state's military forces. Maintaining internal order against the threat of insurgency and/or contributing to regional or global order or justice is more the order of the day.

## Is war inevitable?

Understanding the causes of war – and consequently also the bases for peace – must be the fundamental concern of the study of military security and, many would say, of International Relations as a whole. The precise causes of war are, of course, myriad but they can be distilled down to some general explanatory factors about the nature of the political world. A landmark IR text in this regard was Kenneth Waltz's 1959 *Man, The State and War* which pioneered the widely adopted and adapted explanatory framework of three levels of analysis: man, the state and the international system (see Table 2.4).

### Realists

Waltz, as a Realist, held a Hobbesian view of human nature as being aggressive and selfish and, hence, was of the view that armed conflict over interests was

**Table 2.4** Waltz's levels of analysis

| | Level of analysis | Cause of war |
|---|---|---|
| 1 | Man | Human nature |
| 2 | State | Socio-political factors |
| 3 | International system | Anarchy |

Source: Waltz (1959).

inevitable. Notwithstanding some improvement since the early 2000s, wars have become more frequent and more deadly as time has proceeded, contradicting the idea that humankind has become less savage as it has evolved. From this Realists conclude that violent conflict is an inevitable feature of international politics. They laud Clausewitz for his famous dictum that war is 'a continuation of political intercourse, with the addition of other means' (Clausewitz 1976: 605) and argue that it should not be treated as an aberration but as a rational foreign policy option. This position is not necessarily, as it is sometimes painted, that of the warmonger. The glorification of warfare on the grounds of its usefulness for 'nation building', or even for humanity as a whole by a twisted application of the Darwinian notion of 'survival of the fittest', has permeated Fascism and virulent strains of nationalism but this is not Clausewitzian Realism. The conviction of the Realists is that war is a last resort but still very much a resort. According to this view, war is sometimes necessary and its occurrence cannot be wished away. War, according to Betts, should be viewed as a 'rational instrument of policy rather than mindless murder' (Betts 1997: 8).

However, whilst Waltz buys into the human nature argument, the limitations of this explanation prompted him to additionally consider the higher levels of analysis. With the historic pattern of regular warfare it is quickly apparent that not all countries go to war with the same regularity and some, like Switzerland, appear to be able to avoid becoming embroiled in armed conflicts for many centuries. The foreign policy choice of war may be rational but it is a choice not all governments take and it is evident that some states are more warlike than others. War hence is a political choice as well as a natural human inclination. In Waltz's third level of analysis he then tackled the point that the decision for governments on whether or not to go to war was influenced by wider international factors. The Realist assumption that the international political system of states is anarchic necessitates a readiness of governments to go to war if national interest or a threat to the balance of power make it necessary. Waltz thus pioneered the revamp of Realism into Neo-Realism by adding greater consideration of structural explanations for war and peace alongside the human nature arguments. The levels of analysis methodology also provides a useful means of comprehending alternative, Liberal and Marxist explanations for war.

## Liberals/Pluralists

Liberals dispute the Realist proposition that war is an inevitable feature of international politics in any sort of world. The brutishness of human nature in the Realist analysis is rejected and a more optimistic assessment made on the likelihood of war to remain a central feature of political life in the future. Just as many people lead blameless lives so many states avoid violent conflicts and, though conflict is sometimes unavoidable for the preservation of justice in the world, it could be consigned to the history books given political change. To Liberals the lack of progress of humanity in curbing the resort to war is more about nurture than nature. It is socio-political rather than natural. At the state level, as already discussed, democracies are considered to be more peaceful in their relations with other democracies and so democratization is welcomed.

At the international level the state system is viewed as a further socio-political explanation for war. The arbitrary division of the world into competitive units has seen the populations of these states dragged into wars by self-interested governments, particularly non-democratic ones. This serves to exacerbate disputes beyond what is necessary or rational and leads to wars being prompted by misperception of an adversary and/or the likely gains to accrue from attacking them. If war were truly rational every state which initiated conflict would win which, of course, has not been the case. Hence, for Pluralists, a cure exists to rid humanity of the cancer of war: the removal of its root cause through the erosion of state sovereignty. Interdependence and, to a greater extent, political integration serve to diminish war by revealing that the mutual gains inherent in cooperation outweigh the spoils of individual gain and reducing the likelihood of misperception causing unnecessary wars. The improbability of a new Franco-German confrontation, after three major wars in the course of a human lifespan, is the classic case used to uphold this view. Liberals also distance themselves from the assumption of anarchy in seeing international law, in the guise of collective security, as representing a way in which military order can be maintained in international relations.

### Marxists

Marxism, on questions of war as on most matters, focuses very much on the third level of analysis. Both human nature and state type are held to be largely irrelevant in the face of structural economic forces. The Marxist/Structuralist approach considers economic gain to be the underlying cause of most wars. Lenin famously argued that the First World War was a war of imperialism with the rival factions from Europe and the USA seeking to achieve mastery of each other's colonial possessions. In this view it is the inherent expansionist tendency of capitalism which prompted European imperial expansion and then US-led anti-Communist aggression and economic 'neo-imperialism' in the twentieth century. Contemporary neo-Marxists put particular emphasis on the influence of the military-industrial complex in pushing states towards the use of force to secure economic gains. Wars can be a profitable exercise and it is in the interests of the armed forces and arms industry, two highly influential government lobbies, that war remains a foreign policy option. Hence, in this analysis there were twin economic motivations behind the 2003 Iraq war. As evidence that this proposition is not confined to the far left consider the words of US Republican President Eisenhower at the height of the Cold War:

> In the councils of government, we must guard against the acquisition of unwarranted influence, whether sought or unsought, by the military-industrial complex. The potential for the disastrous rise of misplaced power exists and will persist.
>
> (Eisenhower 1961)

## Social Constructivists

Social Constructivism cannot be plotted onto the levels of analysis table as readily as the other approaches since it is an approach without the normative ideological roots of Realism, Liberalism or Marxism. Constructivists dislike assumptions and there cannot be said to be a 'default position' on human nature or state or inter-state level routes to peace. Social Constructivism has, though, contributed to the debate on the causes of war by bringing into focus the question of human agency and the importance of culture and ideas in understanding conflict. The greater subjectivity of the Constructivist approach lends itself to the contention that wars are often better explained by clashes of culture than abstract concepts such as power vacuums, the economic structure of the world or an absence of democracy. *Some* people are aggressive, but not all and *some* states see the world as anarchic, but not all. Although generally less convinced by the certainties of the democratic peace theory, many Social Constructivists share some common ground with the Liberals in believing that war is not inevitable since governments can come to redefine their interests in favour of collective security (Wendt 2003).

## Conclusions

The 'ending' of the Cold War has not changed the military security threats to the governments or peoples of many states, including those still affected by it (for example Korea or Cuba) or to those for whom it was never the principal concern (for example India or Israel). However, the lifting of the overarching threat posed by that conflict and the nature in which it (at least partially) ended has brought into question a number of long-held assumptions about the study and conduct of military security policy.

Particularly in need of re-appraisal is that most well established and still influential Realist theory, the balance of power. There is a strong case to be made that the preservation or restoration of a balance of power did maintain order in previous phases of history but this is not sufficient reason to believe that a contemporary imbalance will lead to global disorder. Many of the states just down the military pecking order have no interest or desire to topple the USA, since that country does not threaten them and they share many of its general aspirations for the world. Even those amongst that 'second tier' of military powers not as closely aligned to the USA as the UK, such as France and Russia, enjoy sufficiently strong ties to render war unthinkable. Ideological and territorial differences exist between China and the USA but they pale into insignificance when set against the trading links and common economic interests that now link the two countries. US military hegemony has prompted adventurism that alarms much of the world, such as in the 2003 war against Iraq, but this hardly compares to Napoleonic France or Hitlerian Germany. Some Realists have sought to defend the utility of the balance of power theory by advancing the idea of 'soft balancing'. This idea suggests that, although military confrontation against US unilateralism by major powers is unlikely, such countries are beginning to engage in measures to restrain them through the use of international institutions and economic statecraft (Pape 2005; Paul 2005).

This notion of multilateralism and economic interests curbing foreign policy aggression is, however, closer to a Kantian than Hobbesian vision of the world. The balance-of-power theory does still have some applicability at the regional level, such as in the stand-off between India and Pakistan, but when applied to the global political stage, is falsified by the much harder evidence provided by the Kantian peace thesis.

Kantian peace also stands up well to the recent advance of the 'Clash of the Civilizations' thesis. Russett and Oneal, for example, convincingly dismantle Huntington's, theory by clearly demonstrating that no correlation can be shown between recent conflicts and the apparent civilizational setting of the states concerned (Russett and Oneal 2001: 239–70). Islamic and Western states, on past evidence, are no more likely to resort to war than any other combination of countries. Huntington could contend that his thesis was a prediction for the future which cannot be falsified by empirical analysis of the past, but the speculative and sensationalist nature of his writing stands in stark contrast to these Pluralists' more rigorous, reasoned and optimistic view of the way in which the world is likely to evolve.

The three peace prescriptions of Kant, and his protégés like Russett, appear to have passed a number of trials but should not, however, be mistaken for panaceas. Kantian peace does appear to account for the demise of inter-state war but its logic does not explain the persistence of a number of civil wars. Democracy, trade and common political institutions have not deterred some Basque nationalists or British Islamic fundamentalists from pursuing conflict to achieve their aims. In addition it is democracies, including those not predisposed to fight themselves, who do much to fuel conflicts in the undemocratic world through the lucrative trade in arms, usually justified on the national interest grounds of economic expediency. In noting this, however, we can neither conclude that Marxist economic determinism is the catch-all explanation it purports to be, even for explicitly imperial wars. In invading the Falkland Islands in 1982 the Argentine junta were seeking to acquire a British possession which had long been an economic burden to its colonial ruler. It was symbolism which prompted the invasion and principle which prompted the campaign to recapture the islands.

Theories need to change when they are no longer supported by the facts. The balance of power thesis has largely lost its applicability on the global stage. The clash of the civilizations thesis has never had any applicability since its proclamation. Even theories largely supported by the facts need to be taken with a pinch of the Social Constructivist's salt. The 'struggle for power' shorthand of Realist analysis is not redundant, as evidenced by the continued use of the 'national interest' justification of the unjust by many governments, but it is in need of increasing qualification as time goes on. War is often still considered a rational foreign policy choice for some governments but it is not given that this choice will be taken by decision-makers, even if there are tangible gains to be had from them doing so. Germany has not risen again in a quest for military supremacy as much because its government and people have never wished to do so as because of its containment. The recognition that ideas and culture inform decision-making when it comes to the ultimate decision usually to face a government pre-dates the rise of the Social Constructivists in the post-Cold War era. Mueller, in arguing for 'the obsolescence of major war', demonstrated that the historical pattern of cyclical war between the great powers was not being maintained. The nuclear revolution was clearly a factor in this, making such wars irrational, but Mueller posited that an added (and related) dimension to this was a normative change towards seeing war as an unacceptable means of pursuing gain. Slavery had been a profitable venture for many states for a number of centuries but was eventually largely consigned to history because compassion triumphed over economic gain (Mueller 1989; Goldstein 2011). Might war similarly pass into history as a major political phenomenon? After an initial upsurge in the number of military conflicts in the world on the passing into history of the Cold War, there is good evidence for the decline in resort to war. Inter-state wars have become rare events and civil wars have been half as frequent since the early 2000s than they were during the early 1990s. Overall conflict deaths have fallen from 164,000 per year in the 1980s to 92,000 in the 1990s to 42,000 in the 2000s (World Bank 2011: 52; Uppsala/PRIO 2010).

War waged by states has not disappeared but it has become less frequent and, at the same time, a more 'mainstream' political option for some. Other options for resolving disputes are increasingly open to governments but limited tactical wars are also an increasing option for some states. Clausewitz was right to say that war was a form of politics but this affirmation need not cause us to conclude that armed attacks are as inevitable as the differences of opinion that constitute politics.

> Assessment of the risks of war is not in the end a matter of predicting the inevitable or recognizing the fated, but rather of re-emphasizing the fundamental link between war and politics: politics, which cause war, can equally be used to prevent it.
>
> (Halliday 2001: 58)

## Key points

- The twin global issues of the Cold War and decolonization dominated the conduct of international relations in the latter half of the twentieth century and help explain the preoccupation of states today with externally focused military security.
- The 'resolution' of the Cold War and decolonization in the early 1990s brought optimism that a 'New Word Order' would usher in more peaceful inter-state relations and a greater commitment to globally coordinated peacekeeping.
- Not all analysts shared the optimism generated by the apparent New World Order. The legacies of the Cold War and decolonization remain prominent and many Neo-Realists contend that the disappearance of the Cold War balance of power brought with it new, and more de-stabilizing, military threats.
- Realists consider that war is an inevitable feature of international relations, containable by respect for the balance of power between states. Marxists consider war to be inevitable so long as the world remains predominantly capitalist. Pluralists contend that the spread of democracy and interdependence, hastened in the post-Cold War world, offer hope for the eradication of inter-state war, which is becoming less common.

## Notes

1   This figure is made up of 80 'free' and 67 'partly free' states.
2   The other ten Security Council members are elected for two years, by General Assembly vote subject to Security Council approval, on the basis of geographical quotas. Five are chosen from Africa and Asia combined, two from Latin America, one from East Europe and two from 'West Europe/others'.
3   Russian pan-Slavism pre-dates the Cold War and can be seen as a common theme of Russian foreign policy dating back to the Czarist era of the nineteenth century when support for Serb nationalism was demonstrated.
4   Reports suggest that NATO Secretary-General Wesley Clark wanted British troops to confront the Russians but was ignored by General Michael Jackson, leading the British contingent (Tran 1999).
5   The 1922 Washington Conference bound the USA, UK, France, Japan and Italy to specific levels of naval power relative to each other.

## Recommended reading

Clausewitz, C.V. (1976) *On War*, edited and translated by Howard, M. and Paret, P., Princeton: Princeton University Press.
Fukuyama, F. (1992) *The End of History and the Last Man*, London: Hamish Hamilton.
Gaddis, J. (1997) *We Now Know: Rethinking Cold War History*, Oxford: Clarendon.
Goldstein, J. (2011) *Winning the War on War: The Decline of Armed Conflict Worldwide*, New York: Dutton.
Kegley, C. and Blanton, S. (2010) *World Politics: Trend and Transformation*, 2010–11 edn (part 3), Boston: Wadsworth, Cengage.
Nye, J. (2008) *Understanding International Conflicts: An Introduction to Theory and History*, 8th edn, London: Pearson.
Prins, G (2002) *The Heart of War: On Power, Conflict and Obligation in the Twenty-First Century*, London and New York: Routledge.
Russett, B. and Oneal, J. (2001) *Triangulating Peace: Democracy, Interdependence and International Organizations*, New York: Norton.
Waltz, K (1959) *Man, the State and War,* New York: Columbia University Press.
Walzer, M. (1978) *Just and Unjust Wars*, London: Allen Lane.

## Useful web links

NATO: http://www.nato.int/
Stockholm International Peace Research Institute (SIPRI): http://www.sipri.se/
United Nations 'Peace and Security': http://www.un.org/peace/index.html
World Bank, *Conflict, Security and Development: World Development Report 2011,* http://wdronline.worldbank.org/worldbank/a/c.html/world_development_report_2011

# Threats to security from non-state actors

Due to the imbalance of power between our armed forces and the enemy forces, a suitable means of fighting must be adopted, i.e. using fast-moving, light forces that work under complete secrecy. In other words, to initiate a guerilla war, where the sons of the nation, and not the military forces, take part in it.

Osama bin Laden 1996 (O'Neill 2001)

## One man's terrorist . . .

'Terrorism' is, perhaps, the most contentious term in political science. Literally hundreds of definitions have been coined by scholars and practitioners of politics without any clear consensus on how best to articulate what is undoubtedly a significant phenomenon. As far back as 1983 Schmid listed 109 distinct definitions (Schmid 1983). In 2005 the 60th United Nations Summit made the most concerted effort to date to arrive at a universal legal definition but could not reach agreement. A report commissioned by the UK government in 2007 similarly concluded that, 'there is no single definition of terrorism that commands full international support' (Carlile 2007: 47). From 1983 the following definition has been used by the US State Department: 'premeditated, politically motivated violence perpetrated against noncombatant targets by subnational groups or clandestine agents usually intended to influence an audience' (USA 1983).[1] Curiously, this definition would not classify attacks by subnational groups against active but not in-battle US servicemen, such as in the Lebanon in 1983, as terrorist strikes. The definition does, however, capture the essence of the phenomenon we have witnessed as a major issue of global security since the late 1960s, that of political violence waged by non-state actors. The 1968 hijacking of an aeroplane by the Popular Front for the Liberation of Palestine is widely considered to have initiated an era of regular conflict between states and non-state actors in Israel–Palestine and on many other fronts throughout the world. Non-state groups had, though, taken on states before 1968 and left their mark on history. Assassinations of state leaders have a long history and the First World War was sparked by the shooting of the prince of the Austro-Hungarian Empire by a Serb nationalist group. It was from the late 1960s, however, that unorthodox military violence became more routine and increasingly targeted at a wider audience than selected, prominent individuals.

The term terrorism is, though, an unhelpful one to use in describing this phenomenon since it is so value-laden. Terrorism, clearly, is a pejorative word. It is a word bandied about in conflict situations in order to contrast one side's legitimate killing to another side's illegitimate killing. Most frequently this will be by state forces against non-state forces since, in international law, state violence can be legal whereas non-state violence never can. Clearly, however, 'terror' is something that can be inflicted upon people by governments as well as by non-state actors. The term terrorism, indeed, was first coined to describe the state-directed violence and intimidation of French citizens by the Jacobins in the early years of the French Republic after the 1789 revolution. Nazi genocide, Stalin's purges and the 'killing fields' of the Khmer Rouge are amongst the numerous subsequent examples of this phenomenon. At the same time, violent non-state struggles often come to be seen by states and sections of global public opinion as legitimate, as was the case with the African National Congress's (ANC) democratic revolution in South Africa. Hence the oft quoted maxim, 'one man's terrorist is another man's freedom fighter'.

Consider for a moment the US government's terrorism definition minus the clause 'subnational groups or clandestine agents'. The definition now describes perfectly the defence policy of most powerful states, and certainly the USA, in the 'total war' era of the twentieth century. The blanket bombing of civilians in the Second World War and the very essence of nuclear weapons strategy were/are based upon, 'premeditated, politically motivated violence perpetrated against non-combatant targets' and were 'intended to influence an audience'. Even if we accept that state violence deliberately directed at civilians can be legitimate (such as the argument that the atomic strikes on Japan in 1945 ultimately saved lives by ending the Second World War) no one can suggest that the fear of nuclear annihilation is not terrifying. Even in this post-Cold War era, when non-combatant immunity is coming back into fashion, nuclear deterrence as a concept still rests on the fear factor emanating from the extraordinarily destructive power of such weapons.

If we leave aside the nuclear threat, it is clear also that states will often deliberately kill civilians if they consider it necessary for their security interests. 'State terrorism' against foreign citizens can be direct, as in the random scud assaults on Israel by Iraq during the Gulf War in 1991, or indirect through the sponsorship of terrorist cells such as the in anti-Western attacks believed to have been organized by Libya in the 1980s. State terrorism of this form is not solely the preserve of such brutal dictators as Saddam Hussein and Gaddafi, however. The 1985 French destruction of the ship *Rainbow Warrior*, used by the pressure group Greenpeace to protest against nuclear testing in the south Pacific, was evidence that democracies are not adverse to killing civilians outside of a conventional war situation.

Hence the term terrorism is problematic since it seems to conflate two ideas: the deliberate terrorizing of civilians and force used by non-state actors. In the following analysis I will concentrate on the second of those two ideas and accept that terror can be inflicted upon people by their own government, by other governments and by other entities, non-state actors (state terror is considered in Chapter 5). Criminal groups also can, of course, terrify and kill people and this form of non-state actor is considered in a later chapter. This chapter will focus on the form and severity of challenge to states and citizens posed by politically motivated violent non-state actors. 'Terrorism' by non-state actors is just one, relatively minor, aspect of this. Of far greater prominence is the more conventional violence waged in civil wars, which now dominates the military security agenda.

## Types of political non-state military groups

Table 3.1 gives the annual number of incidents of political non-state violence across the European Union, both foiled and 'successful', broken down by type. Whilst the EU experience cannot be synonymous to that of the overall world, similarly thorough global data is not available and the pattern does offer some clues to the wider picture.

**Table 3.1** Number of terrorist incidents in the European Union by type, 2007–11

|  | 2007 | 2008 | 2009 | 2010 | 2011 |
|---|---|---|---|---|---|
| Religious | 4 | 0 | 1 | 3 | 0 |
| Separatist | 532 | 397 | 237 | 160 | 110 |
| Left-wing | 21 | 28 | 40 | 45 | 37 |
| Right-wing | 1 | 0 | 4 | 0 | 1 |
| Single Issue | 1 | 5 | 2 | 1 | 0 |
| Other[a] | 24 | 11 | 10 | 40 | 26 |

Note
[a] Most of these are due to the UK government refusing to specify types to Europol and are mostly separatist.

Source: Europol (2012a).

## Nationalist

### Secessionist

The most prevalent and successful form of political non-governmental violence has come from movements claiming to represent a nation, using force to achieve independence for their people. Nations are socially constructed communities defined subjectively according to common characteristics that a given group feel distinguish them from other nations. Such characteristics vary from case to case but may or may not include language, religion or ethnicity. National self-determination, the belief that nations are entitled to sovereign statehood, has been a powerful force within international politics since the latter part of the nineteenth century. There has never been a precise match-up between nations and states in the world but the struggle to do so has continued on many fronts over the last 150 years as the world has retreated from an age of multi-national empire.

The belief that nations had a right to become nation-states and that it was in the interests of world peace that they achieve it, reached its high point at the 1919 Paris Peace Conference which broke up the Austro-Hungarian Hapsburg and Turkish Ottoman Empires. National self-determination is still a strongly held conviction of most people and statesmen today. As such it is the secessionist 'terrorists' who are most likely to be considered 'freedom fighters' or 'national liberation movements'. A number of contemporary states were founded by successful campaigns of non-governmental violence. Kenya and Algeria were ceded by the UK and France respectively after bloody struggles and, in an earlier age, the USA was born in such circumstances. Many present-day nationalist struggles against states have received large levels of international legitimization. The Palestinians, the Kosovans and, to a lesser extent, the Kurds are cases in point. Violent secessionists represent a major security threat for the states from which they aim to secede but they rarely threaten other states, other than through fear of a copy-cat uprising in their own territory. Such groups do not challenge the Westphalian order[2] since many states consider them simply to be following in their own footsteps and even enhancing international security by moving the world closer to the ideal of the nineteenth-century *risorgimento* nationalists, such as Mazzini, who felt that if all nations became states there would be little left to fight about.

### Counter-secessionist

Nationalism can inspire some people to take up arms to secede but also inspire others to fight to prevent that secession. National self-determination is a messy business in the contemporary world where migration, inter-marriage and integration have made any neat political division of the world on national grounds far more complicated than in Mazzini's era. A secessionist's proposed nation-state will often include enclaves, or even geographically indistinct groupings, of other nationalities who favour the status quo and fear being severed from their present state. Hence Serb nationalists in Croatia and Bosnia-Herzegovina took up arms when those two states seceded from Serb-dominated Yugoslavia in 1991 and pro-British 'loyalist' violence in Northern Ireland emerged in the 1970s to counter Irish nationalist aspirations to unify the province with the Republic of Ireland.

### Liberal

Nationalism is a broad political label and is sometimes also used to characterize movements that are not secessionist or counter-secessionist but popular uprisings seeking to radically change a country in the name of the people. Armed 'Liberal' struggles of this sort occurred in the revolutions of France in 1789, in South Africa in the apartheid era and in several Arab states in 2011 and 2012. The fact that very few would consider labelling these revolutions as terrorist illustrates clearly the point that non-state force can achieve a high degree of international legitimacy.

## Religious

The growth of religious fundamentalism since the 1970s has seen a number of armed groups emerge which are inspired essentially by religious doctrine. Generally seen as a new wave of non-state violence, following the dominance of this form of conflict by Nationalist and Marxist groups in the late 1960s and 1970s, armed religious fanatics, in fact, pre-date the age of terrorism and can be traced back as far as biblical times.

### Judaism

Probably the world's first organized campaign of violence by a non-state group against a government was waged by the Zealots of Israel against Roman rule. As such the Zealots and other similar Jewish insurgency groups could be understood as national liberationists, but a crucial motivation to their campaign was the religious conviction that the arrival of the Messiah would follow a period of mayhem. Hence

Jewish doubters, as well as occupying Romans, were often victims of spontaneous acts of Zealot violence. Many centuries on in Israel groups such as Kach and Kahane Chai have carried out acts of violence since the 1990s against Palestinians in the West Bank in a campaign of biblically inspired Zionism (Jewish nationalist movement to establish a homeland and state).

### Islam

Non-state violence in the name of Islam dates back to the Assassins of the seventh century whose murderous campaign is now immortalized in the English language. The Assassins were Shi'a Moslems who stabbed to death prominent political and religious individuals who were felt to be resisting the advancement of their cause of the preservation of traditional Islamic values. Over a millennium later political violence in the name of Islam returned to become a major feature of international politics. The 1979 Iranian Revolution, which overthrew a Western-oriented royal dynasty and put in its place a fundamentalist Shi'a regime, served as the catalyst for armed Islamist struggles, both Shi'a and Sunni (the two main sects), elsewhere in the Middle East and Africa. This modern wave of political Islam can actually be dated back as far as the 1920s and the anti-colonialist movement in Egypt which founded the Muslim Brotherhood but was inspired, radicalized and internationalized by the Iranian Revolution and the USSR's invasion of Afghanistan which occurred in the same year.

Post-revolutionary Iran gave active support to Shi'a groups such as Hizbullah seeking an Iranian-style revolution in the Lebanon as well as resisting Israeli incursions into that country. Sunni revolutionaries, such as the Armed Islamic Group in Algeria and al-Gama'at al-Islmiyya in Egypt, were also inspired to seek the overthrow of governments they saw as immoral. Some Islamist groups took the fight beyond domestic revolution, rallying to the cause of Palestinian nationalist resistance to Israel and further to the USA and European countries seen as upholding Israel and meddling in the affairs of Islamic states. In this way Islamic violence has come to be seen as so much more of a security threat to Western democracies than other forms of non-state force even though, as Table 3.1 illustrates, it is actually less prevalent than nationalist non-state violence. It tends to be more transnational in character and directly challenges notions of secularity and sovereignty which underpin the Westphalian order. In the aftermath of the September 11th 2001 strikes on the USA Suleiman Abu Gaith, a spokesman of al-Qa'ida mastermind Osama bin Laden (see Box 3.1) stated:

> Every Muslim has to play his real and true role to uphold his religion and his action in fighting and jihad is a duty . . . those youths who did what they did and destroyed America with their airplanes did a good deed. They have moved the battle into the heart of America. America must know that the battle will not leave its land. Go willing, until America leaves our land, until it stops supporting Israel, until it stops the blockade against Iraq.
>
> (Halliday 2002: 235[3])

## Box 3.1 Osama bin Laden

Born in Saudi Arabia in 1957, to a Syrian mother and Yemeni father, surely no individual in modern history has exerted such military influence internationally without the back-up of a state structure. Bin Laden was stripped of Saudi citizenship in 1991 and lived a secretive yet extremely high-profile life after that as a transnational freelance terrorist, drawing support from Islamic radicals across the world in a campaign principally targeting the USA for its foreign policy stance in the Arab world. That one man with a loose, shadowy organization beneath him could confront the world's premier military power and evade for so long its wrath epitomizes the logic of 'asymmetric warfare' and exposes the limitations of the concept of the balance of power. Believed responsible for the original World Trade Centre bombing in 1993, bin Laden was officially the USA's most wanted fugitive by the FBI after a 1996 attack on US servicemen in Saudi Arabia and the 1998 African embassy bombings. Military strikes on what were believed to be his bases in Sudan and Afghanistan in 1998 failed to topple him and he masterminded from afar the massive 2001 New York and Washington attacks. Full-scale war against Afghanistan dislodged the government offering him sanctuary but proved not to have extinguished bin Laden when al-Qa'ida opened their war on a new front against US allies Australia with the 2002 Bali nightclub bombing. He was eventually killed by US troops in Pakistan in 2011 bringing to an end perhaps the most high-profile 'man-hunt' in history.

Bin Laden was a very wealthy man until UN sanctions in 2001 froze much of his financial assets. He grew rich through inheriting his father's construction business and earning lucrative contracts with the ruling al-Saud dynasty in Riyadh. He left Saudi Arabia in the 1980s to embark on his pan-Islamic military career initially fundraising for and then fighting with the 'Arab Afghans' against another superpower, the Soviet Union in Afghanistan. A successful campaign there, aided by US funding and training against their enemy number one of that age, saw bin Laden return to the country of his birth along with many fellow countrymen at the end of the 1980s where his exploits in Afghanistan made him a charismatic cult figure. He fell out with the Saudi government in 1990 over their decision to allow US troops to be stationed in the country in response to the Iraqi invasion of Kuwait. Bin Laden offered the services of his Afghan war veterans to both the Saudi and Yemeni governments but their decline saw him fall out with those governments and turn his al-Qa'ida operatives against a new superpower enemy which was, in his eyes, encroaching on Islam's most holy territory.

The challenge to citizenship and statehood posed by al-Qa'ida and its associates became acutely apparent in 2005 when it transpired that the suicide bombers who killed 56 London public transport passengers were fellow British citizens or 'home-grown terrorists'.

## Hindu

The Thugs, like the Assassins, attracted such fearsome notoriety that their name lives on centuries later as a noun in English and other languages. The Thugs were a Hindu caste who killed, mainly by strangulation, an estimated 1 million people (mainly fellow Hindus) until they were eliminated by the British colonial rulers of India in the nineteenth century (Sleeman 1930). Hinduism is noted as a religion of tolerance and systematic religiously inspired attacks on people of other faiths historically have been rare. Recent years have, though, seen a rise in Hindu fundamentalism and increased attacks on Moslems in India, encouraged by the radical 'hindu nationalism' of the Hindutva movement. Over 2,000 Moslems were killed in a series of orchestrated massacres in Gujurat in February and March of 2002 (Human Rights Watch 2003).

## Christianity

Christian fundamentalism has long been blended with crude racism in US white supremacist groups such as Aryan Nations and the Ku Klux Klan. In recent years the most prolific overtly Christian violent non-state actor has been the Lord's Resistance Army (LRA). The LRA, who are largely based in southern Sudan, have been conducting a civil insurgency against the government of Uganda since the late 1980s aimed at the establishment of a theocratic state governed by the Bible's Ten Commandments. In doing so the LRA have, however, violated most of the Ten Commandments themselves in a horrific campaign which has featured random murders, tortures, rapes and the enslavement of Ugandan citizens and in particular children.

## Buddhism

As a religion noted for its commitment to peaceful relations, Buddhism is less associated with aggressive fundamentalism then other major faiths but it is an indication of how far religious terrorists can bastardize the scriptures which inspire them that it too has also spawned a radical, violent offshoot. The doomsday cult Aum Shinrikyo (Supreme Truth) were established in Japan in 1987 by its spiritual leader Shoko Asahara and have developed an offshoot in Russia. In 1995, in an apparent step towards a take-over of the world, Aum members released the poisonous gas sarin in underground trains in Tokyo, killing twelve people and injuring over 5,000.

## Marxist

Prior to the rise of fundamentalist violence from 1979 the biggest non-governmental security threat for most states came from armed Marxist revolutionaries. As with religious violence, Marxist revolutionaries sometimes represented a threat beyond their country of origin in line with the internationalist doctrine they were fighting for. Many democratic states faced such threats in the late 1960s and 1970s. The Red Army Faction in West Germany, Red Brigade in Italy and Red Army in Japan were amongst the most prominent, becoming a primary security concern in their own countries and a source of international concern because of anti-capitalist actions taken throughout the world.

Leftist revolutionaries of this form are of less significance in Europe and Japan today but have not gone away altogether. The Japanese Red Army is now a tiny cell believed to reside in the Lebanon and groups in Turkey and Greece have continued low-level campaigns. Leftist revolutionaries continue to have a high profile in some Latin America states, most notably in Colombia where the Revolutionary Armed Forces of Colombia (FARC) represents a direct challenge to the government, able even to claim large tracts of 'sovereign' territory, and with the Maoist Shining Path in Peru. Prominent groups also exist in the Philippines, and as elements in the Palestinian nationalist movement and in Nepal the Maoists succeeded in taking partial power in 2006 (see Figure 3.1).

Prior to the contemporary age of terrorism a range of small anarchist groups sent shockwaves around much of the industrializing world between 1880 and 1910 with a series of sporadic, high-profile assassinations that included the Russian Czar (in 1881), French President (in 1894) and US President (in 1901).

## Fascist/racist

Although an equally radical and aggressive ideology, fascism has spawned fewer violent non-governmental groups than Marxism. This is because Fascism is generally associated with the tightening of state authority and tends to be from 'above' rather than 'below'. In addition, of course, fascists tend to be ultra-nationalists who do not to like foreigners so where their actions have occurred they have, until recently, tended to be part of purely domestic compaigns. Armed non-state far-right groups have achieved prominence from time to time, however. Some emerged in the late 1960s and 1970s as counter-responses to Marxist revolutionaries. Ordine Nuovo (New Order) and a spin-off group the Armed Revolutionary Nuclei (ARN) carried out a number of attacks on civilians in Italy between 1969 and 1980. Additionally, racist violence by neo-Nazi groups has risen since the early 2000s. The Boermag in South Africa have targeted black civilians in bombing campaigns, Russian National Unity have carried out a number of anti-semitic attacks and less organized 'skinhead' violence has been a persistent threat to immigrant communities throughout Western Europe. These developments, though, are not properly reflected in the Europol statistics since many countries classify racist attacks as 'hate crimes' rather than terrorism. The fact that right-wing terror hence tends to be underrepresented was made graphically evident in 2011 when a lone gunman in Norway slayed 77 professional and youth politicians he saw as representative of multi-culturalism. This sort of 'lone wolf' terrorism has also been increasingly evident amongst Islamic fundamentalist 'home-grown' activists.

## Other ideologies

### Eco-terrorists

An aggressively militant brand of 'deep green' Ecologism has periodically emerged in Western Europe and North America from the 1970s. Animal liberationists have bombed laboratories known to carry out vivisection and occasional violent tactics have been launched against lumberjacks and building constructors. At a more systematic level, the Canadian-based group Sea Shepherd (a radical offshoot of Greenpeace) have invoked the fury of the Japanese government for carrying out a campaign of ramming and sinking whaling ships in the Pacific. The prominence of the Earth Liberation Front and Animal Liberation Front in the USA has, in the eyes of the Federal Bureau of Investigation (FBI), seen eco-terrorism even eclipse far right anti-federalism to become that country's greatest domestic terrorist threat (Lewis 2005).

### Feminists

Red Zora, an offshoot of leftist German terrorist groups, led a low-level campaign of feminist terror, targeting sex shops and other businesses considered to exploit women, from the 1970s to 1990s.

### Single issue groups

Other politically motivated acts of violence can best be understood as a radicalization of cause groups, rather than part of any broader ideology or religion. Most prominent amongst such groups are anti-abortionists in the USA who have killed medics. Anti-globalization demonstrations at the venues of global economic fora have occasionally turned violent, and been frequently attributed to the bogeyman of yesteryear, anarchists, but might, more rightly also be considered an example of single issue. It is globalization which makes such groups likely to proliferate as the opportunities for international exposure, recruitment and tactical coordination for small-scale organizations are heightened through telecommunications advances.

## The rise of political non-state violence

The rise of this form of conflict can largely be explained by the coming together of two factors. First, it allows the weak to take on the strong. This is not new and not only true of non-state actors. Guerilla warfare dates back to the Peninsular War

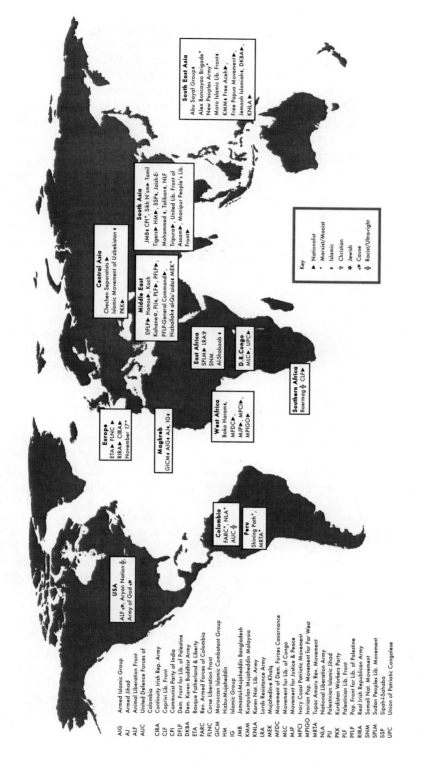

**Figure 3.1** Prominent contemporary armed political non-state groups

early in the nineteenth century when irregular Spanish and Portuguese forces where able to achieve military successes against a far stronger French invading army. Such a feat was repeated in the late twentieth century, in a far more uneven contest, when Vietnamese and Afghan 'Davids' were able to defeat the American and Soviet 'Goliaths'. Soldiers indistinguishable from civilians make an elusive enemy and this is exacerbated when there is no clear link between them and their country.

The second factor behind the rise of 'the age of terrorism' is the advance of communications technology in the latter part of the twentieth century. For political non-state violence to be effective it needs an audience to communicate its message to and to terrify into submission. The first indication of this use of a globalizing audience came with the nineteenth-century anarchist assassins whose acts gained the exposure of an emerging international media. The globalization of the media provides the 'oxygen of publicity' for putting into practice acts of violence. The extensive and sophisticated use of the internet by al-Qa'ida represents the clearest example of this. Cheap and easily available air travel has also served to facilitate international operations of violent non-state groups. Globalization has also assisted non-state groups in raising funds for their campaigns. This has particularly aided nationalist groups since 'ex-pat' communities in other countries are often keen to be remote revolutionaries with a romanticized notion of their brethren's struggle. Irish republicanism greatly benefited from fundraising amongst US citizens of Irish descent, whilst Sikh nationalism in the 1980s was as much orchestrated by migrants in Canada as those residing in the territory seeking secession from India.

Globalization allied to increased state arms surpluses since the end of the Cold War has also contributed to disaffected non-state groups finding it easier to avail themselves of weapons with the proceeds of their fundraising activities. Non-state forces fighting proxy wars during the Cold War, such as the leftist UNITA in Angola or the anti-leftist Contras in Nicaragua, have suffered from losing state sponsorship but other groups have been able to step up their campaigns. The flourishing global trade in arms can help sustain conflicts longer even than the political disagreements which triggered them. In some cases this has led to a blurring of the line distinguishing political from purely criminal violent organizations. 'Conflicts in a number of places (Colombia, Liberia, Tajikistan etc.) have lost any of the ideological motivation they once possessed and instead have degenerated into conflicts among petty groups fighting to grab local resources' (Singer 2001: 196–7).

Political non-state violence has gradually become more and more globalized, but this is not entirely new. Armed Marxist and Marxist-leaning groups coordinated their actions in the 1970s as exemplified by the 1975 kidnapping at an OPEC meeting in Vienna in which the unlikely trinity of the Popular Front for the Liberation of Palestine, Irish Republican Army and Red Army Faction were involved. 'Carlos the Jackal' played the role of the freelance transnational terrorist, linking together such leftist groups in this era, in much the same way as Osama bin Laden did for Islamic radicals in the 1990s and 2000s. The limitations of a balance of power approach to understanding global security politics are starkly exposed by the influence of such individuals and their network. US diplomat Richard Holbrooke summed this up in saying of bin Laden: 'how is it that a man living in a cave can out-communicate the most skilful communications nation in the world?' (Cornwell 2002: 11).

The terror tactics of political non-state military groups are myriad and have evolved over time. The hijacking of aeroplanes ('skyjacking') was the tactic of choice in the late 1960s and early 1970s, the seizing of embassies was popular in the late 1970s and early 1980s and the blowing up of mid-flight aeroplanes took centre stage in the late 1980s. Perennial favourite tactics include hostage taking, the assassination of prominent individuals and detonating bombs in government or public buildings. The September 11th 2001 strikes breathtakingly combined skyjacking and the destruction of public buildings with the added ingredient of suicide bombing in a single, unprecedented enterprise (see Table 3.2). Most non-state political violence is, of course, far more amateurish than the painstakingly planned and precision-timed New York and Washington strikes. Pride of place in the annals of unsuccessful terrorism must go to an Iraqi letter bomber who succeeded only in blowing himself up. Khay Rahnajet failed to put the correct postage on his parcel and detonated his own device when it was returned to his house with a 'return to sender' stamp (Simmons 1996: 84). Overshadowed by al-Qa'ida's actions, the distribution of anthrax spores in the US mail in 2001 offered a small but horrifying glimpse into

**Table 3.2** The top ten bloodiest single acts of non-state terrorist violence

| | Place | Date | No. killed | Action | Perpetrators |
|---|---|---|---|---|---|
| 1 | New York/ Washington, DC/ Pennsylvania | Sept. 2001 | 2,998 | Hijack of aeroplanes and suicide attacks on government and public buildings | al-Qa'ida |
| 2 | Abadan, Iran | Aug. 1978 | 430 | Arson of theatre | Islamic revolutionaries |
| 3 | Beslan, Russia | Sept. 2004 | 331 | Hostages held at a school killed during siege | Chechen separatists |
| 4 | North Atlantic | June 1985 | 331 | Bombing of Indian passenger plane | Sikh nationalists |
| 5 | Mumbai | Mar. 1993 | 317 | Series of bombings | Local Islamic gangsters allegedly working for Pakistani government. |
| 6 | Beirut | Oct. 1983 | 299 | Suicide bombing of US and French troops | Hizbullah |
| 7 | Lockerbie, UK | Dec. 1988 | 259 | US passenger plane bombed | Libyan-backed anti-Western group |
| 8 | Nairobi/ Dar Es Salam | Aug. 1998 | 257 | Bombing of US embassies | al-Qa'ida |
| 9 | Mumbai | July 2006 | 209 | Bombings of train stations | Kashmiri liberationists |
| 10 | Bali | Oct. 2002 | 202 | Tourist (chiefly Australian) nightclub bombing | Jammu Islam |

Note: List excludes casualty figures from full-scale civil wars and counter-invasion insurgencies.

a future nightmare scenario of weapons of mass destruction getting into the hands of non-state actors. Again, however, it is worth emphasizing that most non-state violence is far more 'mainstream' than such tactics and takes the form of sporadic guerrilla insurgency campaigns against state military forces (see Table 3.3). Table 3.3 lists the most bloody of such wars, excluding related civilian massacres, which are addressed in Chapter 5. It has become increasingly common for analysts of terrorism and non-state insurgencies to distinguish between 'old' and 'new' forms of the phenomena. Whilst old terrorism persists, many contemporary violent political non-state actors are small to the point of not being organizations at all and less explicit in their aims. Wilkinson, for example, suggests that only around a quarter of contemporary terror/insurgent groups have over a thousand members and increasingly are 'incorrigible rather than corrigible' (Wilkinson 2011: 7–20).

## State responses to political non-state violence

Table 3.4 attempts to distil the range of political options open to governments seeking to counter the threat posed to them and their citizens by armed non-state political groups.

**Table 3.3** The ten bloodiest civil wars in history

| | War | Date | Battle deaths |
|---|---|---|---|
| 1 | Taiping Revolution (China) | 1850–64 | 20 million |
| 2 | Chinese Civil War | 1945–9 | 2.5 million |
| 3 | Russian Civil War | 1918–21 | 800,000 |
| 4 | American Civil War | 1861–5 | 620,000 |
| 5 | Chinese Nationalist War | 1927–37 | 400,000 |
| 6 | Spanish Civil War | 1936–9 | 200,000 |
| 7 | Mexican Revolution | 1910–20 | 200,000 |
| 8 | Afghan Civil War | 1980–2001 | 150,000 |
| 9 | 1st Sudan Civil War | 1956–72 | 100,000 |
| 10 | Biafran War (Nigeria) | 1967–70 | 100,000 |

Source: White (2001).

**Table 3.4** State counter-terrorist options

| | Domestic | International |
|---|---|---|
| Political | 'No deals' v. appeasement | Diplomacy: carrot and stick |
| Military | Covert operations | War/foreign policy change |
| Containment | Hardening targets | Intelligence sharing |
| Legal | Emergency legislation | UNSC and ICC |
| Educative | Change 'terrorists'/change society | Global discourse |

## *Political*

### *Domestic: 'no deals' versus appeasement*

One option open to governments in facing up to the challenge of non-state violence is to come to some sort of accommodation with the group threatening to initiate or continue a campaign of violence. This may take the form of giving in to the demands made by terrorists in relation to a specific action, such as in agreeing to free 'political prisoners' in exchange for the safe release of hostages. Governments have followed this course of action more frequently than is often appreciated as a simple means of avoiding bloodshed. Concessions are, of course, often kept quiet by governments since they do not want their citizens or other potential terrorists to see them as a 'soft touch'. The Japanese government, for example, secretly made a number of significant specific concessions to the Japanese Red Army in the 1970s. All governments, despite claims to the contrary, have 'given in to terrorism' from time to time in order to avert bloodshed. Though it is not officially admitted, it is known that several governments have paid Iraqi insurgent hostage-takers holdng their nationals during the course of the conflict that has raged there since 2003.

In response to a longer-term campaign of non-state violence a government may come to see that the only way to achieve peace is through some sort of negotiated settlement with the organization in much the same way as inter-state conflicts are often resolved. In fact, concession is more probable in a state war with a non-state actor than in a war with another state since outright military defeat of the enemy is less likely. The Irish Republican Army probably never consisted of more than 1,000 active servicemen but it could not be defeated by the armed forces of the UK since its members were not clearly distinguishable from ordinary citizens. Even the blanket bombing of Ireland, should such an extreme measure have been considered, could not have achieved victory for the UK since many IRA cells operated in London and elsewhere in England. Hence the UK government secretly initiated dialogue with the IRA in 1985, leading eventually to a compromise settlement which saw a former IRA activist take up a position within a power-sharing executive for Northern Ireland.

The Irish peace process represents a two-way compromise, with the IRA abandoning its armed struggle in exchange for a share of power, but non-state violence may succeed in winning a long-term campaign and force a capitulation of the government. The African National Congress (ANC) ultimately forced the white minority government of South Africa to stand down and accept a democratic revolution. In this case the government recognized that its position was hopeless and the capitulation represented the will of the people. In cases where armed groups represent a minority opinion then appeasement becomes more problematic from a democratic point of view. Neumann posits that negotiating with terrorists is the only way a democratic government can expect to end a conflict but nonetheless observes that the process needs to be more sophisticated than making sudden major concessions. Hence the Colombian government's outreach to leftist guerrillas in 1998, which included the surrendering of a huge tract of territory to the FARC (which became known, unofficially, as 'Farcland') empowered and emboldened the guerrillas rather than bringing the conflict to an end. A much more gradual and phased process of incorporating armed rebels into the democratic process is required, as has been seen in Northern Ireland (Neumann 2007).

Whereas appeasement may save lives in the short term the possible downside of this approach, of course, is that it could give encouragement to other disavowed groups that violence pays dividends. The official approach of the US, Israeli and Russian governments, three of the main targets of much non-state violence over recent years, has been most characterized by the phrase 'no deals with terrorists'. President Putin has expressed this in unambiguous terms: 'Russia does not negotiate with terrorists, it destroys them' (Putin 2004). The basis of such a tough strategy is the belief that only by being seen not to back down can terrorism be deterred in the long term. The short-term result may be a loss of lives but the well-known military maxim that you may have to lose a battle in order to win the war holds sway.

Concessions by the Indian government to Islamic militants who skyjacked a passenger plane in 1999 produced some hostile responses in the domestic press, particularly in the wake of the 2001 attacks on the USA and that government's full-scale military response.

> If any state deals with terrorists, it not only encourages stepped-up terrorism against its own interests but also creates problems for other nations. A classic case is India's ignominious surrender to the hijackers of flight IC-814. One freed terrorist hand-delivered by the foreign minister is the suspected financier of Mohammed Atta, the alleged ringleader in the September 11th terrorist strikes. Another released terrorist founded a group in Pakistan that has claimed responsibility for major Kashmir strikes.
>
> (Chellaney 2001)

Evidence as to whether appeasement or zero tolerance is the most successful strategy for dealing with non-state violence is unclear. Walter Laqueur makes the case for zero tolerance in observing that 'the more severe the repression, the less terrorism tends to occur' (Laqueur 1990: 207). Laqueur bases this assertion on observing the relative lack of non-state violence in authoritarian political systems compared to democratic ones, noting that 'terrorism in Spain gathered strength only after General Franco died' (ibid.). There is a certain truth in this argument but, at the same time, there is little likelihood of citizens of most democratic states accepting the idea of living in a police state in order to deter terrorist threats. In addition, the zero tolerance stance of the governments of Israel, Russia and the USA has been accompanied by an increased level of non-state violence being perpetrated on their citizens over the last decade.

A clear illustration of how governments can differ in their approach to non-state terrorism came in 1996 when the Peruvian Marxist revolutionary group MRTA entered the Japanese embassy in Lima and held the ambassador and hundreds of staff hostage (Peruvian President Fujimori was ethnically Japanese). The Japanese government, mindful of successful compromises made to Japanese Marxists in similar circumstances in the 1970s, urged restraint on behalf of the Peruvians who favoured a tough strategy. The Peruvians ignored Japanese caution and sent in commandos, who succeeded in getting the hostages out whilst killing their captors (some allegedly by summary execution after they had been arrested). Ultimately, Fujimori's overall stance against the twin threat posed by MRTA and the Maoist Shining Path gives weight to Laqueur's views on countering terrorism. He used the campaign against them to justify 'emergency rule' of Peru during his presidency, in which democracy was effectively suspended and special powers given to specialist military forces and intelligence services. This policy drew some criticism within Peru, and particularly from other states, but succeeded in imprisoning over 1,000 members of Shining Path and diminishing their murderous campaign which had claimed 35,000 lives since 1980. MRTA, also, have never been the same threat since their 1996 defeat.

It appears, then, there is no simple answer to the question of whether or not governments should talk to terrorists or at least modify their behaviour in line with their demands. The world's worst ever non-state terrorist attack, on the USA in 2001, prompted a major military response which successfully overturned the government seen as hosting the perpetrators and captured many members of the group deemed responsible for the atrocity, but the September 11th strike also stimulated much debate in the USA as to *why* they had been attacked. Although negotiation with those responsible was not a serious option for the USA some re-assessment of Middle East policy, the underlying cause of anti-Americanism in groups such as al-Qa'ida, did take place. Hence in 2001, whilst preparing for war in Afghanistan, we witnessed a president of the USA recognizing the unpopularity of his country's traditionally pro-Israeli stance in the Moslem world by stating his support for a 'viable Palestinian state'. In 2003 US troops began the process of withdrawing from their bases in Saudi Arabia and so satisfied a core demand of al-Qa'ida shortly after going to war to defeat them. The Americans and Israelis have taken a comparatively tough stance in their dealings with non-state forces but the 'no deals' notion is really more rhetorical than real. Israel negotiated with terrorists in the run-up to the Oslo Accords in 1993 and are known to have authorized many Arab prisoner releases. The 'War On Terror' has been more than just a conventional war and there is no doubt that Israel will feel compelled to engage in dialogue again with their foes.

## International: diplomatic carrots and sticks

Increased concern with 'state-sponsored terrorism' from the 1980s onwards led to the increased use of conventional foreign policy tools aimed at pressuring governments believed to be sponsoring or giving refuge to violent non-state organizations. The ultimate diplomatic measure is the severing of all diplomatic links with another state. The withdrawal of diplomatic recognition to governments considered to be sponsoring terrorists sends a powerful political message since, although more a common response than it used to be, this is still a rare act in international relations.

One downside of the modern diplomatic trend of politicizing recognition (as opposed to the traditional *Lauterpacht doctrine* of giving recognition to a regime that is in control whether you like it or not), is that the resulting pariah states are left free from diplomatic leverage. The fact that the Taliban regime in Afghanistan had never been recognized by the USA or any other Western state made it difficult to exercise political pressure on them to give up members of al-Qa'ida based in their territory in the wake of the 2001 attacks on the USA. Where diplomatic and economic links exist governments supportive of violent orgnaizations can be leant upon or given incentives to desist from offering such support. The withdrawal of recognition can induce states 'sponsoring terrorism' to change their ways in order to resume economic links with the countries from which they have become estranged. The Gaddafi regime in Libya, for example, in the 1990s appeared to cease backing anti-Western terror groups in response to the diplomatic stick of isolation and the carrot of lucrative trading links.

One of the first actions of the USA government following the September 11th 2001 strikes was to attempt to build a 'coalition against terror', recognizing that they would need the support not only of their traditional allies but of as many states as possible, in order to pursue a prolonged campaign against those responsible for this and other acts of anti-American terrorism. The diplomatic isolation of Afghanistan made the support of its neighbour Pakistan essential, particularly since it was one of only three states recognizing its government.[4] Pakistan could provide diplomatic leverage on a government it had helped bring to power as well as intelligence information on a country not well understood even by a superpower. Classic diplomatic bargaining was very much to the fore here with Pakistan rewarded by the USA for turning its back on its ally, and risking the wrath of sections of its own population in doing so. Sanctions imposed in the wake of its testing of nuclear weapons in 1998 and military coup which had brought its leader Musharaf to power were lifted and 'rewards' promised. The key regional powers, China and Russia, were also courted by the USA as were countries such as Syria, previously cited by the Americans as sponsors of terrorism, in an exercise of *realpolitik* designed to reduce the options open to an elusive transnational enemy.

That the world's only military superpower should need to coalition-build and horse trade like this was testimony to the fact that the nature of military politics in a unipolar world is not necessarily distinct from previous eras of international relations, even if the sources of insecurity are far different than that encountered by the statesmen of yesteryear. In 1999 Turkey secured the capture of the PKK leader Occalan with the assistance of Israeli secret services and the cooperation of their traditional foe, Greece. The state system itself is challenged by the rise of political actors who defy traditional norms of sovereignty, diplomacy and the resort to arms and its members are increasingly rallying to its defence.

## Containment

The most immediate and predictable response of the government of the USA to the 2001 strikes was to take practical steps to reduce the possibility of such an event re-occurring. All governments faced by a substantial threat of non-state violence look to secure themselves and their citizens by containing such threats through the 'hardening' of potential terrorist targets. Security measures at most international airports were stepped up in the 1970s in response to the popularity of 'skyjackings' and this particular terror tactic became less frequent as a result. The 2001 New York and Washington suicide pilots, of course, avoided encountering extensive security checks on international flights into the USA by hijacking passenger planes on internal flights, notable for much laxer security measures. Even in the wake of the 1995 Oklahoma bombing, by the US anti-federalist Timothy McVeigh, American notions of security remained externalized and moves to tighten checks on internal flights in the late 1990s had been resisted. By contrast, since the 1970s, airport security on internal flights in Israel has been as tight as it is for international flights. From 2001 US security for the first time began to be framed in a manner closer to that of Israel and other parts of the world in which threats of organized non-state violence are part of the political landscape.

Before 2001 the irritation and economic cost of slowing up the USA's dense network of internal flights was enough to outweigh the potential security cost in the minds of most Americans. Such costs and irritations are easily borne by people who perceive that they serve to enhance their personal security. The people of the UK in the 1980s adapted to life without rubbish bins at train stations and in which they were liable to be searched by police on driving into the City of London since they had witnessed the carnage caused by IRA bombs on their TV screens. Most Peruvians initially were happy to tolerate much more serious restrictions on their everyday lives in Fujimori's campaign against Shining Path and MRTA. There is, however, a limit to what citizens of Western democracies will tolerate in the name of containing terrorism. Liberal opinion in the UK was hostile to suggestions by the Labour government in the wake of the 2001 attacks on the USA that ID cards be introduced for British citizens, so that state officials could keep a better track of the activities of foreign citizens. Indeed, the knee-jerk nature of such responses after acts of terror is evident in the fact that the UK government appeared to overlook the fact that the presence of such a scheme in the USA did not prevent the September 11th tragedy nor did it deter the Madrid bombers in 2004. Balancing the security and freedom of its citizens is perhaps the essence of democratic government in the twenty-first century.

## *Legal measures*

### *Domestic legal responses*

A freedom versus security balancing act also faces governments when dealing with the suspected perpetrators of non-state violence (whether their own citizens or not, though most acutely when dealing with their own citizens). Many governments have responded to non-state security threats by issuing 'emergency legislation', introducing measures which essentially suspend normal rights of citizenship for suspects from their own country or withdraw the rights normally enjoyed by non-citizens residing within their country. Amongst the sorts of legal measures enacted by governments in this respect are the following:

## Proscribing the membership of certain organizations

The act of being a member of an organization associated with acts of violence against the state, without necessarily being actively involved in such violence, is frequently criminalized by governments. The UK government made membership of the IRA and other organizations an imprisonable criminal offence as part of their campaign against Irish nationalist violence in the 1970s as have the Turkish government in their struggle with Kurdish separatists. This strategy can lead to violent non-state organizations forming 'legitimate' political wings so that their spokesmen can continue to advance their cause without technically being associated with the violent organization. Examples of this include Sinn Fein, set up as the political arm of the IRA, and Herri Battasuna the sister organization of violent Basque separatists ETA. This strategy proved a successful means of maintaining a twin track approach to forwarding their cause for these two groups in the open democratic systems of the UK and Spain.

## Internment

Emergency legislation enacted in the face of a terrorist campaign may also see the state grant itself the power to arrest suspects without having to resort to normal legal processes. The UK derogated from Article 5 of the European Convention of Human Rights shortly after the September 11th 2001 attacks in order to be able to detain terrorist suspects for longer periods without charging them than ordinarily permitted.

## Trial without jury

Concerns that jurors could be intimidated against finding members of major violent organizations guilty have prompted many governments to suspend the democratic norm of trial by jury for such trials. The UK introduced so called *Diplock courts* (named after Lord Diplock whose report recommended them) for Northern Ireland in 1972 for this reason. In 2007 the USA began trying prisoners held at their naval base at Guantanamo Bay on suspicion of being al-Qa'ida or Taliban operatives by military tribunal. Such was the international unease at this deviation from normal legal practice that even most of the USA's staunchest allies protested and demanded the release of their own nationals held in this way.

## Sentencing

Governments also frequently act against political non-state violence by legislating for the perpetrators of such crimes to be subject to heavier sentencing by the courts than other violent criminals, in the hope of deterring such acts. The logic of deterrence, however, does not always work as well on armed revolutionaries as it does on armed criminals. High-profile imprisonment may serve to advance the cause of the terrorist/freedom fighter (as with Mandela) whilst a death sentence may turn a killer into a martyr and is hardly likely to deter a suicide bomber.

## Restrictions on free expression

Governments have been known to suspend another civil right of democratic citizens when dealing with advocates of political non-state violence, that of free speech and expression. The UK government's frustration with the electoral success of Sinn Fein in the 1980s led them to seek action short of banning a technically peaceful political party that would deprive them of the 'oxygen of publicity'. The results of this action showed the difficulties inherent in balancing democratic norms and action against non-state violence and the pitfalls associated with legislating in haste. The measure introduced denied Sinn Fein members the right to speak directly on television or radio without actually prohibiting their right to express their views. The results of this were farcical as the law was upheld by the use of actors employed to speak the words of Sinn Fein leaders as they appeared on television. Sinn Fein continued to enjoy the oxygen of publicity, denied only the right to have the public hear their actual voices, whilst the government were left to look foolish.

## Restrictions on employment

In the 1970s West Germany introduced a policy of *berufsverbot* (job ban) which prevented any individual considered to be linked to the Red Army Faction or other leftist militia taking up employment in the state sector. Many states, naturally enough, bar revolutionaries committed to the overthrow of the state from Civil Service positions but the German policy was controversial since it applied to any public service position and was believed to have discriminated against people with anti-governmental, but peacefully expressed, views (Wadlaw 1982: 121–6). In 1995 The German government was forced to compensate and reinstate a Communist schoolteacher by a European Court of Human Rights ruling (*Vogt v. Germany 1995*).

## *Global legal responses*

It has taken a surprisingly long time for the Westphalian system as a collectivity to seek to rid itself of the systemic threat posed by non-state violence. The tendency for many states to empathize with nationalist struggles or see advantage in a rival state being weakened by civil strife stifled the development of international law and other collaborative arrangements for many years. UN Conventions outlawing skyjacking and hostage-taking were ratified in the 1960s and 1970s but not until 1985 did Security Council and General Assembly Resolutions (579, 40/61) unite nearly all of the world in condemning all forms of non-state terrorism.[5] Additionally, states have been slower to develop extradition treaties and permit Interpol investigations for politically rather than criminally motivated aggressors. An important breakthrough was the 2004 Security Council Resolution 1566 which declared that terrorist tactics cannot be legitimate under any circumstances.

The end of the Cold War improved solidarity and paved the way for a more systematic approach to tackling political non-state violence. The G7 cartel of the world's most economically powerful states became an unlikely focus for state cooperation against the menace of transnational military forces in the 1990s.

The G7 together with Russia in 1996 held a 'terrorism summit' in Lyon, which sought to harmonize state approaches to the problem in order to avoid such groups exploiting policy differences. Issues addressed included collectively recognizing non-state violence as illegitimate by criminalizing fundraising for such groups, the need to avoid the appeasement of hostage takers and tough sentencing for this sort of crime. In 1993 the Security Council, under Resolution 864, imposed sanctions on a non-state actor for the first time and succeeded in bringing UNITA (National Union for the Total Independence of Angola) to the negotiating table through an arms embargo, travel ban and financial restrictions on the group's membership. The success of these measures prompted similar Resolutions against al-Qa'ida members in the aftermath of the 2001 attacks on the USA. Resolution 1373 (2001) actually goes far beyond just targeting bin Laden and his associates and calls upon all states to criminalize the hosting and/or financing of all non-state military forces.

## Military

### 'Fight fire with fire' #1: covert operations

Much non-state violence has taken the form of 'terrorism' because such strategies are not easily countered by states geared up to resist more conventional military operations. Hence, states faced with persistent non-state security threats have adapted their armed forces in accordance by creating special counter-terrorist units or by adapting existing special forces. The Israeli government authorized their intelligence agency Mossad to implement an operation named 'Wrath of God' as a direct response to the 1972 Munich Olympics massacre of Israeli athletes by the Palestinian nationalist group Black September. A Mossad unit was given the task of wiping out Black September and empowered to do so by whatever means necessary, even where this meant acting outside of international law by entering other states uninvited to carry out assassinations. This controversial strategy was vindicated in that Black September were eliminated by September 1973 but the mistaken killing of an innocent waiter in Norway, unfortunate enough to look like a particular member of the target group, showed the limitations of such an approach.

British counter-terrorism has been led by the Special Air Service (SAS), set up during the Second World War as a crack unit to operate behind enemy lines. The SAS came to the fore in their new role in 1980 when a siege at the Iranian embassy in London was ended with the killing of five and arrest of another of the hostage takers. The SAS were also at the forefront of the British campaign against Irish nationalist violence in the 1980s and early 1990s and their success in killing a number of IRA personnel was a crucial factor in bringing the IRA and Sinn Fein to the negotiating table. Essentially a stalemate had been reached in the conflict with both sides accepting the outright defeat of the other was impossible. In the wake of the September 2001 strikes on the USA many states reviewed their defence arrangements and such units are becoming less 'special' and more of a standard security force.

*'Fight fire with fire' #2: war*

The 2001–2 Afghan War was the only 'full-scale' war to have been waged against an armed non-state actor but conventional military responses at a lesser level have been used from time to time. The USA bombed Libya in 1986 in retaliation for its leadership's links with a number of incidents around the world which had targeted US servicemen. Similarly, in 1998 US air strikes targeted sites in Afghanistan and Sudan linked to al-Qa'ida in a response to the bombing of their embassies in Kenya and Tanzania.

Israel too has used military might to take on an elusive enemy. Controversial invasions of the Lebanon in 1982, 1996 and 2006 sought to flush out PLO and, in the latest incursion, Hizbullah bases in order to secure their northern border. In a similar vein, Turkish actions against Kurdish separatists have included incursions into Iraq, where the PKK have strongholds. These limited military engagements have tended to be largely unsuccessful and, possibly, even counter-productive. The US strikes of 1998 hit an innocent target in Sudan and the Israeli incursion of 1982 is best remembered for a massacre in a Palestinian refugee camp. Additionally, the greatest Libyan-backed anti-American atrocity (the Lockerbie aeroplane bombing) occurred two years after the 1986 Tripoli bombings and the PLO and al-Qa'ida were far from deterred by the state actions targeting them.

## *Educative*

### *Societal or terrorist change*

In the same way that much state criminal policy has come to focus on tackling the 'causes of crime' as well as crime itself, counter-terrorism is evolving towards the more subtle task of seeking to understand the grievances that motivate people to such acts. The UK government's 'Prevent' strategy, launched in 2007, seeks to stop 'home-grown terrorism' by better understanding what societal explanations there might be for some of its citizens choosing to become suicide bombers like the Islamic fundamentalists who killed 52 in London in 2005. Such exercises in 'anger management' are not about 'giving in to terrorism' as hardliners may complain but are about the longer game of 'preventive diplomacy' through appreciating the underlying causes of such threats. This is an approach which, as discussed in the previous chapter, has become mainstream in inter-state military security politics and, as outlined in the proceeding chapters, has emerged as a key strategy in countering most other areas of security. Such an approach also does not preclude the deployment of accompanying hardline counter-terrorist strategies since it can give greater legitimacy to being tough on those who do resort to excessive means to highlight their grievances when there are other, peaceful avenues open to them. In this way the freedom fighter/terrorist dichotomy is more clearly resolved since, as Wilkinson memorably put it: 'one democracy's terrorist is another democracy's terrorist' (Wilkinson 2011: 207).

### Global discourse

The task of understanding the grievances that prompt political non-state violence must also be the stuff of international politics. At the global level equitable facilities to address grievances, such as a responsible UN Security Council with clear provision for dealing with civil conflict and the International Criminal Court, can perform a similar service if permitted to do so. Set against a functioning and just global polity, unjust non-state grievances, or grievances which persist in using unjust means, will be more easily identified as such and be able to be singled out for concerted global action, political or military, of the sort traditionally reserved for unlawfully aggressive states. International recognition of educative solutions was evident at the United Nations' 2005 Madrid Summit. The summit was widely reported on as a failure for not securing an agreed definition of terrorism but, nevertheless, did get consensus on the key methods needed to diminish the phenomenon. Five pillars, or five Ds, were identified and subsequently fleshed out in a Global Strategy Against Terrorism released in 2006:

> **D**issuade disaffected groups from choosing terrorism as a tactic to achieve their goals.
> **D**eny terrorists the means to carry out their attacks.
> **D**eter states from supporting terrorists.
> **D**evelop state capacity to prevent terrorism.
> **D**efend human rights in the struggle against terrorism.
> (UN General Assembly 2006 – emphasis added)

## Conclusions: can political non-state violence be defeated?

The depressing truth is that there is no easy answer for dealing with non-state political violence and it probably can never be entirely defeated. That, though, is not to say that we cannot learn how to deal with insurgencies and non-state terror and minimize its impact. Cronin, drawing on extensive empirical evidence, suggests that there are six ways in which terrorist campaigns can come to an end:

- *'Decapitation'*: the terrorists are defeated, as appears to be the case with the Tamil Tigers in Sri Lanka.
- *Negotiations*: a two-way compromise ends the struggle, as with the UK–IRA peace settlement.
- *Success*: the 'terrorists' win, as with the ANC revolution in South Africa and many anti-colonial independence movements.
- *Failure*: the terrorists implode due to a loss of support owing to public revulsion at tactics or a perceived loss of relevance. Many Marxist groups have declined in this way and al-Qa'ida may similarly fade away as democracy begins to emerge following the Arab Spring revolts.
- *Repression*: tough counter-terrorism subdues the terrorists without defeating them, as with the Russian suppression of the Chechens.

- *Re-orientation*: the terrorism metamorphosizes into a full-scale insurgency or into criminal enterprises (such as 'narco-terrorism' in Latin America).

(Cronin 2009)

Cronin's analysis supports the notion that countering non-state political violence requires the careful blending of a range of the strategies previously outlined to fit the particular circumstances. Traditional military responses by the state can achieve some success but only where the foe is closely linked with a government and a clear target can be aimed at, as was the case with the US war against Afghanistan in 2002. This campaign assisted the US 'war on terror' by removing a key support base for its principal enemy, al-Qa'ida, and killing a number of that organization's operatives but, of course, it could never be as complete a victory as it would have been had the Afghan government itself been the direct enemy. Wars between states usually reach a definitive conclusion but wars against non-state actors rarely do. Non-state actors are unlikely to surrender since they can usually run away rather than face the music of a post-war settlement. Hence al-Qa'ida continued their campaign against the USA after 2002, depleted but not defeated and still carrying the same grievances. The very notion of a war against al-Qa'ida's terror may even have been counter-productive since it elevated a loose protest movement to the sort of status previously reserved for great powers like Nazi Germany or the Soviet Union. The same can be said of Israel's 2006 campaign against Hizbullah in the Lebanon. Few observers of this comprehensive military victory consider that it actually advanced the Israelis in their aim of defeating this enemy and securing their borders. Invoking the language of national security in countering non-state violence is often not appropriate or helpful to the state. Horrific though 9/11 was it is worth remembering that the 'national security' threat posed by al-Qa'ida to the United States cannot be compared to the Soviet Union during the Cold War or Japan in the early 1940s. Insurgencies can become matters of national security but 'new' global terrorism is invariably a human security matter not soluble by traditional security methods.

It is this limitation in the application of state power which prompted Paul Wilkinson famously to liken wars against non-state forces to 'fighting the hydra', the mythical beast that could respond to having its head cut off by growing another one (Wilkinson 1986). Non-state foes can be subdued for periods of time but, if the same grievances persist, others are likely to take up arms again for the cause. Indeed, the longer grievances fester the more they become socialized and second and third generation 'freedom fighters' are no more likely to abandon their fathers' and grandfathers' cause than state citizens are to meekly submit to foreign invasion. Peace deals after long-term civil insurgencies tend to be particularly difficult since sections of the non-state force frequently become more absolutist in their stance. Hence in Northern Ireland, Israel/Palestine and the Basque country attempted settlements have split the nationalist movements and created hardline splinter groups.

The unpalatable fact is that whilst grievances remain in the world violence will always resurface. Acts of international terrorism by non-state actors are an unfortunate side-effect of a more open and closely connected world. Short of closing all state borders and rolling back the democratization of the world and licensing the even greater threat of unrestrained state terrorism, non-state violence can never be comprehensively defeated. 'Anyone who claims to have a total solution to terrorism in a democracy is either a fool or a knave' (Wilkinson 1990: 253). To admit this is not to say that nothing can be done about political non-state violence or that it is the fault of democracy and globalization. Grievances that prompt violence can be addressed, either through direct bargaining with the aggrieved or by the general evolution of a more just world. The same point made in the previous chapter with reference to inter-state war holds for its sub-state variant. Since war is political, politics can resolve war (Halliday 2002: 58). Democracy and globalization can facilitate this. 'Terrorists' can become democrats and negotiate their position around a table rather than through force. Violent Irish nationalism was largely transformed into democratic Irish nationalism by giving the movement some legislative power in exchange for abandoning the use of military power. Begin, Makarios and Kenyatta made the transition from terrorist/freedom fighter to respectable and respected democratic politicians in Israel, Cyprus and Kenya respectively. Extensive empirical research by Marshall and Gurr, comparing conflict resolution during and after the Cold War, gives some scope for optimism in this regard, suggesting that secessionist conflicts by 2004 were at their lowest level since 1960 (Marshall and Gurr 2005).

The perpetuation of sovereignty as a sacred political concept beyond its practical existence serves to obscure the simple fact that war is war whatever communities the combatants purport to represent. International cooperation has done much to lessen the recourse to military action by states and, given the opportunity, it can have the same effect for non-state actors. International law can directly target globally operating groups and individuals through implementing effective travel bans and freezing their bank accounts in a way that state legislation or war cannot. The same increased interconnectedness of the modern world that has breathed life into political non-state violence can also help to suffocate it.

## Key points

- The term 'terrorism' is typically applied to non-state political violence but this is analytically unhelpful since states frequently terrorize their own and other states' citizens.
- Political non-state violence has been dominated by three types: nationalist, Marxist and religious.
- A range of tactics have been used by governments to combat threats of this kind with no clear consensus on the most effective.
- Political non-state violence is now far more common and persistent than state-to-state conflict suggesting that greater recourse to negotiated solutions are required, however unpalatable this may be for governments.

## Notes

1    'Noncombatants' is taken to include off-duty or unarmed troops.
2    The sovereign state system. So named after the 1648 Treaty of Westphalia often seen as having initiated the concept of state sovereignty.
3    As published in the *Financial Times*, 10 October 2001.
4    The others were Saudi Arabia and the United Arab Emirates.
5    Cuba was the only state to vote against the General Assembly Resolution.

## Recommended reading

Cronin, A. (2009) *How Terrorism Ends*, Princeton: Princeton University Press.
Halliday, F. (2002) *Two Hours That Shook the World, September 11, 2001: Causes and Consequences*, London: Saqi.
Wilkinson, P. (2011) *Terrorism versus Democracy: The Liberal State Response*, Abingdon: Routledge.

## Useful web links

Europol, EU Terrorism Situation and Trend Report TE-SAT: http://www.europol.europa.eu/content/press/eu-terrorism-situation-and-trend-report-te-sat-2012–1567
University of St Andrews Centre for the Study of Terrorism and Political Violence: http://www.st-andrews.ac.uk/academic/intrel/research/cstpv/
US State Department Counterterrorism Office: http://www.state.gov/s/ct/

# Economic threats to security

> We have the means; we have the capacity to wipe hunger and poverty from the face of the Earth in our lifetime. We need only the will.
> (President John F. Kennedy of the USA, World Food Congress, Washington, DC, October 1963)

## Economic insecurity

The concept of human security accommodates the consideration of a wide range of threats to life, of which poverty is undoubtedly the most significant. Poverty kills directly in huge numbers when people are unable to secure sufficient food to live because they lack the economic means to purchase or produce it. This situation can arise in a number of ways which are considered in this chapter. A famine can occur when an acute shortage of food is incurred across a broad swathe of people. More persistent is the continual threat posed by hunger to millions of people across the world due to economic circumstances. Additionally, people may be periodically exposed to life-threatening economic insecurity due to a sudden deterioration of economic circumstances due either to a recession or the imposition of trade sanctions for political reasons. Poverty is also an underlying cause of human death by other security threats. As Thomas states, 'the pursuit of human security must have at its core the satisfaction of basic material needs of all humankind. At the most basic level, food, shelter, education and health care are essential for the survival of human beings' (Thomas 2000: 7).

Satisfying the 'basic material needs of humankind' is not solely an economic task but it is, without doubt, principally achieved by the possession of money, personally and societally. Money is not the root of all of humanity's ills nor the sole cause of starvation and hunger. On the one hand, droughts and other natural phenomena can disrupt the food supply, and on the other, it is possible to feed yourself without buying the food. Money, however, can be used to secure yourself against natural hazards and insure you against fluctuations in the food supply caused either by natural or economic disruptions. In addition, self-sufficiency in food production, either for individuals or states, is an increasingly difficult means of achieving security. Money, so the saying goes, 'can't buy you love' but it can buy you a certain measure of that other of life's most precious commodities, security. Table 4.1 illustrates the point that the wealthy of the world live longer whilst the poor die young. There is not a precise correlation between wealth and life expectancy but the match-up, particularly at the bottom of the scale, is still striking. The world's poorest people are also, by and large, the world's most insecure.

There are, however, some anomalies which emerge from comparing income and life expectancy which demonstrate that there is more to security than money. Equatorial Guinea is Africa's richest country and ranked 45 in the world by GDP per capita but its citizens have a life expectancy of only 51, the thirteenth worst in the world. The country has acquired great export earnings from oil production but is, at same time, beset with corruption, poor governance and civil turmoil. At the other end of the scale, the prominence of gun crime and lack of state health-care provision in the USA are factors in that country's citizens having an average life expectancy not in line with its wealth and below, for example, Cuba. The United

**Table 4.1** The price of poverty: wealth and life expectancy

| | 2009 ranking by GNP per capita, PPPª | 2009 ranking by life expectancy (out of 194) | 2009 ranking by HDI (out of 187) |
|---|---|---|---|
| **Top (over $40,000)** | | | |
| 1 | Qatar | 39 (79.4) | 37 |
| 2 | Luxembourg | 26 (80) | 25 |
| 3 | United Arab Emirates | 49 (76.5) | 30 |
| 4 | Norway | 13 (81.1) | 1 |
| 5 | Singapore | 3 (81.1) | 26 |
| **Bottom (under $700)** | | | |
| 183 | Niger | 171 (54.7) | 186 |
| 184 | Eritrea | 154 (61.6) | 177 |
| 185 | Liberia | 166 (56.8) | 182 |
| 186 | Burundi | 184 (50.4) | 185 |
| 187 | Dem. Rep. of Congo | 194 (48.4) | 187 |

Note
ª GNP is 'Gross National Product', the total earnings of all citizens of a country. This divided by the population of the country gives the GNP per capita. This figure is factored by PPP 'purchasing power parity', the relative worth of that country's money.
Source: UNDP (2011).

Nations Development Programme (UNDP), to get over the limitations of judging development purely in economic terms, calculates a 'Human Development Index' to rank a country's progress (see Table 4.2). This figure combines income, life expectancy and educational attainment to give a more thorough picture of whether a state's wealth is being utilized to the benefit of its people. Hence states which, for various reasons, do not utilize their resources for the benefit of all of their people, like Equatorial Guinea, or higher up the scale like Kuwait, are judged to be less developed than their GDP would suggest. Equally some countries, such as Cuba and Madagascar, under HDI can be understood as more developed than their income would suggest due to relatively good health and educational systems securing their citizens. At the same time, the most developed countries by HDI are rich but not necessarily the richest (see Table 4.2). Although there is more to it than money, when it comes to achieving human security there is no doubt that it helps.

## Famine

The most acute and immediate economic threat to human security comes in the form of famine.

**Table 4.2** Human development indicators

| Top 10 by HDI | Top 10, HDI compared to GDP PPP | Bottom 10, HDI compared to GDP PPP | Bottom 10 by HDI |
| --- | --- | --- | --- |
| 1 Norway | 1 Cuba (+52) | 1 Eq. Guinea (−91) | 178 Guinea |
| 2 Australia | 2 Georgia (+36) | 2 Kuwait (−57) | 179 C. African R. |
| 3 Netherlands | 3 N. Zealand (+30) | 3 Botswana (−56) | 180 Sierra Leone |
| 4 USA | 3 Grenada (+30) | 4 Oman (−50) | 181 Burkina Faso |
| 5 New Zealand | 5 Palau (+29) | 5 S. Africa (−44) | 182 Liberia |
| 6 Canada | 6 Tonga (+26) | 6 Gabon (−40) | 183 Chad |
| 7 Ireland | 6 Madagascar (+26) | 7 Angola (−38) | 184 Mozambique |
| 8 Liechtenstein | 8 Ukraine (+24) | 8 Bhutan (−36) | 185 Burundi |
| 9 Germany | 9 Palestine (+23) | 9 Djibouti (−28) | 186 Niger |
| 10 Sweden | 10 Samoa (+22) | 10 Swaziland (−27) | 187 Congo D.R. |
| | 10 Armenia (+22) | 10 UAE (−27) | |

Source: UNDP (2011).

The information in Table 4.3 is highly approximated in a number of ways. First, famines are functionally related to other threats to human security such as disease, drought and flooding, which are considered elsewhere in this book. Floods and droughts wipe out crops and can cause famine but they can also kill directly, whilst diseases are generally more virulent when infecting a malnourished population. Hence, determining the precise cause of death for people beset by such natural catastrophes is problematic and, as such, figures on famine fatalities are inexact. Second, even allowing for the blurring of the causal factors of death, disaster mortality statistics are notoriously unreliable. Governments tend to underestimate figures whilst anti-government voices often exaggerate them for opposing political purposes. Most of the figures quoted in Table 4.3 are contested and it is difficult to verify precise totals even with painstaking research. This problem is not solely one of authenticating historical records. Modern-day statistics also tend to be arrived at through educated guesswork. The highly secretive North Korean government denied any problem of starvation for a number of years and have subsequently admitted to 'only' around 200,000 deaths due to this. Natsios's estimate of 2–3 million was largely derived from making extrapolations based on interviews with refugees (Natsios 1999). The true picture will probably never be known.

## The causes of famine

A further abstraction in Table 4.3 comes from indicating the principal cause of each famine. Invariably there are a combination of factors which can explain such humanitarian disasters. As with the mortality figures, the causes of famines are frequently disputed by analysts and politicians. Most famines are the result of a

**Table 4.3** The top ten famines in history

|   |   | Deaths | Principal cause |
|---|---|---|---|
| 1 | China 1958–62 | 30 million[a] | *Political*: forced urbanization and collectivization of agriculture |
| 2 | N. China 1876–8 | 12 million[b] | *Natural*: drought |
| 3 | Bengal 1770 | 10 million[c] | *Natural*: drought |
| 4 | C. India 1876–8 | 6 million[b] | *Natural*: drought |
| 5 | Ukraine 1932–3 | 5 million[d] | *Political*: harsh USSR quotas on Ukrainian grain collected centrally |
| 6 | N. Korea 1995 | 2 million[e] | *Natural*: drought and floods |
| 7 | Bengal 1943–4 | 1.9 million[d] | *Political*: supply and price of rice negatively affected by the Second World War |
| 8 | Rajputana, India 1869 | 1.5 million[f] | *Natural*: drought |
| =9 | Orissa, India 1865–6 | 1 million[f] | *Natural*: drought in 1865 followed by floods in 1866 |
| =9 | India 1897 | 1 million[f.] | *Natural*: drought |
| =9 | Ireland 1845–7 | 1 million[g] | *Natural*: potato blight |

Sources: [a] Becker (2000); [b] Davis (2001); [c] Sen (1981); [d] Disaster Center (2003); [e] Natsios (1999); [f] Hazlitt (1973); [g] Ó Gráda (1999).

combination of both natural and political factors and disputes on causation centre on determining the relative weighting of the two contributory factors (hence, this section is included here rather than in the chapter on natural disasters). The famines in India and Ireland, for example, had natural causes but are generally considered to have been exacerbated by an ignorance of the local situation born of colonial rule. The North Korean famine had natural origins but has, undoubtedly, been greatly worsened by the government's drive for economic self-sufficiency, which has seen food imports reduced at the same time as the domestic food supply has dwindled.

Marxist analysis argues that structural economic factors account for famines as much as the inadequate political responses of particular governments to crop failures. It is, indeed, striking that so many of the worst famines in history occurred in the late nineteenth century, an era of as-then unparalleled global economic liberalization when the trade in foodstuffs greatly increased. Marx himself considered the famines of his era to be the product of capitalism and his latter day protégés, such as Davis, cite persuasive evidence that colonized or semi-colonized countries, like India and China, thrust into a global market economy, exported food to the developed world whilst their own nationals starved (Davis 2001: 27). The late nineteenth century, however, was also an era marked by extreme climatic conditions in Asia owing an increased prevalence of the 'El Nino' effect. El Nino is a periodically occurring phenomenon whereby equatorial areas of the Pacific Ocean warm up causing atmospheric disturbances which can manifest themselves in periods of drought and flood, in place of the characteristic seasonal changes in weather. It appears that a combination of profound changes in both the natural and economic environments transpired to kill millions in Asia and elsewhere in the late nineteenth century. Those deaths should serve as a powerful warning from history of the need to temper contemporary economic globalization with political measures in order to be ready to deal with the rise of unexpected threats to economic security.

The clearest cases of human-made, political famine are the horrific twentieth-century disasters in Communist China and the USSR. The Chinese famine was influenced by the effects of excessive rainfall on harvests but there is little doubt that its principal cause was Mao Tse Tung's determination to pursue his 'Great Leap Forward' economic reform plan, regardless of the human consequences. The Ukrainian famine did not have any obvious natural causes and appears to have been entirely political, deliberately engineered by Stalin to punish farmers of the region for their lack of enthusiasm for Soviet collectivization.

There are three fundamental explanations for any particular famine related to the balance between the supply and demand for food.

1    A fall in the food supply.
2    An increase in the demand for food.
3    Disruptions to the normal distribution of food.

The third of these is most particularly influenced by politics and economics. As will be explored in the next section, if considered from a global perspective, all famines can be attributed to explanation 3 since there is demonstrably sufficient food in the world for all people to be adequately fed. We do not yet live by effective global governance, however, and all three explanations can variously be applied to the situation in states where famines are occurring. The food supply in countries can fall below the level sufficient to meet demand because of poor harvests or the population can grow at a rate that the food supply is unable to match.

Overpopulation is a condition that has certainly affected most of the principal arenas of famine over the last century, such as in China and India where it has prompted domestic political action to curb population growth. A provocative argument from prominent American economists the Paddock brothers in the late 1960s went as far as to argue that India and other countries prone to famine had only themselves to blame and should be left to suffer for their own and everyone else's good. Overpopulation added to endemic poor government meant that, for some states, food aid was a waste of time and that they should be considered to form a 'can't be saved' group and ignored by the USA and other benefactors. 'Waste not the food on the "can't be saved" and the "walking wounded". Send it to those nations which, having it, can buttress their own resources, their own efforts, and fight through to survival' (Paddock and Paddock 1967: 229).

The economist Garret Hardin advanced a similar idea in formulating the analogy of lifeboats in an ocean to characterize states in a world where food supplies will eventually be used up in the face of population growth. Hardin's thesis argued for the application of 'lifeboat ethics' to combat this, which essentially argued that international action to tackle famine was folly as wealthy countries would risk sinking their own 'lifeboats' in doing so. Better to let the overcrowded lifeboats of the Third World sink than ensuring that we all drown (Hardin 1996). Such apocalyptic views of the global security implications of overpopulation were common in the 1960s and 1970s and can be dated back as far as the eighteenth century and the works of Thomas Malthus. They are, though, rarer today since the central plank of the Malthusian and neo-Malthusian prediction, that world population will come to exceed world food supply, has not happened and does not look likely to do so. The demand for food continues to increase in the less developed world and natural disasters continue to blight many of the same countries, creating food shortages, but most contemporary analysts of famine emphasize distributive factors in their explanations of particular cases. Modern governments can insure against future crop shortages by stockpiling reserves of food and protecting the price of agricultural products.

The leading writer in this approach to explaining famine is economist Amartya Sen (see Box 4.1). Sen expounds the 'entitlements approach' in which he argues that all individuals should by rights be able to expect to be protected from famine by their government, regardless of changes in food supply or population. In a convincing application of the democratic peace argument to economic rather than military security Sen draws on extensive evidence to propose that:

> No substantial famine has ever occurred in any independent and democratic country with a relatively free press. . . .
>
> Even the poorest democratic countries that have faced terrible droughts or floods or other natural disasters (such as India in 1973, or Zimbabwe and Botswana in the early 1980s) have been able to feed their people without experiencing a famine.
>
> (Sen 1999: 6–7)

Democratic governments are compelled to be responsive to the needs of ordinary people whose security is imperilled, whether directly or indirectly through the pressure of the media or other concerned citizens, in a way in which tyrannical

---

### Box 4.1 Amartya Sen

The winner of the Nobel Prize for Economics in 1998, Sen is an Indian academic from Bengal who experienced the 1943–4 famine first hand as a young boy. He was born on a university campus to Bangladeshi parents (his father was a Chemistry lecturer) and has graced most of the leading universities of the world in a glittering academic career. Sen has lectured in Economics at Cambridge, Oxford, the London School of Economics and Harvard and his research has focused on the economic dimensions of poverty, famine and human rights. As such Sen's work has found influence outside of the confines of Economics and he is revered in political science for his contribution to bringing a much neglected ethical dimension to the 'miserable science'.

dictators or neglectful colonialists are not. Democracy saves people as well as empowers them and the spread of democratization in the world will help in the fight against famine. Food shortages will still occur from time to time but these can normally be planned for by governments and, when they cannot be dealt with, the international community can step in. Countless lives in North Korea would have been saved were it not for the fact that the state had virtually cut itself off from the rest of the world and external assistance had not been possible. Being part of the global economy would have saved the lives of many North Koreans. Being a democratic state within the global economy would have saved more still.

## Global policy on famine relief

The principal instrument for coordinating famine relief at the global level is the UN's World Food Programme (WFP) a hybrid of the Food and Agricultural Organization (FAO) and World Health Organization (WHO). Created in 1963, initially as an ad hoc three-year project, the WFP has evolved into the 'food arm of the UN' (WFP 2002a: 1) with all of the characteristics of an IGO. Based, like the FAO, in Rome, the WFP is governed by an Executive Board and served by a permanent secretariat. The Executive Board votes on where to allocate food aid from an annual budget of around $5.5 billion (WFP 2011). Through the course of its working life this food aid has increasingly been targeted at countries suffering food shortages due to the effects of natural disasters or conflict rather than for general development purposes.

The stated aim of the WFP's work is 'eradicating hunger and poverty. The ultimate objective of food aid should be the elimination of the need for food aid' (WFP 2002b: 1). In reality, though, the WFP is a global emergency service and the broad aim of achieving 'food security' – 'access of all peoples at all times to the food needed for an active and healthy life' (FAO/WHO 1992) – is a more profound goal beyond the reach of its budget and operations.

## Hunger

Global political action, coordinated inter-governmentally by the WFP and non-governmentally by pressure groups such as Oxfam, CAFOD and War on Want has, in recent decades, succeeded in curtailing the escalation of famines but such groups are quick to point out that such periodic disasters are merely the tip of the global hunger 'iceberg'. Far more people in today's world die of starvation through plain poverty rather than as a result of short-term regional imbalances between the supply and demand for food. The WFP claim that some 25,000 people every day die as a result of hunger and related ailments and that over 1 billion in the world suffer from malnutrition (WFP 2002c).[1] Some consider this a conservative estimate but this death toll undoubtedly outstrips any other threats to human existence.

Why then does this relentless carnage persist in a world in which the food supply is sufficient to permit every person in the world at least 2,720 calories per day (FAO 2002)?

## 1 Ignorance

One explanation is that, in spite of the best efforts of pressure groups, the general public of states wealthy enough to help alleviate the problem (and possibly some government ministers) are simply not sufficiently aware of the scale of the problem to feel compelled to 'find the will' called for in President Kennedy's speech in the early 1960s. Whilst famines have become less prominent since the 1980s, partly due to international political and charitable responses, the underlying issue of basic hunger remains a persistent problem that is harder to highlight in the news media than through dramatic pictures of emaciated children amidst cracked earth and flies after a drought. '[B]ecause we view hunger in the background of life, the terrible toll does not enter our headlines, nor, for most of us, our concerns' (Hunger Project 1985).

A reformist *Alter-Globalist* (as opposed to being pro or anti globalization/capitalism) does not accept that hunger is inevitable in a capitalist world economy but argues that global political failings are still culpable for the persistence of poverty. Alleviating hunger is possible without abandoning global capitalism by reforming international institutions and encouraging governments to act less selfishly in international trade. The 'make poverty history' campaign of the 2000s, for example, sought to increase public awareness of the daily death toll due to hunger and pressure governments into structural political actions to alleviate this tragedy. The agricultural industry in the Global North has managed to remain largely exempted from the international trade liberalization since the mid-twentieth century and, in many countries, enjoys heavy government subsidization and protection. This undermines the capacity of the Global South countries to export their food produce to Northern markets. The losses resulting from this distortion of the free market – an estimated annual $100 billion – far exceeds the sums given to the Global South in aid (Watkins 2002). Hence 'trade not aid' became a mantra of the Make Poverty History campaign in contrast to the charity-focused Band Aid/Live Aid movement of the 1980s which had inspired it. Hence Alter-Globalists argue for a 'mixed economy' for the world in which more political intervention is required in some cases but, in other instances, the invisible hand of the free market should be allowed to do its work.

## 2 Structural violence

More radical, Marxist explanations for the persistence of poverty-induced starvation hold that it is, like famine, actually caused by the global economy and more a case of wilful ignorance by the world's wealthy. In the 1960s Galtung, using language deliberately designed to 'securitize' the issue of global poverty, coined the phrase 'structural violence' to encapsulate the nature of the phenomenon:

> if people are starving when this is objectively avoidable, then violence is committed, regardless of whether there is a clear subject–action–object relation, as during a siege yesterday or no such clear relation, as in the way economic relations are organized today.
>
> (Galtung 1969: 170)

The conventional notion that economic development was a stage that all states would eventually reach if they underwent social and economic 'modernization' came to be challenged from the 1960s by Galtung and 'dependency theory' advocates led by Frank (Frank 1971). From this 'Structuralist' perspective *developing* states are nothing of the sort, they are dependent states, systematically and deliberately exploited by their wealthy counterparts. The global economic system requires underdeveloped states in order to feed the voracious capitalist appetite for more wealth in the developed states. Hence, building on evidence that some Latin American states' economic fortunes improved rather than worsened when their principal trading partners were distracted in the Second World War, Frank and others advanced the notion that the poor states of the world would be better off by cutting themselves off from the Global North and concentrating on developing their own resources.

Wallerstein's 'World Systems Analysis' is a more sophisticated version of Structuralism which builds on Galtung's notion of a *core* and a *periphery* inevitably occurring in dependent states by applying this to the global level. In this view it is not so much the rich states of the world exploiting the poor states as a transnational wealthy class (including elites in less developed countries) exploiting a transnational class of the poor (including the poor in developed countries) (Wallerstein 1979).

## 3 Failure of certain states to encourage modernization

The orthodox position on poverty argues that it can be eradicated by those countries affected pursuing economic development of the kind experienced by Northern states. This view stands in direct opposition to the Marxist-Structuralist perspective by advocating that less developed countries (LDCs) can best mimic Northern development by integrating themselves into the global economy to permit export-oriented industries to flourish and gain from the inward investment provided by multi-national corporations (MNCs). In this way the conditions for modernization can be created: wealth, democracy, education, state-welfarism and smaller families; all of which serve to alleviate poverty. The clearest articulation of this view came from the influential US Economic Historian Rostow with his 'Stages of Growth' thesis in the 1960s. Rostow analysed the process of development in the North and concluded that all states pass through five similar stages of progression towards 'take-off' and an end stage of a wealthy consumer-driven society (Rostow 1960).

The failure of many LDCs to show any sign of such progression since the 1970s has dented the rigour of Rostow's thesis but the orthodox position on development remains dominant in the discourse on international economic relations. The successful economic development of the newly industrialized countries (NICs), such as the 'Asian Tigers' of Taiwan, South Korea, Hong Kong and Singapore, after opening themselves up to foreign investment and developing export-oriented manufacturing industries, served to reinforce the notion that a global route out of poverty is available for those states stuck in pre-modernity.

## *Global policy on hunger*

The new 'Liberal International Economic Order' that emerged from the 1944 Bretton Woods Conference was not, however, pure Economic Liberalism since the international development policy was founded on the notion that interventions from Global North states could and should stimulate economic growth in the South. The capitalist world had learned from the Great Depression of the 1930s that free markets do not always correct themselves when in a downturn and *Keynesian* Economics (named after the UK economist and politician John Maynard Keynes who was his country's head delegate at the Bretton Woods Conference) had become mainstream in domestic economic policy. Keynesian economics advocates government interventions and spending to combat unemployment and boost the demand for goods in order to kick-start a slumping economy. In line with this thinking, President Roosevelt had sought to regenerate the US economy in the 1930s by pumping money into the poorest areas of the country in his New Deal package (an approach not followed at the time in the UK). It was in this framework of thinking that the idea of a 'New Deal' for the capitalist world emerged in the mid-1940s with a US-led international drive to give foreign aid and developmental loans to the world's poorest countries and offering incentives for businesses to locate there in order to stimulate growth. The very new political landscape at the end of the Second World War was where the idea of development in international politics took hold. Harry Truman first used the term 'underdevelopment' in his inaugural US Presidential Address of 1949. With Western Europe no longer the source of political power in the world the one thing the two new superpowers could agree on was that the former colonies of Britain, France, The Netherlands and Portugal should be free to pursue their own destiny and given a helping hand to make their way in the world. Of course, Cold War realpolitik as well as empathy was at work and the USA and USSR each saw the emergent 'Third World' as an arena in which they could secure strategic allies in the context of the unfolding ideological conflict. Many parts of Latin America, Asia and Africa became the focus of superpower competition, most prominently in Korea, Vietnam and Cuba.

The first systematic challenge to the orthodoxy which had dictated development policy from the Second World War was the New International Economic Order (NIEO). The NIEO was announced as a manifesto of the 'Third World' at a Non-aligned Movement[2] summit in 1973, riding on the wave of the oil crisis that was already challenging the supremacy of the developed 'First World' in global economic relations. Utilizing the change in composition of the UN, due to the wave of decolonization that had swept Asia and Africa, the list of reformist demands making up the NIEO was adopted by the General Assembly in 1974 by 120 votes to 6 (including among the dissenters the USA and UK). The NIEO did not aspire to take LDCs out of the global marketplace but, rather, offer them certain protections within the framework of the world's 'Liberal International Economic Order' and promote a more endogenous form of economic growth. The demands included:

- full sovereign control of Northern MNCs operating in their territories (the key theme of the oil crisis);
- debt relief;

- reallocation of military expenditure in the developed world on Third World development;
- preferences in trading rules to allow LDCs to be able to compete with other countries and gain access to protected developed world markets;
- greater emphasis on 'technology transfers' from North to South in aid and development programmes;
- establishment of 'Common Funds' to stabilize the global price of primary products on which many LDCs are dependent;
- reform of the World Bank and IMF so that LDCs have a greater say in decision-making and that the conditions for IMF loans are less austere.

As the 1974 General Assembly vote indicates, the NIEO was something broader than a wish list of the world's underprivileged. Many similar themes were taken up by the Reports of the Independent Commission on International Development Issues (Brandt Reports) of the late 1970s and early 1980s, a fairly conservative think-tank set up at the suggestion of the American President of the World Bank Robert McNamara. The Brandt Reports upheld the virtues of liberalizing trade but advocated greater international cooperation to cushion LDCs from the insecurities of free trade and help them to help themselves. Specifically on the question of hunger the Brandt Reports advocated: greater food aid, the establishment of a global grain reserve, less agricultural protectionism (global trade liberalization had concentrated on industrial protectionism) and, more radically, land reform in LDCs to empower the poor (ICIDI 1980: 90–104).

The 1990s, however, witnessed a revival of the orthodoxy in development politics, often encapsulated in the expression 'the Washington Consensus' (so named to highlight the importance of the US government and the IMF, based also in Washington). The end of the Cold War, although giving an opportunity for non-military issues to gain global attention, represented a setback for the Third World since there was no longer a First and Second World to play off each other. In the 1970s many African, Asian and Latin American countries were able to compete for the attention of two superpowers who saw it as in their strategic interests to help them. Additionally the ending of the Cold War shifted the focus of Western Europe and North America to the transition of the former Communist countries and further marginalized the Global South.

The twenty-first century, however, has witnessed the renaissance of an NIEO-like agenda and a *post-Washington consensus* emerge which, while still advocating economic development through modernization, acknowledges structural failings in the contemporary global economic system. The New Right tide, which had seen Economic Liberals like Reagan and Thatcher rise to power, ebbed away in the 1990s as evidence of the limitations of purely free market solutions to poverty became apparent. The Asian Tigers had followed a broadly orthodox script (albeit with a stronger role for government than many Economic Liberals would favour) but many Global South countries found the prescription of opening up their economies to foreign competition a bitter medicine with no remedial effects. In Mozambique, for example, their once major cashew nut industry collapsed in the early 2000s when they were compelled to stop subsidizing the sector as a condition of World Bank loans. With more interventionist administrations coming into power in London and Washington civil society criticism of Structural Adjustment became more prominent and, as a consequence, the World Bank came to listen to different voices and further re-oriented itself on a reformist and socially conscious path.

> The overall goal of development is therefore to increase the economic, political and civil rights of all people across gender, ethnic groups, religion, races, regions and countries.

> (World Bank 1991: 31)

The World Trade Organization, launched in 1995, whilst undoubtedly dominated in its decision-making by the Global North, has nevertheless given a prominent platform for the Global South to again project its voice. Global civil society, with campaigns such as 'Make Poverty History' has also played its part in giving momentum to an agenda for reform. Hence some of the NIEO demands, having been largely ignored in the 1990s, have come back to the fore and, to some extent, been acted upon. The debts of some of the most hopelessly impoverished states have been written off or restructured and the IMF, and particularly the World Bank, have come to be more socially conscious in their dealings with developing countries. The issue of opening up Northern agricultural markets to competition from the South has yet to be fully acted upon but is very much to the fore in global economic negotiations.

Institutionally, the Food and Agricultural Organization (FAO) of the UN is at the centre of global policy with regard to global food production. Its principal tasks have been to increase food production in the world and create a framework of standards for the distribution of this food. The FAO, whilst acknowledging the scale of global hunger, makes a case for its contribution to tackling the problem: 'Food production has increased at an unprecedented rate since the FAO was founded in 1945, outpacing the doubling of the world's population over the same period' (FAO 2002). The FAO has, nevertheless, been the focus of much criticism. Uvin, in an angry polemical work on global hunger in the mid-1990s, described the combined work of the FAO and its offspring the WFP as amounting to an 'international hunger regime' (Uvin 1994: 73–4). Uvin contends that the FAO, in line with other UN agencies and IGOs, is interested in facilitating greater international trade through mechanizing agricultural production in LDCs rather than confronting the nutritional needs of people in poverty. The FAO stands accused of having undergone a value shift from its original aspirations and becoming an agent of Northern economic gain rather than that of relieving human suffering. The FAO has, however, done much to achieve one of its central aims and undoubtedly assisted in improving agricultural productivity since the mid-twentieth century. Its role in food trading has possibly served Northern interests more than those of the South since the epistemic community on whose advice it draws is far more corporate than other UN agencies. The FAO, however, cannot to be held responsible for the persistence of the root cause of inequitable food trading, excessive government protectionism. The fact that developed states have shown little enthusiasm for freeing up agricultural trade in the same manner that has been achieved for industrial produce has stifled a potential economic way out of the quagmire for many LDCs. Global governance guided by more than the profit motive of wealthy states is needed to ensure that the FAO's success in promoting food production is put to best use.

In line with this post-Washington Consensus, and in order to move international development policy beyond rhetoric and build a genuine consensus, a new global reformist agenda, the Millennium Development Goals (MDGs), were adopted by the UN General Assembly in 2000. Importantly, unlike the NIEO, the MDGs were also adopted by the IMF, World Bank, Organisation for Economic Co-operation and Development and G7; institutions dominated by the Global North and with more political muscle than the UN's talking shop. The eight broad goals of the MDGS are as follows:

- Reduce extreme poverty and hunger by half.
- Achieve universal primary education.
- Promote gender equality and empower women.
- Reduce child mortality by two-thirds.
- Reduce maternal mortality by three-quarters.
- Reverse the spread of HIV/AIDS, malaria and other diseases.
- Ensure environmental sustainability.
- Develop a Global Partnership for Development (fair trade and more aid).

As can be seen, the MDGs are far from a utopian wish-list and represent an attempt to set pragmatic and verifiable targets by which the international community can be judged. The baseline for the calculations are the various indicators as of 1990 and the judgement on meeting the goals will be made in 2015.

Progress towards meeting the Millennium Development Goals in 2015 can best be described as 'mixed'. The proportion of the world living on less than $1.25 has fallen significantly but hunger levels have not improved. The World Food Programme estimates that the number of malnourished people in the world topped the 1 billion mark for the first time in 2009, significantly up on the 1990 level (WFP 2009). On unpicking these figures a general trend for all the goals emerges. Asia, Latin America and North Africa have seen significant progress, and are likely to meet many of the targets on a regional basis, but sub-Saharan Africa is out of step with this improvement.

## Depression

The creation of the present global economic system at the Bretton Woods Conference in 1944, and its persistence and growth ever since, was/is inspired by the desire to safeguard economic security. The USA, finding itself in the position of global hegemon in the wake of Europe's devastation during the Second World War, bore the burden of funding the new international financial institutions intended to stabilize the world's currencies and usher in free trade. To be sure, the US government took up the costly role of entrepreneur and manager of the new Liberal International Economic Order for some more conventional political motivations. Military security was seen as being enhanced by propping up the capitalist world against the potential spread of Communism and it is customary for the world's premier economic power to promote free trade because, ultimately, they should enjoy the greatest spoils from the increased volume of world trade which follows. The UK actively supported free trade in the nineteenth century for much the same reason.

In addition to these two motivations of economic gain and military security, however, the LIEO was moulded by the belief that building a system to support Economic Liberalism was the best way of guaranteeing human security. In this way the LIEO differs from the nineteenth-century economic system, which was concerned only with free trade and did not have institutions intended to act as a safety net for states struggling with financial difficulties. The International Monetary Fund (IMF) was designed as an international source of liquidity for governments to borrow from when facing balance of payments difficulties and the World Bank was created as a source of development loans.

The Great Depression of the 1930s, in which thousands of people starved to death and others experienced abject poverty in both the developed and under-developed world, loomed large in the minds of the Bretton Woods negotiators and strengthened the resolve of capitalist states to move away from the protectionism of the first part of the twentieth century seen as responsible for the economic meltdown (and, ultimately, the Second World War also). Clark describes the Great Depression, rather than either world war or ideological conflict as 'the greatest formative event of twentieth century history' (Clark 2001: 28). The LIEO outlived the Cold War, even contributing to its termination through its success, and has widened (in terms of the states involved) and deepened (in terms of the extent of its political impact) in the years following, with the distant memories of the 1930s still lingering.

Since the 1930s and subsequent creation of the Bretton Woods system, financial turbulence has recurred periodically and had profound effects on the economic security of a number of states and their populations. The oil crises of the 1970s were the economic making of a number of oil-producing countries but their hiking-up of the price of this crucial commodity prompted economic recession for much of the rest of the world. In 1997 the huge bubble that was East Asian economic growth burst, causing a loss of income for Japan and more serious hardship for some of the poorer countries affected. Around 40 million Indonesians were plunged into poverty. Argentina's financial meltdown in 2002 had profound social and political effects in that country and in some of its neighbours. The *British Medical Journal* that year reported that around 2 million Argentine children were suffering from malnutrition which had claimed at least forty-nine lives (Arie 2002).

Despite the spread of financial contagion through East Asia and South America, the North American and European economies remained relatively unaffected and the fashion for allowing currencies to 'float' rather than be pegged to other currencies and liberalizing capital markets (relaxing government rules on financial firms) persisted. After a decade of economic growth in Europe and North America, however, another sudden – and this time global – economic recession caused by financial turbulence threatened the remaining Bretton Woods edifice.

From 2008 a financial crisis spread through the world triggered by the collapse of the US housing market. Banks had been granting loans to people to buy houses much more readily than in the past and then selling on the money based on this debt to other financial companies to fund investments. These financial companies assumed these loans were 'secure' because mortgages have traditionally been viewed in this way (because the sum is seen as guaranteed by the fact that the banks have people's homes as collateral) and credit rating agencies in the city assured them that they were. House prices had been rising for several years, allowing this sort of lending to appear viable, but when this financial bubble inevitably burst it became apparent that it was not. The loans were not traditional mortgages and were not secure because the banks had been increasingly lending to: (1) poor people unlikely to be able to make the repayments; and (2) rich people who had bought property purely for investment purposes. Hence, when the poor borrowers started to default on repayments and rich borrowers responded to a fall in prices by simply handing back the house keys, the mortgage lenders were left owning property nowhere near the value of the sums of money they had lent. When it became obvious that banks had been lending sums far in excess of what they owned, businesses lost confidence in them and the whole financial system was plunged into chaos. Many major international banks collapsed, many others had to be bailed out with $ multi-trillion injections of government (i.e. taxpayers') money, and a slump in production occurred as businesses became starved of bank loans, creating a huge growth in unemployment. Across the world at least $4 trillion was lost (to put this in context global GDP or 'all the money in the world' is around $60 trillion) in the worst economic recession since the Great Depression of the 1930s.

The persistence of the recession undermined the position of the *Globalists* or *Economic Liberals*. This is a temporary setback: the bursting of another economic bubble after which the market will correct itself and allow the normal pattern of economic growth – which has dominated the period since the 1950s to resume. For *Anti-globalists or Marxists* the scale of the downturn provides damning evidence that capitalism is simply unsustainable as a global economic system. However, the post-Washington Consensus has persisted and the *Alter-globalist* view that the recession represents a political failing that can be rectified has, if anything strengthened. The international consensus is that the fault for the recession lies in the failure of certain governments to properly control banks and the financial markets and the lack of robust international mechanisms to monitor financial flows. The dominant view is that, learning from the 2008 recession and putting reforms in place, the global economy can be resurrected in a better, more regulated, form. Hence the IMF has been beefed up rather than slaughtered and the Bretton Woods system lives on, albeit with a wider cohort of economic giants, including the likes of China, India and Brazil, now calling the shots alongside the Western powers.

## Economic statecraft

Whereas poverty can variously be attributed to natural disasters, domestic political disorder or global structural forces, the economic security of particular states and individuals also can be threatened systematically and deliberately by a state (or grouping of state's) foreign policy through various forms of economic statecraft.

Some argue that the use of blockades on food and other essentials from entering an enemy state in wartime constitutes a weapon of mass destruction, a term generally applied to nuclear, chemical or biological weapons (Baylis, Wirtz, Cohen and Gray 2002: 256–7). In instances such as the UK-led blockade on Germany and its allies in the First World War the aim was to starve the government of war-making materials but also to starve the population of the target state into surrender, in line with the prevailing ethos of the time, that civilians were legitimate targets. In accordance with the retreat from *total war* and the revival of *just war* in recent years, the use of economic instruments of foreign policy has attempted to be more discriminating and target governments and state structures rather than civilian populations. As with just military campaigns, however, the collateral damage associated with economic statecraft can be considerable.

Economic instruments of foreign policy have grown in significance since the end of the Second World War and come in a range of forms, the severity of their likely impact related to the importance of the foreign policy aim they are intended to realize. At the lesser end of the scale a state may withdraw trade preferences or raise the taxes it imposes on the import of certain goods (tariffs) from a target state to express disapproval at its behaviour on a particular issue. The USA and a number of other states imposed such limited sanctions on India and Pakistan in 1998 in protest at their testing of nuclear weapons. Such actions are common in international trade disputes, even amongst political allies. The so-called 'banana wars' of the late 1990s, for example, saw the USA raise tariffs on a few token imports from the EU to symbolically protest at the EU's trade preferences for Caribbean banana producers. Such measures have been legitimized in international law, so long as they are proved to be just, by being written into the statutes of the World Trade Organization. Economic statecraft can also take the form of 'carrot' as well as 'stick' with states offering incentives to others to change their behaviour in a way the sanctioning state desires.

Such limited economic sanctions, however, are not intended to threaten the security of states and individuals (although people can lose money and employment as a result of such actions). Comprehensive economic sanctions, which prohibit all trade, barring essentials to life such as medicines and certain foods, are far more profound in their aim and in their effects. Comprehensive economic sanctions may be imposed on a target state unilaterally, such as those operated by the USA against Cuba since the Communist revolution of 1959 and by states on their enemies at times of war. Unilateral sanctions of this kind are usually more symbolic than security threatening since the target state invariably will simply import its required goods from other states. Detailed research by Hufbauer, Scott and Elliott found that two-thirds of all of the 116 cases of economic sanctions (nearly all unilateral or by a small number of states) imposed between 1914 and 1990 failed in terms of meeting their stated aims and that most of the other third worked only partially (Hufbauer, Scott and Elliott 1990: 92–3). Cuba, however, has undoubtedly suffered from the continuation of US sanctions since the 1990s owing to the size and proximity of their foe and the fall of their chief economic ally during the Cold War, the USSR.

In most cases the economic security of states and their peoples is only likely to be threatened by global economic action, depriving them of any legitimate trading partners. Economic sanctions were an option open to the League of Nations, for the purpose of deterring aggression, but were only ever used in a limited and symbolic manner owing to a lack of resolve amongst its member-states. Fascist Italy's invasion of Abyssinia (Ethiopia) in 1935 prompted only meek measures which, crucially, did not include an oil embargo. The League was hampered by the UK and France's reluctance to antagonize Italy too greatly through fear of war and by the fact that many significant economic powers, such as the USA and Germany, were not members and so not obliged to follow suit.

The collective international imposition of significant economic sanctions originated in the 1960s under the auspices of the UN Security Council, empowered by Article 41 of the UN Charter to act against threats to international peace and security. Cold War geopolitics limited this to resolutions forbidding trade with the racist regimes in Rhodesia and South Africa and it was not until the 1990s that Article 41 became widely utilized. The significance of Security Council-backed sanctions is that they become binding on all UN members, whether they individually support the measure or not. Bearing in mind the limited operation of collective security, UN sanctions represent the most significant example of global supra-national policy seen to date. The success of UN economic sanctions as a means of conducting coercive diplomacy is not easy to judge. The use of economic sanctions has increased greatly since the end of the Cold War but they are often controversial and, some feel, counter-productive. Criticisms levelled at the use of comprehensive economic sanctions include the following:

## 1 They cause collateral damage

Economic sanctions have aroused most controversy on the grounds that they represent a blunt instrument that tends to have more impact upon ordinary civilians in the target state rather than the government. These fears became most pronounced in the 1990s with evidence of starvation amongst Iraqis in the wake of long-standing UN sanctions but, either way, they led to thousands of deaths. There is a good case to be made that these deprivations were more the fault of the Iraqi government than the UN sanctions. Saddam Hussein's regime, undoubtedly prioritized rearmament over famine relief in allocating expenditure from their shrinking budget and milked the suffering of their people in order to gain support for a lifting of the measures. Wherever the fault ultimately lies, however, there is no doubt that thousands of Iraqis died as a result of economic hardship resulting from political action rather than any natural disaster. This illustrates another, related, argument against economic sanctions: their success rests on the assumption that the target state government will act in a rational way.

## 2 They can have negative effects on neighbouring states

The fall out from economic sanctions can spread beyond the civilians of the target state, across the border to neighbouring states. States which have strong trading links with a state subjected to mandatory sanctions are in danger of suffering from the effects of having such ties cut. The UN sanctions on South Africa, for example, had profound implications for small states like Lesotho and Swaziland which were virtually economically dependent on their neighbour.

## 3 Full implementation is impossible

As with many areas of global policy, the business of getting agreement to impose economic sanctions is difficult but represents less than half of the battle. Implementing economic sanctions is a highly complex matter in an increasingly interdependent global system. Getting every company in every country to end all interaction with a target state is a huge task for the United Nations, particularly when some governments are unenthusiastic about the sanctions or lack the capacity to control firms based in their territory. The evasion of sanctions was a major problem for the UN actions against Rhodesia. The South African government continued to trade out of sympathy for its fellow minority white settler regime and many European and American MNCs blatantly ignored the Security Council Resolutions.

## 4 They can mobilize the population of a target state behind their government

Even if the hardships endured by the population of a state under UN economic sanctions are more the responsibility of their own government's negligence than that of the international community, it is predictable that they may focus their resentment on the latter, particularly if this view is encouraged by the state media. Milosovic and Saddam had their support bases bolstered by using UN sanctions both as a scapegoat for domestic economic failings and for mobilizing nationalistic 'us against the world' fervour. Hence the result of sanctions can actually be a bolstering of the position of the government they are aimed at influencing.

## From 'dumb' to smart sanctions

As a consequence of points (3) and (4) economic sanctions have tended to be slow acting and, as a result, it is difficult to evaluate their success. The racist governments of Rhodesia and South Africa were overthrown but not until many years after economic action was taken. Iraq was forced out of Kuwait, but this was the result of military action rather than the initial sanctions imposed upon them, and they continued for many years to defy UN demands for weapons inspectors to be allowed into the country until eventually facing military action again. The Yugoslav wars, also, ended more as a result of military and diplomatic interventions by the USA than by the economic measures imposed by the international community.

Despite such reservations, the use of UN economic sanctions has increased in recent years and this trend looks set to continue. The popularity of sanctions principally lies in the fact that, when compared to military action, they are a cheap peacekeeping option, both economically and in terms of peacekeeper lives. They provide an option 'between words and war', allowing the Security Council to do more than merely condemn aggression where the will or need for collective military security is not present. In addition, despite the controversy surrounding economic measures against Iraq, the advent of 'smart sanctions' since the mid-1990s has served to counter the chief criticisms levelled at this political tool.

Smart sanctions aim to be less blunt than comprehensive sanctions by focusing more specifically on the government and state officials of the target state. The case of Haiti served to highlight the potential of smart sanctions. A conventional package of measures, including an arms and oil embargo, making up the 1993 sanctions appeared to have little impact on the military government, who reneged on a peace deal with the ousted President Aristide, so new measures were adopted in 1994. Security Council Resolution 917 added some highly targeted instruments of economic coercion in an attempt to tighten the thumbscrews on the violent and corrupt military regime. Officers in the Haitian military, their families and personal employees had their bank accounts frozen. This, more personalized economic security threat, appeared to do the trick and within four months Aristide was back in power and all UN sanctions were lifted.

All UN sanctions have become more targeted and less comprehensive, both to increase their effectiveness and in an effort to avoid collateral damage. A notable 'smart' feature of economic sanctions is the imposition of travel bans on selected individuals (in the cases of Libya, UNITA, Sierra Leone, Liberia and Afghanistan) which have, 'lowered the state revenues of government-owned airlines and restricted the movement of privileged elites who travel internationally' (Lopez and Cortright 2002: 2). The restriction on personal movement, and resultant curtailing of international business opportunities, gives such a seemingly trivial measure its impact and is believed to have been influential in inducing changes in behaviour in the Libyan government in the late 1990s. More targeted sanctions have helped alleviate some of the humanitarian side-effects, although in Iraq, even after the shift from blanket sanctions to the 'oil for food programme', hunger amongst the general population and evasion remained major problems. The Iraqi case indicates that even the sharpest of instruments can be blunted when used against a stubborn and despotic leader.

If the record on collateral damage is still mixed, improvements in the design of economic sanctions regimes have certainly helped counter the problem of states suffering from the effects of sanctions on a neighbouring target state and improved implementation. The possibility for states to seek financial assistance from the international community towards the costs of implementing Security Council decisions has always existed under Article 50 of the UN Charter and was taken up by a number of states affected by the sanctions against Iraq and Yugoslavia. Work has been undertaken by the UN in recent years to find further ways to cushion such states from the harmful effects of economic sanctions.

The imposition of sanctions by the Security Council is followed up by the creation of a Sanctions Committee which utilizes expert opinion to consider the humanitarian effects of new economic measures, their effects on third-party states and also seeks to oversee their effective implementation. Implementation has become much tighter in recent years and the sorts of 'sanctions-busting' seen in the Rhodesia case are unlikely to be repeated. A major breakthrough in this regard was the Security Council decision in 2001 (Resolution 1343) to impose sanctions against Liberia (additional to existing sanctions against them) for its failure to comply properly with mandatory UN sanctions against Sierra Leone. A permanent mechanism to manage and implement sanctions, rather than convening ad hoc groupings once a resolution has been agreed, is a likely next step for the UN as the use of sanctions continues to grow.

## Achieving global economic security

Very different prescriptions exist about how best to lessen the human security threat posed by economic want. The study of *International Political Economy*, conventionally has three main approaches which, as well as being paradigms for conceptualizing the economic world, can be understood as ideologies for enhancing economic security.

### Marxists

Marxists (or *Structuralists*), consider the chief source of human insecurity, economic or otherwise, to be the global economy itself. Hence, as referred to earlier in the chapter, Dependency Theorists advocate that LDCs are best advised to concentrate on their own economies rather than integrate themselves more into an exploitative global trading system. From this perspective global economic security can only be achieved by radical global change with the LIEO making way for international socialism in which the inequalities inherent in the class structures that underpin capitalism are swept away.

### Economic Liberals

Economic Liberals contend that more rather than less liberalization of the global economic order is needed for human security to be enhanced. The LIEO has allowed the people of the world to get richer by limiting the capacity of their governments to buck the market in claiming the money for themselves in tariffs. Free from meddling governments, international trade can increase in volume and serve the interest of humanity though the logic of 'comparative advantage'. Rather than having states pursue self-sufficiency, freer global trade allows countries or regions to produce what they are best suited to rather than 'a bit of everything'. Hence, in the logic of Liberalism, more is produced and more is traded. The pioneer of this perspective was eighteenth-century Scottish economist Adam Smith who greatly influenced British international policy in the following century.

Some of Smith's contemporary protégés put the world's economic failings down to the LIEO not being sufficiently liberal and are concerned at recent shifts towards more socially minded 'compensatory liberalism' in global bodies like the World Bank. Peter Bauer, an exponent of true global free-market economics once said of foreign aid that it is 'an excellent method for transferring money from poor people in rich countries to rich people in poor countries' (*Economist* 2002b). This view that charity from the North tends to be squandered by elites in the South and produces dependency provides an interesting instance of the political right and left reaching the same conclusions about the world.

## Mercantilists

Mercantilism, the economic sibling to political Realism, views the world through a lens in which the state is the referent object of security. This is mainly for the ontological reason that 'that is how it is', but also through the normative belief that people's lives and livelihoods are best safeguarded by the policies of their governments. At the extreme level Mercantilism has manifested itself in the foreign policy of autarky, whereby states have sought to enhance their power (and hence also theirs and their people's security) by foreign conquest to gain economic resources. In a more mainstream form, what has been distinguished as 'Neo-Mercantilism' both sees and advocates the state putting their interest over that of the wider international community by promoting economic protectionism. Just as Realism has dominated foreign policy practice in military security, traditionally Mercantilism has guided governments in their international economic relations and continues to do so. The Liberal International Economic Order has advanced the logic of Smith further than at any point previously in history but all states, including the liberal democracies, still have a reluctance to fully integrate themselves into the global marketplace. In this view one state's comparative advantage is another's disadvantage.

There is some compelling logic behind all three approaches to IPE when thinking about human security. The famines of the late nineteenth century bear testimony to the failings of laissez faire economics at the global level. The persistence of hunger in a contemporary world of unprecedented wealth indicates that the system is still fundamentally flawed. The dependency theory solution of going it alone, however, is no longer a serious option, such is the interconnectedness of the world today. Isolated, dogmatic North Korea stands as a stark illustration of that. The Structuralist contention that global economic forces determine people's lives and deaths is no longer an argument aired only at Marxist rallies, it is demonstrably true and now part of mainstream thinking in IPE. The notion that North–South interactions in the global system are inherently exploitative does not, however, entirely stand up to scrutiny. Without doubt, the economic gap between the world's rich and poor continues to widen and many countries remain undeveloped and appear unlikely to develop in the foreseeable future. Many countries have achieved economic development, however, and nearly all have achieved human development. Of all states in the world only Zambia recorded a lower HDI rating in 1999 compared to 1975 (Goklany 2002) and life expectancies have risen more quickly in LDCs than the developed world since the mid-twentieth century (see Chapter 6).

There can be little doubt that liberalizing trade leads to more produce and wealth for the world collectively but it is unsurprising that governments are reluctant to abandon Mercantilism given that there is a certain risk inherent in opening up your country in this way. The collective spoils of free trade are not likely to be distributed evenly and governments fear not getting their slice of the pie if it is a global free-for-all. Comparative advantage might make global economic sense but it might also represent governmental political suicide. Governments abandoning large swathes of their country's industrial or agricultural firms to allow more efficient foreign competitors in in their place, of course, risk courting huge unpopularity. This, however, does not indicate that protectionism is the best method of achieving human security, if seen from the global perspective. Agricultural protectionism in the Global North keeps Northern farmers and food producers wealthy but abandoning it would not imperil their lives. Lives in the Global South, however, are threatened by the distorting effects of this protectionism. This illustrates clearly the failings of statecentricism in the pursuit of human security. Globalization, if driven purely by the economic interests of some states, can represent a threat to much of the world but, a more fully rounded form of globalization, with a social and political dimension, can do much to enhance human security.

## Key points

- Poverty is both a major direct threat to life, as a cause of famine and hunger, and a major indirect threat to life, since it heightens vulnerability to other threats.
- Famines usually have natural triggers but, ultimately, are human-made phenomena since they are sometimes politically motivated and nearly always politically avoidable.
- Famines are high-profile peaks of suffering dwarfed by the general, persistent threat of hunger.
- Hunger is avoidable since there is sufficient food in the world for all people but remains a major problem due to global political failings which can, variably, be attributed to negligence or wilful exploitation in the Global North or the failure to modernize in the Global South.
- Life-threatening societal poverty may also occur as a result of economic recession or as a side-effect of sanctions targeting governments.
- Economic security from an Economic Liberal perspective is best achieved by more globalization, from a Mercantilist perspective by less globalization and from a Marxist perspective by radical global change.

## Notes

1   Malnutrition is defined by the WFP as a daily intake of below 1,800 calories; 2,100 is the recommended intake.
2   The NAM was obstensively an organization of states declaring themselves to be aligned to neither Cold War superpower but became a vehicle of 'Third World' solidarity.

## Recommended reading

Commission on Human Security (2003) *Human Security Now,* New York: CHS.

Galtung, J. (1969) 'Violence, Peace and Peace Research', *Journal of Peace Research,* 6(3): 167–91.

Payne, A. (2005) *The Politics of Unequal Development,* Basingstoke and New York: Palgrave.

Rostow, W. (1960) *The Stages of Economic Growth,* Cambridge: Cambridge University Press.

Sen, A. (1981) *Poverty and Famines: An Essay on Entitlement and Deprivation,* Oxford: Clarendon Press.

Thomas, C. (2000) *Global Governance, Development and Human Security,* London: Pluto Press.

## Useful web links

Food and Agricultural Organization: http://www.fao.org/

Millennium Development Goals: http://www.undp.org/mdg/

World Food Programme: http://www.wfp.org/

World Bank *World Development Indicators Database*: http://www.worldbank.org/data/databytopic/GNIPC.pdf

# Identity, society and insecurity

I love my country far too much to be a nationalist.

(unknown)

## Security and society

Undoubtedly the most influential idea to emerge from the conceptual widening of Security Studies in the 1990s by the Copenhagen School was that of societal security. This concept seeks to encapsulate the fact that the process of securitizing issues could sometimes be witnessed when what is thought to be being threatened is neither the state nor individuals within it, but a particular kind of society. 'Societal security concerns the ability of a society to persist in its essential character under changing conditions and possible or actual threats' (Waever, Buzan, Kelstrup and Lemaitre 1993: 23). This security is threatened when 'societies perceive a threat in identity terms' (ibid.). Hence the heightened political prominence given to the issue of immigration in many Western European countries in the 1990s could be construed as a securitizing of that issue, by nationals fearful of threats to their traditional values and customs.

In many ways the 1990s did witness a resurgence in violent nationalism in the form of groups inspired by the self-preservation of their socially constructed nation (as opposed to the 'nationalism' of states pursuing self-advancing foreign policies). From the rise of far right political parties and racist attacks in wealthy cosmopolitan democracies like France, Germany and Austria through to outright ethnic conflict in states beginning to embrace democracy like Yugoslavia, Moldova and Romania, Europe appeared to be awakening old spectres. This, added to earlier revivals in radical regionalism in Europe (such as Basque and Corsican separatist violence) and anti-Western nationalism in some Islamic states, appeared to represent a new essentially societally driven dimension of security politics.

In line with the other threats to security considered in this book, however, this chapter will focus on the existential security of individuals rather than considering how societies can be threatened. Issues such as the abandonment of a state currency in favour of monetary union with neighbouring countries or the cultural dominance of foreign films and food outlets may threaten many people's notion of their societies but they are not, in themselves, life threatening. Globalization and integration are very important political topics in many ways and have framed the context of many security issues but they represent a separate dimension of the study of International Relations. Though this study favours a broad approach to the subject, security becomes too diluted a concept if cultural change is accommodated alongside matters of life and death. In addition, on an ontological level, social constructs make very awkward referent objects on which to base analysis. McSweeney makes this point in challenging the approach of the Copenhagen School. Societies, by definition, evolve and individual identities change with them, making any inquiry into challenges to identity problematic (McSweeney 1996). There may even be practical dangers inherent in this approach since the arbiters of what is society and who are threatening it will be likely to be those with the loudest voices in the 'speech act' of securitization. Frequently such people will be ultra-nationalist elites seeking to justify the exclusion of minority 'others'. 'Despite his liberal sensibilities, Buzan's conceptualization of security provides him with no theoretical grounds for disputing, say, Radovan Karadzic's claims that Bosnian Serb security depends on the creation of an ethnically pure territory' (Wyn Jones 1999).

In spite of these reservations about societal security, the Copenhagen School did a service to International Relations in further releasing the discipline from its statecentric straitjacket. Surely one of the clearest limitations of the traditional notion of 'national security' (where the referent object is the state) comes from the fact that it excludes from consideration the political killing of people by their own government or other sections of their society. Individuals die because of social constructions, however abstract and subjective they may be.

## Forms of violent discrimination

### National identity

Nations, certainly, are abstract and subjective social constructions. Famously described by Benedict Anderson as 'imagined communities' (Anderson 1991), nations defy simple, objective definition yet have been for the last two hundred years the most significant referent object of security in international politics. What is taken to constitute a nation varies considerably from case to case. The 'we feeling' that distinguishes one's own nation from the rest of humanity is determined by various different factors. Ethnicity is linked to nationality in some states, such as Germany and Japan, but is less significant in countries with a tradition of multi-national citizenship, such as France, the UK and USA.

Where ethnicity is considered to define the nation, minority ethnic groups are not likely to be accommodated by or assimilated into the dominant, indigenous national group and risk becoming marginalized. At the lesser end of the scale this might be in the form of being denied the rights of citizenship in their country of residence (as with most ethnic Turks in Germany today) and in the extreme manifests itself in the horrors of genocide and 'ethnic cleansing'. 'Ethnic cleansing' entered the language in the 1990s to denote a policy less extreme than an outright attempt to annihilate a national group but which aims to remove them from a given territory. The term was widely applied in relation to the Yugoslav war over the secession of Croatia and Bosnia-Herzegovina but was, in fact, a wholly inappropriate description. Croats, Serbs and Bosnian Moslems were/are not ethnically distinct since they are all Slavs. National hatred seemed to appear from nowhere with archaic historical and religious distinctions suddenly acquiring great significance. The deadly vagueness of national identity and its propensity towards promoting 'ethnocentricism', by stressing the difference between 'self' and 'other', became all too apparent to a horrified onlooking world.

Table 5.1 attempts to rank the worst genocides in history but it should be borne in mind that, due to difficulty in verifying wildly fluctuating figures, some historical massacres are probably denied their rightful place in this list. In addition, the distinction between genocide and war in the age of total war is not always clear-cut. However, since national identity is very much a phenomenon of modern

**Table. 5.1** The top ten ethnic/national genocides in history

| | Victims | Perpetrators | Date | Numbers killed (m) |
|---|---|---|---|---|
| 1 | Chinese | Mongols | 1215–79 | 18.8[a] |
| 2 | Slavs | Nazis, Germany | 1940–5 | 10.5[a] |
| 3 | Jews | Nazis, Germany | 1933–45 | 6[a, b] |
| 4 | Persians | Mongols | 1220–2 | 6[a] |
| 5 | Nuer, Nuba & Dinka | Sudan | 1983–present | 1.9[b] |
| 6 | Tibetans | China | 1959–present | 1.6[b] |
| 7 | Germans | Poland | 1945–8 | 1.6[a] |
| 8 | Bengalis | Pakistan | 1958–87 | 1.5[a, b] |
| 9 | Armenians | Turkey | 1915–17 | 1.5[b] |
| 10 | Ibos | Nigeria | 1966–70 | 1[b] |

Sources: [a] Rummel (2003); [b] Genocide Watch (2003).

history,[1] it is safe to assume that the desire to exterminate 'the other' must also reside principally in the modern era. Pre-modern imperial conquests certainly claimed millions of lives but, in most cases, the aim was the conversion or subjugation of the conquered peoples rather than their annihilation. The Mongols were unusually savage in their ransacking of cities and so merit an inclusion but the list excludes some notable long-term slaughters, such as the fate that befell African slaves and native Americans in the imperial era. It was in the twentieth century when ideas of nationhood began to be conflated with 'ethnic purity' in the extreme nationalism of Nazi Germany that 'genocide' entered the political lexicon and landscape (see Box 5.1).

The subjective nature of nationality heightens the importance of perception in this area of security politics. The perception that a minority nationality is a human security threat to the majority nationality, such as in the association of certain migrants or resident minorities with crime and terrorism, is a common trait. At a lesser level, and more commonly, the minority nationality may be perceived as a threat to the economic well-being of the dominant group. Minority nationalities may even be perceived as threats to state security, as in the Nazi and neo-Nazi portrayal of Jews, formerly as Communists and latterly as part of a global conspiracy to control economic life.

The minority nationality may also perceive threats to their human or societal security from the state or dominant nationality. When two or more national groups each perceive that another threatens their lives or identities a 'societal security dilemma' (Waever, Buzan, Kelstrup and Lemaitre 1993) can be the cause of conflict. Such threats may be very real but frequently they will not be, given the ambiguous yet compelling nature of national identity. Roe describes how an escalation of misperceptions about 'the other' led to the 1990 Tirgu Mures riots between Magyars and the dominant nationality in Romania. A revival of demands by Transylvanian Magyars for linguistic and educational rights was wrongly interpreted by Romanians as a bid for secession, prompting violence in which six people were killed. Roe considers that the misperception occurred because of the interplay of a number of

### Box 5.1 Rafael Lemkin

Rafael Lemkin, an International Law lecturer at Yale University, both coined the term *genocide* and played a leading role in the formulation of the UN's 1948 'Genocide Convention'. Lemkin was a Polish Jew who fled Nazi persecution in 1939, moving initially to Sweden before then embarking on an academic and activist career in the USA. Lemkin's 1944 book *Axis Rule in Occupied Europe* was the first publication to use the term genocide which he defined as 'a coordinated plan of different actions aiming at the destruction of essential foundations of the life of national groups, with the aim of annihilating the groups completely' (Lemkin 1944: 79). The word, which combines the Greek *genos* (meaning race/family) with the Latin 'cide' (to kill), had particular resonance to him since forty-nine members of his family and 6 million of his fellow nationals had been murdered in the Nazi genocide by what Churchill called the 'crime without a name'. Lemkin went on to play the leading role in the drafting of the UN convention on genocide and participate as an adviser at the Nuremberg trials against Nazi war criminals. Something of a forgotten hero, Lemkin's grave at the Mount Hebron Cemetery, New York, refers to him aptly as the 'Father of the Genocide Convention' (Korey 2001).

factors. The Magyars did not explain the true nature of their demands and the Romanians (both societally and governmentally) could not comprehend that demands for reform could mean anything less than secession and the destruction of the Romanian state. Underlying all of this, of course, was the recent history of Romania as a brutal, authoritarian political system where minority identities were stamped upon and no mechanisms for dealing with such issues existed (Roe 2000).

## *Religion*

Religion as a basis for conflict or discriminatory violence is, of course, as old as religion itself. Religious identity pre-dates national identity by many centuries and was the chief cause of wars and massacres within and between the rudimentary states of the pre-Westphalian era, aside from the age-old and perennial motive of straight territorial gain. The 1648 Treaty of Westphalia marked the end of a major religious war across much of Europe, the Thirty Years War between Catholicism and Protestantism, and also the end of an era of religious domination over the kingdoms of Europe. From 1648 the sovereignty of kingly states began to supersede the supranationality of the Pope and the loyalty and identity of citizens shifted accordingly from their religion to their monarch and nation. In subsequent centuries the Westphalian system spread beyond Europe to the rest of the world but nations have never entirely replaced religions as a social identity for which individuals are prepared to kill and be killed. In many cases national identity succeeded rather than superseded religious identity and provided a framework for pre-Westphalian conflicts of faith to persist in a sovereign, secular age. The Wars of the Reformation (which culminated in the Thirty Years War) were still being fought in Northern Ireland in the 1990s, although by then this was very much about national self-determination rather than Papal authority.

Since some nationalities are defined in religious terms the presence of individuals of other religions is often portrayed as a threat to national cohesion and, hence, they can become the victims of state or societal repression. This was starkly illustrated by the phenomenon of so-called 'ethnic cleansing' in Bosnia-Herzegovina in the 1990s. Slavic Serbs, Slavic Croats and Slavic Moslems, speaking the same language and having cohabited peacefully for decades, fought along religiously determined battle lines in the middle of a secular state. The Bosnian Moslems, natives of the region whose ancestors had converted to Islam in the fifteenth century and who were no more religiously devout than the Catholic Croats or Orthodox Serbs, suddenly came to be seen as outsiders in their own country because of a societal security struggle between the other two nationalities. Serbian nationalism was reawakened by the break-up of the multi-national state they had dominated and rallied to its traditional cause of Islamophobia, fuelled by historic memories of their centuries of domination by the Ottoman Turks.

Whereas the break-up of Yugoslavia and the lower-level dispute over the status of Northern Ireland are really national conflicts with ancient religious roots rather than genuine clashes of faiths, there are numerous contemporary instances of blood being shed over insecurities rooted firmly in religion. Secular, Westphalian states today are still wary of the alternative lure religious identity may hold for their citizens. The radicalization (or politicization) of many religions in the last quarter century has led to state and societal insecurity frequently being triggered by more 'real' challenges than the use of religion as a label of difference. Religious *fundamentalism* first came to the attention of the international community in 1979 when an absolute monarchy was transformed into Shi'a Moslem semi-theocracy in Iran. For Iranians Shi'a Moslem clerics, who had always been their spiritual leaders, would now be their political leaders also. Revolutions in other countries have always made governments nervous of their own citizens following suit and, just like the French and Russian revolutions in earlier eras, the Iranian revolt prompted copy-cat uprisings in other societies and pre-emptive strikes against this possibility by other governments. In Sunni Moslem states, such as Egypt, Algeria and Uzbekistan, the undisputed national religion, in fundamentalist form, has come to be seen as a threat to the government, prompting civil war and societal fissures.

Where a radicalized religion is that of a minority group the insecurities of the dominant culture often leads to heightened persecution of 'the other'. Traditionally poor relations between Hindus and Moslem minorities in India have worsened since the last 1990s with Islamic fundamentalism prompting the rise of more militant strains of Hinduism. Western European societal anxieties over migration have, in some cases, taken a more specific form than a more generalized distinction between self and other. The rise to prominence in The Netherlands of the populist nationalist Prime Ministerial candidate Pim Fortuyn in 2002 was based on a campaign which called not for a general tightening of non-EU migration, as favoured by most European far right politicians, but specifically for curbs on the entry of Islamic people. Fortuyn, openly homosexual and with some black members in his party, cut an unusual figure for an ultra-nationalist. His campaign, which saw the 'Pim Fortuyn List' finish second in the elections after his assassination, won support principally by arguing that Islamic culture was specifically at odds with permissive, liberal Dutch society. The September 11th 2001 al-Qa'ida attacks in the USA have increased the tendency for Moslems in Europe and North America to be specifically targeted, above minorities in general, in attacks by militant nationalists.

Although many 'religious conflicts' are best understood as nationalist rather than theological struggles, religious issues can sometimes serve to enflame essentially national conflicts. Serb nationalist atrocities perpetrated on the Kosovar Albanians in the 1990s were partially explained by the sacred significance of Kosovo to the Serbian Orthodox Church (who, themselves, were active in promoting Serb nationalism in the region leading up to Milosovic's campaign). Similarly, the Palestinian–Israeli dispute is especially complicated by the religious importance attached to Jerusalem by both sides (and indeed by Christianity), particularly in regard to the Temple Mount.[2] Hindu–Moslem and Hindu–Sikh tensions in India have periodically worsened following incidents relating to mosques and temples, respectively. The Tamil secessionist campaign in Sri Lanka, too, came to have a much greater religious dimension after their 1998 attack on the Temple of the Buddha's Tooth.

Table 5.2 illustrates the range of recent violent clashes involving both governments and societal groups which are overtly religious in character. For convenience's sake, atheistic Communism is included as a 'religion' since much religious violence occurs *vis-à-vis* this ideology.

## *Gender*

The Societal Security approach, characterized by Buzan and Waever, has focused almost exclusively on national and religious identity. A further form of social identity which is frequently the basis of life-threatening discrimination, but which is not addressed either by traditional approaches to security or by the Copenhagen School, is gender. Hansen, in a seminal article, highlights the 'striking absence of gender' (Hansen 2000: 286) in the Copenhagen School approach. This oversight arises, she contends, because the Copenhagen School's 'epistemological reliance on speech act theory presupposes the existence of a situation in which speech is indeed possible' (Hansen 2000: 285). Hansen uses Copenhagen's little mermaid statue (who in the story from which it is derived is silent) as an analogy, to make the point that much organized and ritualized violence against women is excluded by the societal security approach since the victims are less able to 'securitize' the threat than religious or national minorities.

In illustration of this critique Hansen uses the issue of 'honour killings' in Pakistan, where women are often killed for having committed adultery. Men too, in theory, are subject to the death penalty for this 'crime' but, in practice, are able

**Table 5.2** Typology of contemporary religious violence in the world

| Victims: | Islam | Hindu | Christianity | Buddhism | Judaism | Other religion |
|---|---|---|---|---|---|---|
| **Perpetrators:** | | | | | | |
| Islam | 1 Sunni v. Shi'a in Iraq, Pakistan and Saudi Arabia 2 Secular v. fundamentalist in Algeria, Egypt and Uzbekistan | Persecution of minorites in Pakistan and Bangladesh | Persecution of minorities in Egypt, Sudan, Indonesia, Nigeria and Lebanon | State persecution of the Jumma in Bangladesh | 1 Persecution of minority in Iran 2 Terrorist strikes in non-Islamic countries | |
| Hindu | India – societal attacks on Moslems | 1 Hindu v. Sikh in India 2 Violence associated with the caste system | Societal attacks in India | Tamil Tigers in Sri Lanka | | |
| Christianity | 1 Far right attacks in Europe and USA 2 Civil conflicts in former Yugoslavia, Ivory Coast, Philippines and Uganda | | Orthodox v. other (e.g. Georgia) | | Far right attacks in Europe | 1 South Africa: persecution of Animists and 'witches' 2 USA: attacks on 'neo-pagans' |
| Buddhism | State and societal persecution in Myanmar | Sinhala Buddhist resistance v. Tamils in Sri Lanka | State persecution in Bhutan | | | |
| Judaism | Zionist groups in Israel/ Palestine | | | | Orthodox v. secular in Israel | |
| Communism | China | | Laos | China (Tibet) Laos | | Persecution of Falungong in China |

to escape punishment or make a deal to save their lives. Pakistani women, as a collective entity, are not being threatened but individual Pakistani women are subject to threats **because** of their gender. In addition, the pervading threat hanging over Pakistani women as a collective serves to deter them from voicing their fears and so highlighting their plight. A very different sort of security dilemma emerges for individuals who, far from being able to securitize their concerns, may actually increase their insecurities in doing so. Human security issues pertaining to women, such as 'honour killings', have little chance of receiving attention in the traditional statist paradigm of International Relations since women tend to suffer a double discrimination. Women's security issues frequently suffer from being doubly marginalized, first, in domestic politics (as a private, 'domestic' family matter) and, then, in international politics (as a private, domestic sovereign state matter).

In addition to the limitations of the 'speech act' approach to security when applied to gender-based discrimination, Hansen also criticizes the Copenhagen School for subsuming such problems in the focus on national and religious identity (Hansen 2000). Female insecurity is often a by-product of religious or national/ethnic societal security concerns. Women are often constructed as the embodiment of national and/or religious culture and, as such, treated more harshly than men when they step outside of the culturally prescribed notion of a 'good woman' (Yuval-Davis 1997: 46). Hence adulterous women in some Islamic states are seen as a greater threat to cultural norms than their male equivalents and, as a result, are punished more severely.

The insecurity of women can also be seen to be both heightened and obscured by the rise of military security threats to the state in which they live. Although wars continue (in the main) to be fought between men, the threat posed to women in such conflicts has risen greatly in recent history. Feminist IR writers have drawn attention to this as an antidote to the 'myth' of war being fought by men on behalf of the women and children of their society or state. Those women and children have had to bear the brunt of the rise of the systematic targeting of civilians in war over the last century, make up the bulk of refugees and displaced persons resulting from war and have suffered the greatest deprivations due to states re-aligning their economies to the war effort.

In addition, the sexual abuse of women in wartime, although by no means a new phenomenon, has, in recent years, become more common without being fully appreciated. Tickner argues that 'rape is not just an accident of war but often a systematic military strategy' (Tickner 2001: 50). Rape has long been practised by invading military forces, to symbolize their power and the subjugation of the occupied peoples, but the scale of the attacks in recent ethnic conflicts does suggest something more orchestrated. Some 250,000 women are believed to have been raped in the Rwandan civil war of 1994 (Tickner 2001: 50) and at least 20,000 in the Bosnian War of 1991–5 (Pettman 1996: 52). Both of these wars were classic 'societal security' conflicts where single countries were ravaged by internal national conflict. The demonizing of and the desire to humiliate the 'other', promoted by nationalists, directly or indirectly legitimized sexual savagery beyond the norm in military conflict. In the civil wars raging in Sierra Leone, the Congo and Angola in the 1990s the threat posed to women by mass rape became even more acute due to likelihood of contracting HIV/AIDS in the assaults. There can be no more stark an illustration of how women's insecurity is heightened by perceptions of national insecurity.

The most common threat to the lives of women arising from their sexual status, however, comes from a less obviously violent source than foreign soldiers or domestic executioners. Mary Anne Warren first coined the term 'gendercide' to highlight the scale of female-specific abortions and infanticide (Warren 1985). The general preference for male heirs in most societies is exacerbated in countries where overpopulation has prompted government measures to restrict the number of children per family. Though the scale of this phenomenon is uncertain, and the ethics of killing unborn infants unproblematic for many, it is clear that hundreds of thousands of female lives are not lived every year as a result. Rummel is unequivocal in ranking this phenomenon alongside other, better-recognized human security threats.

> the accumulation of such officially sanctioned or demanded murders comprises, in effect, serial massacre. Since such practices were so pervasive in some cultures, I suspect that the death toll from infanticide must exceed that from mass sacrifice and perhaps even outright mass murder.
>
> (Rummel 1994: 65–6)

Baby girls in a number of countries are frequently murdered soon after birth, usually by starvation or wilful neglect when ill, whilst ultrasound scans of pregnant women also make gender-based abortions increasingly common. In China, where families with more than one child are strongly 'discouraged', the 2002 population census revealed a sex imbalance of 116 males to every 100 females. The disparity was as high as 135 to 100 on the island of Hainan (Gittings 2002). The Chinese government's alarm at the social effects of such an imbalance prompted them to restrict the availability of ultrasound scans meaning that infanticide must now be the major explanation for the disparity. Similarly, the 2011 census in India, where government policy combating overpopulation also encourages single offspring, revealed that the country had 7.1 million fewer girls under 7 than boys mainly due to gender-specific abortions.

The fact that an individual's sex can be the source of their insecurity cannot be seen more clearly than in them being fatally discriminated against before even being able to live their life. During a woman's lifetime sex-based domestic violence remains a significant threat. It has been estimated that half of women in the world who are murdered are killed by male partners (Krug et al. 2002). The inaccuracy of the conventional externalizing of security threats is never more apparent than in this instance, where the threat comes not only from within the individuals own country but from within their own, immediate family.

It is important to note, however, that the victims of 'gendercide' are not always women. In both inter-state and intra-state war the systematic culling of men 'of fighting age' amongst enemy non-combatants has long been a military tactic. The mass killing of potential soldiers was a feature of the early German campaign in the USSR in the Second World War and was evident in the Serb massacres of Kosovar Albanians in the run-up and duration of the 1999 Kosovan War (Jones 2000). Additionally, it is males who form the bulk of war casualties, as they do of criminal murders and industrial accidents. It is a paradox of human life it is far safer to be born a boy but grow up as a woman.

## Sexual orientation

Aside from nationality, ethnicity, religion and gender, a further form of identity subject to life-threatening discrimination is homosexuality. Many people have been killed and continue to be killed purely on the grounds that they practise consensual sexual activities with other people of the same sex. Homosexuals were targeted alongside minority ethnic groups and the disabled in the Nazi holocaust and many thousands were sent to death camps.[3] Nazi discrimination represented an extreme manifestation of state prejudice against homosexuality evident in nearly all countries at the time (far less frequently against lesbianism) and still apparent in many states today. Domestic legal restrictions on homosexuality have greatly lessened in most of the developed world over recent decades but in 2009 there were still 80 states legally prohibiting same-sex relationships and five which retained the death penalty for homosexuality (Iran, Mauritania, Sudan, Saudi Arabia and Yemen). In many of these states illegality is a technicality which does not necessarily lead to prosecution but several Iranians have been hanged in recent years for consensual, adult homosexuality (Ottoson 2009).

Even where homosexuality is not a capital crime being gay can cost you your life. Violent political non-state groups, of various shades, have targeted homosexuals and other sexual minorities in campaigns in a number of countries. Right-wing death squads have murdered homosexuals in Colombia as have the left-wing MRTA in Peru (Narrain 2001–2). In some states the government may be complicit in such attacks, even if they are not directly responsible. President Mugabe's remark in 1995 that homosexuals were 'less than human' undoubtedly contributed to the subsequent proliferation of attacks on gay Zimbabweans in the course of the internal conflict raging there. Even in some countries where homosexual rights are firmly entrenched, 'gay bashing' remains a significant problem. The bombing of a Soho pub, known as a favourite haunt of London's gay community, by a lone neo-Nazi fanatic in 1999 served to illustrate this fact.

## Disability

Disabled people, too, were amongst the array of 'undesirable' minority groups targeted in the Nazis' reign of terror in Germany. An estimated 200,000 mentally ill or physically disabled people were killed between 1939 and 1945 under the 'T-4' programme in Germany and the occupied territories (Burleigh 1994). The policy was presented as 'euthanasia' but the practice of deliberate starvation and the administering of lethal injections was far from the contemporary notion of consensual 'mercy killings'. The T-4 programme represented an escalation of the war against the handicapped, which had previously concentrated on sterilizing rather than killing those with physical or mental impairments. Between 1934 and 1937 around 225,000 of Germany's disabled population were made incapable of reproducing new disabled (or, indeed, able-bodied) people (Kevles 1995: 117).

This initial Nazi strategy of ridding their country of the disabled was, however, largely uncontroversial. Many other states at the time were introducing similar, if less extensive, schemes as the science of eugenics gained popularity. Eugenics is the science of 'improving' humanity by restricting reproduction of those deemed imperfect. The USA had sterilized 36,000 disabled people by 1941 (Kevles 1995: 116) and eugenics programmes had been introduced in Sweden, Denmark, Finland and in one Swiss Canton between 1929 and 1939 (Kevles 1995: 115). 'Democratic Eugenics' (Drouard 1998: 174) continued in the Nordic states (including Norway) until the 1970s. The ethical tide has ebbed away from eugenics in democracies but the sterilization of the disabled persists in many contemporary states. China in 1995 enacted a law forbidding marriage to couples carrying genetic or infectious diseases unless they first agreed to be sterilized.

## Politicide

Strikingly absent from the UN definition of genocide is the mass, systematic killing of political and/or social opponents by radical governments or non-governmental forces. Since the targets of such action are not necessarily national, ethnic or religious minorities, the distinct category of *politicide* is necessary for a complete understanding of the phenomenon of societal massacres. The omission of politicide from the UN Convention is the result of the predictable opposition of the USSR in the late 1940s to classifying their extermination of opponents and undesirables alongside that of the Nazis. As Table 5.3 indicates, the USSR regime represented at the UN drafting of the Convention on Genocide can claim the dubious distinction of being history's most brutal ever. Rummel estimates that some 62 million political

**Table 5.3** The top ten politicides in history

| | Perpetrators | Victims | Date | Numbers killed (m) |
|---|---|---|---|---|
| 1 | Stalinist USSR | Class enemies, dissidents | 1928–1953 | 49.5[a] |
| 2 | Maoist China | Class enemies | 1949–1976 | 35[a,b] |
| 3 | Nationalist China | Communists, other opponents | 1927–1949 | 10.2[a] |
| 4 | Chinese Communist opposition | Nationalists | 1927–1949 | 3.5[a] |
| 5 | Khmer Rouge | Class enemies | 1975–1979 | 2[a,b] |
| 6 | North Korea | Class enemies | 1949–present | 2[a] |
| 7 | North Vietnam | Class enemies | 1954–1975 | 1[a,b] |
| 8 | Ethiopia | Class enemies | 1974–1979 | 0.75[a] |
| 9 | Lenin's USSR | Class enemies, dissidents | 1917–1922 | 0.75[a] |
| 10 | Indonesia | Communists | 1965 | 0.5[b] |

Sources: [a] Rummel (2003); [b] Genocide Watch (2003).

and social opponents were killed during the three-quarter-century lifespan of the USSR and the Stalin era, alone, can lay claim to having been the largest single cause of human mortality bar the Black Death. Rummel observes that the average Soviet citizen was more at risk of being killed by their own government than the average smoker is from lung cancer (Rummell 2003: Table 1.3).

Politicide is very much a twentieth-century phenomenon owing to the polarization of political ideologies in this period. Ruthless leaders have long slaughtered opponents away from the battlefield in order to buttress their power or through the paranoia that autocracy frequently brings but, in the last century, this blended with ideological zeal in a deadly cocktail. As Table 5.3 indicates, major politicides have invariably been carried out either by or against Communists/Marxists of various shades. The limitations of conventional approaches to Security Studies, which hold that significant threats come only from other states and that the Cold War was a period of peace, are surely exposed by the unparalleled human suffering resulting from twentieth-century politicide.

## Securing the individual: the global politics of human rights

The notion of governments taking politico-legal steps to protect individuals other than one's own nationals/citizens is a relatively recent one in international affairs and still a long way from being firmly established in international law.

### *Empowering the individual: international human rights law*

Table 5.4 charts the progress of international human rights law over the last two centuries. Developments have tended to occur amidst the optimism of reconstruction following major international wars, dating back to the end of the Napoleonic Wars in Europe. The unparalleled human suffering associated with the Second World War predictably provided the major catalyst.

*Genocide*

Though the word did not exist at the time, the first systematic international political response to an act of genocide occurred during the First World War when a declaration was made by the allied powers, France, Russia and Great Britain about the Turkish massacres of Armenians. The 1915 declaration stated that the allied powers would hold the Ottoman government responsible for the various atrocities going on as well as the mobs directly responsible. The allies, however, were only partly true to their word on the termination of the war. Under the terms of the Treaty of Sevres Turkey was obliged to bring to justice those responsible for the massacres. Some Turks were prosecuted internally and Great Britain even took the step of holding some of the suspects themselves, incarcerating them in Maltese jails before returning them to Turkey in 1921. The 'Young Turk' revolution of 1922, however, brought about a reconciliation between the allied powers and the new

**Table 5.4** Key developments in human rights law

| 1815 | Congress of Vienna | The 'Concert of Europe' powers agreed to end the slave trade |
|------|--------------------|--------------------------------------------------------------|
| 1864 | 1st Geneva Convention | First of series of conventions giving legal protection to wounded or surrendered individual combatants in war and to non-combatants |
| 1890 | Brussels Convention on Slavery | Outlawed the slave trade |
| 1901 | International Labour Office workplace standards | Origins of notion of universal workers' rights. Not highly influential but paved the way for the creation of the International Labour Organization in 1919 as part of the League of Nations system |
| 1919 | League of Nations Minorities Section created | The League did not develop a systematic human rights regime but made guaranteeing the right of national minorities a condition of membership for some states and condemned state discrimination against minorities in the PCIJ *Minority Schools in Albania 1935* case and other Advisory Opinions |
| 1926 | Slavery Convention | Made slavery itself (in addition to slave trading) illegal |
| 1946 | United Nations Commission on Human Rights established | Authorized by Article 68 of the UN Charter, the Commission worked on wording a Declaration. A full-time Commissioner of Human Rights was initiated by the 1993 Vienna Convention |
| 1948 | Universal Declaration of Human Rights | Declaration adopted by the UN General Assembly establishing a Bill of Rights for the world comprising 30 short articles of mainly civil and political rights |
| 1948 | Convention on the Prevention and Punishment of Genocide | The convention proscribed acts which aim to 'destroy in whole or in part a national, ethnic, racial or religious group'. This legislation was reinforced by 1951 ICJ declaration that genocide is a crime in customary international law (i.e. binding on all states regardless of whether they ratified the convention) |
| 1951 | Refugee Convention | Makes it illegal for a receiving state to deport a refugee to a country where they are likely to be persecuted |
| 1966 | Covenants on i. Economic, Social & Cultural Rights and ii. Civil & Political Rights. | The legal machinery to implement the Universal Declaration came in two instruments. ESCR lists entitlements individuals can expect *from* their states (such as work and education). CPR lists individual freedoms *against* the state (such as free speech) |
| 1969 | Convention on the Elimination of All Forms of Racial Discrimination | Outlaws racial or national discrimination and holds the states accountable for societal violations. A CERD Committee monitors implementation and can investigate individual complaints |
| 1981 | Convention on the Elimination of All Forms of Discrimination Against Women | A Bill of Rights for the women of the world outlawing violent and social state discrimination |
| 1984 | Convention against Torture | Followed up Article 5 of the UN Declaration to criminalize state torture under any circumstances |
| 1989 | Convention on the Rights of the Child | Declares that 'the best interests of the child' should be respected in legal actions (e.g. in decisions on imprisoning or deporting their parents) |
| 1990 | Convention on Rights of all Migrant Workers and Members of Their Families | Protection of economic migrants from exploitation |
| 2006 | Convention on the Rights of Persons with Disability | Protection of disabled people from economic exploitation or social discrimination |

secular Turkish republic and a new treaty (the Lausanne Treaty) in 1923 absolved the new government of responsibility for pursuing crimes committed in the Ottoman era (Schabas 2000: 14–22).

In 1951 the International Court of Justice declared that, since the 1948 convention was so widely ratified, genocide came into the category of 'customary international law', making it a crime anywhere in the world. This means that genocide can be understood as a rare case of Public International Law functioning as 'proper' law. Countries which have not ratified the convention are not excluded from its jurisdictional reach[4] and there is a duty on all states which have ratified to prosecute those guilty of the crime where they can. The precedent for the universal jurisdiction of the Genocide Convention was established by the 1962 *Eichmann case* when Israeli secret agents kidnapped the former Nazi General and tried him in Israel for anti-Jewish genocide.[5] Twenty years later the USA agreed to Israel's request for another suspected mass-murderer, Demjanjuk, to be extradited for trial. Additionally, Canada and Australia had trials in the 1990s against naturalized citizens for participation in the Second World War atrocities against Jews in which the accused were acquitted but the principle of universal jurisdiction confirmed.[6] The 1990s revivals of both genocide and international morality gave fresh impetus to the principle of enforcing the 1948 convention and saw, amongst others, successful cases brought in Germany and Belgium for crimes against humanity committed in Bosnia and Rwanda.[7]

## Racial discrimination

For ethnically based abuses short of genocide (i.e. not systematically seeking to eliminate a whole national group) the Convention on the Elimination of All Forms of Racial Discrimination (CERD) came into force in 1969 outlawing racial or national discrimination and holding the ratifying states accountable for societal as well as governmental violations. Since it is near universally and unreservedly ratified CERD is significant enough to amount to 'an international law against systemic racism' (Robertson 2000: 94). Many liberal democracies have followed the lead of CERD in framing domestic race relations laws and criminalizing the incitement of racial hatred. The CERD regime also permits individuals to take up cases against governments. Set against this, however, countries with the most serious ethnic tensions have systematically failed to report to the CERD Committee which implements the regime.

## Torture

The 1984 Convention against Torture followed up Article 5 of the UN Declaration to criminalize state torture under any circumstances (including the theoretical 'ticking bomb' scenario – where an apprehended terrorist refuses to reveal the whereabouts of a weapon primed to imminently inflict mass casualties – frequently offered as a defence of such tactics). The Torture Convention is considered part of customary international law but has seen its rules bent even by Western liberal democracies. The US government's approval for 'torture lite' techniques such as sleep deprivation and 'water boarding'[8] at its Guantanamo Bay, on the island of Cuba, camp holding prisoners of the Iraq and Afghan Wars was a clear case of this.

## Refugees and migrants

The 1951 Geneva Refugee Convention continued with the League of Nations' refugee regime by declaring it illegal for a receiving state to deport a person fleeing persecution to a country where they are likely to be imperilled. The Geneva regime at the time was largely seen as a 'mopping-up' operation for living victims of Nazi oppression in the same way that the League's regime was aimed at resettling people uprooted by the Russian Civil War, but it has become much more than that. By 1967 it was clear that long-running conflicts, such as in Palestine and the Congo, were making refugees far more than a temporary phenomenon and a protocol to the convention removed geographical and time limits from its scope and effectively universalized and made permanent its core provisions. By 2010 147 states were covered by these provisions.

In recent years, however, the permanence and universality of the Refugee Convention has started to come into question. Countries have always differed in how readily they will grant asylum to a refugee but some governments have begun to question whether they should continue to be bound to give refuge at all. This is largely the result of the unforeseen rise in numbers of refugees. In 2008 there were an estimated 16 million refugees and asylum seekers in the world, up from around 3 million in the early 1970s (UNHCR 2008). The increased prevalence and persistence of civil wars is a major factor behind this. People in many democratic countries have pressured their governments for action to curb the numbers of asylum seekers through the belief that many are really economic migrants using political unrest in their countries as a pretext for moving. As a result of this, many governments – such as Australia and the UK – have made the process of applying for asylum more rigorous and even resorted to incarcerating asylum seekers until their applications have been processed.

## Women

The 1981 Convention on the Elimination of All Forms of Discrimination Against Women (CEDAW) is, on the face of it, impressively universal, having amassed some 187 ratifications by 2012. Robertson, however, argues that CEDAW is far less influential than its close relation the 1969 Convention on the Elimination of All Forms of Racial Discrimination owing to the number and nature of reservations to its provisions lodged by the ratifying parties (Robertson 2000: 94). The most frequently derogated from articles are 5 and 16 which deal with, respectively, the role of women in relation to customs/culture and the family. Since these two factors are those that most threaten the security of women this is a serious limitation on the convention's effectiveness. Hence the sex discrimination inherent in certain aspects of Sharia law as applied in some Islamic states is out of the reach of the convention. It should be added, however, that many Western European states have ratified with reservations and that the USA has not ratified at all.

Despite this, the 1981 Convention is not a paper tiger and it has made a contribution to protecting the rights of women. The Committee on the Elimination of Discrimination Against Women (CEDAW Committee), set up by the convention, is at the heart of an international regime which, at least to a limited extent, empowers individual women in a number of countries with rights not adequately covered in the twin Human Rights Covenants. An optional protocol to CEDAW was adopted in 1999 and by 2012 had been ratified by 104 states giving the CEDAW Committee the power to pursue cases brought by individual women in those states. Even amongst those states who have ratified CEDAW but not the optional protocol, the convention has on occasion been cited in defence of women in domestic legal cases. The Constitution of Brazil, for example, was amended to bring it into line with the provisions (International Federation of University Women 1999). The 1993 UN Declaration on the Elimination of Violence Against Women and the 'Platform for Action' agreed at the 1995 Beijing Conference have deepened the range of global norms concerning women's rights but these instruments lack the legal force of the CEDAW regime, limited though that is. Violence and wider discrimination based on sex remains endemic in much of the world and much remains to be done to properly secure women.

## The disabled

Around 700 million people, or one-tenth of the world, are restricted by mental, physical or sensory impairment but they have only recently come to be covered by international human rights legislation. A series of General Assembly declarations initiated this process in the early 1970s. The 1971 Declaration on the Rights of Mentally Retarded Persons and 1975 Declaration on the Rights of Disabled Persons sought to ensure that the disabled were covered by the UN Covenant on Civil and Political Rights. A World Programme of Action Concerning Disabled Persons was adopted by the General Assembly in 1982 and launched alongside the UN Decade for Disability (1983–92). Also established at this time, a Special UN Rapporteur on Disability was appointed within the Commission for Social Development. This sought to advance the economic rights of the disabled and led to the General Assembly in 1993 adopting the Standard Rules on the Equalization of Opportunities for Persons With Disabilities (a non-binding agreement).

Thus it has gradually been confirmed in international law that the disabled are 'human' and entitled to the same protective rights as others but transforming this into a legal instrument granting special protection, akin to that afforded to women, migrants and children, has been a slow process. 1987 discussions in the General Assembly over a Convention on the Human Rights of the Disabled were postponed when a number of states' delegates indicated that they considered the disabled to already be adequately covered in existing human rights legislation (O'Reilly 2003). Disabled rights have advanced significantly in most countries over recent decades but the fact that 80 per cent of the world's disabled people live in LDCs, where the means of facilitating their involvement in social and economic life may be absent even if the will is present, serves to heighten their vulnerability. An umbrella pressure group network, the International Disability Alliance, was at the forefront of the campaign to plug this gap and establish a UN convention for the disabled. A strong campaign persuaded the General Assembly to set up an ad hoc committee to draft a Convention on the Rights of Persons With Disabilities, which was then adopted unanimously by the Assembly in 2006 and entered into force in 2008. The articles of the convention, in general, look to ensure a better quality of life for the disabled through fuller participation in society with economic and social rights such as employment and a right to an education to the fore accompanied by civil liberties such as reproductive rights.

## Abuses not specifically covered by global human rights regimes

### Homosexuals

Even more clearly than with women's rights, the difficulties of overcoming cultural differences in establishing global standards are apparent when considering the rights of homosexuals and other minority sexualities. The UN has been unable to reach a consensus to give the same status to sexual freedom as religious or political freedom in international human rights law. The right to have same-sex relationships is not covered in the UN Declaration or Covenants and the extermination of people on grounds of their sexual practices is not included in the 1948 Genocide Convention. Some tentative steps in the direction of securing global human security for homosexuals have been taken, however. In 1991 Amnesty International began including within their category of 'prisoners of conscience' (those whose release they demand) homosexuals imprisoned for private consensual sexual activity. The European Court of Human Rights have interpreted Article 8 of the European Convention on Human Rights, which upholds 'Respect for Private and Family Life', to include gay rights. As a result of this, homosexuality was decriminalized in Northern Ireland (1981), the Republic of Ireland (1988) and Cyprus (1993). The UN Human Rights Committee similarly ended the criminal prosecution of homosexuals in Tasmania, Australia, with a ruling in the 1994 *Toonen Case*. The Human Rights Committee does not have official judicial powers but was asked for its opinion on this case by the Federal Government of Australia before repealing the Tasmanian law. Despite such developments, the state-sanctioned incarceration, and even execution, of people for private, consensual acts persists in many parts of the contemporary world. Persecution on these grounds is still persistent enough in the liberal, democratic world to ensure that enthusiasm for extending the reach of global protection to individuals for this particular form of discrimination has not, as yet, been sufficient to overcome the usual barriers of sovereignty.

### Politicide

The 1999 *Pinochet Case,* when the British government rejected a Spanish prosecutors' request to extradite the former Chilean President who was visiting the UK, proved to be key test case for the status of politicide in international law.

UK courts would not accept the Spanish grounds of genocide as a basis for handing over the former tyrant since his crimes were targeted against leftist opponents rather than a national or religious minority (Robertson 2000: 229). However, although the Pinochet Case outcome disappointed human rights activists, it was still a significant step forward for global policy. Pinochet was released and allowed to return to Chile due to ill-health but the UK law courts made it clear that his crimes did amount to 'crimes against humanity' against which sovereignty was no defence. The ICC, which has the authority to act on crimes against humanity, looks set to finally end the anomaly of this most heinous and widespread of cries being overlooked in international human rights law.

## Implementing human rights

Codifying law is only part of the process of developing human rights. Implementing international law is always a more difficult task than with domestic law because of the barrier presented by the notion of sovereignty and this is especially so when law is focused on individuals, traditionally considered the preserve of governments and domestic courts.

### United Nations

There are UN mechanisms for implementing human rights but they have been limited and uneven in their impact. The UN Commission on Human Rights' record on encouraging the implementation of the Declaration and Covenants it crafted is, according to the esteemed human rights lawyer Geoffrey Robertson, 'woeful' (Robertson 2000: 45). The Commission, restrained by intergovernmental politicking, failed even to condemn the horrific politicides/genocides in Cambodia and Uganda in the late 1970s. In Uganda dictator Idi Amin had massacred political opponents and expelled thousands of ethnic minorities from his country. In Cambodia Pol Pot's reign of terror had seen up to a million of his own citizens slaughtered for the ideological mission of returning his country to 'year zero'. The Commission was beefed up in the 1990s, with the appointment of a full-time Commissioner at its head, but still lacked any enforcement powers beyond 'naming and shaming'. Hence, in 2006, the General Assembly approved the creation of a new body to take over from the Commission, the Human Rights Council (HRC). The HRC meets three times per year (the Commission met only once per year) and comprises representatives of 47 states elected by the General Assembly. Concerns that the voting procedure would continue the trend established under the Commission of electing members from countries with poor rights records and that its actions may be politicized was cited by Israel for their non-involvement in the organ.

Also contributing to the implementation of human rights standards are committees established with some of the covenants and conventions that have entered into force. The Human Rights Committee was set up to monitor the implementation of the Covenant on Civil and Political Rights. However, only a small number of admissible cases had been lodged with the HRC by this time and many governments – including the USA, UK and China – have shown no inclination to be committed to the procedure.

The Committee on the Elimination of Racial Discrimination (CERD) and the Committee on the Elimination of Discrimination Against Women (CEDAW Committee) have the capacity to take up individual cases for states that permit this. CEDAW has on occasion been cited in defence of women in domestic legal cases. Within the Children's Rights regime a UN Committee on the Rights of the Child examines parties' progress in implementing the convention and has made some progress in embarrassing some governments into implementing legal changes, such as separating juvenile from adult war criminal suspects detained in Rwanda. The HRC and implementing committees have had some successes in informing legal cases but these instances are few and far between and, of course, the countries concerned are not the ones where the most serious human rights violations are occurring, which are invariably – though not exclusively – undemocratic states.

## Civil society

Pressure groups have played a big role in facilitating the implementation of international law on human rights by forming a key partnership with the United Nations. Amnesty International, which has grown from a one-man campaign, launched by British journalist Peter Benenson in 1961, to a multi-million pound operation with over 2 million members in over 150 countries, work on highlighting non-compliance with the UN Covenant on Civil and Political Rights and have a particular focus on judicial rights (e.g. fair trials). As well as helping implement existing legislation, Amnesty have taken the lead in promoting the development of new law to be taken on by the UN, such as with the Torture Convention. The US-based group Human Rights Watch, whilst also working in conjunction with the UN, have focused on facilitating the implementation of the Helsinki Accords, established during the Cold War to improve human rights in the context of East–West relations, and most of their activities serve to highlight violations of free expression. Over 200 other pressure groups perform similar functions in the world today, mainly in the area of civil and political rights.

## National courts

Since genocide, torture and 'crimes against humanity' are part of customary international law some national courts have come to assume the right to pass verdicts on crimes committed on individuals other than their own citizens. In the 1990s new impetus was given to the politics of human rights by the end of the Cold War but the world also witnessed the spectre of genocide revived in Rwanda and Yugoslavia. This prompted successful cases brought in Germany and Belgium for such crimes committed in Bosnia and Rwanda.[9] The 1999 *Pinochet Case* in the UK was a test case in international human rights law, not only in confirming a right to arrest suspects of crimes against humanity but also setting a precedent that diplomatic immunity (Pinochet claimed this as a former president and 'life senator') was no protection against such crimes.

A setback to the development of this method of implementing global human rights came with a 2002 verdict by the UN's court, the International Court of Justice, which ruled that Belgium was not entitled to try a government minister of the Congo, Ndombasi, for his role in a massacre of Tutsis in Kinshasa.[10] Belgian authorities were instructed that they had no right to strip Ndombasi of diplomatic protection, even in view of the gravity of the offences of which he was being accused. This development was to the relief of some in the Belgian government who had become alarmed at the likely diplomatic fallout from their country vainly seeking to bring a long list of recent tyrants to justice in Brussels. The ICJ verdict brought dismay to human rights activists for setting back the cause of universality in human rights law but, ultimately, the case may help strengthen the arguments in favour of global justice. The prospect of dozens of states around the world simultaneously pursuing various individuals in the name of international law could also be said to demonstrate the necessity of a global judiciary less vulnerable to criticisms of partisanship and more likely to be able to meet success in pursuing individuals traditionally protected by sovereignty. The International Criminal Court (ICC), considered in the next section, could yet fulfil this function.

## Global courts

The idea of an international court to try individuals, alongside the International Court of Justice dealing with state-to-state conflicts, was around at the birth of the United Nations but, like many other global aspirations, was frozen in time by the Cold War. An international criminal court had earlier been proposed during the time of the League of Nations in relation to a stillborn 1937 convention dealing with terrorism. An early draft of the Genocide Convention floated the idea of a court to enforce its provisions but this was soon shelved as too radical a notion to put to the bifurcating international community (Schabas 2001: 8). Instead Article VI of the convention provides for justice to be dispensed either in the courts of the country where the crimes occurred or else in a specially convened international tribunal. This was the case with the Nuremberg and Tokyo trials, which prosecuted Nazi and Japanese war criminals in the 1940s, and the ad hoc tribunals established by the Security Council to try individuals for genocide and war crimes in Yugoslavia and Rwanda in the 1990s.

The idea of the ICC did not perish during the Cold War years and, when the opportunity then presented itself at the close of the 1980s, the UN's International Law Commission (ILC), a body responsible for the codification of international law, revived the plan. In 1992 the General Assembly gave the go-ahead to the ILC to draft a blueprint for the ICC, paving the way for the 1998 Rome Conference, at which the statute for the court was agreed upon and opened for signature. By 2002 the statute had received enough ratifications to enter into force and the court was born. Only seven states opposed the court at the Rome Conference (USA, Israel, China, Iraq, Sudan, Yemen and Libya) and, by 2012, it has 121 parties. The USA declined to ratify the Rome Convention that underpins the ICC largely on the grounds that it would be unconstitutional to permit a US citizen to be tried outside of the US legal system for an alleged US-based crime and that, as the world's only superpower, they would be more likely to have cases brought against them than other states, whether through the fact that they are more prominent in UN military operations than most or due to trumped-up charges based on anti-Americanism.

How influential the ICC can become remains to be seen (by 2012 it had only taken up cases in seven countries) but it could eventually give real meaning to international human rights law by exercising the sort of supranational authority witnessed only sporadically and selectively to date. A key difference between the ICC and previous ad hoc human rights courts is that it will not have to get approval to act from the 'Big 5' in the UN Security Council and so will be less vulnerable to criticism of partiality to the Great Powers and of only ever being an arbiter of 'victor's justice'. In 2005, a significant boost to the credibility of the court was given by an agreement by the UN Security Council to refer to it the Darfur (Sudan) genocide case despite the initial hostilities of the USA to involving a body it does not support and the fact that Sudan is not a party. In time, the court could also potentially widen the grounds upon which it can launch a prosecution beyond the current remit of genocide, war crimes and crimes against humanity since Article 10 of its Treaty refers to the evolution of its statutes in line with customary international law.

## Regional courts

### European Convention on Human Rights

The regime, centred on the Council of Europe, an older and wider body than the European Union, is undoubtedly the most extensive international human rights system in the world. The system was established in 1950 and now covers 47 states (essentially all of Europe, including Turkey and Russia, bar Belarus, the continent's last dictatorship). Individual petition by citizens is the main channel for taking up cases, although some cases taken up by one government against another have also occurred.

The convention originally sought to implement the UN Declaration in Western Europe but has evolved into something much more extensive than anything within the UN system. The European Court of Human Rights (ECHR) has gradually assumed the right to be 'creative' in interpreting the articles of the convention thereby allowing it to pass verdicts – binding on all government parties – that go well beyond the most blatant forms of human right abuses. The ECHR, for example, have interpreted Article 8 of the European Convention on Human Rights, which upholds 'Respect for Private and Family Life', originally intended to give protection against forced sterilizations, to include gay rights and so greatly advance this.

### Organization of American States (OAS)

The OAS's Declaration on the Rights and Duties of Man actually pre-dates the UN Declaration (by seven months) but the western hemisphere's human rights regime lags well behind its European counterpart. There is a similar institutional set up with an Inter-American Convention Commission to take up cases from individuals as well as states and a court but the system has had very little influence. Gross human rights violations in most of its 26 parties throughout much of its history have undermined the regime's credibility as has the non-participation in the court of its potentially two most influential members: Canada and the USA.

## Africa

The African Union's (AU) African Charter on Human and People's Rights (Banjul Charter) of 1981 covers nearly all of Africa and features a commission that promotes human rights but there is, as yet, no implementing body. A 1998 protocol did set up a court but it has yet to function. The Economic Community of West African States (ECOWAS) does, however, have a functioning court – though not ostensibly a human rights judiciary – and in 2008 this passed a landmark verdict against the government of Niger for failing to protect a girl from being sold to slavery.[11]

## *Foreign policy*

The 1990s saw something of a rise in 'ethical foreign policy' with countries declaring that human rights would be allowed to enter the calculations of foreign policy objectives long dominated by the geopolitics of Cold War. In the UK Robin Cook was explicit in stating this on becoming foreign minister of the Labour government in 1997 and, in the USA, the 'Clinton Doctrine' emerged with greater emphasis on the diplomatic encouragement of democracy and human rights than seen since the Wilson government of the 1920s. In fact, however, the starting point of this development can be traced back the détente era of the Cold War in the 1970s when it appeared that the conflict was coming to an end with a significant thaw in East–West relations. The Helsinki Accords of 1975 was the high point of détente: a wide-ranging diplomatic/human rights treaty which saw the West agree not to interfere in the affairs of the Eastern Bloc in exchange for the Soviets improving human rights in their empire. A notable reduction of political persecution in the USSR did occur after this and also in the West since the USA was now vulnerable to charges of hypocrisy if they persisted in propping up oppressive military dictatorships who took an anti-communist line. An ethical foreign policy is always a hostage to fortune, however, and numerous claims of hypocrisy have been levelled at the USA, UK and other countries when lurches back to following the 'national interest' have occurred.

On a more consistent level human rights have been clearly stated as an objective of Dutch and Norwegian foreign policy since the early 1970s. Norway and The Netherlands together with Sweden and Canada came to be known as the 'Like Minded Countries' for their generous foreign aid budgets and particularly for linking this to the human rights record of recipient countries. The governments of Norway and Canada have subsequently played the lead roles in launching the Human Security Network, an alliance which advocates the development of global policies focused on the human interest, whether or not these happen to coincide with state interests. Cynics have suggested that this sort of strategy is just a tactical move by less powerful governments to raise their diplomatic profile through populist gimmicks and that it is easier to take the moral high ground when you can more easily avoid the tough politics of the 'low ground'. IR human rights specialist Jack Donnelly, for example, comments that 'small states rarely have to choose between human rights and other foreign policy goals' (Donnelly 2007: 135). The USA and UK have used such arguments in defending something of a return to Cold War realpolitik in controversial actions taken in the 'war against terror' since 2001, such as the prolonged British derogation from Article 5 of the European Convention (covering rights on arrest), to allow for legal principles in place since Magna Carta to be suspended for arresting terrorist suspects.

## Fighting for the rights of others: humanitarian intervention

Wars prompted by the abuse of another country's citizens are a relatively recent historical development and still shrouded in controversy. Declaring war against a country for the mistreatment of one's own nationals resident there is far more solidly established in international law. Perhaps the most liberal interpretation ever of this doctrine came in 1850 when the UK threatened Greece with war for a Greek mob's attack on the home of Don Pacifico who was part-Gibraltarian and hence a British subject.

Table 5.5 presents a chronology of military interventions which have purported to have been inspired, at least partially, by the motivation of relieving the suffering of nationals distinct from the interveners. Differentiating between a humanitarian military action and one motivated by more traditional spurs of gain, self-defence or ideology is nearly always a difficult judgement. In all of the listed cases one or more of these more familiar reasons to take up arms have been claimed by some observers to be the real cause of war.

The legal basis for humanitarian intervention is a moot point and it has come in and out of fashion in international affairs over the last three centuries. Grotius, in the seventeenth century, considered rescuing imperilled non-nationals to come into the category of just war but it was not until the Concert of Europe era in the nineteenth century that the concept was put into practice. Humanitarian intervention, along with just war in general, fell out of favour amidst the amoral realism of twentieth-century state practice but rose to prominence again in the 'New World Order' that was heralded by the demise of the Cold War in 1990. Robertson provides a striking illustration of this by contrasting the UK government's enthusiasm for the 1991 'Safe Havens' action in Iraq and 1999 Kosovan War with a Foreign Office assertion in 1986 that: 'contemporary legal opinion comes down against the existence of a right of humanitarian intervention' (Robertson 2000: 401[12]).

Despite more frequent recourse to it in recent years, humanitarian intervention remains a highly contentious concept in international relations since it challenges that fundamental underpinning of the Westphalian system, state sovereignty. International Law is unclear on the issue. The UN Charter appears both to proscribe and prescribe the practice. Articles 2.4 and 2.7 uphold the importance of sovereignty and the convention on non-interference in another state's affairs but Chapter VII

**Table 5.5** Notable 'humanitarian interventions' in history

| Intervention | Interveners | Humanitarian spur |
|---|---|---|
| Greece (Ottoman Empire) 1827 | France, UK and Russia | Turkish massacre of Greeks |
| Lebanon (Ottoman Empire) 1860 | France | Massacre of Christians by Druze |
| Serbia, Montenegro, Bosnia-Herzegovina, Romania and Bulgaria (Ottoman Empire) 1877–8 | Russia | Massacres of Bulgarians by Turkish partisans |
| Cuba (Spanish Empire) 1898 | USA | Atrocities against Cubans by Spanish colonialists |
| Macedonia (Ottoman Empire) 1905 | Bulgaria, Greece and Serbia | Oppression of Christians by Turks and nationalist violence |
| Congo 1960–4 | 1 Belgium, 2 UN, 3 Belgium and USA | Civil war and massacres following independence (from Belgium) |
| Dominican Republic 1965 | USA | Protect foreign citizens from new military dictatorship |
| East Pakistan 1971 | India | Pakistani genocide against breakaway region (Bangladesh) |
| Zaire 1978 | France and Belgium | Massacres of civilians by anti-government guerillas |
| Cambodia 1978 | Vietnam | 'Autogenocide' of various sections of own people by Khmer Rouge government |
| Uganda 1979 | Tanzania | Expulsions, massacres and human rights abuses against ethnic minorities and opponents |
| Central African Republic 1979 | France | Overthrow of Bohasia government responsible for massacres of civilians |
| Grenada 1983 | USA and Organization of East Caribbean States | Protect foreign citizens after military coup |
| Panama 1989 | USA | Protect foreign citizens in civil unrest |
| Liberia 1990–7 | 1 Nigeria 2 ECOWAS | Restore order amidst civil war |
| Iraq 1991 | UN | Protect Kurds in North and 'Marsh Arabs' in South from government massacres |
| Yugoslavia 1992 | UN | Protect Bosnian Moslems from Serb massacres |
| Somalia 1992–3 | UN | Restore order amidst civil war |
| Haiti 1994–7 | UN | Restore democracy and order following military coup |
| Sierra Leone 1997 | ECOWAS | Restore order amidst civil war |
| Kosovo (Yugoslavia) 1999 | NATO | Protect Kosovar Albanians from Serb massacres |
| East Timor (Indonesia) 1999 | INTERFET[a] (Australia, UK, Thailand, Philippines and others) | Maintain order in transition to independence |
| Libya 2011 | NATO (on behalf of UN) | Protect anti-government protestors from massacre |

Note
[a] International Force East Timor. Also involved were; Brazil, Canada, Denmark, Egypt, Fiji, France, Germany, Ireland, Italy, Jordan, Kenya, Malaysia, New Zealand, Norway, Portugal, the Republic of Korea, Singapore and the United States.

of the UN Charter suggests that extreme humanitarian abuses can constitute a 'threat to peace' legitimizing intervention.

The main arguments against humanitarian intervention can be summarized as follows:

## Abuse of the concept

One man's humanitarian intervention is always another man's imperialist or balance of power-inspired venture. All of the interventions listed in Table 5.5 were opposed by some states, unconvinced by moral assuagements of the intervener. In all cases other motivations for intervention can easily be found. The Tanzanian and Vietnamese interventions of the late 1970s overthrew two of the vilest governments in history but were widely condemned in the democratic world, assuming the missions were driven by power (in the former) and both power and ideology (in the latter). It was notable that NATO's 1999 action in Yugoslavia, ultimately, was 'sold' to the general public of the intervening countries more on the grounds of maintaining European order than as averting humanitarian catastrophe. Some measure of self-interest, alongside compassion for others, appeared to be necessary to justify going to war.

## Inconsistency in application of the concept

The various European interventions in the Ottoman Empire which set the precedent for applying Grotian morality in international affairs also helped to undermine the concept of humanitarian intervention and increase cynicism about it as a workable doctrine. Although abuses did occur under the Ottomans they were no more despotic rulers than some of the interveners and it is hard to escape the conclusion that the interventions really represented clashes of the civilizations with Europeans rallying to the cause of Christians under the yoke of Moslem rule.[13] More recently, the willingness of the UN and NATO to act in defence of anti-government protestors in Libya in 2011 stood in stark contrast to the lack of response to similar crackdowns on protestors elsewhere in Yemen, Bahrain and Syria that same year. Libyan oil and its leader Gadaffi's previous sponsorship of anti-Western terrorism made it easier to get international agreement than for the other Arab despots. Equally, humanitarian intervention is always more likely to be considered an option where the target state is not going to be too tough a military opponent. Power politics dictates that Chinese genocide in Tibet or Russian aggression in Chechenya were/are never likely to be awarded the same response as Serb or Iraqi atrocities. Selective justice undermines the principle of humanitarian intervention, many claim.

## Cultural relativism

A core argument against humanitarian intervention is that rights and cultures vary so significantly from state to state that judging a country as being a danger to its own citizens is likely to be prejudicial. Such judgements are likely to be made by the dominant power of the day and so, in effect, represent a hegemonic imposition of a particular ideology. Nearly all (if not all) states have seriously violated their citizen's rights at some time. Based on this would it follow that an invasion of just about any country by any other country could be legitimized?

## May worsen the situation

Additionally, even where a clear case of tyranny can be established, there is the concern that intervention may not be the answer to the problem in that it can only inflame the situation. Is the use of violence an appropriate response to the use of violence? Many critics contended that NATO's action in defence of the Kosovar Albanians led to an escalation of the Serb campaign against them.

## Counter-arguments

It is clear that humanitarian intervention can probably never be a perfect method for combating tyranny. Inconsistent application of the principle is inevitable given that it might not be practical to intervene in some cases since the target state may fight back and lead to more bloodshed than might have been the case if no action had been taken. However, does this mean that no action should ever be taken and the world should sit on its hands whilst avoidable slaughters are being carried out? Should the realism of doing something to avert catastrophe when it is clearly achievable be subsumed by the Realism of doing nothing unless the interests of the intervener are at stake? If an individual walking through a city witnesses two assaults, one by a large armed man and another by a small unarmed man, is it better to be morally consistent and walk past both incidents? The just war principle of avoiding conflict escalation can be applied to humanitarian intervention to give a practical working doctrine which, if not perfect, is surely better than doing nothing.

## Towards universalism

As previously referred to in considering the case of humanitarian intervention, the chief moral objection to the universal application of human rights is the position commonly known as cultural relativism. This position argues that the world's cultural diversity makes any attempt to apply rights universally, at best, difficult and, at worst, an immoral imposition of dominant cultural traits. President Jiang Zemin of China articulated this view on his state visit to the USA in 1997 in defending his government from criticisms on its human rights record. 'The theory of relativity worked out by Mr Einstein, which is in the domain of natural science, I believe can be applied in the political field. Democracy and human rights are relative concepts and not absolute' (Kaiser 1997).

**Table 5.6** Regional human rights regimes

| Regime | Year began | Membership | Political impact |
| --- | --- | --- | --- |
| European Convention | 1953 | Most of Europe | Commission and Court able to make supranational verdicts. Individual petition possible |
| Banjul Charter | 1981 | Most of Africa | Commission promotes human rights but there is no implementing body |
| Inter-American Convention | 1978 | N. and S. America | Commission and Court but has little influence |
| Arab Commission | 1968 | Arab states of Middle East | No Convention developed. Speaks out on Arab rights in Israel |
| The Commonwealth | 1931 | Former British colonies | Has suspended membership and imposed political sanctions on member-states for human rights abuses |

Zemin's statement in support of cultural relativism came fifty years after the first major articulation of this viewpoint in international politics in the run-up to the 1948 Universal Declaration of Human Rights. Concerns at the notion of a global bill of rights riding roughshod over the minority cultures of the world prompted leading anthropologists, including Melville Herskovits and Ruth Benedict, to petition the UN Commission for Human Rights.

> Standards and values are relative to the culture from which they derive so that any attempt to formulate postulates that grow out of the beliefs or moral codes of one culture must to that extent detract from the applicability of any Declaration of Human Rights to mankind as a whole.
>
> (American Anthropologist Association 1947: 542)

In Benedict's view, and that of most traditional anthropologists, the notion of what is morally right can only equate to what is customary within a given society (Benedict 1934). Hence the notion of rights pertaining to all humankind is not 'natural'. Rights are the rules of mutual give and take which develop over time within a society in order for it to function peacefully and survive. Rights are, in effect, implicit agreements arrived at within societies. The American Anthropologist Association (AAA), as a counter to criticisms from human rights activists that they and their discipline were immoral, issued a declaration in 1999 giving qualified support for UN human rights legislation. The AAA now argue that human rights are 'an evolving concept' and that they have come to see global policy as a way of campaigning to preserve human cultural difference (American Anthropologist Association 1999). Anthropology as a discipline, however, continues to be very influenced by the positivist epistemological belief that value judgements over cultures other than one's own are an imposition of those values.

In contemporary philosophy perhaps the leading exponent of relativism is Gilbert Harman, whose writings may have influenced Zemin since he argues the case that scientific relativity ought to inform our understanding of morality. '[T]here is no single true morality. There are many different moral frameworks, none of which is more correct than the others' (Harman 1996: 8). Cultural relativism comes in various strengths. The strongest position is to reject any notion of universal human rights, but the more moderate form asserts that the rights of the collective should temper the prescription of individual liberty.[14] There is a flavour of moderate relativism in the Banjul Charter's emphasis on the rights of 'peoples', alongside individual rights. 'They [peoples] shall freely determine their political status and shall pursue their economic and social development according to the policy they have freely chosen (Article 20).'

Neither the Banjul Charter nor an anthropologically enriched UN regime, of course, have had to stand the course of practical implementation. Simultaneously upholding both individual and collective rights is highly problematic. Rwandan Hutus as a collective freely chose to slaughter 800,000 individual Tutsis for their own social, political and economic development. Existing universalist human rights for sure did not save the Tutsis, but this was due to lack of will to implement existing legislation. Prioritizing collective cultural rights and state sovereignty over those of individuals would not only fail to stop genocide but even offer a defence of it.

The 1948 Universal Declaration of Human Rights was written and signed up to at a time when the membership of the UN was far from universal. Much of Africa and Asia was still under the colonial yoke and hence not represented amongst the independent states making up the General Assembly. The declaration does reflect Western liberal philosophy in its focus on protecting the individual from the tyranny of the state and resembles in particular the US and French constitutions. The cultural imposition argument, however, is overstated. No state voted against the declaration and most of the abstainers were later brought on board. Although Saudi Arabia objected to the notion of religious freedom other Islamic states such as Syria, Iran and Pakistan did not (Robertson 2000: 32). The USSR and its East European allies objected to the lack of emphasis in the declaration given to economic and social rights but this was rectified in the development of the twin covenants that followed 1948. The twin covenants stand as a broad legal instrument empowering individuals both with rights against states and entitlements from states going beyond many Western bills of rights.

A fundamental weakness with relativist arguments in regard to human rights is that they presuppose that societies or cultures can secure the rights of their individual constituents endogenously. Nations as social entities are rarely, if ever, directly represented in the political world. Multinationalism, whether arrived at through migration or historical accident (such as in the partitioning of Africa), is the norm in the modern state system. If the states of the world mirrored its distinct 'cultures', ethical/cultural relativism would stand as a realistic alternative to universalism in protecting human rights. In the real world, however, how are the rights of cultural minorities within states to be fully safeguarded? The fact that national or religious minorities are frequently imperilled rather than protected by states cannot be questioned. The homogeneous 'traditional' culture advanced by relativists is rarely found in the countries to which it is attributed and complaints of the inappropriateness of 'Western' human rights are usually made by tyrannical regimes trying to justify repressive policies in the name of 'nation building'. Women, the disabled, homosexuals and people linked by any other form of collective identity stand little chance of having their 'cultural differences' respected when they overlap with far more influential 'cultures'. Entrusting states to be the arbiters of human rights frequently leads to the imposition of dominant cultural norms on minority cultures in precisely the fashion that relativism purports to prevent. Rhoda Howard has referred to this as 'cultural absolutism', as a counter to the relativist claim that human rights are a form of absolutism (Howard 1995).

Even if a more optimistic view of the relationship between governments and individuals than that encouraged by recent history is taken states still offer a limited guarantee of future human security since their own position is far from secure. The lifespan of many states during the twentieth century has been much the same as that of their citizens. The economic rights afforded to its people by the USSR and its allies, such as employment, disappeared with the fall of Communism as quickly as the civil and political rights of Latvians, Estonians and Lithuanians had been snuffed out by their annexation by the USSR.

It can further be argued that relativism in regard to ethics and rights is not only unhelpful but ontologically flawed. The temptation to want to protect the weak from the strong in international affairs is obvious but think for a moment about the implications of applying cultural relativism in other situations. If cultural relativism should apply at the global level should it not also be applied at the domestic level to recognize the impunity of criminal culture from the imposition of state values? If it is wrong to universally apply values then why is it not wrong to universally apply cultural relativism? If all cultural moralities are equally valid does this mean that contradictory moral opinions can both be valid?

The (strong) relativists' answer to the final of these three questions is to adopt the position of 'methodological relativism' or 'truth relativism' and suggest that the idea of validity has no bearing in ethics, or indeed in any social scientific context. This position, associated in Sociology with Bloor (1976) and in Philosophy with Davson-Galle (1998), posits that moral judgements have no rational basis and are, in effect, no more than matters of taste. This position, however, can lead only to a nihilistic abandonment of reason and the tolerance of intolerance. Abandoning reason and any notion of right and wrong in ethics is not only unhelpful in terms of giving the green light to genocide and any other form of human abuse; it can also be argued to be logically flawed. Proving truths in a social context is more difficult than in natural science but some philosophical methods have been advanced to show that moral judgements can be rationalized. Apel, for example, demonstrates that people necessarily accept certain fundamental ethical norms as binding in the process of making everyday communication possible. In any form of communication the idea of truth and lies must implicitly be accepted by someone communicating or communication would have no meaning (Apel 1990). The strict observance of truth relativism would mean that you could not participate in any discussion on ethics. Those philosophers, anthropologists and others who deny the universality of rights do so by making arguments grounded in reason. Zemin in upholding the relativity of human rights on his 1997 visit to the USA did so by justifying China's different interpretation of the concept to that favoured in the West. In a world in which transnational communication is ever more prominent and cultures increasingly intersect surely the notion of relativism unravels.

It is right to be concerned about ideologies that oppress other cultural values, whether blatantly through nationalist hatred or more subtly through economic domination, but this itself is a moral judgement. You cannot properly respect another culture if you cannot also criticize another culture. Instead of reducing ethnocentrism, relativism in this way can actually encourage its proliferation by reinforcing in all cultures the sanctity of their own values. The moral isolationism promoted by such an approach has been the basis of the various forms of societal discrimination which have so blighted recent history and which humankind, as a global society, must at least try to eradicate.

## Key points

- The security of individual people is frequently threatened by their own governments and other groups in their society because of their social identity.
- The chief forms of social identity subject to life-threatening discrimination are nationality, religion, sex, sexual orientation, disability and ideology.
- Global political action to protect individuals against discrimination on national or religious grounds has evolved significantly since 1945 but has been patchily implemented. Global policy relating to discrimination on the grounds of the other forms of social identity is far more limited.
- Sovereignty and the belief that rights are culture-bound, and hence not appropriate for global policy, remain significant obstacles to the further development of global policy in this area.

## Notes

1   It is generally accepted that national identity evolved from the late eighteenth century when ordinary people, through greater communication, began to be more aware of people from other countries and were hence able to perceive of their own societies as having certain distinguishing characteristics.

2   Ironically, as the site of Abraham's offer to sacrifice his son to God, Temple Mount unites the three great monotheistic faiths. It is also, however, the site of Solomon's Temple in Judaism and of Mohammed's ascent to heaven in Islam (marked by the Dome of the Rock Mosque).

3   The numbers killed are unclear. See Grau (1995) for a detailed account of this, often neglected, episode in history.

4   In 2012 there were still fifty-one UN member-states that had not ratified the Genocide Convention. Amongst this number were several who had joined the UN only since 1990 and may be expected, in time, to ratify. Included amongst the others, though, were a number of states against whom since the last 1960s charges of genocide could have been levelled such as Somalia, Indonesia and the Congo. More curious non-ratifying states include Japan and Malta.

5   *Attorney General of Israel v. Eichmann*, 36 International. Law Report 277.

6    *Regina v. Finta* (1994) Supreme Court of Canada 24 March. *Polyukhovich v. Commonwealth* (1991), 172 C.L.R. 501 (Australia).

7    *Public Prosecutor v. Djajic*, No. 20/96 (Sup. Ct. Bavaria 23 May 1997).

8    A procedure in which the prisoner has water poured into their mouth so that they imagine they are drowning.

9    *Public Prosecutor v. Djajic*, No. 20/96 (Sup. Ct. Bavaria 23 May 1997).

10   *Democratic Republic of the Congo v. Belgium*, ICJ verdict 14 Feb 2002 General List no. 121.

11   *Hadijatou Mani Koraou v. Niger*, 2008.

12   UK Government (1986) Foreign Policy Document No. 148, *British Yearbook of International Law,* 56, Section 2, para. 22.

13   Individuals rallied to these causes such as the English poet Byron who died in Greece preparing to fight in their independence struggle.

14   Frankena uses the term 'meta-ethical relativism' for the stronger version (Frankena 1988). Some contemporary anthropologists now distinguish between cultural and ethical relativism; the former being purely descriptive whereas the latter is normative (Rosaldo 2000).

## Recommended reading

Donnelly, J. (2007) *International Human Rights*, 3rd edn, Cambridge, MA: Westview.

Hansen, L. (2000) 'The Little Mermaid's Secret Security Dilemma and the Absence of Gender in the Copenhagen School', *Millennium Journal of International Studies*, 29(2): 285–306.

McSweeney, B. (1996) 'Identity and Security: Buzan and the Copenhagen School', *Review of International Studies*, 22(1): 81–93.

Robertson, G. (2007) *Crimes against Humanity: The Struggle for Global Justice*, 3rd edn, London: Penguin.

Schabas, W. (2009) *Genocide in International Law: The Crime of Crimes*, 2nd edn, Cambridge: Cambridge University Press.

Tickner, A. (2001) *Gendering World Politics: Issues and Approaches in the Post-Cold War Era*, New York: Columbia University Press.

Waever, O., Buzan, B., Kelstrup, M. and Lemaitre, P. (1993) *Identity, Migration and the New Security Agenda in Europe*, London: Pinter.

## Useful web links

Amnesty International: http://www.amnesty.org/

Genocide Watch: http://www.genocidewatch.org/

International Criminal Court: http://www.icccpi.int/php/show.php?id=home&l=EN

Rummel, R. 'Freedom, Democracy, Peace: Power, Democide and War': http://www.hawaii.edu/powerkills/welcome.html

# Environmental threats to security

We want the islands of Tuvalu, our nation, to exist permanently forever and not to be submerged underwater merely due to the selfishness and greed of the industrialized world.

Saufatu Sopoanga, Prime Minister of Tuvalu, at the 2002 World Summit on Sustainable Development (Sopoanga 2002)

## Introduction

Security threats emanating from the 'environment' present humanity with three key political dilemmas:

1    The threats are usually less clear-cut and direct than the other types of threat considered in this study. They are, as Prins describes, 'threats without enemies' (Prins 2002: 107). The threat posed by issues like global warming and ozone depletion may be profound but they are, in the main, still perceived as longer-term creeping emergencies rather than imminent disasters and attacks.
2    Countering the threats is usually costly and requires a significant compromising of economic interests.
3    The threats often can only be countered by globally coordinated political action.

The scale of the human security threat posed by environmental change is difficult to quantify but it is undoubtedly significant and, to a large extent, avoidable given the political will. Probably the most 'securitized' issues of environmental change, at different times since the 1970s, have been: resource scarcity due to population growth, ozone depletion and global warming. The fact that the first of these 'crises' never really materialized and the second one was partially averted by reasonably effective global political action has served to reinforce the notion that contemporary threats posed by environmental change, such as global warming, are potential rather than actual threats and perhaps exaggerated. As a result, despite gradually becoming more of a feature on the global political agenda, environmental issues have tended not to be placed towards the top of the international political 'in tray' of most governments.

However, whilst some of the gravest threats posed by global warming are potential ones which could yet be averted, it is also increasingly apparent that future threats can only be averted by immediate action and that some of the human security impacts are already being felt throughout the world. Even allowing for the lack of certainty in ascribing any given death to global warming, there can be very little doubt that the phenomenon already represents a bigger human security threat (and, for countries like Tuvalu and many others a much clearer national security threat) than terrorism: widely held as the primary concern of global security since the early 2000s. The World Health Organization suggest that around 150,000 deaths a year since the early 1970s can attributed to the gradual rise in temperatures across the world (McMichael, Campbell-Lendrum and Kovats 2004). Even if this is taken to be a wild exaggeration, it must still dwarf the death toll attributable to terrorism.

Indeed, even if we take global warming out of the equation, the WHO estimate that 5 per cent of all deaths in the world due to heart disease are a consequence of air pollution (WHO 2004a). Environmental threats, thus, are not just theoretical future scenarios of apocalypse, they are a 'clear and present danger', as illustrated in Table 6.1.

Some domestic political systems have evolved to a position where the first and second of the aforementioned dilemmas can be overcome. Pressure group advocacy and government learning have gradually led to more long-termist policies being developed mitigating against threats to both human and non-human state residents. Environmental policies in Western Europe and North America have seen economic interests compromised to limit uncertain threats posed to human health and to wildlife. The third dilemma is, of course, beyond governments acting in isolation but is slowly coming to be addressed by an evolving global *epistemic community* and polity. Transnational pressure groups and scientific communities are simultaneously pushing governments to rethink the first and second dilemmas and provide the means for achieving the third. Central to this process is the slow but inexorable realization by governments that environmental threats are 'real' and the apparent 'national interest' may not always serve their citizens' interests. Political dilemmas can always be resolved when this is understood. The three dilemmas presented here are not, in fact, unique to environmental politics. For most states very similar compromises have been made in the name of military security, since – as explored in Chapter 2 – military threats are usually not immediate and require great expense and international diplomatic cooperation to deter. Global, rather than state, political action is necessary for the enhancement of human security in all of the issues considered in this study but it is most crucial in the realm of environmental security.

## The rise of environmental issues in global politics

Global environmental politics is a relatively 'new' dimension of international relations, and of politics in general, but that is not to say that problems of environmental change are in any way new. The extinction of certain species of animals due to human recklessness (for example the dodo) and the diminution of woodland areas through overexploitation are centuries-old phenomena. Ecologism emerged

**Table 6.1** Global deaths from environmental risk factors, 2004

| | | |
|---|---|---|
| 1 | Indoor smoke | 1,965,000 |
| 2 | Water pollution | 1,908,000 |
| 3 | Urban air pollution | 1,152,000 |
| 4 | Lead poisoning | 143,000 |
| 5 | Climate change | 141,000 |
| | Total | 5,309,000 |

Source: Hughes *et al.* (2011).

as a science in the nineteenth century, bringing recognition of natural systemic phenomena like food chains, the carbon cycle and evolution and an understanding of humanity's place within the environment. George Perkins Marsh's *Man and Nature* in 1864 is widely regarded as the first book to use empirical data to prove the effect of human activity on woodlands and waterways (Marsh 1965). Policies to conserve nature, and pressure groups campaigning for conservation, began to emerge in the USA and Western European states in the latter part of the nineteenth century. Yellowstone became the USA's first National Park in 1872 and the British Royal Society for the Protection of Birds (RSPB) became the world's first conservation pressure group (and later the first international pressure group when it extended its membership to countries of the British Empire).

The origins of international policy on an issue of environmental change can be traced back as far as 1889 and an international convention to prevent the spread of the disease *phylloxera* in grapes. This and other agreements such as the 1902 Convention on the Protection of Birds Useful to Agriculture (the first international instrument on animal conservation) were, however, motivated by economic rather than environmental concerns. Wine and internationally traded food were the stake at issue rather than the flora and fauna. At this stage the more abstract value of conservation for reasons of aesthetics or empathy with animals beginning to be witnessed in the politics of North America and Western Europe could not find its way onto the international political agenda, dominated by issues of military and economic security (and particularly the former).

The 1960s saw a significant rise in prominence of environmental issues in North America and Western Europe and the emergence of environmental politics, beyond purely economic concerns, on the international political agenda. A major factor in this was the publication of Rachel Carson's hugely influential pollution polemic *Silent Spring* in 1962 (see Box 6.1). *Silent Spring* most notably highlighted the effects of the insecticide dichloro-diphenyl-trichloroethane (DDT) on wild animals, vegetation and rivers, and quickly influenced US insecticide policy on conservation grounds. The book also, however, considered the implications for human health of indiscriminate insecticide use and this aspect began the process of forcing environmental change onto the global political agenda and securitizing some of the many issues in this area. In the wake of *Silent Spring* new political concerns began to be voiced, such as with the effects of *acid rain* (rainwater polluted by industrial emissions), and older issues such as oil pollution by tankers were given far more prominence.[1]

Heightened concern with the human health effects of pollution and other forms of environmental change at the global level was confirmed by the convening by the UN of the 1972 Conference on the Human Environment (UNCHE) at Stockholm. The Conference was boycotted by the USSR and its Eastern Bloc allies but attended by representatives of 113 states. The Stockholm Conference did not directly produce a new body of international law but had a catalytic effect in identifying some key principles which challenged the conventions of state sovereignty and in putting environmental change permanently on the agenda of international politics. 'Principle 21' confirmed that states retained full sovereign authority over resources located in their own territory but charged them with the responsibility to exploit them with regard to the effect of this on the environment

## Box 6.1 Rachel Carson

Rachel Carson, correctly, is widely feted as having launched environmentalism as a political ideology in the early 1960s with her hugely influential magnum opus *Silent Spring*. The title of the book forewarns of a future world without the songs of birds and is best remembered for highlighting the harmful effects of DDT on wildlife. The book also, however, pioneered awareness of the human health repercussions associated with the use of DDT and other chemicals.

Born in Pennsylvania in 1907, Carson became a marine biologist in an age when women scientists were extremely rare. Her determination to succeed against the odds saw her publish *Silent Spring* in 1962 despite a long-standing fight with cancer and attempts to block its publication by a hostile chemical industry. The book had been serialized in the *New Yorker* magazine prior to its release and caused such interest that chemical companies began fearing a consumer backlash against their products and mounted vitriolic attacks on the scientific authenticity of the work. The attacks failed to prevent the book becoming a major success commercially and politically, both in the USA and across the developed world. Carson succumbed to cancer just two years after the release of the book; a disease the causes of which she had done so much to increase the understanding of. She was at least able to witness before her death the beginning of legislation being passed to curb the use of polluting chemicals and the birth of a new political era.

of other states ('the polluter pays principle'). The parties to the Conference also agreed to acknowledge the concept of a 'common heritage of mankind' whereby resources located outside of territorial borders (such as minerals on the deep seabed) should be considered as belonging to the international community collectively, rather than being subject to a 'finders keepers/losers weepers' approach to their ownership. Stockholm did have a direct institutional legacy with the creation of the United Nations Environmental Programme (UNEP) giving a degree of permanence to the policy area on the international stage. Overall, the conference's most significant legacy was in putting environmental questions firmly on the political agenda by prompting many governments to create new ministers and departments of the environment and greatly deepening and widening a global network of environmental pressure groups.

Although Stockholm did not securitize environmental change and put it at the top of an international political agenda still, in spite of détente, dominated by the Cold War and impending global recession, some 'high politics' was witnessed at the Conference. Swedish Prime Minister Olaf Palme used the event to denounce the use of herbicides in war as 'ecocide'. Palme made no explicit reference to the recent American use of the infamous jungle defoliant *Agent Orange* in Vietnam, but the implied criticism caused grave offence to the Nixon administration, who responded by withdrawing the US ambassador from Stockholm. Full diplomatic relations between the two countries were suspended for over a year (January 1973–May 1974).

By the 1970s the appreciation by the international community of two key factors help explain the rise to prominence of an issue area which so challenged the traditional logic of international relations.

## Pollution does not respect frontiers

Acid rain became a contentious issue in the 1960s not just because of the emergence of evidence that rainwater could become contaminated and that this could contaminate ground water and threaten wildlife, but also because it was a problem in some states that could not be resolved by that state's government. Sulphur dioxide and other emissions from the burning of fossil fuels which accumulate in the Earth's atmosphere can return to the surface as precipitation, hundreds of miles from where they departed as fumes. Hence countries particularly faced with this problem, such as Sweden, Norway and Canada, which were at the forefront of the greening of governments that was occurring at the time, found that they could not resolve the problem since the root of it lay in other sovereign states. This form of transboundary pollution most graphically demonstrated the need for international cooperation to resolve certain environmental issues, which was already obvious in the case of states sharing rivers and other forms of water.

In 1979 the Long Range Transboundary Air Pollution Agreement was signed up to by the USA, Canada and most Western European states, establishing cuts across the board in sulphur dioxide and other industrial emissions. That it took so long to reach what was a modest agreement between such friendly states is testimony to the challenges presented by environmental problems to those traditional determinants of government policy: sovereignty, self-sufficiency, the national interest and economic growth. The 1970s also saw the rise of international cooperation on curbing pollution between states sharing common stretches of water. UNEP oversaw the birth of a series of 'Regional Sea Programmes', such as the Mediterranean Action Plan and North Sea Convention, whilst many regimes already in operation for riparians, such as the world's oldest international organization, the Rhine Commission, began to take on environmental as well as navigational dimensions.

## The idea of a global commons

More radical than the utilitarian notion that neighbouring states who shared a problem should work together to resolve it was the idea that emerged in the late 1960s that sovereign control over the common 'goods' of water, air and natural resources was unsustainable. In 1968 the ecologist Garret Hardin used as a parable a warning first aired in the nineteenth century by the economist William Foster-Lloyd on the finite quality of shared resources, known as the 'Tragedy of the Commons'. Foster-Lloyd described how the traditional English village green was endangered because of overgrazing by cattle conventionally open to all villagers. As the practice had gone on for centuries it was assumed that it always could but it had emerged that an increase in the number of cattle above an optimum level could erode the land and ruin the common resource for all. Hardin argued that the village green was analogous to global commons such as clean air, fresh water and high seas fish stocks, endangered by states continuing to exploit or pollute them oblivious to the fact that the cumulative effect of this would eventually be their ruin or depletion (Hardin 1968).

The Tragedy of the Commons concept became influential in the early 1970s with concerns that the economic security of the developed world could be imperilled by the Earth as a whole exceeding its 'carrying capacity'. One manifestation of this was the rise of international political action on population control (see Chapter 4); another was the popularization of the 'limits to growth' thesis which argued that increases in industrial production and economic growth in developed countries would have to be checked. Two very different solutions to the Tragedy of the Commons parable can be found. First, you could have informed collective management to regulate use of the village green for the benefit of all. Second, you could abandon the idea of common land and divide the green up into individual holdings in the expectation that each plot holder would graze sustainably, as it would be in their own interests to do so since the costs could not be externalized as before. At the global level both types of solutions are evident in the development in the 1970s of international law for a 'commons' already subject to many centuries of contention, the high seas. The 'Common Heritage of Mankind' principle agreed to at Stockholm crystallized ten years later as part of the Third UN Conference on the Law of the Sea (UNCLOS III) with the agreement that deep seabed minerals would be the property of the International Seabed Authority. This form of collective management to sustain collective goods can be contrasted with the encroachment on the tradition of the 'freedom of the seas' by the huge growth of waters claimed by states in the legitimization at UNCLOS III of 200-mile 'Exclusive Economic Zones (EEZs)'. Although EEZs, on the one hand, could easily be accounted for by a conventional Realist analysis of coastal states maximizing their power, the rationale offered for their creation was that fish stocks and other resources would be utilized more sustainably if under sovereign jurisdiction rather than subject to a 'free for all'.

The gradual appreciation of three other challenges posed by environmental change questions to conventional state-to-state relations since the mid-1980s has elevated this realm of international politics to a higher diplomatic level and securitized some of the issues.

## *Localized environmental problems can become global problems*

Although transboundary pollution and the management of the global commons were, by the 1980s, firmly on the international political agenda, the majority of the harmful effects of environmental change seemed only to be felt locally and, as such, were of little concern to the international community. Domestic legislation in the developed world had banned the use of notoriously polluting chemicals like DDT and curbed the excesses of industrial emissions and waste disposal, leading to visible improvements in animal conservation and better standards of human health. However, the emergence of evidence that seemingly remote problems, experienced primarily in LDCs, had wider repercussions served to bring a number of new environmental issues to global political prominence.

Deforestation, seen for a number of years as a problem for forest-dwelling wildlife and humans, was cast in new light by the discovery of the 'carbon-sink effect', the fact that trees absorb atmospheric carbon dioxide. Carbon dioxide in the atmosphere above a certain level is poisonous to man and at a lesser level contributes to global warming. It has been estimated that the loss of trees in the world contributes more to global warming than the much-trumpeted impact of transport (Stern 2006). The realization that the net loss of tropical rainforest could, ultimately, harm North American and European urban residents as well as Amazonian Amerindians helped bring this issue to the global political agenda. Similarly, seemingly localized 'Tragedy of the Commons' issues such as desertification have repercussions beyond the most directly affected peoples since the world food supply will be influenced by the removal of once-fertile land from production. The increased economic globalization of the world can bring external environmental problems into the domestic arena. Harmful organochlorine insecticides may have been virtually eliminated from use in developed countries by the 1980s but their continued use, promoted by Northern MNCs, deprived of a domestic market, was seeing them return to their places of origin in imported foodstuffs.

## Some environmental problems are global in scale

The securitization of certain environmental issues on the global stage has tended to occur when full realization dawns amongst governments that the problem is genuinely global in its scale. Deforestation and desertification have not been securitized because, ultimately, they are still perceived by many as localized problems with some wider implications. By contrast, it is widely accepted that ozone depletion and global warming are not problems that governments can protect their citizens from by domestic legislation or by regional political cooperation with like-minded neighbouring states. In addition, these are not problems caused by LDCs that are being exported northwards. They are problems that are principally caused by Northern democracies with potentially dire consequences for the whole world, or 'global security' in its full sense.

## Environmental issues are inseparable from global economic issues

The vast majority of environmental problems are related in some way to the processes of economic development and growth, which have dominated how governments frame their policies both domestically and in the global marketplace.

Industrialization and urbanization, the classic ingredients of development, put increased strain on a country's resources, whilst changing its pattern of land use and altering nature's own 'balance of power'. Increased industrial and agricultural production invariably brings more pollution as well as more raw materials, food and wealth. The fundamental paradox of how to reconcile economic security with environmental concerns was apparent at Stockholm but shelved through the desire to demonstrate solidarity but, by the 1980s, it could no longer be ignored. By then it had become clear that global environmental policy was being stymied because, although the developed world was coming to terms (albeit partially) with the need to embrace a 'limits to growth' approach, LDCs would not compromise economic security since the stakes were so much higher. As Indian President Indira Gandhi announced at Stockholm in 1972 the world should not forget that 'poverty is the worst pollution'.

In an effort to get around this problem, the UN General Assembly in 1987 set up a World Commission on Environment and Development, chaired by Norwegian Prime Minister Gro Harlem Brundtland (see Box 7.1). The 'Brundtland Commission' produced a report entitled 'Our Common Future', which identified *sustainable development* as the solution to the economic–environmental paradox, and this soon became the guiding ethos for future global environmental policy. Sustainable development sought to win the backing of LDCs for environmental policy by reassuring them that this would not compromise their political priority of achieving economic development. The Global North would have to take the lead in implementing costly anti-pollution measures and recognize that the South would need more time to follow suit. To the South this was only fair since the North was responsible for most global pollution and had been able to develop without constraints being put on their industrialization; to many in the North this was the only way to win support from LDCs who would eventually come to be major global polluters also.

Sustainable development is less pessimistic than the 'limits to growth' thesis, which dominated environmental policy thinking in the 1970s, in that it does not consider economic growth to be anathema to avoiding pollution and the depletion of the Earth's resources. Economic growth, even for wealthy states, is fine so long as it is at a level that can be sustained in the long run and not at the cost of degrading the environment. Hence sustainable development tries to speak the language of the 'rational actor' by calling upon governments to be more long-termist in their economic policy. Rapid economic growth today may enrich the present generation but risk impoverishing or endangering future generations if resources are not utilized in a sustainable and responsible manner. Sustainable development is also, however, less optimistic about the future than the approach to the Earth and its resources adopted by a number of thinkers and statesmen. The non-arrival of a demographic doomsday of the sort forecast by Malthus back in the eighteenth century or by the 'neo-Malthusians' in the 1970s has prompted some 'Cornucopians' to suggest that economic growth need not be restrained at all since technological progress and human ingenuity can be relied upon to surmount future problems. Lomberg's 2001 work *The Sceptical Environmentalist*, for example, attracted great interest (and great derision from ecologists) for questioning whether implementing international policy on global warming made any rational sense. Lomberg did not deny that global warming was a human-caused problem but suggested that it is not as significant a threat as it had been painted and that the expenditure to be allocated to tackling the problem would be better spent on addressing global poverty (Lomberg 2001). Cornucopians and neo-Malthusian 'limits to growth' advocates are still prominent positions in the dialogue on global environmental policy but sustainable development, holding the middle ground, has become the principal guiding ethos of the international regimes that have emerged since the 1990s.

The Brundlandt Report prompted the UN General Assembly in 1989 to approve a twenty-year follow-up conference to Stockholm to flesh out the concept of sustainable development. As the title indicates, the 1992 UN Conference on the Environment and Development (UNCED), held in Rio de Janeiro, recognized the need to couple together the two issue areas and was a much larger and more diverse gathering than in 1972. A total of 170 states were represented, most at some stage by their heads of government, and some 1,400 pressure groups were also present at the myriad formal and informal meetings that characterized the conference. In contrast at Stockholm, twenty years earlier, only two heads of government and 134 pressure groups had attended. Although decision-making authority was reserved for government delegates the pressure groups at Rio played a pivotal role in organizing the event and in the extensive lobbying of the decision-makers.

Amongst twenty-seven general principles agreed to in the 'Rio Declaration' at the summit were two particularly important breakthroughs. Principle 7 identified the 'common but differentiated responsibilities' of developed and less-developed states in environmental protection, a key aspect of the sustainable development concept. The Global South were part of the process but the North would have to take the lead and incur most of the initial costs. Principle 15 acknowledged the legitimacy of the 'precautionary principle' in developing environmental policy. This strengthens the meaning of sustainable development by proposing that a lack of absolute scientific certainty over the harmful side-effects of some form of economic activity widely believed to be environmentally damaging, should not be used as an excuse to continue with it. This was an important agreement because issues of environmental change tend to be complex and subject to some level of scientific disagreement. In the face of this, excuses can readily be found for ignoring environmental demands and the case for continuing to favour unhindered economic growth strategies appear stronger.

Like Stockholm, the Rio Summit did not create international law at a stroke but, unlike Stockholm, it did explicitly set the signatory governments on a legislatory path. 'Agenda 21' of UNCED set out a programme of action for implementing sustainable development across a range of environmental issues. Some forty chapters, detailing the issues to be regulated and the means of effectively doing so, made up Agenda 21. Issues debated in recent years but not yet subject to conventions, such as deforestation and hazardous waste management, were formally given approval for action. A Commission for Sustainable Development was established to regularly review progress towards establishing and implementing the conventions that were to follow. In addition, a crucial tenet of sustainable development was realized in the creation of a fund subsidized by developed countries, the Global Environment Facility, upon which LDCs could draw.

The ten-year follow-up to Rio, the World Summit on Sustainable Development (WSSD) in Johannesburg in 2002, represented the third environmental 'mega-conference' but was more low key than its predecessor. It was also noticeably more focused on development rather than the environment. Little progress was made in advancing the agenda on species conservation (biodiversity) established at Rio and, although global warming policy was kept alive it was not developed in any significant way. New proposals to erect a framework for phasing in the use of renewable energy sources and improving LDC access to developed world food markets were side-stepped but some new goals were set. The target date of 2015 was set for the realization of two new human security aims: halving the number of people who lack access to clean water and achieving sustainability in global fishing.

## The environment and military security

The 1990s also saw environmental issues given greater concern in foreign policy-making circles through the partially widened security notion that some issues of environmental change should be considered the stuff of high politics, because they can have knock-on military effects. The end of the Cold War, again, was significant in widening the focus of foreign policy-makers to see dangers other than those facing them at the other side of the balance of terror 'seesaw', but the roots of this idea can be traced back to the rise of concerns about securing key economic resources in the 1970s.

The oil crises of 1973–4 and 1979 shook international relations practically and academically. The academic dominance of Classical Realism, which stressed the uppermost primacy of military power in calculating the 'national interest' by which state foreign policy should be guided, was toppled by a recognition of the importance of economic power in state relations. Neo-Realists, such as Waltz (1979), revamped the old paradigm to accommodate non-military components of power into its framework of analysis based on competitive state-to-state relations. At the same time Pluralists, such as Keohane and Nye (1977), felt vindicated that a more cooperative-based and multi-faceted model of how politics is conducted at the international level was shown to be needed by the rise to prominence of military dwarfs such as Saudi Arabia and Kuwait in the global arena. In the 'real' world of international relations the 'Carter Doctrine', announced in 1980, made it plain that questions relating to the economic resources of distant states would enter into the calculations of the US national interest by stating that military action to secure oil imports and other economic interests was a possibility.

The rise to high politics of oil pricing prompted greater scrutiny of the importance of threats to the supply of key economic resources to states. The 1970s also saw the rise in concerns that global overpopulation could drain the world's resources (see Chapter 4) and greater recognition that resources could be threatened by environmental degradation as well as through political action. It was not until the 1990s, however, when the agenda of international politics was allowed to broaden, that environmental degradation as a potential state security threat began to take prominence in academia and mould the thinking of foreign policy-makers. Economic statecraft had been revived as an instrument of foreign policy by the oil crises but, interestingly, it was not until the strategic constraints of the Cold War had been lifted that a full manifestation of the Carter Doctrine was put into practice with the US-led action against Iraq in the Gulf War. A just war and long-awaited display of collective security it may have been, but few would dispute that securing oil supplies was a key motivation for the allied forces action.

Whether one takes a positive (moral) or cynical (wealth maximization) view of the allied action, the Gulf War represented a use of military might to preserve stability rather than counter a direct military threat (apart from the perspective of the Gulf States). In this light a strand of IR inquiry emerged in the New World Order era to consider if threats to stability due to environmental degradation were possible and hence something that should be of concern to Realist-minded foreign policy-makers. Canadian academic Homer-Dixon has been at the forefront of this area of study, leading teams of researchers since the 1990s in exploring the possibility of causal links between environmentally induced resource depletion and military conflict. His extensive research leads him to claim that links can be shown to exist. 'Environmental scarcities are already contributing to violent conflicts in many parts of the world. These conflicts are probably the early signs of an upsurge of violence in the coming decades that will be induced or aggravated by scarcity' (Homer-Dixon 1994: 6).

Homer-Dixon's research focused on LDCs since his belief was that such states were less likely to adapt to the social effects of environmental degradation than developed countries and thus are more prone to this form of conflict. Hence, Homer-Dixon does not postulate that environmental scarcity leads directly to conflict but that it can be a root cause of social unrest that can spill over into violent unrest. In line with explanations of famine, environmental scarcity (of, for example, fish or fertile soil) occurs through the interplay of three factors: the supply of resources, the demand for resources, and changes in the distribution of resources. Two phenomena, emerging from changes in the three factors, are identified by Homer-Dixon as the key link between environmental scarcity and social unrest: 'resource capture' and 'ecological marginalization'. Resource capture occurs when elites within a state respond to falls in supply or rises in demand by appropriating more resources for themselves and leave the poorer sections of society to bear the brunt of scarcity. Ecological marginalization is said to occur when population growth and/or changes in access to resources for certain sections of the populus produce migrations which cause the overexploitation of resources in certain areas (Homer-Dixon 1994: 10–11).

Case studies, undertaken by colleagues of Homer-Dixon to illustrate his thesis, included the Senegal River conflict of 1980 and the civil war in Peru between the government and Shining Path. The Senegal River conflict was considered an illustration of how 'resource capture' can lead to conflict. An ethnic conflict between the politically dominant Arabic Mauers and black Mauritanians followed the expropriation of black land by Mauers. This land grab was in response to scarcity resulting from a rise in land prices due to a damming project. Ethnic Senegalese number amongst the black Mauritanian population and Maures number among the population of neighbouring Senegal, causing the ethnic unrest to become internationalized. In Peru the rise of Shining Path can be attributed more to the 'ecological marginalization' of peasant farmers in the mountainous areas of the country than their ideological conversion to Maoism (Homer-Dixon and Percival 1996).

The spillover of conflict from Mauritania to Senegal led Homer-Dixon to consider that river water is the only renewable resource likely to precipitate inter-state conflict (Homer-Dixon 1994) but his research has generally concluded that environmentally inspired conflict is most likely to be civil rather than international. The weakening of states, however, contributes to regional instability and can still be construed as a security issue for other states, it is contended.

The work of Homer-Dixon, and other prominent US academics such as Kaplan (1994), certainly convinced the US government in the early 1990s that environmental degradation represented a potential source of military insecurity. In 1993 a new government position in the Defense Department was created, the Deputy Under Secretary for Environmental Security, and the Environmental Task Force was set up as part of Washington's intelligence network. The introduction to the 1994 National Security Strategy Document, an annual government statement of foreign policy aims, states that 'an emerging class of transnational environmental issues are increasingly affecting international stability and consequently present new challenges to U.S. strategy' (USA 1994: 1). The launch of a UK National Security Strategy in 2009 similarly focused on climate change and was accompanied by the appointment of a new 'Climate and Energy Security Envoy' Rear Admiral Neil Morisetti.

Despite its influence on US government thinking the approach of framing environmental scarcity as military security has not been without its critics. The empirical evidence linking environmental degradation and political conflict is, by Homer-Dixon's own admission, not straightforward, prompting scepticism as to whether other variables are the real causes of conflicts in situations where environmental scarcity can be demonstrated. Smith, for example, points out that the Senegal River conflict was more about ethnic and class conflict than access to river water (Smith 1994). Levy criticizes the Homer-Dixon-led research on the grounds that the fact that only LDCs are chosen as case studies is a tacit admission that general poverty, rather than environmental change, is the root cause of the conflicts analysed.

> it is difficult to imagine how conflict in any developing country could not involve renewable resources. Developing country elites fight over renewable resources for the same reason that Willy Sutton robbed banks – that's where the money is.
>
> (Levy 1995: 45)

The environmental scarcity literature focuses on the competition for non-renewable resources as a new, de-stabilizing trend in post-Cold War international relations, referred to by Rogers as 'prologue wars' heralding a new era (Rogers 2000: 79). However, just as it can be shown that resource wars are nothing new, neither are conflicts with a non-renewable resources dimension. The 1969 'Football War' between El Salvador and Honduras, despite its linkage to a volatile World Cup qualifying match between the two national sides, echoed the River Senegal dispute in that its main cause was ethnic tension created by migration and its effects on land rights. Even two of the wealthiest and most democratically mature states, Iceland and the UK, had a major diplomatic dispute with a limited military dimension over fishing rights in the 1970s 'Cod Wars'. In respect to the much vaunted coming of 'water wars', Gleick points out that such conflicts go back five thousand years and lists a number of them including an ancient 'dambuster' raid by Alexander the Great of Greece against Persia between 355 and 323 BC (Gleick 1994). If the focus is narrowed to domestic upheaval then it is probably fair to suggest that most popular revolutions have had questions relating to access to productive land at their core. Equally, an abundance of resources can be a source of contention as much as a scarcity. Iraqi oil has made it the foremost international military battleground of recent years and the geological fortune to possess rich diamond reserves has been the political misfortune of countries such as the Congo and Sierra Leone. Of course access to resources causes political upheaval. It was ever thus.

Not only are 'water wars' nothing new, they barely register in an analysis of modern military history. Despite a spate of publications warning of the likelihood of conflicts fought to secure freshwater supplies, particularly in the arid and volatile Middle East (Starr 1991; Bullock and Adel 1993), no war of this kind was fought in the twentieth century and it has played little part in Arab–Israeli hostilities (Libiszewski 1995). A burgeoning 'anti-resource war' literature has emerged providing empirical evidence that cooperative responses to increased resource scarcity are more common than conflictual ones (Salehyan 2008; Reuveny 2008; Nordas and Gleditsch 2007). A three-year empirical project carried out by a team at Oregon State University provides solid grounds for suggesting that international quarrels over water resources are invariably dealt with cooperatively rather than inducing conflict. The study found that there had been 1,831 international political interactions over water in the previous 50 years of which none had produced war and only 507 instigated a dispute (two-thirds of these disputes were purely verbal and only 37 had any armed dimension). In contrast 1,228 of those international water interactions produced cooperative responses including 157 treaties (Wolf 2007). There is no evidence that fighting over depleting resources is in any way a distinguishing feature of the contemporary world.

Securing access to resources, it could be argued, is becoming more critical when parts of the world are depleting life-supporting non-renewable resources, such as in the process of desertification, but responsible management and cooperation is a more rational and fruitful political response than conflict. Again, as with problems of famine, the democratic peace thesis leaves room for optimism that we are not entering an era of resource wars. Democracies are forced to confront resource allocation questions as a matter of course and, increasingly, act on environmental degradation even if no obvious human side-effect is apparent. In addition, democracies (and some non-democracies) long ago came to the conclusion that resources are more easily secured through trade and common management than conflict. Access to fishing beds on the high seas is an issue of great importance in many states and international competition to secure rights remains fierce, but the threat of the global depletion of certain species has prompted unilateral acts such as the Canadian suspension of cod fishing from the 1990s and the EU's unpopular but necessary conservation co-management strategy, the Common Fisheries Policy. There is scope for optimism that resources can be managed by most states in the present state system but the much increased likelihood of scarcity due to global warming could yet see the resource wars scenario become a reality.

## Environmental issues themselves as threats to security

Whereas much of the 'environmental security' literature to emerge in the 1990s focused on adding environmental degradation to the list of conventional concerns used to discern the potential military threats emanating from other states, a more profound school of thought arose around the same time arguing for a deepening of the meaning of security to incorporate issues of environmental change. Ullman, in pioneering the re-evaluation of security in 1983, sought to cast the concept in a less statist light by including within its remit the security of individuals imperilled by resource scarcity rather than just tacking on a new category of threats to the security of states (Ullman 1983). By the end of the decade it was not only warming East–West Cold War relations but the apparent actual warming of the Earth that brought environmental threats to security to the fore of international political concern.

In a 1989 article for the conservative and influential journal *Foreign Affairs*, Jessica Mathews, a former member of the US government's National Security Council, followed Ullman's line of reasoning in a more state-centred analysis. In addition to calling for greater consideration of the effects of resource depletion on the political stability of poorer states, Mathews argued that environmental problems with global ramifications, such as ozone depletion, climate change and deforestation, should become issues of state security concern because they were the underlying cause of regional instability (Mathews 1989).

### Environmental threats to human security

#### Ozone depletion

In 1985 the British Antarctic Survey were able to prove conclusively what had been suspected by scientists for at least a decade, that the Earth's ozone layer had a hole in it. The ozone layer is a protective gaseous shell in the upper atmosphere which absorbs ultraviolet rays from the sun before they reach the Earth's surface. This is a vital service for humanity (and other life forms) since ultraviolet radiation can claim lives in the form of skin cancer and other serious ailments.

The 'clear and present danger' posed by the loss of this defensive shield prompted an unusually rapid international response. Within a few months of the British Antarctic Survey discovery the Vienna Convention on Protection of the Ozone Layer established a framework treaty, fleshed out two years later in the 1987 Montreal Protocol on Substances That Deplete the Ozone Layer. The 1987 Montreal Protocol saw twenty-four industrialized states bind themselves to an agreement for major cuts in the future use and emission of chloro-fluoro-carbons

(CFCs) and some other chemicals known to be agents of ozone depletion. In the years since 1987 the regime has been strengthened in a series of amendments deepening the cuts to be made by states and widening its application to most of the world. This was achieved by the application of key sustainable development principles agreed on at Rio with LDCs allowed to take a slower track towards phasing out CFCs than the developed states and a Multilateral Fund created to overcome the costs of implementing the agreements. The success of the regime can be witnessed by growing recent evidence that the ozone layer has begun to repair itself (World Meteorological Organization/United Nations Environment Programme 2006).

## Global warming

Surely the clearest case of how environmental change can become an issue of security is in the threat posed by global warming. The Earth's average temperature has risen consistently over the last century and it is now almost universally accepted that this is more than a natural development and likely to accelerate if not responded to. The central cause of global warming is an exacerbation of the natural phenomenon of the 'greenhouse effect', caused by increased industrial emissions. Increased releases of carbon dioxide and methane over the years, principally through the burning of fossil fuels, served to exaggerate the natural tendency of the atmosphere to trap a certain amount of infrared sunlight after it is reflected from the Earth's surface. The implications of this are various but include increased desertification and a raising of sea levels due to the polar ice caps melting, both carrying significant threats to human life (see Table 6.1).

The *Framework Convention on Climate Change* emerged two years after Rio and was fleshed out in the Kyoto Protocol of 1997. Most of the world's states committed themselves to cuts in 'greenhouse gases', to be phased in over time and differentiating between developed and less developed states. The costs to developed states of implementing the cuts were significant enough to prompt a rebellion not seen in the ozone regime negotiations. The USA, most notably, broke ranks and failed to ratify the protocol despite signing the framework treaty. The US government under Bush Junior cited the lack of scientific certainty over global warming and concerns over the lesser constraints imposed on LDCs but also, crucially, admitted that the treaty is simply not in their 'national interest' because of the economic cost. Although scientific uncertainties inevitably still exist over an issue as complex as climate change, a definitive epistemic consensus has emerged from the UN's Intergovernmental Panel on Climate Change since its establishment in 1988. By their fourth report in 2007 this substantial grouping of the world's top climatologists were able to pronounce, in the cautious words of science, that it was between 90 and 95 per cent certain that global warming was caused by human action (Intergovernmental Panel on Climate Change 2007). Despite the undoubted costs to the US exchequer of implementing Kyoto, which would be far beyond those for any other state, this hard-headed economic calculation is increasingly questionable. The 2006 'Stern Review', compiled by a British economist on behalf of the UK government, calculated the cost of non-action on climate change as amounting to at the very least 5 per cent of global GDP for ever more. Set against this, the costs of effective action to curb climate change would cost around 1 per cent of global GDP per year (Stern 2006).

Global warming is a global problem, in both cause and effect, but the scale of human security threat is not equal across the globe. For low-lying island states the prospect of a rise in the level of the oceans is a human and state security threat of the utmost gravity. The governments of the Maldives and Kiribati have already made plans to shift there entire populations to other locations. For other states the threat is seen as far more remote, both geographically and chronologically, and the urgency to act, which is generally needed for governments to ratify costly environmental agreements, is not there. Indeed, it should be noted that the Stern Review was very much a cost–benefit analysis and, whilst noting that globally the balance is undoubtedly weighted in favour of the former, it makes clear that some parts of the world could experience net gains from fewer cold-related deaths, and the increased revenue from tourism and improved agricultural fertility. Even in the part of the world most dramatically affected by climate change opinion in divided. A Greenlandic government minister has articulated this: 'Because of the warming of the sea the halibut are multiplying faster, and the fisheries have never been so good as they are now ... Because of global warming our rivers and lakes have never been so full. We have lots of water and we want to use it for hydro power' (Cathcart 2007). It is also apparent that many of the threats identified in Table 6.2 could be averted by human adaptation to a changing landscape. Technological solutions have also come to be suggested in the emerging science of *geoengineering*. One example of this is solar radiation management through measures such as releasing reflective aerosols into the atmosphere. The technical and economic feasibility of such measures remains to be established.

The threat posed by global warming, however, is not just a theoretical future scenario. The human cost is already significant and is not just confined to the developing world, where other factors can more easily be employed to explain mortality figures. The Global North has been rocked by events such as the heatwaves that struck Western Europe in 2004 and Russia in 2010, both of which killed around 50,000 people. Whilst proving categorically whether such single

**Table 6.2** Ten major security threats posed by global warming

* More frequent and lengthy heatwaves
* More frequent droughts
* Coastal flooding due to sea level rises
* Reduced crop yields due to reduced rainfall
* Spread of tropical diseases north and south
* Increased rate of water-borne diseases in flooded areas
* Ocean acidification due to carbon dioxide affecting fish stocks
* More frequent and stronger riverine flooding in wet seasons due to glaciers melting/reduced water supply in dry season
* Increased incidences of wildfires
* More frequent and stronger windstorms

events are attributable to global warming is impossible, the changes noted in Table 6.2 are already occurring and this overall trend cannot be put down to chance.

## Persistent organic pollutants (POPs)

The 1992 Rio Summit was also the catalyst for significant global political action in the area of human health-threatening atmospheric pollution. UNEP's Governing Council in 1997 endorsed the opinion of the UNCED-born Intergovernmental Forum on Chemical Safety that an international, binding treaty be set up to phase out the production and use of twelve POPs including eight organochlorine pesticides and polychlorinated biphenyl (PCB) (Decision No: 19/13c). The Treaty was signed by 127 governments at a Diplomatic Conference in Stockholm in May 2001, initiating a regime that will continue to consider adding new chemicals to the original twelve through a Review Committee. Born of UNCED, forged by UNEP and long promoted by environmental pressure groups, the POPs regime, on the face of it, appears to represent a triumph of environmentalism. There is little doubt, however, that the primary motivation of the signatories was the alleviation of the suffering of their own nationals by these chemicals rather than concerns for the fates of birds, fish or atmospheric quality. 'This new treaty will protect present and future generations from the cancers, birth defects, and other tragedies caused by POPs' (Buccini 2000).

The production and use of the twelve outlawed chemicals has long ceased in most developed countries but their properties ensure that they remain a domestic hazard to their populations. The listed chemicals are all highly persistent, have a propensity to travel globally in the atmosphere through a continual process of evaporation and deposition and tend to bioaccumulate in human foodstuffs. Hence, sterility, neural disorders and cancer in peoples of the developed world can be attributed to the use of organochlorines in other parts of the planet. The political significance of this is such that even President George W. Bush, already known as the 'Toxic Texan' for his administration's lack of enthusiasm for environmental concerns, declared the USA to be a firm supporter of international political action on POPs.

## Deforestation

An appreciation of the role of forests as *carbon sinks* gave the problem of the overexploitation of forests throughout the world a clearer human security dimension and prompted efforts, principally by Northern states, to set up a convention on forests at the Rio Summit. These negotiations failed, resulting only in a weak, non-legally binding agreement known as *The Forest Principles* which proclaims the virtues of sustainable forestry management but, in effect, gives the green light to states to continue deforesting by asserting that forests are sovereign resources. Effectively regulating deforestation is too much of an economic burden for most prolific 'logging' states to countenance and it is not seen as sufficiently threatening to human security to prompt other states to exercise greater leverage on them. Again, however, this attitude is a case of not being able to 'see the trees for the wood'. Deforestation exacerbates global warming and can be seen as a causal factor behind natural disasters such as mudslides down once naturally secure hillsides (see Chapter 8) (Humphreys 2006: 1).

## Desertification

Perhaps the clearest manifestation of the 'Tragedy of the Commons' effect in the world over recent years has been the process of desertification, whereby deserts have grown in size at the expense of fertile lands surrounding them. Once land becomes arid in this way it is effectively lost forever in terms of its productive value and so can have food security implications for the local population and, to a limited extent, humanity at large. Recognition of this prompted the 1994 Convention to Combat Desertification which sets out a code of practice for the management of semi-arid lands. The convention was unusual in global environmental politics in that it was prompted by LDCs rather than the industrialized states. It was principally African states, affected by the spread of the Sahara and Kalahari deserts, who championed the inclusion of this issue in Article 21 of the Rio Summit (Chapter 12). The regime has evolved slowly since 1994 and, although it is now virtually global in scope, it lacks any of the legal rigour of its ozone depletion or global warming counterparts. The lack of a clear human security dimension for all states has stunted its development.

## Biodiversity

Other issues of environmental change have come to be framed in anthropocentric or human security terms. In 2008 The Economics of Ecosystems and Biodiversity (TEEB), a think-tank funded by the EU and German government 'did a Stern Report' on a classically ecocentric issue somewhat put in the shade by the politics of climate change. The TEEB review posited that global GDP would be likely to decline by 7 per cent by 2050 if greater commitment to preserving fish stocks, forests and other species needed by humanity was not given (Sukhdev 2008). Released against a backdrop of unprecedented rises in global food and energy prices this seemed a particularly pertinent warning.

## Evaluating environmental security

Deudney is a foremost challenger to the inclusion of environmental issues within the remit of security politics. He cites three key arguments for not extending the reach of Security Studies to incorporate issues he, nonetheless, considers as important political concerns.

> 1. It is analytically misleading to think of environmental degradation as a national security threat, because the traditional focus of national security – interstate violence – has little in common with either environmental problems or solutions.

2. The effort to harness the emotive power of nationalism to help mobilize environmental awareness and action may prove counterproductive by undermining globalist political stability.

3. Environmental degradation is not very likely to cause interstate wars.

(Deudney 1990: 461)

Deudney's reasoning, unlike that of many critics, is not that of the refusenik military strategist irritated by greens encroaching on his turf but comes from a sincere belief that securitizing the environment undermines rather than enhances the likelihood of finding appropriate political solutions to environmental problems. Point three is a direct rebuttal of the Homer-Dixon-led approach of coupling certain environmental issues with military security which, as discussed in the previous section, is open to challenge. Point two rightly implies that global problems require global responses rather than relying on individual state calculations of rationality, a standard challenge presented by environmental problems to the traditional statist national interest-based model of how foreign policies should be constructed. The weakness in Deudney's argument, however, comes from a statist bias in another way. Nationalism is, indeed, an inappropriate political ideology to tackle most environmental problems but who has ever proposed this as a solution to global warming or pollution? Environmental problems are, indeed, fundamentally distinct from the problem of interstate violence but why does this preclude them from being security concerns? Deudney, in common with most traditionalists, conflates 'security' with 'something that requires a military response by the state' rather than seeing it as a condition which relates to people's lives and which can be acted upon at various political levels. 'Both violence and environmental degradation may kill people and may reduce human well-being, but not all threats to life and property are threats to security' (Deudney 1990: 463). This represents an explicit admission that 'security' can have no meaning other than as a synonym for 'military defence against other states'. Real security needs of people and of the whole planet are excluded by such blinkered logic. The fact that a problem cannot be solved by conventional thinking and means does not indicate that the problem should be ignored but rather that the thinking should be improved and new types of solution sought.

Threats related to the environment confront the inadequacies of conventional state-centred thinking in International Relations most profoundly of all. Dyer argues that global environmental change represents the greatest security challenge to the world because it is 'seen as an externality to the international system, rather than an internal variable which can be addressed in terms of familiar political structures and their supporting social values' (Dyer 2000: 139). Global warming potentially threatens the security of all life on Earth (and the states they inhabit) and it is a threat which does not emanate from any particular state and which cannot be averted by any particular state, regardless of its economic or military capabilities. Dyer refers to this conundrum as a new type of *security dilemma* soluble only by new, global political structures (2000: 139). In a similar vein, Myers has termed environmental security 'ultimate security' (Myers 1993).

The failings of individualistic, rather than collective rationality in decision-making in certain problem-solving situations is familiarly portrayed in game theory analogies such as the 'prisoner's dilemma' (Box 6.2). The Prisoner's Dilemma can easily be recast as a 'polluter's dilemma' facing states operating in the international system when confronted with certain environmental issues. The question 'to pollute or not to pollute?', when applied to the atmosphere or waters, can yield different 'rational' answers. The economic costs incurred by curbing pollution allied to the fact that the negative effects of the pollution might be slight or even borne elsewhere, could lead the rationally acting state to favour continuing to pollute, particularly if other states choose to curb pollution and lessen the collective problem. If all states were to take such a selfish stance, however, the results for the polluter may become negative, with 'environmental costs' exceeding the costs of political action. Recent political diplomacy on measures to combat global warming illustrate this dilemma neatly, particularly since the potential costs of failing to think and act collectively are catastrophic.

## Conclusions: towards ecological security?

Global political action on environmental change has seen many issues politicized and put on the international agenda but few securitized at the top of that agenda.

---

### Box 6.2 The Prisoner's Dilemma

Two prisoners are arrested by police for a minor crime both have committed but the police are more interested in securing a confession to convict for a more serious offence they are both implicated for but for which there is no proof. The two prisoners are offered a deal by the police whilst being held in separate cells. Each prisoner is told separately:

1   If they confess to the serious crime they can go free, whilst the other prisoner gets a three year sentence.
2   If they both confess they each get a two year sentence.
3   If they both fail to cooperate they will each be convicted of the minor crime and receive a one year sentence.

Thus, each prisoner has two options yielding four possible outcomes; freedom and one, two or three years in prison.

The dilemma demonstrates the complexity of rational decision-making when other decision-makers are involved in the process. Simultaneously, the best and worst option is to cooperate with the police. The 'safe' option of staying silent depends on a level of trust in the other prisoner in order to avoid the heavier sentence. According to individual rationality the best choice might be to confess but, if collective rationality is employed, then the best outcome is for both to stay silent.

---

Myriad international regimes have emerged since the high water mark of environmental governance at Rio in 1992 but global policy today stands in stark contrast to the domestic environmental laws of Western European and North American states which are marked by precautionary consumer standards and non-human conservation measures. Where successful international environmental regimes have emerged it has been where a clear and unambigious human health threat is apparent.

It is far rarer for the value of environmental protection to be prioritized at the global level than it is at the domestic level. Global politics is such that international agreements, to which governments remain the signatories in spite of the growing role of pressure groups, are still somewhat reliant on a perception of utilitarian gain. Although it is becoming ever more blurred, a 'high politics–low politics' distinction is still evident in international politics. Governments are still prone to taking blinkered decisions informed by economic interest in the face of epistemic consensus and longer-term utilitarian calculations of 'national interest', as witnessed by the USA's stance on global warming.

There is a need for global environmental policy to go beyond knee-jerk reactions to disasters or imminent disasters if it is to properly enhance human (and indeed non-human) security. The evolution of global governance should eventually realize this. Only through the holistic management of environmental threats can the Prisoners Dilemma scenario be escaped and states be freed to act in their and their people's real interests rather than being compelled by domestic political constraints to conserve harmful human practices. The European Union's Common Fisheries Policy is often vilified in its maritime member-states because it stops fishermen fishing as they have always done but is still a highly necessary system since it prevents the exhaustion of fish stocks to everyone's detriment. Seeing the bigger picture is difficult in a politically compartmentalized world but it is gradually happening through the growth of a global civil society and epistemic communities persuading governments and citizens that it is in their own interests to think global.

Dalby argues that the key to safeguarding human security in issues such as climate change and resource depletion is to cease framing such problems in the context of 'environmental threats'. Considering human activity as an integral part of the Earth's biosphere, rather than something related to but distinct from 'the environment', is a central tenet of Ecologism and its emphasis on giving greater value to non-human life forms, but can be understood also as a means of preserving the human species. Dalby defines security in terms of a referent object which is the global totality: 'the assurance of relatively undisturbed ecological systems in all parts of the biosphere' (Dalby 2002: 106). Thinking in terms of ecological rather than environmental change means that social and economic transformations are not treated as distinct from atmospheric or biological developments in terms of their consequences. Appreciating that human phenomena like urbanization or increasing consumption have effects in the natural world with implications for human security can improve the management of threats. Security threats can be more subtle than the rapid emergence of a hole in the ozone layer and the solutions more complex than switching from the use of CFCs to replacement chemicals. A better appreciation of this complexity could help alleviate these difficulties before they become imminent crises.

Ecologism might be a minority ideology in today's world but most democratic states have political systems that have evolved over time to act in the public good even where this incurs some individual or commercial cost. US environmental policy is robust enough to restrain business interests for the good of the environment and society even though its government has not always behaved this way on the global stage. There is no reason to suppose that global environmental policy cannot evolve in a similar manner but it needs to do so soon before it is too late.

## Key points

- The threat to human security posed by environmental change is mainly an indirect one, by heightening vulnerability to other threats like disease, or a long-term potential one.
- This lack of imminent threat has limited the development of global environmental policy much beyond acting against obvious threats like global warming and ozone depletion.
- The notion that environmental scarcity can prompt military conflicts has attracted much attention in recent years but the case is not proven.
- Tackling many environmental problems necessitates international or global action, exposing the limitations of the sovereign state system as a means of enhancing human security.

## Note

1    The 1967 *Torrey Canyon* disaster, when an oil tanker was wrecked and spilled its load off the coast of the Scilly Isles, UK, was particularly influential in stimulating awareness of and an international political response to oil pollution.

## Recommended reading

Carson, R. (1962) *Silent Spring*, Penguin: Harmondsworth.
Dalby, S. (2009) *Security and Environmental Change*, Cambridge: Polity.
Dyer, H. (2000) 'Environmental Security: The New Agenda', in Jones, C. and Kennedy-Pipe, C. (eds) *International Security in a Global Age: Securing the Twenty-First Century*, London and Portland: Frank Cass.
Hardin, G. (1968) 'The Tragedy of the Commons', *Science*, 162: 1243–8.
Homer-Dixon, T. (1994) 'Environmental Scarcities and Violent Conflict: Evidence from Cases', *International Security*, 19(1): 5–40.
Lomberg, B. (2001) *The Sceptical Environmentalist*, Cambridge: Cambridge University Press.

## Useful web links

Stern Report: http://www.hm-treasury.gov.uk/independent_reviews/stern_review_economics_climate_change/stern_review_report.cfm
United Nations Environment Programme: http://www.unep.org/
World Summit on Sustainable Development (Johannesburg 2002): http://www.johannesburg summit.org/

Chapter 7

# Health threats to security

> The heart of the security agenda is protecting lives – and we now know that the number of people who will die of AIDS in the first decade of the 21st Century will rival the number that dies in all the decades of the 20th Century
> US Vice President Al Gore, UN Security Council
> Opening Session, 10 January 2000

## The globalization of ill-health

Disease has long been the biggest threat of all to humankind and, despite the unrelenting advances of medical science, looks set to continue to be for the foreseeable future. The Black Death of the fourteenth century claimed more lives than any military conflict before or since, whilst the great influenza epidemic of 1918–20 killed far more than the First World War that it closely followed. The 'Plague of Justinian', which started in sixth-century Constantinople and then spread throughout the Mediterranean, was a classic 'national security' issue since it precipitated the fall of the Byzantine Roman Empire (McNeill 1989: 101–6). In addition, the threats posed by diseases, like some environmental problems, tend to be transnational and as such represent a security challenge not easily countered by a human race artificially subdivided into independent, though not impervious, units. Today, AIDS (acquired immune deficiency syndrome) represents a far greater threat to life than armed conflict for most sub-Saharan Africans and for many millions more in all of the inhabited continents of the world.

As with famines and hunger, however, major epidemics and pandemics (international epidemics) of diseases represent only dramatic periodic escalations of an underlying and persistent threat. Tables 7.1 and 7.2 give an indication of the scale of this threat, the greatest challenge of all to human security. By the end of the 1970s there was optimism that humanity's war against disease was being won. Disease is an enemy of humanity which can probably never be entirely defeated, but in the decades which followed the Second World War a growing belief emerged that scientific and medical advances could eliminate many diseases and at least contain the others. The attack was led by the use of synthetic (organic) insecticides, following the 1939 discovery of dichloro-diphenyl-trichloroethane (DDT), against disease-carrying insects such as mosquitoes and tsetse-flies. The defence against disease was strengthened by significant medical advances which discovered and refined antibiotics, such as long-acting penicillin, which could directly attack the microbes themselves or immunize whole vulnerable populations against threatening diseases. Coordinating this joint strategy was a new global body set up as part of the United Nations, the World Health Organization (WHO).

A WHO-led immunization campaign entirely eradicated smallpox in 1978, saving around 2 million lives a year, whilst the use of DDT in WHO-led operations quickly curbed the annual death toll attributable to malaria to a similar degree without actually eradicating the disease. In line with these and many other successes, the WHO optimistically declared in 1977 that victory against disease was in sight in setting the target of 'Health for All by the Year 2000'. By the end of the century, however, the WHO's hope that it could shift its main focus to Primary Health Care (ensuring all people have access to health care, clean water and

**Table 7.1** The ten deadliest disease epidemics and pandemics of all time

| | Epidemic/pandemic | Location | Date | Death toll |
|---|---|---|---|---|
| 1 | Black Death | World | 1347–51 | 75 million |
| 2 | AIDS | World | 1981– | 30 million |
| 3 | Influenza | World | 1918–20 | 21.64 million |
| 4 | Plague | India | 1896–1948 | 12 million |
| 5 | Typhus | Eastern Europe | 1914–15 | 3 million |
| 6 | 'Plague of Justinian' | Eastern Mediterranean | 541–90 | 'millions' |
| =7 | Cholera | World | 1846–60 | 'millions' |
| =7 | Cholera | Europe | 1826–37 | 'millions' |
| =7 | Cholera | World | 1893–94 | 'millions' |
| 10 | Smallpox | Mexico | 1530–45 | up to 1 million |

Sources: Ash (2001: 31); UNAIDS (2009).

**Table 7.2** The ten most significant global communicable, maternal and nutritional threats

| | Disease | Cause | Main areas affected | Annual deaths (m) |
|---|---|---|---|---|
| 1 | Lower respiratory diseases | Influenza and pneumonia viruses, passed by coughing and sneezing | Global but most deadly in LDCs | 3.5 |
| 2 | Perinatal | Infections contracted by babies via their mother such as streptococcus | LDCs, particularly sub-Saharan Africa | 2.6 |
| 3 | Diarrhoeal | Various diseases carried by water-borne viruses, bacteria and parasites (e.g. Cholera, dysentery, E coli) | LDCs, particularly sub-Saharan Africa | 2.5 |
| 4 | AIDS | Virus transmitted by bodily fluids | Global but principally sub-Saharan Africa | 1.8 |
| 5 | Tuberculosis | Bacterial infection transmitted by coughs and sneezes | LDCs, principally Africa and SE Asia | 1.3 |
| 6 | Malaria | Parasites transmitted by mosquito | The 'tropics' | 0.8 |
| 7 | Upper Respiratory diseases | Infections of the upper respiratory tract such as Pertussis ('whooping cough') | LDCs, particularly sub-Saharan Africa | 0.7 |
| 8 | 'Childhood cluster' | Viruses affecting children such as measles | Global | 0.4 |
| 9 | Nutrition | Disorders associated with malnutrition such as iodine or iron deficiency | LDCs, particularly sub-Saharan Africa | 0.4 |
| 10 | Maternal | Infections contracted by the mother such as tetanus | LDCs, particularly sub-Saharan Africa | 0.4 |

Source: Figures from WHO (2011).

sanitation) had been overtaken by events with the revival of apparently dormant illnesses and the arrival of new even-more virulent diseases.

Although human history is replete with peaks and troughs of disease a number of factors particular to the contemporary world can be offered as partial explanations for the deepening and widening of disease since the 1980s.

## Increased travel and migration

History shows that epidemics and pandemics of diseases have tended to occur when previously isolated human populations mix. The Roman Empire was beset by periodic plagues of previously unknown magnitude, new diseases entered Europe from Asia in the wake of Marco Polo's establishment of links in the thirteenth century, and diseases left Europe for the Americas with Columbus and his successors from the late fifteenth century (Pirages and Runci 2000: 176–80). Human groups over time can evolve immunities to certain strains of disease which when encountered by humans who have evolved (genetically) from other geographical areas can be deadly. The prevalence of holiday ailments, often erroneously blamed on foreign food, bears testimony to the fact that this phenomenon persists. Ever-greater levels of contact between people ultimately should diminish the deadliest impacts of this by making human immunities more similar but, in the meantime, contemporary global social change is a root of the problem rather than the cure.

The much more frequent movement of people around the globe also serves to transport diseases dangerous to all to new parts of the world in ever-greater quantities. Aeroplanes and international shipping are well-established hosts for the spread of dangerous pathogens, carried either directly by the tourists or on insect or rodent vectors. Between 70 and 86 per cent of measles outbreaks in Europe are believed to have been imported from travellers returning from Asia and Africa (Chen and Wilson 2008: 1421). Immigrants will, of course, tend to be 'vetted' for alien diseases by state authorities before admission into the country but this is neither feasible nor politically acceptable for tourists and other visitors entering or, particularly, for citizens returning from abroad.

## Increased trade

As with travel, the link between trade and the spread of disease is well established. The Black Death arrived in Europe directly via goods imported from the Orient and, although trading standards have evolved somewhat since that time, the rapid proliferation of trade links in recent years has opened up more potential routes for disease to spread. In particular, the globalization of food production and movement has been accompanied by the globalization of food-borne illnesses. In 2011, for example, over forty people were killed by a sudden outbreak of *Escherichia coli* (E coli) in Germany. Despite the high levels of bureaucracy that characterize the European Union's Common Agricultural Policy, scientists could not be sure where the vegetables infected by the bacterium originated whilst politicians in Germany, Spain and elsewhere pointed the blame at each other. Once localized outbreaks of disease, due to hygienic failings in food production, are now more likely to become globalized since consumers come from increasingly far afield.

## Displaced persons

Just as more frequent voluntary movements of people have increased outbreaks of diseases, so have more frequent enforced movements, as a consequence of natural or human disaster. People fleeing countries beset by war or famine will obviously be far more likely to be carrying diseases and also more vulnerable to contracting them. Recipient countries, though, can help refugees and prevent the further spread of disease. At much greater risk are peoples coerced into moves to other parts of their own state rather than abroad, who technically are not refugees but 'internally displaced persons (IDPs)'. Such people are less likely to receive assistance, either domestic or international, and tend to be forced to settle in overcrowded and unhygienic locations. For example, in 2011 cholera claimed hundreds of lives in Mogadishu, Somalia amongst IDPs crowded into unsanitary accommodation to escape civil conflict.

## Insect and microbe resistance

A major factor behind the counter-attacks of disease against man in the war against disease since the 1970s has been the increased redundancy of human weaponry. The globalization of the human strategy has had the side-effect of globalizing resistance. Both pathogens and the pests by which they are transmitted have increasingly developed immunities to the pesticides and antibiotic drugs used against them. Many insects and rodents have become resistant to insecticides and rodenticides used against them since the mid-twentieth century, with diseases like malaria resurging from near elimination as a result. Similarly, many antibiotics have become increasingly ineffective in treating illnesses they once could be relied upon to combat. That most renowned panacea, penicillin, for example, can no longer be guaranteed to treat gonorrhoea or pneumonia. Additionally, resistance requires increased innovation in antibiotic development, increasing the costs of treatment and exacerbating the vulnerability of people in the world's poorest states. For both pesticides and antibiotics overuse has been a part cause of target resistance and more cautious application is now understood as the best strategy against an enemy more ingenious than imagined in the 1950s and 1960s. That period of the conflict between man and disease looks ever more like a victorious phase in a protracted war.

## Urbanization

The trend for population growth in urban areas at the expense of rural areas has been witnessed since industrialization began in Europe in the eighteenth century but has become particularly prominent in the Global South over recent decades. This has had profound implications for the spread of disease in two dimensions:

1    Overcrowding in megacities has led to many people living in squalor, providing the conditions for diseases associated with poor sanitation to emerge and for other diseases to be more readily transmitted amongst a large population. Examples of this include dysentery and cholera, chiefly spread by unsanitary food and water.

2    Urban encroachment on traditionally, distinct rural areas can cause diseases associated with the rural environment to contaminate the urban population. Deforestation, for example, has contributed to the spread of tropical diseases such as malaria and leishmaniasis since the tropical insects have come into contact with more people. In addition, entirely new human ailments are believed to have emerged as a result of greater contact with other animal species allowing for cross-species transmission of 'zoonotic' diseases. Some 60 per cent of the 300 new diseases to have emerged since 1940 have crossed to humans from other animals (Laurance 2010).

## Development projects

Human-driven changes to the environment other than urbanization can also upset the equilibrium in a given ecosystem and cause a resurgence of certain diseases. Large dam projects in Africa, for example, have been known to have contributed to the proliferation of water-breeding disease vectors such as mosquitoes and water snails, causing the spread of rift valley fever and schistosomiasis (NIC 2000).

## Technological advances

A further but inverted link between economic development and disease can be seen in the spread of certain diseases associated specifically with technologically advanced societies. There can be no doubt that modern medicine saves more lives than it claims but the death toll attributable to it is still considerable. Around 37,000 people a year across the European Union die of nosocomial infections (hospital-acquired) such as *staphylococcus aureas* (the bacterium causing 'toxic shock syndrome'), are associated with modern invasive medical procedures and over-reliance on antibiotics (WHO 2010).

## Global environmental change

Even if a small number continue to question whether global warming is natural or human-made, it is beyond dispute that average temperatures on Earth have risen over recent decades and this has had and will continue to have a considerable bearing on the spread of certain diseases. Tropical diseases, associated with insect vectors native to equatorial areas, are becoming increasingly common in areas with traditionally more temperate climes. The warmer the weather the more readily mosquitoes breed and bite and malaria and other diseases have recently become a health threat in countries outside of the insects' usual habitat. The USA, for example, has been hit by West Nile virus as far north as New York every summer since 1999. A record number of cases of the bacterial lung infection 'legionnaire's disease' in the UK in 2006 led the Health Protection Agency to claim that the country had suffered its first casualties from infectious disease due to global warming (Laurance 2006). The WHO estimate that air pollution accounts for 5 per cent of the annual global deaths from heart disease and climate change is responsible for 3 per cent of malaria and diarrhoea fatalities (Hughes *et al.* 2011: 93).

The erosion of the ozone layer is believed to be a significant factor in the rise of cases of skin cancer (malignant melanoma) over recent years. Increased levels of ultraviolet radiation resulting from ozone depletion appear a major explanation for why the disease should have risen in prevalence in the USA by 1,800 per cent from 1930 to the end of the century (the increased popularity of sun bathing is another factor) (UNEP 2002: ch. 3: 4).

## 'Failed states'

As with the growth of other causes of human insecurity, the increased number of politically chaotic states, associated with the contemporary age, has exacerbated the dangers posed by disease. Political upheaval in sub-Saharan African states such as Sudan, Somalia and the Democratic Republic of Congo has contributed to poverty and the limited development of public health and sanitation provision. Even in states less anarchic and less naturally prone to disease epidemics than sub-Saharan Africa health threats to security have emerged in line with political upheaval. One of the side-effects of Russia's difficult process of political, social and economic transition since the fall of Communist rule in 1991 has been the rise of vaccine-preventable diseases like tuberculosis and diphtheria, largely attributed to poverty and cuts in health expenditure. Failed states also, of course, encourage migration and the global spread of disease in addition to localized resurges.

## Global market forces

Economic globalization has some negative implications for human health beyond the side-effects of creating a single market for food. The profits from trade and tourism have become such a major element of the state exchequer that governments have been known to downplay or deny disease outbreaks for fear of the economic costs of doing so. Pirages and Runci note that a pneumonia outbreak in India in 1996 was not reported to the WHO as is customary for these sorts of fears (Pirages and Runci 2000: 190). This decision was, doubtless, influenced by the estimated loss of $1.7 billion to the country as a result of a well-publicized plague epidemic two years earlier (Heymann 2001: 12). States have lost huge slices of income as a result of international panic in response to an epidemic. Tourism to the UK was affected by the 2001 outbreak of 'foot and mouth' even though it was a cattle disease and represented no threat to human life. The likelihood is that many human lives have been sacrificed on the altars of profit and national pride.

## Cultural globalization

The diffusion of disease around the world is not entirely a one-way process of transmission from South to North. Globalization has also seen certain non-communicable 'lifestyle illnesses', associated with mass-consumption societies of the Global North, head southwards as people in LDCs adopt some of the unhealthy practices associated with modernization. The consumption of high-fat and high-sugar foods, for example, has led to previously minor health problems such as obesity, heart disease and diabetes becoming more prominent in many LDCs and even in the societies on the margins of highly developed states. A rise in rates of obesity and diabetes amongst indigenous peoples of the Arctic has resulted from the nutrition transition to Western consumption patterns. The mechanization of travel and decline in hunting in some communities has also added to the obesity problem as the Arctic lifestyle has become less active (Sharma 2010). Diabetes claims as many lives in Asia as AIDS and is estimated to become the sixth leading cause of all deaths by 2030 (Mathers and Loncur 2006). Tobacco smoking has become more common in a number of LDCs (encouraged by Northern MNCs faced with a declining market at home), leading to a rise in lung cancers. Native Alaskans are nearly nine times more likely to die of alcohol-related health problems than the average US citizen (Seale, Shellenberger and Spence 2006). Cancers were near non-existent in the Arctic until the last hundred years but lung, colon and breast cancers have soared due to social change (Friborg and Melbye 2008). Overall, non-communicable diseases account for 63 per cent of all deaths in the world (WHO 2009) (see Table 7.3).

## The development of global health policy

The transnational threat posed by infectious disease epidemics has long been apparent to statesmen and participants in international commerce but counter-measures were slow to develop owing to an absence of any real epidemiological understanding of contagious diseases not spread directly by human to human (such as leprosy). The first systematic political measures to contain the international spread of disease can be dated back to fourteenth-century Venice and the origins of imposing a *quarantine* on people arriving from certain countries. Ships which had come from or visited ports known to be afflicted with the Black Death were required by law to wait docked at sea for thirty days, before being allowed to land if no evidence of the plague was apparent. This procedure was referred to as 'trentina' from the Latin for thirty, and when in the next century the time scale was extended to forty days it became known as 'quarantine' from the Latin for forty days.

Other European states adopted similar quarantine measures over the next three centuries but coordinated international action to combat the spread of disease was not attempted until the mid-nineteenth century, when the unprecedented growth in international trade and birth of Liberal internationalism prompted the 'Concert' powers to consider a response. In 1851 the first International Sanitary Conference was held in Paris but failed to agree on a Convention to establish

**Table 7.3** The ten deadliest non-communicable diseases in the world

| | Disease | Contributory factors | Main areas affected | Annual deaths (m) |
|---|---|---|---|---|
| 1 | Cardiovascular: ischaemic and cerebrovascular heart disease | Poor diet, obesity | Global, particularly significant in East Asia and Europe | 17.3 |
| 2 | Cancers | tobacco smoking, poor diet | Global, particularly prevalent in East Europe and N America | 7.6 (lung cancer 1.4, stomach 0.7, liver 0.7) |
| 3 | Respiratory disorders, e.g. bronchitis | tobacco smoking | Global, particularly significant in East Asia | 4.2 |
| 4 | Digestive, e.g. cirrhosis, peptic ulcers | Poor diet, alcohol consumption | Global, particularly significant in Asia | 2.2 |
| 5 | Neuropsychiatric, e.g. epilepsy, Alzheimer's | Poverty, depression | Global | 1.3 |
| 6 | Diabetes mellitus | poor diet, excessive sugar | Global, particularly prevalent in N America, E Europe and Middle East | 1.3 |
| 7 | Genito-urinary, e.g. kidney diseases | Diabetes and high blood pressure | Global | 1.0 |
| 8 | Congenital abnormalities | lack of pre-natal diagnosis | Global, particularly prevalent in SE Asia and Middle East | 0.4 |
| 9 | Endocrine disorders (other than diabetes) | Poor diet, obesity | Global | 0.3 |
| 10 | Musculoskeletal, e.g. arthritis | Work strain | Global North | 0.2 |

Source: Figures from WHO (2011).

harmonized quarantine practices for cholera, plague and yellow fever which were ravaging Europe and much of the world. Subsequent International Sanitary Conferences also made little progress in coordinating controls in an era when barriers to free trade and navigation were anathema to the great naval and commercial powers. A breakthrough, however, occurred in 1892 at the seventh International Sanitation Conference when an International Sanitary Convention for cholera was agreed upon by most of the European maritime powers. The onset of a major cholera epidemic the following year prompted two further International Sanitary Conventions at the eighth and ninth Conferences, which furthered measures to control the spread of that disease. At the tenth International Sanitary Conference in 1902 a fourth Convention was agreed upon dealing with the age-old threat of the plague.

The four Conventions were merged into a single International Sanitary Convention in 1903 and the seeds of today's global health polity were sown with the emergence of the International Sanitary Bureau in the USA (later to become the Pan American Health Organization, now the World Health Organization's arm for the Americas) and the intensification of talks for a global IGO for public health. In 1907 L'Office Internationale d'Hygiene Publique (OIHP) was agreed upon with a Parisian headquarters, permanent staff and decision-making body made up of (eventually) representatives of over fifty governments and colonial administrations. The OIHP sought to disseminate medical information as well as codifying quarantine agreements and expanding the scope of the International Sanitary Convention.

The OIHP continued to function despite the creation of a new global health organization as part of the League of Nations system established after the First World War. The Health Organization of the League of Nations (HOLN) was established amidst the carnage of typhus, cholera and influenza epidemics which dwarfed even the horrors of the world's greatest ever military conflict which had prompted the creation of the League and the implementation of the concept of collective military security. The OIHP continued to have authority over the International Sanitary Conventions (which were expanded by conventions for smallpox and typhus in 1926 and for aerial transport in 1935) whilst the HOLN focused on advising particular countries on containing the spread of epidemics and set up specialist commissions of experts to coordinate information and advice for governments to utilize in dealing with particular diseases. Hence, in 1923 a Malaria Commission and a Cancer Commission were established.

The HOLN's role decreased sharply at the outset of the Second World War as the whole League project crumbled in the face of a pronounced failure of collective military security. The League's well-documented peacekeeping failings, however, detract from the fact that the HOLN (and other specialized agencies) had proved quite successful. The HOLN had succeeded in containing the spread of typhus from East Europe in the first year of its operation in 1921 and fostered the development of an international 'epistemic community' of health specialists who, undoubtedly, contributed to the rapid improvement in human health standards throughout the world in the twentieth century.

During the Second World War a new international body was set up to offer humanitarian assistance to countries on the cessation of fighting. The United Nations Relief and Rehabilitation Administration (UNRRA) started operations ahead of the rest of the planned United Nations system set to replace the League of Nations at the full conclusion of the war. From 1944 to 1946 UNRRA supplied food and equipment to countries where fighting had stopped and in many cases this came to be accompanied by medical personnel and drugs for countries racked with disease. A 1946 cholera outbreak in China, for example, was brought under control by the supply of an effective vaccine from the USA. UNRRA also assumed control from the OIHP (which continued to exist until officially absorbed by the World Health Organization) for administering the International Sanitary Conventions.

UNRRA, however, was only ever intended to be a temporary programme and it was wound up in 1946 when its work was considered to be complete. The 1945 San Francisco Conference which founded the United Nations system did not envisage a successor to the HOLN but a resolution of the first UN General Assembly in 1946 paved the way for the creation of the World Health Organization.

## World Health Organization

A WHO Interim Commission came into operation in 1946 prior to the establishment of the WHO proper in 1948 and had a notable success in controlling a 1947 cholera epidemic in Egypt. The organization was from the start marked by an independent streak and it was agreed that the term 'United Nations' should not feature in its official title and that it would have a far more decentralized structure than any other UN Specialized Agency. The decision to devolve a great deal of the work of the WHO to six regions (Africa, the Americas, Europe, Eastern Mediterranean, South-East Asia and Western Pacific[1]) was partly a practical decision as it facilitated the continuation of the world's oldest health IGO as the American arm of the new global body.

Centrally, the work of WHO is directed by an annual World Health Assembly (WHA), held in Geneva, in which delegates of its 194-member governments vote on budgetary matters and overall policy. The WHA elect a geographically balanced 34-member Executive Board to oversee the implementation of WHO policy. The Executive Board members are intended to be public health specialists rather than government delegates, although the six Regional Committees are made up of health ministers. The WHO Director-General is elected by the WHA, on the recommendation of the Executive Board and serves a five-year term at the Geneva headquarters supported by 30 per cent of the WHO's 8,000-strong secretariat. A further 30 per cent of the Secretariat serve the regions whilst the remaining 40 per cent are represented throughout the world in field programmes or as resident advisers to government (WHO 2012b). The WHO is financed by two distinct budgets. The regular budget, made up of assessed governments' contributions, finances the central institutions: the extrabudgetary funds made up of voluntary additional contributions from government and donations from other UN agencies (particularly the World Bank) and private sources. These funds can be targeted at specific programmes at the donors' request. The American information technology tycoon Bill Gates, for example, has made contributions to campaigns on guinea worm disease eradication and HIV research.

The undoubted high point of the WHO's history was the global eradication of smallpox, declared in 1978 after a vast immunization campaign. This momentous effort, which had to overcome obstacles such as a cultural reluctance to accept injections in some parts of India, saw many millions of people vaccinated and around 2 million lives a year saved. Other successes include greatly reducing the impact of *onchocerciasis* (river blindness) through pesticide sprayings of the larvae of the *simulium* black fly and the development of the drug *Ivermectin* and bringing *yaws* and *poliomyelitis* close to eradication through antibiotic and vaccination campaigns.

Fuelled by the breakthrough inventions of penicillin and DDT in the 1940s, global health security appeared to be a realizable dream for the WHO, but many of the battles in this major war have not been won. In 1955 a global eradication programme for malaria was launched, the largest of its kind in public health history. The use of DDT around human dwellings in the late 1950s and 1960s rapidly killed all mosquitoes that came into contact with it, and virtually eliminated the disease in all areas in which it was used. An illustration of DDT's success in eliminating malaria comes from comparing the numbers of infections before and after its extensive use in Sardinia, Italy. There were 78,000 cases of malaria on the island in 1942 prior to the use of DDT, compared with only 9 in 1951, after several years of treatment with the insecticide (McEwen and Stephenson 1979: 23). Replacement insecticides have not matched the success of DDT in its early years, and malaria has resurged in Africa, South-East Asia and South America. In Ceylon (now Sri Lanka), where DDT had reduced the annual number of malaria outbreaks to 17 by 1963, its withdrawal prompted a resurgence of the disease to greater levels than ever, reaching an estimated 2 million cases in 1970 (Hicks 1992). By the 1990s malaria was claiming around 1.5 million lives a year worldwide, with the disease gaining resistance to drugs such as chloroquine and mefloquine, in addition to the *anopheles* mosquito's increased resistance to DDT and other insecticides. In 1998 the WHO, abandoning all aspirations to eradicate the disease, instead launched the far more conservative 'Roll Back Malaria' campaign which declared as its aim the halving of malaria cases by 2010. This was to be achieved by improving access to treatment in Africa and increasing the use of insecticide-laden nets to deter rather than eliminate the mosquitoes (WHO 2002a).

In spite of its achievements the WHO, along with other specialized agencies under the UN umbrella, became the target of criticism in the 1980s and 1990s for being over-bureaucratic and inefficient. The 'New Right' philosophy of US and UK premiers Reagan and Thatcher sought to challenge what it considered to be complacency in global public bodies in the same way as it had done for state bureaucracies in the USA and UK. The clearest manifestation of this challenge came with the withdrawal of those two countries from the United Nations Educational, Scientific and Cultural Organization (UNESCO) in 1984 and the withholding of a proportion of the US regular budgetary contributions to UN agencies from 1985. Criticisms of the WHO from the 1980s, however, went beyond the confines of cutting 'global red tape' and freeing up international trade. The Japanese WHO Secretary-General from 1988 to 1998, Nakajima, was widely vilified for running the organization like a personal fiefdom in which nepotism, discrimination and vote-buying were alleged to have occurred. Things came to a head during the campaign for his re-election in 1993 when a bizarre protest saw his prized pet carp and ornamental goldfish expertly filleted and left as sushi by the side of the fishpond at the Geneva headquarters.

The election of the highly respected Dr Gro Harlem Brundtland (see biographical Box 7.1) in 1998 heralded a reform of the structure of the WHO still widely considered necessary in spite of the ebbing of New Right ideology and the existence of more internationalist governments in London and Washington. In an

## Box 7.1 Gro Harlem Brundtland

Few individuals can have had the influence over such a range of international political issues as three times Norwegian Prime Minister Gro Harlem Brundtland. The daughter of a doctor-turned-politician, in the early 1970s Brundtland followed in her father's footsteps by swapping the physicians coat for a political career.

A socialist, though married to a conservative politician, she quickly entered government as environmental minister from 1974 to 1979.

A decade later, Brundtland's credentials as an environmentalist saw her appointed as chair of the UN-sponsored World Commission on the Environment and Development (WCED), charged with the task of advancing global environmental policy. The commission helped forge the concept of sustainable development, which became the guiding ethos of future global policy, finding expression at the landmark 1992 UN Conference on the Environment and Development (UNCED) at Rio de Janeiro. Sustainable development not only put the environment firmly on the international political map but revamped thinking and policy on global poverty. In recognition of her contribution to this, Brundtland was awarded the Third World Foundation Prize in 1988.

Brundtland's role on the WCED coincided with her second stint as Norwegian head of government, leading the most female cabinet in history, having been the country's first woman Prime Minister in her first stint. After a third spell as premier in the 1990s, she returned to her roots in public health in becoming elected as Secretary-General of the WHO in 1998. A popular leader, she did much to restore the vibrancy and credibility of a position and organization that had been much criticized under her predecessor and oversaw an unprecedented global fundraising effort to help fight disease. One of Brundtland's many reforms on taking up her position at the WHO was to increase the number and prominence of women in managerial positions at the institution. Hence, at the turn of the millennium, the work of Gro Harlem Brundtland had left a clear mark on four major international political issues: environmental change, economic development, public health and the role of women.

exercise reminiscent of the overhauling of welfare systems in most developed states, Brundtland's measures were taken to streamline bureaucratic procedures and incorporate greater financial accountability aided by the utilization of private managerial expertise and greater levels of transparency. The fifty-two old WHO programmes were transformed into thirty-five departments, with 'sunset' programmes abandoned to free up resources (Brundtland 1999a). The new departments, in turn, were consolidated into nine 'clusters' each headed by an Executive Director, who together form a cabinet which meets weekly to discuss policy with the Director-General.

The WHO has also been subject to criticism from an opposing coalition to the New Right, made up of some medical professionals, humanitarian NGOs and functionalists (proponents of greater internationalization led by specialist organizations), concerned that the organization has lost its political influence and has been relegated to a purely technical advisory role to global financial institutions which carry the real influence in terms of health security. The history of the WHO can be characterized by periodic shifts in overall strategy towards achieving the aim, specified in its charter, of the 'attainment by all peoples of the highest possible level of health'. The strategy of the WHO in its early years was 'vertical' in that the emphasis of its work was on targeting specific diseases for eradication campaigns. At this stage the role of the WHO was essentially non-political since its approach of applying technical fixes to problems was universally accepted as effective and appropriate. However, once it became evident that insect and microbe resistance to antibiotics and pesticides made combating the spread of disease more complicated than had at first been anticipated 'horizontal' strategies for achieving global health security came to be advocated in opposition to the 'vertical' orthodoxy and the whole issue area became politicized. Horizontal strategies favour tackling underlying problems that exacerbate the effects of disease as the best means of advancing global health and this became characteristic of WHO activities from the mid-1970s. Godlee comments that the new strategy of Primary Health Care 'marked a new policy direction for WHO, leading the organisation out of the quiet waters of technological consensus into the much more troubled waters of political controversy' (Godlee 1994: 1492).

The horizontal approach to global health has met resistance from some states because technical quick-fixes remain popular in spite of some notable setbacks. As seen in other global issue areas, disasters trigger responses from the international community better than 'routine' suffering and tackling epidemics head-on remains an instinctive response. In addition, despite the retreat over malaria, other 'fire fighting' successes, such as with smallpox and polio, continue to encourage the vertical strategy. The extrabudgetary funds allocated to the WHO, which finance the disease-specific programmes, have grown since the late 1970s whilst the regular budget has frozen. This has had the effect of counteracting the horizontal ethos expounded by the World Health Assembly and Executive Board and, in the minds of some, has served to undermine the achievement of global health security. Garrett contends that the international community's emphasis on HIV/AIDS has actually worsened the overall health of many countries particularly blighted with the infection because HIV medics are often segregated from other health workers and money has drained out of public health budgets. This separation occurs because of the stigma associated with the disease and the preference of international donors for working through NGOs and is exacerbated by the brain drain of Global South medics to the North.

> Guinea-Bissau has plenty of donated ARV [HIV anti retroviral drug] supplies for its people, but the drugs are cooking in a hot dockside warehouse because the country lacks doctors to distribute them.
>
> (Garrett 2007)

The WHO's horizontal strategy also steered it into troubled waters by challenging the orthodoxy on economic development by seeming to favour greater LDC independence and local empowerment over MNC investment. This was most clearly demonstrated in the 'essential drugs' campaign, launched in 1977, which promoted the domestic development of pharmaceuticals in the Third World over their import from the First World. A contributory factor here was that the WHO, like the UN General Assembly, had become radicalized by the arrival of new member-states from Africa and Asia, keen to vent their frustrations against their past and present dominators and able to do so through its egalitarian voting system. The USA, as the state most supportive of the spread of MNC influence, became increasingly exasperated with the new, bolder WHO. A humiliating 118–1 vote at the 1981 World Health Assembly, on adopting an international code to curb the export of infant milk substitutes[2] to LDCs, and long-running disagreement over the essential drugs programme contributed to the USA's general disillusionment with the whole UN system which saw them cut their regular budget contributions in the mid-1980s.

The USA's protest had the effect of tempering WHO 'radicalism' and, although Primary Health Care remains a core ideal, Godlee contends that the organization in the 1990s had 'sunk into a political vacuum' (Godlee 1994: 1495). In evidence of this she contrasts the modest 1990s WHO crusade to discourage cigarette smoking in LDCs to the vigorous and successful 1980s campaign against infant milk substitutes, which followed on the back of the adoption of the International Code. Similarly, the esteemed medical journal *The Lancet* contended that the WHO had lost its direction and suffered a 'loss of the intellectual leadership' (*Lancet* 1995: 203). The WHO in the 1990s continued to be attacked by the US right, however, as epitomized by the article 'WHO Prescribes Socialist Medicine' which appeared in the *Wall Street Journal* in 1996 (Peeters 1996).

Hence, entering the twenty-first century, the WHO found itself criticized on two fronts and its overall direction caught between that advocated by vertical 'eradicationists' (Godlee 1995) and horizontal proponents of containment. Brundtland's stewardship saw the WHO become more open and cost-efficient, to the satisfaction of the USA and other major donor states, but it has not been afraid to court corporate displeasure. This was evident in the revamping of the anti-tobacco campaign, which in 2005 culminated in the entry into force of the Framework Convention on Tobacco Control. It was also evident in a campaign in support of the 'essential drugs' programme which spawned two significant legal victories in 2001. Several US pharmaceutical firms and the US government were persuaded to drop legal challenges preventing South African and Brazilian firms from marketing cheaper versions of generic HIV drugs. In both instances the legal cases had sought to uphold WTO Trade Related Intellectual Property Rights (TRIPS). A global public outcry over the cases prompted the backdown and marked a significant victory in this particular recurring clash between competing international laws satisfying the sometimes-rival values of wealth maximization and human security.

The WHO's twin funding mechanism may cause confusion and attract criticism from two directions, but it does allow the organization to continue to attract public and private monies for high-profile campaigns, whilst persisting with a more socially oriented functionalist political direction driven by the organization itself. The *British Medical Journal* in a 2002 editorial declared its qualified support for the twin-track approach: 'both (horizontal and vertical programmes) are needed. Vertical programmes will be unsustainable without well functioning healthcare systems, but vertical programmes on, for example, immunization can achieve a great deal rapidly' (Smith 2002: 55).

## Global public and private partnerships

The bureaucratic centralization of WHO introduced by Brundtland 'to make WHO one – not more than fifty' (Brundtland 1999b) has been accompanied by the partial outsourcing of some of its vertical operations into 'Global Public and Private Partnerships (GPPPs)' (Buse and Walt 2000). Enterprises such as the Global Programme to Eradicate Filariasis (GPEF), Guinea Worm Eradication Programme and (the largest of all) the Global Fund to Fight AIDS, Tuberculosis and Malaria have brought in substantial extrabudgetary funds, whilst retaining links with the WHO as only one of a number of 'partner' institutions. This represented a trend throughout the UN system from the 1990s in an effort to bring in funds and revitalize the specialized agencies. Public health has been the most prominent of the issues affected owing to the centrality of the private chemical manufacturing industry to any immunization or pest control scheme. Corporations in recent years have become more concerned with their public image and have provided much needed cash injections to public health programmes but concerns have been expressed that this could be detrimental to the public-service ethos and work of the WHO. Concerns have focused on the possibility that the independence of the WHO could be compromised by the need to satisfy sponsors and that its overall strategy might become more diluted and/or fragmented (Buse and Walt 2000: 705). Corporations involved, at least partially, for public relations purposes may be keen to focus resources on projects likely to succeed rather than those that are most deserving and be more hesitant to tackle more stigmatizing diseases such as sexually transmitted diseases (Walt and Buse 2000).

Some voices are more cynical about the whole concept of directly involving industry in global public health ventures. Oxfam's response to the development of partnerships between the UN and manufactures of HIV-retroviral drugs has been particularly sceptical: '[C]orporations in the pharmaceutical sector are offering islands of philanthropy, while promoting a global patents system which would enhance their profitability, but which could also consign millions to unnecessary suffering' (Oxfam 2002: 8). Similarly, a 2002 study by the pressure group Save the Children and the London School of Hygiene and Tropical Medicine (LSHTM) criticized the Global Alliance for Vaccines and Immunizations (GAVI). The report, based on extensive field research in four African countries, expressed concern that the focus on supplying vaccines overlooked the fact that the means of implementing immunization campaigns might not be sufficient and that the programme would be unsustainable if GAVI funding was not replaced after the five years of its operation (LSHTM 2002).

The behaviour of several American pharmaceutical firms in protecting their own products against South African and Brazilian competition gave some credence to the Oxfam claim. The governance of the GPPPs, however, is not as skewed in the direction of donors and corporations as might be imagined and efforts have been made to achieve a balance of stakeholders on the governing Boards, in a similar manner to that employed on WHO programmes and Expert Groups. The sort of dominance by MNCs highlighted in studies of the membership of Boards of the Food and Agricultural Organization (FAO) and the Joint FAO/WHO food standards agency, the Codex Alimentarius Commission, is certainly not replicated in the public health GPPPs (Avery, Drake and Lang 1993). The Executive Board for the Global Fund to Fight AIDS, Tuberculosis and Malaria comprises fourteen government ministers (seven from donor states and seven from LDCs), two pressure-group representatives, one representative from the Gates Foundation (as a major private sponsor not functionally involved) and one representative of the salient private sector (Global Fund to Fight AIDS, Tuberculosis and Malaria 2002). The Board acts on the advice of a Technical Review Panel made up of experts selected from individual applicants chosen by the Executive Board according to geographical and gender quotas. GAVI is governed by a fifteen-member board composed of four permanent members, WHO, UNICEF, World Bank and the Gates Foundation, and eleven rotating members; three donor governments, two LDC governments, one NGO, one LDC industry representative, one developed world industry representative, one foundation, one technical health institute and one research/academic body. The Global Fund board, in particular, safeguards against excessive influence from actors for whom the value of profit may be the chief motivation, whilst recognizing the reality of a situation where the involvement of those actors is necessary in pursuit of the value of minimizing human suffering. Despite some reservations and concerns, Save the Children still concluded in their study that 'GAVI was generally seen as a positive development in all four countries' (LSHTM 2002: 44). Similarly, Brugha and Walt writing in the *British Medical Journal* accepted that: 'It is only through a global fund that this kind of concerted global action between major corporate and public sector players can be achieved' (Brugha and Walt 2001: 154).

That business is driven by profit and that market forces are not always compatible with the public good is obvious and something to be safeguarded against in politics but, if the public good can be served by uniting actors with disparate reasons for achieving a similar goal, then socially conscious politicians should not instinctively dismiss such alliances. More money on global health should be welcomed but there is a need to ensure that the public good is not compromised and the bigger picture is appreciated.

> Instead of setting a hodge podge of targets aimed at fighting single diseases, the world community should focus on achieving two basic goals: increased maternal survival and increased overall life expectancy.
>
> (Garrett 2007)

## *Other UN agencies contributing to global health*

### *UNAIDS*

UNAIDS was set up as a programme of the WHO in 1986 in response to the spread of the new disease along similar lines to its other disease-fighting arms. In 1996, however, UNAIDS became a UN programme in its own right co-sponsored by ten

UN agencies including the WHO, World Bank, UNESCO, United Nations Population Fund (UNFPA), UNDP, United Nations Children's Fund (UNICEF) and United Nations Office on Drugs and Crime (UNODC). This reflected the scale of the threat posed by AIDS, necessitating a response beyond the means of the WHO, but also, according to some, a lack of faith in the WHO to lead such a venture (Godlee 1994: 1494–5). UNAIDS is based in Geneva with a secretariat of over 900, divided between the headquarters and various country offices (UNAIDS 2009). It was the first UN organ to include pressure group representatives in its executive, although voting rights in the Programme Coordinating Board are restricted to the twenty-two government representatives, elected by ECOSOC according to geographical quotas. The ten co-sponsors also have permanent representation on the board without voting right and many of their field workers carry out UNAIDS work in developing countries. UNAIDS' annual budget has grown from a modest $60 million in 2001–2 to $469 million for 2008–9 and it has been widely lauded for its fundraising activities. Global health 'Horizontalists' though have sometimes been critical of UNAIDS for not considering underlying problems in countries most affected by the disease, such as the criminalization of homosexuality or neglect in helping drug users, and have advocated handing responsibility for leading international policy back to the WHO (England 2008; Das and Samarakera 2008).

## World Bank

The World Bank from the outset was intended to play a role in promoting public health in LDCs through its Health, Nutrition and Population division (HNP), although it was not until 1970 that it granted a loan via this arm of its organization (Abbasi 1999). By the 1990s, however, the NHP was outstripping the WHO in its outlay on projects (Stott 1999). The 1993 World Development Report 'Investing in Health' heralded this new direction for the World Bank, inspired by a desire to be more compassionate in its development projects and the pragmatic logic that economic growth is more likely in a healthy population.

## UNICEF

UNICEF was established by the General Assembly in 1947 before the creation of the WHO with the aim of providing emergency food and health care to children affected by the Second World War. It became a permanent agency in 1953 and by 2010 had a staff of 5,600 based in New York with eight regional offices around the world (UNICEF 2009). UNICEF is widely seen as having shifted since the 1980s from a horizontal approach to global health, in line with the WHA, to a more selective, vertical strategy (Werner 2001; Koivusalo and Ollila 1997: 209). From standing shoulder to shoulder with the WHO at Alma Ata in 1978 when the 'Health for All' crusade was launched, by the mid-1990s UNICEF had moved closer to the World Bank in focusing on the implementation of specific projects rather than the gradualist advancement of Primary Health Care. Werner considers this not to be a shift in ideology by the organization but, rather, the effect of UNICEF being a voluntary fund and so constrained by the preference of its donors for programmes of vaccinations and drug administrations over education and structural improvement. A key factor in the rise to prominence of UNICEF and particularly the World Bank has been that their point of contact with governments is through finance rather than health ministries, which are usually more politically powerful (Koivusalo and Ollila 1997: 207–8; Abbasi 1999; Godlee 1994: 1405).

## The state securitization of health

The WHO Constitution states that 'the health of all peoples is fundamental to the attainment of peace and security' (preamble). Hence it was recognized at the birth of the United Nations that military stability and the security of states, the chief aims of the overall UN system, rested on more than the blend of collective security and concert power politics that made up the Security Council. This reflected both the spirit of Idealism and an appreciation of security in a fuller form that marked international relations at the time, but was soon transformed by the Cold War. Though the WHO proceeded to carry out some remarkable public health work during the Cold War years, greatly enhancing human security, the state security dimension to health was largely forgotten until the Idealist renaissance that came with the passing of that conflict.

The WHO Secretary-General Nakajima took steps to re-establish the state security–world health link and revive state interest in the organization's work in a 1997 article and series of speeches (Nakajima 1997). A further development came in 2000 when the UN Security Council adopted a resolution in response to the threat to the international community posed by AIDS. The Resolution calls upon the UN agencies to increase collaboration and is modest in its assessment that the 'HIV/AIDS pandemic, if unchecked, *may* pose a threat to stability and security' (UN Security Council 2000: 2) (emphasis added). Such understatement in the face of a scourge killing millions of people and economically undermining many states is, on the one hand, breathtaking but, on the other hand, still significant in that it marked the first occasion a health issue was debated at the high table of realpolitik. The US government, in a manner similar to their embracing of environmental threats in the 1990s, began considering the national security implications of infectious disease in the first years of the third millennium. The Central Intelligence Agency (CIA) in 2000 published an extensive report on the threat posed to the USA by a range of diseases (National Intelligence Council 2000) and the State Department in 2001 hosted a conference entitled 'Global Infectious Disease and US Foreign Policy'.

The 'securitization' of infectious disease has, like the securitization of the environment in mainstream politics, been simply a case of considering the implications of this threat for military security rather than the general security of individual people. The term *microbialpolitik* was coined by Fidler to describe this phenomenon (Fidler 1999). The Security Council Resolution refers to the dangers posed by UN peacekeepers being infected with HIV, whilst the US State Department interest has focused on the potential for disease to 'exacerbate social and political instability in key countries in which the United States has significant interests'

(National Intelligence Council 2000: 2). Southern Africa is most frequently cited in this context. In Zambia three government ministers died of AIDS in the 1990s and, at the turn of the millennium, it was estimated that half of the police and armed forces were HIV positive (Price-Smith 2001: 14). In particular, the threat of diseases being deliberately unleashed in acts of warfare has, since the 2001 anthrax attacks in the USA, elevated questions on the availability of antidotes and the preparedness of emergency forces for combating epidemics to matters of high politics. A 2003 article by Prescott in the avowedly 'traditional' security journal *Survival* argued for greater Northern aid for Southern health problems and applauded the greater international cooperation of medics in the wake of the SARS outbreak as it augured well for preparing for a bio-terrorism attack (Prescott 2003). Horrific though the spectre of biological warfare is, it is pertinent to remember that only a handful of people have ever died in this manner whereas millions every year perish as a result of diseases which, although naturally occurring, are nonetheless preventable by human endeavour.

The state securitization of health has had some positive benefits for enhancing human security. The USA was better able to deal with recurrences of West Nile virus in 2002, which had been an annual summer event since 1999, because of a strengthening of information links between hospitals motivated by fear of biological terrorism (*Economist* 2002c). Essentially self-motivated policy can contribute to the global common good. President Bush (Jr), as clear an exponent of the 'national' interest as you could find, in his 2003 'State of the Union' address announced a major increase in the US contribution to the global campaign against AIDS, malaria and tuberculosis. Political stability in Africa may have been the chief aim of the initiative but human security was additionally enhanced as a result.

As with other non-military issues, though, the national security framing of health threats can lead to inappropriate solutions. In 2011 a cholera epidemic occurred amongst Haitians being rehoused by UN troops after the earthquake due to the installation of inadequate sanitary systems in the new dwellings.

## The human securitization of health

The impact infectious epidemics can have on one's own or another state's power capabilities is certainly something governments should factor in to their foreign policy decision-making, but the security most threatened by disease is that of ordinary people rather than states. The inappropriateness of the high politics–low politics distinction in international relations is most clearly apparent when considering health issues. Recognition of this can be dated back to the 1940s, when the discipline of International Relations was still in its infancy. David Mitrany took on the mantle of internationalism from Kant, Bentham and the Idealist statesmen of the 1920s and 1930s and developed the theory of functionalism, prescribing and predicting a future post-Westphalian world order in which people's needs would be met by functional INGOs rather than by states. Functionalism is both normative and descriptive. Mitrany considered the growth of functional international organizations (organizations with a specific function such as the OIHP) in the late nineteenth and early twentieth century to have been a boon to ordinary people's lives and something around which to build a new, better post-war world. The international system of states was alien to the needs of people since it artificially divided humanity into competitive units which overemphasized the 'high politics' of securing the state through military means at the expense of welfare. Hence Mitrany and the Functionalists advocated the growth of functional international organizations run not by government delegates but by internationalists specializing in the particular function concerned. The belief was not that this would happen overnight but that gradually and inexorably people would come to see that their interests were better served by such organizations and switch their loyalties away from their own states and nationalities. Thus a world revolution would occur quietly and slowly by a process referred to as 'spillover', as the functions of government transferred to a more appropriate polity which would emerge over time. Crucially, Functionalism very much advocates revolution from below and opposes world or regional federalism since this would be the creation of political institutions by politicians rather than their natural evolution, and thus risk replicating the illogical high–low politics distinction. Functionalism favours a farewell to states rather than their amalgamation into larger ones (Mitrany 1975).

The WHO is an intergovernmental rather than a true non-governmental functional organization but it has developed an independent and global perspective from its epistemic community of experts and serving medics. It has frequently been criticized by both Functionalists and intergovernmentalists for not being fully in either of these camps, but its track record in the provision of the global good of public health is unprecedented in human history. It is inconceivable that the charitable cooperation of governments could have achieved the eradication of smallpox and so saved the lives of 2 million people a year. The logistics of mounting a genuinely global vaccination campaign, which had to overcome political and cultural obstacles to the intervention of foreign doctors, could only be dealt with by a body representing the whole world, rather than a powerful sub-set of it. In spite of its setbacks, the WHO has presided over a period of unprecedented improvements in human health. Life expectancies in the Global South have improved markedly despite the fact that these countries continue to bear the brunt of health problems. World life expectancy (at birth) in the first fifty years of the WHO increased from 46.5 to 64.3, an increase of 38 per cent. Whilst some of this can be attributed to economic growth, great improvements have occurred in parts of the world where economic development and modernization has not significantly advanced. African life expectancy has increased by 36 per cent (from 37.8 to 51.4) whilst US–Canadian life expectancy has increased by 11 per cent (from 69 to 76.9). The highest growths have been in Asia where both economic and health developments has been significant (41.3 to 66.3/61 per cent) (WHO 1999b). Public health interventions, however, are the major explanation for longer life. In a major study to evaluate the reasons for reduced mortality in the twentieth century, Preston estimated that, contrary to popular assumption, economic development accounted for only 15–20 per cent of the global improvement in life expectancy between the 1930s and the 1960s. Overwhelmingly this improvement was attributable to better public and professional knowledge with regard to disease prevention and cure (Preston 1975). Subsequent studies by the World Bank (1993) and World Health Organization (WHO 1999b) have corroborated this finding.

## The globalization of health security

In common with the other areas of global security, globalization is for health a two-edged sword. It brings with it new threats and challenges but also new opportunities for better coping with threats both old and new. Although the opportunities for diseases to diffuse throughout humankind are greater than ever before, the means of mobilizing resistance to this are also greater than ever before and can only get stronger. The widening and deepening of politics characteristic of the modern global condition offers a number of possibilities which can enhance the health security of all people and, in particular, those most insecure in the Global South.

## *The use of information technology to advance the global dispersion of medical knowledge*

Over recent years there have been major advances in the use of computer and communications technology to advance the knowledge of and means to contain and control the spread of disease. The WHO launched the HINARI Programme for Access to Health Research in 2002 in an effort to offset the perennial criticism that the fruits of globalization are rarely enjoyed globally. To improve medical knowledge in LDCs, in line with its horizontal strategy, the WHO has promoted free or low-cost internet access to over 8,000 online medical journals and helped make available cheap software for improving medical delivery systems. Private information systems, such as ProMED and TravelMED, perform similar services but the WHO's global reach and public orientation give their network greater significance and scope for future development.

## *The use of information technology to strengthen global policy*

IT advances have also served to strengthen the capacity to detect and respond to disease outbreaks at the global level. Despite concerns over the dilution of its political leadership in global health the WHO, with its near universal membership and undoubted epistemic leadership, has been able to put itself at the forefront of this development and give greater authority to existing global rules on disease notification and open the way for the development of further ones. An Outbreak Verification System was initiated in 1997, to improve upon the previous system of relying on official state notifications to the WHO of significant disease outbreaks. As mentioned earlier, some governments can be coy about releasing such information whilst some might lack the capacity to do so effectively. Part of this system is the Global Public Health Intelligence Network (GPHIN), which routinely scans media sources for epidemiological information and passes it on to the WHO to verify and inform relevant authorities in an early warning system. The significance of this development is shown in the figures that of all initial reports gathered under the system in the first two years of its operation 71 per cent came from unofficial (generally media) sources rather than official ones (Grein *et al.* 2000: 100).

The Global Outbreak and Alert Response Network (GOARN) in 2000 further developed this capability by globalizing and coordinating various regional and disease-specific surveillance networks into a single 'network of networks'. GOARN has also worked on pooling the resources of participating states and organizations so that international teams of experts can be quickly assembled and dispatched to outbreak scenes. The 2000 Ebola outbreak in Uganda, for example, prompted a rapid international response led by GOARN whilst, in 2003, the notoriously secretive Chinese government was quickly forced into coming clean after initially attempting to downplay the outbreak of severe acute respiratory syndrome (SARS). China is estimated to have lost $1,000 billion due to the SARS outbreak of 2003 but, when the second wave of the disease struck the following year, the government reported it immediately and fired the officials deemed responsible for covering up the facts in the original outbreak (Upton 2004: 76). David Heymann, head of the WHO's communicable diseases operations, has even gone so far as to suggest that: '[h]ad this system been in place in the early 1980s, AIDS might never have become a global epidemic on the scale we see today' (Heymann 2001: 12). In line with such developments the keystone of WHO policy the International Health Regulations (IHR), which require governments to give international notification of epidemics, entered into force in 2007. The IHRs, which can be dated back to the International Sanitary Conventions at the dawn of global health policy, aim to extend notification obligations beyond the long-standing requirements for cholera, plague and yellow fever to all diseases constituting an international threat.

## *The strengthening of global civil society*

Many pressure groups, such as Oxfam and Save the Children, have a long history of highlighting the plight of disease victims but recent years have seen a significant deepening of NGO activity in this field. A new breed of pressure groups are increasingly using advanced communications technology to assist medics in LDCs. The US-based group SatelLife, for example, make use of satellites to link medics in LDCs to their developed world. TEPHINET (Training Programs in Epidemiology and Public Health Internventions Network) was set up in 1997 and disperses help on a not-for-profit basis. The medical profession itself increasingly lobbies at the global level. MedAct is a group comprising health professionals which campaigns for governments to give greater consideration to the health impact of their policies in areas such as military security and economic development. This is a more overtly political stance than the traditional neutrality of groups such as the Red Cross, seeking to provide relief to human suffering in crisis situations. The radicalization of pressure groups, in public health and in international relations in general, is best characterized by the work of the group Médecins Sans Frontières (MSF) (Doctors Without Borders). MSF consciously chooses to ignore the constraints of sovereignty in its operations, sending in medical teams to countries without being specifically requested to enter by the government and making overtly political statements on the right of individual people to receive medical attention: a global 'right to life'. The UN–NGO symbiosis, best known in the global politics of the environment and human rights, is also evident in health. Public health pressure groups enjoy a healthy relationship with WHO and have been extensively consulted and utilized in initiatives such as GOARN.

## Greater public scrutiny of business

As with the 'greening' of petrochemical firms witnessed in the politics of the environment, greater consumer awareness has prompted MNCs operating in the developing world to improve their public image. The cynic can point to tax breaks often open to MNCs who make charitable contributions and to the advertising pay-offs of apparent philanthropism, but the fact remains that businesses are donating significant sums to global public health and contributing to a global good. At the same time, blatantly cynical activities by MNCs which undermine public health are increasingly likely to be highlighted by pressure groups and be used to damage their image in the eyes of ever more enlightened consumers. The backtrack of the pharmaceutical firms and US government over the patenting of HIV drugs in Brazil and South Africa, referred to earlier, provides a clear instance of this.

## Democratization and more socially responsive government

The logic of the Sen 'Entitlements thesis', that famines are less likely under democratic conditions, holds also for public health in general. Citizens empowered with the vote are unlikely to tolerate governments negligent in securing their health. The Indian state of Kerala has been highlighted by Sen and others as a case study of human development in the face of economic adversity. The state government of Kerala in the 1970s introduced a major reform package of social security provision and land redistribution in the face of significant political protest. Despite insignificant economic growth in the state, Keralan citizens' lives improved remarkably over the next two decades, including a major advance in life expectancy. Sen's advocacy of a 'support led' approach to development does not simply equate democratic political systems with better health since he emphasizes how countries like China and Cuba have achieved better health for their people than wealthier, democratic states by having well-funded public health and education systems (Dreze and Sen 1991: 221–6). Marxist/Maoist governments generally have an instinctive, ideological commitment to public health which does not need to be prompted by society (the Keralan government was also leftist). It is the globaliza-tion, then, of socially responsive government rather than simply democratization that has contributed to improved standards of public health.

## The globalization of the public service ethos

The injection of private money into global health programmes has brought with it fears that policy could be transformed from the 'Health for All', social security approach expounded by the WHO to a more uneven charitable approach. Similar fears were expressed when developed democracies began undergoing a 'welfare backlash' from the mid-1970s, after the cost of state support began to spiral due to ageing populations and higher levels of unemployment causing more people than ever envisaged to fall into the welfare safety net. Countries of Western Europe and North America responded, to varying degrees, by incorporating private solutions to public health in what has been described as a 'welfare mix' (Rose and Shiratori 1986). However, the wholesale dismantling of welfare state provision has not happened in any country, despite economic and political arguments favouring this, partly because public opinion considers state health provision a right and partly because public health practitioners have powerfully resisted this. Similarly, medics and scientists operating at the global level provide a powerful lobby in favour of maintaining the WHO's horizontal strategy. The epistemic community for global public health is an influential one since its opinions are generally seen as informed and clearly inspired by the provision of a public good rather than any sectional interest. The standing of the WHO was evident in 2003 during the SARS outbreak when governments and the general public interpreted their recommendations not to travel to the affected cities of Beijing and Toronto as authoritative 'bans' and they again became the source of global authority when the swine flu pandemic caused panic in 2009. The growth of new NGOs, internationally oriented doctors and the persistence of the WHO have together helped formulate a culture in the politics of global health which the dominant discourse is based on a right to health for all, even though this is proving harder to achieve than imagined in the 1970s.

Aside from the human security logic of acting on global public health issues a simple widened security state-utilitarian logic also supports action. Benatar, Daar and Singer argue that:

> it is both desirable and necessary to develop a global mindset in health ethics, we also suggest that this change need not be based merely on altruism, but could be founded on long-term self interest. For example, it has been shown by mathematical modelling for hepatitis B that resources needed to prevent one carrier in the United Kingdom could prevent 4,000 carriers in Bangladesh, of whom, statistically, four might be expected to migrate to the UK. Thus it would be four times more cost-effective for the UK to sponsor a vaccination programme against hepatitis B in Bangladesh than to introduce its own universal vaccination programme.
>
> (Benatar, Daar and Singer 2003: 133[3])

Appreciation of the WHO from the global general public is increasing on both a pragmatic level, spurred by personal security fears, and, on an empathetic level, due to greater awareness of the suffering of others. In this way we are beginning to witness a globalization of Sen's entitlements thesis and the gradual realization of Mitrany's dream of Functionalist world revolution.

## Key points

- Increased human movements and societal changes, associated with contemporary globalization, have heightened the cross-border threat posed by both transmittable and non-transmittable illnesses.
- Technical solutions to combat diseases were successful from the 1940s to the 1970s, most notably in the eradication of smallpox by the WHO, but increased resistance to drugs and pesticides has prompted a resurgence of some diseases like malaria.

- This setback prompted the WHO to advocate a more 'horizontal' approach to global public health in which alleviating the underlying causes of vulnerability to disease is stressed. At the same time the 'vertical' approach of seeking to eradicate diseases continues to be pursued by the WHO in alliance with private donors.
- The traditional state security implications of diseases like AIDS have attracted greater governmental interest in global public health policy.
- Globalization may be a cause of global health problems but it also offers opportunities for enhancing global health security through the harnessing of transnational information flows to disseminate medical knowledge and by empowering the WHO to coordinate policy.

## Notes

1  Some of the regions are only loosely geographical: 'Eastern Mediterranean' comprises most of the Arab world, Iran, Afghanistan and Pakistan; South-East Asia includes India and North Korea; Australia and New Zealand are linked to much of East Asia in the 'Western Pacific region'.
2  These were controversial because of the dangers inherent when mixing milk powder with water in countries with poor water sanitation levels.
3  This estimate is based upon N. Gay and W. Edmunds (1998) 'Developed Countries Should Pay for Hepatitis B vaccine in developing countries', *British Medical Journal*, 316: 1457.

## Recommended reading

Benatar, S., Daar, A. and Singer, P. (2003) 'Global Health Ethics: The Rationale for Mutual Caring', *International Affairs*, 79(1): 107–38.
Elbe, S. (2010) *Security and Global Health: Toward the Medicalization of Insecurity*, Cambridge: Polity Press.
Garrett, L. (2007) 'The Challenge of Global Health', *Foreign Affairs*, 86(1): 14–38.
Lee, K. (2008) *World Health Organization*, London: Routledge.
Pirages, D. and Runci, P. (2011) 'Ecological Interdependence and the Spread of Infectious Disease', in Cusimano, M. (ed.) *Beyond Sovereignty: Issues for a Global Agenda*, 4th edn, Boston: Wadsworth, Cengage: 264–81.

## Useful web links

Global Alliance for Vaccines and Immunization: http://www.vaccinealliance.org/home/index.php
Global Fund to Fight AIDS, Tuberculosis and Malaria: http://www.globalfundatm.org/TRP.html
UNAIDS: http://www.unaids.org/
World Health Organization: http://www.who.int/en/

# Natural threats to security

> We cannot stop the forces of nature, but we can and must prevent them from causing major social and economic disasters.
>
> Kofi Annan, UN Secretary-General (Annan 1999)

## Natural disasters

A major source of insecurity for much of the world's population is rooted in the natural, non-living world, from physical phenomena originating in the Earth's interior, its atmosphere and even from beyond our planet. The phrase 'Acts of God' encapsulates the notion of human helplessness in the face of such dangers which are out of our control, but the truth is that natural disasters are as much socio-political as geological or meteorological phenomena. '[A] disaster is the intersection of two opposing forces: those processes generating vulnerability on one side, and physical exposure to a hazard on the other' (Blaikie, Cannon, Davis and Wisner 1994: 22). It is socio-political factors that make people vulnerable to hazardous natural events. The fact that people live, whether through their own choice, ignorance or compulsion, in places known to be prone to disaster is one such factor. Another is the capacity and/or willingness of governing authorities to take steps to alleviate the potential human cost of events known to be likely to occur.

Tables 8.1 and 8.2 illustrate not only the horrific scale of human casualties that can accrue from natural disasters but also the importance of the socio-political component in such events. The Huang Ho and other Chinese rivers are more prone to dramatically bursting their banks than most of the world's waterways but this has been well known in China for centuries. Overpopulation, poor government and the human propensity to risk residing in such hazardous places for the benefits of farming on the fertile soils deposited by the flooding are major contributors to the shocking death toll that has accumulated over time. The death toll by natural disaster is somewhat variable, as can be seen in Figure 8.1 but, in terms of sudden deadly impact, events like the 2010 earthquake in Haiti and 2004 Tsunami in South

**Table 8.1** The ten worst natural disasters in history

| | Place | Date | Type | Fatalities |
|---|---|---|---|---|
| 1 | Huang Ho River, China | 1931 | Flood | 3.7 million[a,b] |
| 2 | China | 1959 | Flood | 2 million[a,b] |
| 3 | Upper Egypt and Syria | 1201 | Earthquake | 1.1 million[d] |
| 4 | Huang Ho River, China | 1887 | Flood | 900,000[c] |
| 5 | Shaanxi, Shanxi and Henan, China | 1556 | Earthquake | 830,000[c] |
| 6 | Huang Ho River, China | 1938 | Flood | 500,000[d] |
| 7 | China | 1939 | Flood | 500,000[a,b] |
| 8 | Bangladesh | 1970 | Cyclone | 300,000[a,b] |
| 9 | Tang-shan, China | 1976 | Earthquake | 242,000[a] |
| 10 | Indian Ocean | 2004 | Tsunami | 227,000[a] |

Sources: [a] CRED (2011); [b] Disaster Center (2003); [c] Castello-Cortes and Feldman (1996); [d] NGDC (2003).

**Table 8.2** Average annual death toll by types of natural
disaster, 2000–10

| | | |
|---|---|---:|
| 1 | Earthquakes | 40,888 |
| 2 | Tsunamis | 22,798 |
| 3 | Windstorms | 15,636 |
| 4 | Extreme temperatures | 13,884 |
| 5 | Floods | 5,673 |
| 6 | Avalanches/landslides | 1,038 |
| 7 | Wildfires | 71 |
| 8 | Volcanic eruptions | 54 |

Source: CRED (2011); excludes droughts.

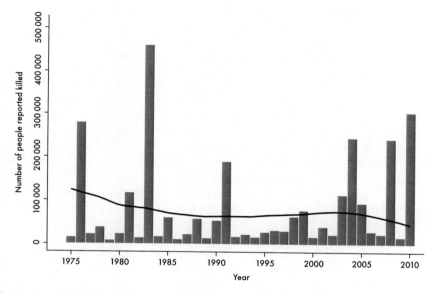

**Figure 8.1** Global deaths by natural disaster, 1975–2010

Asia – which both claimed well over 200,000 lives – far outstrip any recent wars or insurgencies.

Historically, floods and earthquakes have presented the greatest natural hazards to human life but, in the 1990s, windstorms claimed more lives. These three categories of disaster have continued to account for thousands of deaths per year in the early years of the twenty-first century, as Table 8.2 illustrates. Statistics for the last decade, however, differ from previous eras since three particular events, the 2003 and 2010 heatwaves in Western Europe and Russia and the 2004 Indian Ocean tsunami, were far and away the most calamitous incidents of their kind in history and have elevated the position of these phenomena to higher than ever before.

## *Earthquakes*

Earthquakes, more clearly than any natural hazard, demonstrate the centrality of the social component in the onset of a disaster. Though the scale of seismic shocks in the Earth's crust cannot be entirely predicted, the places where such shocks occur is well established. Seismic activity is most pronounced on the margins of the Earth's tectonic plates, such as along the San Andreas Fault Line, which marks the point at which the Pacific plate meets the North American plate. The threat to humanity posed by earthquakes is almost entirely due to the secondary effects of seismic waves destroying the human-made infrastructure built in such susceptible areas rather than the event in itself.

1   *Surface faulting*: Direct death by earthquake is rare but possible if someone is killed by a fall into a fault line, which has been widened or moved by seismic waves. More commonly, though still a relatively minor form of earthquake-related fatality, people can be killed by buildings being dislodged in this way.

2   *Ground motion*: Of far greater significance than faulting is the shaking effects of seismic waves on the Earth's surface. A combination of the waves' amplitude, frequency and duration will determine how much ground motion they create. This is generally most pronounced near the earthquake's *epicentre* (the point on the surface directly above the source of the seismic wave, the *focus*). Ground motion in itself is not especially hazardous to man but the effects it has on the human environment can be devastating.

    i   FALLING BUILDINGS: The most common cause of death during an earthquake is as a result of the collapse of dwellings or other constructions. Recent history's most calamitous earthquakes, in Tang-shan, China in 1976 and Haiti in 2010, killed nearly a quarter of a million people in this way. Most of the cities' buildings were destroyed during the principal earthquake and those that survived were then toppled by the *aftershocks* that followed. Hence, the design and location of buildings in earthquake-prone areas is a critical factor in the scale of security threat they represent. In some cities in locations vulnerable to earthquakes, such as Tokyo and San Francisco, the security threat to citizens is significantly diminished by the implementation of regulations requiring particular safety-conscious engineering techniques in the construction of buildings.

    ii   FIRE: The structural damage caused by earthquakes can prove lethal in ways other than crushing victims with masonry or causing them to fall to their deaths. A common knock-on effect is the spread of fire through a town hit by an Earth tremor. Most of the casualties of the famous earthquakes that hit San Francisco in 1906 and Tokyo in 1923 were killed in fires instigated by damage to cookers and heating equipment. In Tokyo fire swept through wooden dwellings specifically designed to avoid the sorts of casualties associated with the fall of stone buildings.

    iii   LIQUEFACTION: Deaths may also result from earthquakes when geological conditions permit ground water to seep to the surface due to seismic disturbance in a process known as *liquefaction*. This can result in major land subsidence or flooding. It is in this way that many of the victims of the 1985 Mexico City earthquake perished.

iv  LANDSLIDES: Earthquakes can also pose a hazard by prompting the fall of stones or soil from a hillside overlooking a town.

## Tsunamis

The Japanese term 'tsunami' (meaning literally 'harbour wave') is the correct term for what are still sometimes referred to as 'tidal waves'. These giant sea waves are not produced by tides but by seismic activity such as volcanic eruptions and earthquakes. Tsunamis have a wavelength of between 100 to 150 kilometres (around 100 times the size of an ordinary sea wave) and can travel hundreds of kilometres at speeds ranging between 640 and 960 km/h. On the high seas, however, they can be very difficult to detect since their height may be no more than a metre (Whittow 1984: 554). By far the most devastating tsunami in history occurred in December 2004 in the Indian Ocean, triggered by earthquakes along the margins of the Indian and Eurasian tectonic plates near Aceh, Indonesia and the Andaman Islands of India. Over 220,000 people were killed as a result of rapid coastal flooding in Indonesia, Sri Lanka, India, Thailand, Malaysia, the Maldives and Somalia (CRED 2011).

Though historically they are comparatively rare, tsunamis appear to have become more common and deadly in recent years. In 2011 the most powerful earthquake ever recorded to have struck Japan (9.0 on the Richter Scale) triggered a tsunami that swept vast waves over towns along the north-east coast of the country leaving 28,050 people dead and many thousands more homeless (CRED 2011). The Japanese authorities were well prepared for an earthquake – even of this intensity – but less so for the consequent tsunami.

## Windstorms

### Cyclones

Known variously as hurricanes (in North America) or typhoons (in East Asia) cyclones are storm systems based on an area of low atmospheric pressure in tropical climes. Gale force winds circulate around the calm 'eye' of the storm (anti-clockwise in the northern hemisphere, clockwise in the South) accompanied usually by torrential rains. The most devastating consequence of a cyclone is coastal flooding caused by a *storm surge*, when winds create huge sea waves. It was in this way that upwards of 300,000 people were killed around the Ganges delta in Bangladesh in 1970. Wind damage and riverine flooding can also result from cyclones and claim lives.

### Tornadoes

Similarly to cyclones, tornadoes are storms which rotate around an eye of low atmospheric pressure. However, in contrast, they tend to be narrower and faster and generally originate inland rather than at sea. The world's most deadly tornado occurred again in Bangladesh when 1,300 people were killed around the town of Saturia in 1989 (Castello-Cortes and Feldman 1996: 27). Owing to their narrow, funnel-like shape the destruction caused by tornadoes tends to be quite localized, although they move across the surface in a somewhat unpredictable manner. Damage by tornadoes tends to be of three forms:

1    *High winds*: Extremely strong winds associated with tornadoes can cause significant damage to buildings, either directly or through the propelling of debris.
2    *Updraught*: The circulatory winds and low pressure vortex can cause large objects and even people to be 'sucked up' the tornado funnel and deposited up to several kilometres away.
3    *Effect of low pressure*: The extremely low air pressure in the eye of the tornado is the most hazardous element of the phenomenon. Buildings caught in the eye are prone to explode because of the difference in pressure inside and outside of the walls.

## Floods

Floods, historically, are far and away the biggest security threat to humanity from the non-living world. Although overtaken by windstorms in recent years, most of these fatalities were also the result of flooding triggered by the effect of cyclones. Floods often occur as secondary effects of other natural phenomena but can present a direct hazard to human life in a number of ways.

*Flash floods* occur when heavy rainfall exceeds the capacity of the ground to absorb the water and causes a rapid, widespread deluge. Nearly 2,000 people were killed in northwestern Pakistan in this way in 2010 (CRED 2011). *Riverine floods* occur when precipitation causes a river to burst its banks. This is the most dangerous type of flooding since it is relatively common and rivers frequently run through densely populated areas. The Huang Ho river system in China can lay claim to being the most hazardous natural feature on Earth having claimed millions of lives over the centuries. Additional flooding hazards can occur when an excessive inflow from rivers or as a result of snow melt causes lakes or seas to flood.

Drowning, obviously, is the major means by which floods can kill but this can happen in a number of ways. People may simply be engulfed by rising waters, become trapped in buildings or cars or caught in river sediment deposited by the waters. Collapsing buildings and trees form an additional significant hazard and structural damage may also lead to deaths by electrocution and even, with grim irony, fires. Hypothermia and water-borne diseases are also often associated with flooding. Flooding only represents a hazard when it is not predictable. The regular, seasonal flooding of rivers can not only be managed but utilized for its benefits to humankind since silt deposits from rivers bursting their banks provide fertile soils. It is instructive that the Bengali language has two, distinctive words for 'flood'. *Barsha* refers to the usual and beneficial floods, whilst the word *bona* is reserved for more infrequent and destructive large floods.

## Avalanches/landslides

Sudden mass movements of snow and ice down a mountainside, known as ava-lanches, can kill by directly smothering people in a valley or, more commonly, by destroying buildings. 'Wet' snow avalanches, which tend to occur in spring when mountain snows begin to melt, tend to be the most destructive. The biggest ever avalanche disaster occurred in Peru in 1970 when nearly all of the 20,000 inhabitants of Yungay were killed when an earthquake triggered a wet 'slab avalanche' of ice and glacial rock to fall down the side of the country's highest mountain Nevado Huascaran. Airborne-powder-snow avalanches are less hazardous but can also kill as they are frequently preceded by avalanche winds which can cause houses to explode as a result of rapid changes in air pressure (Whittow 1984: 45).

Landslides are a common knock-on effect of other geothermal and meteoro-logical phenomena and are sometimes human-made, but can occur independently by the natural process of gravity acting on soil and rock accumulated on a hillside. Typically, rainwater is the catalyst for this process. A period of torrential rainfall in Northern China in 2010, for example, prompted mudslides in Gansu which led to 1,765 fatalities (CRED 2011).

## Extreme temperatures

Both 'hot waves' and 'cold waves' can kill. The deadliest recorded heatwaves hit Western Europe in 2003 and Russia in 2010, both claiming over 50,000 lives (CRED 2011). Excessive cold represents the first and excessive heat the second biggest annual causes of death by natural hazards in the USA (Goklany 2007). Dramatic short-term rises in temperature can kill through heatstroke and cold waves can kill directly by hypothermia or frostbite. Most cold wave deaths, however, are caused indirectly as a result of power lines freezing or heavy snow crushing dwellings. Unpredictability is the key danger in these events. The 38°C temperatures that Moscow and other Russian cities experienced in August 2010 would not have killed in other parts of the world but there they were unprecedented and the resultant heat and smog led to a sudden rise in heatstrokes and exacerbated illnesses in the old and infirm.

## Wildfires

Wildfires are prominent in woodland regions with an arid climate and strong winds. Droughts and hot winds can dry vegetation which may then be ignited by lightning or other forces causing fires which spread to other trees or shrubs carried by the wind. The USA and Australia are particularly prone to wildfire in the summer. The worst ever disaster occurred in 1871 in the US states of Wisconsin and Michigan, when around 1,500 people perished (Smith 2001: 248). Australian bushfires of 1974–5 burned around 15 per cent of the whole country (ibid.) and, in 2009, claimed 180 lives (CRED 2011).

It is debatable, however, whether wildfires should be considered natural disasters at all since an estimated 80 per cent of them ultimately are human-made, resulting from negligence or ignorance in forestry, farming or some other form of land use (Goldammer 1999: 69). Indeed, it has become increasingly apparent in recent years that many wildfires are not only not natural but are not accidents either. It has been suggested that around a quarter of wildfires in California occur as a result of arson (Smith 2001: 256). There was a public outcry in Australia in 2002 when it transpired that the 2001–2 'Black Christmas' fires that devastated large areas of New South Wales were deliberately started by a number of youths and young adults for no clear motive. The human aspect, whether deliberate or accidental, has become more significant with the increased encroachment of settlements into wooded areas and wildfires are becoming more common and even a regular phenomenon in certain places.

## Volcanic eruptions

The threats to human life from volcanic activity come in many, diverse forms:

1   *Lava flows*: The most familiar threatening image of volcanicity is the sight of molten lava flowing down the hillside. Today, however, lava flows represent a minor threat to life since they are generally slow enough and well enough observed to permit the evacuation of nearby settlements.

2   *Pyroclastic flows*: More deadly than lava flows are the movement of mixtures of volcanic gases and debris that can be formed on the side of a volcano. The Roman city of Pompeii, famously, was destroyed in this way and the highest death toll by volcanicity in the twentieth century was also accounted for in this way when 29,000 people were killed near Mount Pelee, Martinique, in 1902.

3   *Lahars (volcanic mudflows)*: Volcanic debris mixed with water can also form a deadly agent, principally since this moves further and more quickly than lava or pyroclastic flows. The 1985 Nevada del Ruiz eruption in Colombia killed 23,000 people in this way when a relatively small eruption produced pyroclastic flows which mixed with snow at the summit and flowed many kilometres down the valley, engulfing the town of Armero.

4   *Tephra*: Various solid objects can be spat out at high speed during a volcanic explosion. Chunks of molten lava chilling in the air to form 'volcanic bombs', volcanic glass and ash may be showered onto residential areas. Eruptions of Mount Pinatubo in the Philippines in 1991 killed over 200 people, principally as a result of tephra collapsing the roofs of houses in nearby setlements. Tephra may also create knock-on disasters by downing aeroplanes, instigating lightning and damaging infrastructure and crops. A famine occurred following the 1815 Tambora eruption in Indonesia, the largest and most deadly volcanic eruption in history, killing 82,000 people in addition to the 10,000 direct deaths from tephra and pyroclastic flows (University of North Dakota 2002).

5   *Poisonous gases*: Many toxic chemicals can be emitted by volcanic eruptions including: carbon dioxide, carbon monoxide, sulphur dioxide, hydrogen

sulphide and gaseous forms of hydrochloric and sulphuric acid. It is even possible for poisonous gases to be released from a volcano without any eruption. In Cameroon in 1986 1,700 people were killed by a cloud of carbon dioxide released from Lake Nyos, a crater on a dormant volcano (a *caldera*). The gas had seeped out of underground magma into the lake and was then released into the atmosphere owing to some sort of disturbance to the water (Coch 1995: 97).

## *Space invaders: natural threats to security from other worlds*

Although they have yet to greatly impact human society, natural phenomena emanating from beyond the Earth must also be seen to represent a security threat. 'An asteroid of size 1km or more hitting our world at the minimum possible velocity (11km/s – the escape velocity of the Earth) would release at least as much energy as 100,000 one-megaton hydrogen bombs' (Kitchin 2001: 54). Asteroids are minor planets within our solar system which vary in size from a diameter of a thousand to less than one kilometre. Most lie between the orbits of Mars and Jupiter but some, the 'Earth Crossing Asteroids' (ECAs), can cross this planet's orbit of the Sun. The ECAs together with comets and meteoroids (debris from asteroids or comets) which pass close to the Earth are collectively referred to as 'Near Earth Objects' (NEOs). The possibility of one of these celestial objects striking the Earth, and the likely effects, has been the subject of increasing speculation in recent years and some measures have been taken to improve the capacity to predict if such a collision could occur and initiate thinking on how it could be avoided. The 'Torino Scale' has been devised to rationalize the likelihood of asteroid collision (Peiser 2001) (see Table 8.3).

**Table 8.3** The Torino Scale[a]

| | | |
|---|---|---|
| 0 | Events having no likely consequence | Collision will not happen |
| 1 | Events meriting careful monitoring | Collision is extremely unlikely |
| 2 | | Collision is very unlikely |
| 3 | Events meriting concern | 1% chance of localized destruction |
| 4 | | 1% chance of regional destruction |
| 5 | | Significant threat of regional devastation |
| 6 | Threatening events | Significant threat of global catastrophe |
| 7 | | Extremely significant threat of global catastrophe |
| 8 | | Localized destruction (occur every 50–1,000 years) |
| 9 | Certain collisions | Regional destruction (occur every 1,000–100,000 years) |
| 10 | | Capable of causing global climate catastrophe (occur less than once per 100,000 years) |

Note: [a] This scale was devised by Professor Richard Binzel.

There are no validated records of human deaths due to NEO collisions but there is evidence that such events have occurred. Meteoroids regularly enter the Earth's atmosphere (what are referred to as *meteors*), where most burn up and disappear, but some survive long enough to strike the surface (*meteorites*) or explode close to the surface (*bolides*). Evidence that comets can collide with planets was provided in 1994 when *Shoemaker-Levy 9* was observed crashing into Jupiter. The 'Cretaceous/Tertiary Impact', caused by either a comet or an asteroid, 65 million years ago created the 250 km wide Chicxulub crater in the Gulf of Mexico and is widely held as responsible for the extinction of the dinosaurs and various other life forms. A bolide is believed to be responsible for the 1908 phenomenon around the River Tunguska in Siberia when over a thousand square kilometres of uninhabited forest where flattened (Chyba, Thomas and Zahnle 1993).

Surveillance of the night sky for early detection of NEOs has increased since the launch of the 'Spaceguard' initiative by NASA in the early 1990s and its subsequent linking up with other national schemes. What could be done if an NEO was set for collision with the Earth remains to be established, however. Military solutions have figured prominently in discussions. The possibility of destroying an NEO by nuclear strike has been aired regularly, particularly in the USA, the state most likely to be able to attempt such an action. Nuclear deterrence is always a divisive security measure, however, and a less dramatic strategy of deflecting an NEO off course by crashing an unmanned spacecraft into it is now more commonly suggested. Other, non-military suggestions for defending the Earth from such collisions border on the surreal. British politician Lembit Opik, for example, has proposed that: 'You could have a big plastic condom or space sheath to collect near-Earth objects and tow them to safety' (Brown and Goodchild 2000).

## The rise of human vulnerability to nature

Natural disasters are, of course, as old as humankind. Even older, if the risk posed to other animals from natural events, such as the fate that befell the dinosaurs, is considered. Although the overall historical trend has been downwards since the 1930s, the frequency and deadliness of natural disasters has increased since the early 1990s. A number of factors have contributed to this:

### *Poverty*

Between 1991 and 2005 the death toll by natural disasters in developing countries was ten times that in OECD countries (Ferris and Petz 2011). Clearly money can buy some degree of security from natural disasters. More particularly it is the sort of well-evolved legal environment associated with economic development that brings security to people. 'It is not an "Act of God" that no more than 10 per cent of the multi-storey structures in Indian cities are built according to earthquake resistant norms' (Wisner 2000). Striking evidence of this was provided in 2010 when two major earthquakes struck the Americas. A month after the Haiti disaster devastated the western hemisphere's poorest country comparatively wealthy Chile was rocked by a earthquake that was 500 times as powerful but claimed only 500 lives.

Bankoff, however, cautions that shifting the focus for dealing with natural disasters from technical responses to tackling underlying vulnerability carries a danger of conflating securing those at risk with modernization and traditional notions of economic development. Designating large proportions of the population of the Global South as 'vulnerable' reinforces the notion that such people can only be 'saved' by technical assistance from the North (Bankoff 2001). Some aspects of economic globalization have served to make LDC populations more vulnerable at the same time as furthering their economic development. Prioritizing economic growth over safety has sometimes served to make LDC populations more vulnerable at the same time as advancing their 'development' by encouraging them to live in overcrowded cities. Additionally, the 2005 New Orleans flooding in the wake of Hurricane Katrina demonstrated that inadequate governance and social exclusion can render sections of the population of wealthy, developed countries insecure. The devastation caused by the 2011 Japan tsunami and 2010 New Zealand earthquake also served as reminders that development, democracy and experience do not guarantee human security.

## Better information

There is a case to be made that one key factor behind the rise in natural disasters is simply that more are being reported in the world's media. The ever-extending lenses of the global media and concerted efforts of a developing global epistemic community continue to bring more events than ever before into focus. The annual number of recorded natural disasters in the world was consistently in double figures in the 1970s and 1980s but has been in triple figures since 1990 (Swiss Re 2012).

## Population growth

Since 'if people are not involved there is no disaster' (Loretti 2000) the more people there are in the world the increased likelihood there is of a natural hazard having human security consequences and becoming a natural disaster. As significant population growth in the world is now largely confined to the Global South, where disaster mitigation policy tends to be as underdeveloped as the economy, ever greater numbers of people are being exposed to natural hazards.

## Urbanization

The burgeoning population of the Global South in the main manifests itself in the growth of major cities. Around half of these new *megacities* which have emerged are located in areas prone to seismic or storm activity. Most of the quarter of a million people who perished as a result of the Haiti earthquake in 2010 were residents of shanty towns clinging to the hillsides that surround the capital, Port au Prince.

## Land degradation

In many cases natural disasters are triggered or exacerbated by a lack of natural defences. Hence, changes in land use can have disastrous side-effects. For example, the loss of traditional vegetation on river banks can increase the likelihood of flooding, and on hillsides can make land slips more likely (UNEP 2002: ch. 3, p. 10).

## Refugees

Increased flows of refugees and internally displaced people over recent years has contributed to the increase in number and deadliness of natural disasters. Desperate and, frequently, unwelcomed people are likely to settle in insecure places. The exodus of over 2 million Afghanis to neighbouring Pakistan since the 1980s has presented many of these people with a choice of relocating either in urban slums or rural margins, such as mountain sides (Matthew and Zalidi 2002: 74–5). Either option brings heightened vulnerability to natural hazards: the former from earthquakes and the latter from landslides.

## Climate change

Natural hazards can be understood to occur for rational, natural reasons. Tropical cyclones, for example, can be viewed as 'safety valves' which dissipate the build-up of excessive heat in the ocean or atmosphere (Ingleton 1999). This has led many climatologists to suggest that the increased prominence of *El Nino* events since the 1990s, associated with more frequent cyclones and other extreme weather phenomena, is linked to global warming (Mazza 1998; Trenberth 1998). The 2003 and 2010 European heatwaves provided even clearer evidence of a correlation between global warming and natural disasters.

## Global economic forces

In the same way that new health and environmental threats can be linked to social change prompted by global economic forces promoting modernization, so too can natural hazards. Changes to the human–environmental equilibrium can prompt natural hazards or make people more susceptible to 'regular' hazards. Lopez noted how Filipino subsistence farming tribes had, in the 1980s, become more at risk from tropical storms and landslides as a result of being pushed into higher ground by the establishment of modern farmsteads (Lopez 1987). In addition, the traditional relationship between people and natural phenomena may be weakened by globalization. Societal coping mechanisms can develop over time in areas prone to extreme meteorological or geothermal events and these might be undermined by profound socio-economic changes related to modernization and development. Well-meaning outside interventions can sometimes even prove unhelpful. Traditional tactics for dealing with flooding in Bangladesh, which include building portable houses, burying precious possessions and responding to certain behaviour patterns in animals associated with an imminent cyclone, have tended to be overlooked by outside agencies. A report on NGO activity in Bangladesh found that well-equipped relief agencies were sometimes less prepared for a flood than the local population, with serious consequences since they had assumed control of response operations (Matin and Taher 2000).

Preparedness for coping with natural disasters might also be diminished by outside pressures in a more overt way. It has been suggested that the capacities of Nicaraguan and Honduran social services to deal with the effects of Hurricane Mitch in 1998 were diminished by Structural Adjustment policies put in place in both countries to meet the conditions of IMF loans (Comfort *et al.* 1999).

In thinking about natural disasters, then, 'vulnerable' should not simply be conflated with 'undeveloped' or 'poor', even though there is clearly some correlation. Various factors, natural and social and local and global, combine to render certain individuals vulnerable to natural hazards. From a 'horizontal' perspective, the strategy most effective for securing vulnerable people from the risks presented by natural hazards is by reducing their vulnerability through societal learning and empowerment. The less vulnerable of the world can assist in this with emergency assistance and technical applications to tame the effects of natural hazards but also by tackling their own contribution to exacerbating the effects of such hazards. Progress on the former has, to date, been much more impressive than the latter.

## Preparing for the unexpected: the global politics of natural disaster management

The horizontal versus vertical approaches debate seen in combating global disease resurfaces in the global politics of natural disasters.

### Traditional security responses

Natural disasters present a straightforward basis for governments to widen state security since armed forces can easily be utilized for relief operations. The post-Cold War 'peace dividend' in Europe has seen armies increasingly engaged in this non-military function as is illustrated by the increased prominence of NATO in this sphere of activity.

#### The role of NATO in natural disaster relief

In a classic instance of traditional security widening, part of the post-Cold War restructuring of NATO saw, in 1998, the establishment of a unit at its Brussels headquarters to utilize military resources to protect citizens from natural rather than military threats. The Euro-Atlantic Disaster Response Coordination Centre (EADRCC) is a tiny cog in the NATO machine but its creation epitomized not only a widening of its notion of security but also the widening of its sphere of operations beyond the defence of NATO member-states. The EADRCC is, in fact, coordinated by the Euro-Atlantic Partnership Council (EAPC), in which the twenty-eight NATO states are linked to twenty-two non-NATO partner states, and emerged from a proposal by one of those partners, Russia. NATO has had a role in disaster relief dating back to 1953 when North Sea floods prompted the initiation of a 'Policy on Cooperation for Disaster Assistance in Peacetime', but the EADRCC has enhanced this significantly.

The EADRCC helps coordinate international relief programmes responding to natural or industrial disasters occurring in any of the fifty EAPC states.[1] To avoid any duplication of roles with the UN, a permanent Office for the Coordination of Humanitarian Affairs (OCHA) Liaison Officer is based at the centre alongside EAPC state representatives and permanent NATO staff. Hence the EADRCC represents a means of assisting UN relief when disaster occurs in a EAPC state or of coordinating assistance within the EAPC area if the UN-OCHA is distracted elsewhere. In the first year of its operation, for example, the EADRCC helped coordinate an international response to problems caused by flooding in Ukraine at a time when the UN-OCHA was preoccupied with the devastations being wreaked on Central America by Hurricane Mitch. When UN-OCHA is active in an EAPC state, the EADRCC cooperates closely with it and supplies material support, such as vehicles and medical facilities, or logistical support, such as in facilitating the wavering of visa restrictions for relief workers. A Euro-Atlantic Disaster Response Unit (EADRU), comprising both military and civilian experts from the EAPC countries, has been dispatched by EADRCC to many prominent recent disasters within the EAPC area, such as to the USA for Hurricane Katrina and most notably outside of this area to Pakistan in 2005 when the government requested help with earthquake relief operations. The success of the EADRCC prompted the emergence of a similar regional international mechanism for the Association of South East Asian Nations (ASEAN), the Agreement on Disaster Management and Emergency Response (AADMER), which entered into force in 2009.

Disasters can sometimes inspire acts of security cooperation and conciliation which are at odds with diplomatic hostility. A special edition of the *Cambridge Review of International Affairs* in 2000 dedicated to 'disaster diplomacy' demonstrated how security communities can emerge between neighbouring states facing a common threat, in which information is shared to minimize a common risk. The warming of relations between Greece and Turkey after earthquakes ravaged both countries in 1999 is a classic case of two governments and societies overcoming cultural and political differences when faced with a common foe. At the one level this was a case of basic human empathy at the societal level triumphing over realpolitik and then being reciprocated but Ker-Lindsay demonstrates that the case is more revealing than that. The level of cooperation between the two governments, which surprised the rest of the world, was a result of an agreement reached at a meeting of foreign ministers a few months before the earthquake (Ker-Lindsay 2000). Turkish Foreign Minister Cem and his Greek counterpart Papandreou had met principally to discuss the regional military security implications of the crisis going on at that time in Kosovo. Sharing a common concern about the possible spread of conflict to other parts of the Balkans and the flow of refugees from Yugoslavia which was already happening, the two traditional foes engaged in uncharacteristically cordial dialogue. One dimension of this, barely noticed at the time, was to offer reciprocal help in the instance of a deadly earthquake striking either country. Relations between the two governments remain somewhat frosty on certain issues but have certainly continued to be better than for many years prior to 1999 and societal contact has increased since the disasters. This represents a clear case of spillover, with sectoral cooperation promoting wider cooperation between governments and bringing people closer together through realizing their common interests.

A similar scenario was witnessed in 2001 when the destruction wreaked by earthquakes in India prompted offers of relief from Pakistan and the first contact between the two countries' leaders for two years. Such occurrences may assist in improving relations but security communities require more systematic levels of cooperation and information-sharing to be able to develop. NATO's role in natural disaster relief looks set to increase and become a routine feature of risk sharing and mitigation between its member-states and associates. The functional spillover logic which drives EU integration saw natural disasters added as a new policy area to the European Commission's roster with the creation of the Natural and Environmental Disasters Information Exchange System (NEDIES) in 1997. The 2002 floods across existing and future member-states in central Europe emphasized the need for further cooperation in this area.

## The rise of horizontal policy

Proponents of a horizontal approach have become more prominent in recent years, challenging traditional assumptions that the best way to minimize human suffering from 'Acts of God' is through the refinement and better application of technological solutions (a vertical approach). It has long been apparent in domestic politics that security from disaster comes from the 'long game' of reducing vulnerability. An added factor behind the disparity in death toll between the 2010 earthquakes in Haiti and Chile, referred to earlier, is the democratization of the latter set against the political instability of the former. Stringent national building safety codes have evolved in the recent era of democratic stability in Chile and the Bachelet government responded rapidly and efficiently to the disaster (Smith and Flores 2010). There is good evidence that democratic citizenship provides some measure of security from natural disaster. Civil society in Turkey was jolted into life by the 1999 earthquakes and a major pressure group campaign critical of the government and existing legislation of a kind not seen before emerged. Consequently a crisis centre was created by the government and responses to a second earthquake that year were much more efficient (Smith and Flores 2010).

The appliance of science, indisputably, is vitally important in developing strategies to predict when disasters are likely to occur, lessen their human impact when they do occur and assist in the process of recovery from damages that do accrue. 'Horizontalists', however, contend that securing people from the effects of natural disasters is as much a social as a technical task. Security for people threatened by natural hazards cannot be achieved by tackling the physical causes of their risk if social factors making them vulnerable are not addressed. 'In many cases nature's contribution to "natural" disasters is simply to expose the effects of deeper, structural causes' (IFRC 2001: introduction).

## The International Decade for Natural Disaster Relief (IDNDR)

The 1990s were designated as the International Decade for Natural Disaster Relief by UN General Assembly Resolution 46/182 in 1989, following the recommendation of a specially commissioned ad hoc group of experts. The decade inspired unprecedented levels of international cooperation in this policy area and the formation or deepening of numerous epistemic communities for particular disaster forms. The decade also, however, witnessed an upsurge in the number of fatalities from natural disasters, which served to illustrate that transnational scientific cooperation, though welcome, was not enough.

The IDNDR approach was largely technical and vertical. A number of sectoral initiatives were launched such as the Global Fire Monitoring Centre, Tsunami Inundation Modelling Exchange Programme and Tropical Cyclone Programme which improved transnational early warning capacities. A number of pilot studies were also activated during the decade by coordinating the work of existing international organizations. UNEP, WHO and the World Meterological Organization (WMO) collaborated in trial runs for a Heat/Health Warning System to better anticipate extreme weather. The International Association of Volcanology and Chemistry of the Earth's Interior (IAVCEI) instigated a scheme monitoring sixteen active volcanoes to assess how public awareness of the various hazards could be improved.

The arch-'horizontalist' Ben Wisner says of the decade: 'Science was exchanged all right, but generally it has not been applied' (Wisner 2000). This view is echoed by Britton: 'There is little doubt that IDNDR was effective in encouraging nations to focus attention on the threat posed by natural hazards and in creating an environment wherein greater international collaboration was fostered. Nevertheless, the fundamental task of reducing societal consequences of disaster reduction remained' (Britton 2001: 45). The Secretariat of the IDNDR itself admitted: 'The application of science and technology was recognized as being essential for reducing the risk of natural disasters, but in the early years of the decade, it became evident that this was not sufficient by itself' (Jeggle 1999: 24).

## The International Strategy for Disaster Reduction (ISDR)

To continue the work undertaken under the IDNDR a successor UN body was established in 1999 and launched in 2000. The ISDR was adopted at the 1999 IDNR Programme Forum and then ratified by both the UN General Assembly (54/219, 22 December 1999) and ECOSOC (E/1999/63, 30 July 1999). The ISDR has a small secretariat based in Geneva under the authority of the Under-Secretary-General for Humanitarian Affairs and a policy-making body, the Inter-Agency Task Force on Disaster Reduction (IATF/DR), chaired by the same person.

The ISDR declare that their overriding aim is: 'To enable all societies to become resilient to the effects of natural hazards and related technological and environmental disasters, in order to reduce human, economic and social losses' (ISDR 2002a: 1). This aim is to be achieved in four ways: (1) stimulating public awareness; (2) obtaining the commitment of public authorities; (3) promoting interdisciplinary cooperation; and (4) fostering greater scientific knowledge (ISDR 2002a: 2).

The ISDR has incorporated more horizontal, mitigation-based approaches in its overall strategy than during the IDNDR. 'Vulnerability to disasters should be considered in a broad context encompassing specific human, social/cultural, economic, environmental and political dimensions, that relate to inequalities, gender relations and ethical and racial divisions' (ISDR 2002b: 21).

At the global level, in a similar manner as seen in the politics of health, the horizontal approach to securing people against natural hazards has come to prominence from epistemic communities and operates alongside more prominent vertical strategies. The ISDR maintains research on technical solutions to particular forms of hazard but has a far more holistic approach than that seen during the IDNDR. UN agencies have also shifted the emphasis towards a more horizontal strategy. From 2001 the UNDP began work on the first World Vulnerability Report, an annual index to aid disaster mitigation based on identifying where the world's most vulnerable populations, from a socio-economic perspective, are located. Whilst it might be expected that the UNDP would approach the problem of natural hazards from a socio-economic perspective a more surprising convert is the World Bank, who have moved well beyond lending money just for post-disaster reconstruction. The Disaster Management Facility (DMF) established in 1998 aims to improve state preparedness through insurance and better public education (Arnold and Merrick 2001). In the sphere of global civil society the Global Disaster Information Network was launched in 1998 linking experts from academia, industry, IGOs, pressure groups and governments with the express purpose of providing information to potential victims rather than money to victims after the event.

In 2005 the Central Emergency Response Fund (CERF) was established after a resolution of the UN General Assembly to manage the dispersal of emergency aid (for war and disease as well as disasters). Despite this, there is still a notable unevenness in international disaster aid donations. In 2010 eight times as much was spent on each earthquake-affected Haitian as on each flood-affected Pakistani (Ferris and Petz 2011: 23).

Additionally, international responses to disasters still tend to be after the event rather than pre-emptive. This is not only ineffective but also often wasteful. In 2006 the government of Mozambique requested £2 million of emergency aid which would have been sufficient for them to prepare against imminent floods but, shorn of tragic images to project to the world, no supply of funds was forthcoming. When the subsequent floods duly arrived the international community dug deep, but too late, to find £60 million (Ashdown 2011). Hence there remains dissatisfaction with the capacity of the 'international community' to respond to disasters, as illustrated in Box 8.1.

### Box 8.1 Paddy Ashdown

The UK Liberal politician Paddy Ashdown was commissioned by the British government to lead a review of international disaster relief operations in 2011. After a distinguished military career, Ashdown entered politics and served as leader of the Liberal Party between 1988 and 1999. He subsequently has worked in a variety of diplomatic roles with the UN, most notably serving as High Representative for Bosnia and Herzegovina between 2002 and 2006.

Ashdown's Humanitarian Emergency Response Review considered that 'the UN is the only legitimate authority that can lead but is often too weak and slow to do so' and proposed the following key factors to be given greater emphasis in its work on disasters:

- Resilience: invest in infrastructure to avoid disasters occurring.
- Leadership: the UN should invest in 'leadership cadre'.
- Innovation: more thought is needed on how best to respond to disasters: e.g. money may be more effective than blankets or food.
- Accountability: recipients of relief aid must be consulted so that social issues, such as vulnerability and gender, can be accounted for.
- Partnership: relief should be multilateral and involve NGOs.
- 'Humanitarian space': there is a need to think about the political context of a disaster: e.g. work with 'neutral' NGOs where states are not welcome, be prepared to get UN support for military support where this is necessary.

(Ashdown 2011)

## Conclusions

As with the global politics of health, the horizontal approach to securing the lives of those most prone to natural disasters has steadily gained credibility in epistemic communities and in the global polity, but struggles to win the hearts and minds of governments and the general public of countries moved to help those people. Despite efforts at improving global management, humanitarian aid still tends to be after the event rather than pre-emptive. The long game of promoting education, economic development and local empowerment is simply less sexy than sending in relief workers and raising charitable donations. 'It is hard to gain votes by pointing out that a disaster *did not* happen' (Christopolos, Mitchell and Liljelund 2001: 195). When Gerhard Schroeder regained the Chancellorship at the 2002 German elections it was widely felt that his crisis management during recent devastating floods secured victory in a tight election. To put it another way, Schroeder won *because* German flood defences failed. Had they succeeded he would have been denied the opportunity to don his waders and demonstrate compassion and leadership in the media spotlight.

The 2004 Indian Ocean tsunami and 2010 Haiti earthquake prompted impressive global relief operations but also demonstrated how unnecessarily insecure large swathes of humanity are in the current world. Global governance, driven by human security rather than sporadic bouts of human compassion, could have saved most of the tsunami victims: specifically through the implementation of an early warning system of the kind operated in the wealthier Pacific rim and, more generally, through the appreciation of the way in which vulnerability turns natural hazards into human tragedies. Additionally, the very fact that such calamitous tragedies would not register on the 'seismographs' of narrow (and some wider) security scholars serves as a reminder as to the irrelevance of such an approach to the discipline.

Inter-state competition and sovereignty have little to offer when it comes to dealing with natural disasters, other than the occasional deployment of troops to help after the event. Sharing security information in this context carries no risks and can only serve to make states more secure. As with other issues, 'securitization' by widening rather than deepening can lead to a misallocation of resources. The concern that the 'war on terror' may be hampering governments in dealing with other threats to their citizens became apparent in 2005 with the US administration's response to the New Orleans disaster. The first batch of relief supplies sent to the area by the Federal Emergency Management Agency (FEMA) was made up of materials intended for dealing with the aftermath of a chemical terrorist strike.

Natural disasters are global problems in both a geological and human sense and state borders are irrelevant in both regards. The natural dimensions can better be countered by a pooling of human efforts and ingenuity and the socio-economic dimensions of vulnerability can better be addressed by global action. Global problems require global solutions and natural disasters are doubly global problems.

## Key points

- Natural disasters are socio-political phenomena since it is human vulnerability to natural hazards, rather than the hazards themselves, which chiefly accounts for the security threat they pose.
- Earthquakes represent the biggest contemporary 'natural' human security threat followed by tsunamis, which are usually triggered by earthquakes.
- Human vulnerability to natural hazards has increased in recent years due principally to population growth and movement in the Global South.
- Global policy to mitigate the effects of natural disasters has traditionally been dominated by technical fixes, such as increasing predictive capacity, but recently has begun also to address the underlying socio-political issue of human vulnerability to hazards.

## Note

1    EADRCC operations have been dominated by natural disasters, particularly floods.

## Recommended reading

Blaikie, P., Cannon, T., Davis, I. and Wisner, B. (2005) *At Risk: Natural Hazards, People's Vulnerability, and Disasters*, London and New York: Routledge.

Coppola, D. (2011) *Introduction to International Disaster Management*, 2nd edn, Oxford: Butterworth-Heinemann.

Ferris, E. and Petz, D. (eds) (2011) *A Year of Living Dangerously: A Review of Natural Disasters in 2010*, London: Brookings Institute.

Smith, K. and Petley, D. (2009) *Environmental Hazards: Assessing Risk and Reducing Disaster*, 5th edn, London and New York: Routledge.

UNEP (2002) *Human Vulnerability to Environmental Change*, GEO3, ch. 3, http://geo.unep-wcmc.org/geo3/.

## Useful web links

Centre for Research on the Epidemiology of Disasters(CRED): http://www.cred.be/

NATO 'Euro-Atlantic Disaster Relief Coordination Centre': http://www.nato.int/eadrcc/home.htm

United Nations International Strategy for Disaster Reduction: http://www.unisdr.org/

# Accidental threats to security

> If the daily global casualty rate at work would be concentrated in one place, it would be all over the first pages of the world's newspapers.
>
> Karl Tapiola (ILO 2005)

## Accidents will happen? The nature and form of human-made accidents

Of all of the issues considered in this volume (entirely) human-made accidents, in their various forms, are least frequently thought of, and hence acted upon, as matters of security. However, unnatural structural or mechanical failings represent a major risk to human life throughout the world and it is a risk that has grown over time and looks likely to continue to do so. The absence of explicitly threatening causal factors, be they non-human or human with 'malice aforethought', has led to accidents being, to a certain extent, accepted as 'one of those things' and safety from them not becoming securitized in the same way as other causes of harm. Most accidents, though, are wholly unnatural and rooted in contemporary human societal practices that are becoming more widespread throughout the world. As such 'technological' and 'traditional' accidents are actually no more unavoidable than other social systemic problems like war and crime. In particular, accidents have underlying socio-economic causes inextricably linked to the global politico-economic system. As for all the issues of global security, with accidents the not so fickle finger of fate points in familiar directions: towards the poor and the weak. This is clearly illustrated in a telling statistic about globalization and security: the Global South has 20 per cent of the world's cars but 80 per cent of the world's fatalities from car crashes (WHO 2004b).

### Transport accidents

Major transport disasters have politicized safety issues over the last 100 years with domestic security measures frequently enacted by governments after the event. Many states rewrote maritime safety legislation after the infamous *Titanic* disaster exposed weaknesses in the provision of lifeboats and other procedures. This 'closing the stable door after the horse has bolted' approach was witnessed following a number of the disasters listed in Table 9.1.

However, just as the iceberg that sank the *Titanic* revealed but a tiny fraction of its full dangerous form to the doomed ship, the chief risk to life posed by travelling is largely unappreciated. As illustrated in Chapter 1, road traffic accidents claim well over a million lives per year worldwide, the biggest cause of all deaths apart from disease and it is a figure that continues to rise. Such deaths occur so regularly and so universally that they tend not to attract the sort of attention given to sporadic ferry, rail or air crashes and have for some time been almost uncontroversial. This complacency has, to some extent, begun to change in recent years as data, showing significant disparities in deaths between countries, has proved that the toll can be reduced through governmental action. Hence the French government in 2003 initiated a campaign focused on better enforcement of existing

**Table 9.1** The world's worst transport disasters

| | Place | Date | Type | No. killed |
|---|---|---|---|---|
| 1 | Philippines | 1987 | Ferry crash (*Dona Paz*) | 4,000[b] |
| 2 | Salang Tunnel, Afghanistan | 1982 | Fire in road tunnel | 2,000[a] |
| 3 | Haiti | 1993 | Ferry sunk (*Neptune*) | 1,800[a,b] |
| 4 | Mississippi, USA | 1865 | Steamship exploded (*Sultana*) | 1,800[c] |
| 5 | North Atlantic | 1912 | Ship sunk by iceberg (*Titanic*) | 1,500[b] |
| 6 | Senegal | 2002 | Ferry sunk (*Joola*) | 1,200[b] |
| 7 | Japan | 1954 | Ferry (*Toya Maru*) | 1,172[a,b] |
| 8 | Egypt | 2006 | Ferry sunk (*al-Salam*) | 1,028[b] |
| 9 | Canada | 1914 | Ship sunk (*Empress of Ireland*) | 1,014[b] |
| 10 | New York, USA | 1904 | Ship fire (*General Slocum*) | 1,000[b] |

Sources: [a] Ash (2001); [b] CRED (2011); [c] Potter (1992).

speeding restrictions which saw an immediate 20 per cent cut in annual deaths (WHO 2004b). Invariably where domestic safety standards are relatively lax, deaths on the road are relatively high. Sometimes, as in the case of France, cultural factors associated with risk and motor travel can explain laxer standards but, usually, the most secure motorists drive on roads regulated by the most stringent legislation in the most developed and wealthy states.

Domestic political action on accidents has tended to be more stringent, however, for public rather than private transport. The greater bursts of killing in train, aeroplane or ferry crashes tend to be more newsworthy and heighten both public anxiety and governmental sense of responsibility. Again, however, insuring against such events is a cost much more likely to be absorbed in countries developed enough to sacrifice some profit for safety. The prominence of ferry disasters in the Global South in Table 9.1 bears this out. Packing more bodies on a ferry pushes up the profits but also the danger level. It is a similar story with air travel. A downward trend in global deaths since the mid-1990s has reversed since the mid-2000s, largely due to an increase in flights with older aircraft in the Global South[1] (*Flight International* 2006; ICAO 2011).

## Structural accidents

Like transport accidents, disasters due to structural failure have occurred for as long as such human activity has occurred but have become far more common and dangerous in the industrialized age. In contrast to transport accidents, however, Table 9.2 gives a fuller representation of the overall death toll and indicates that the threat posed by structural accidents has lessened over recent decades rather than coming to be accepted.

Improved safety standards for public buildings in most countries have seen deaths reduced from a high point of the latter half of the nineteenth and first half of the twentieth centuries. However, accidents of this form cannot be eliminated

**Table 9.2** The world's worst structural accidents

| | Place | Date | Type | No. killed |
|---|---|---|---|---|
| 1 | Santiago, Chile | 1863 | Fire in a church | 2,000[c] |
| 2 | Chungking, China | 1949 | Spread of dockside fire | 1,700[a,b] |
| 3 | Canton, China | 1845 | Theatre fire | 1,670[a] |
| 4 | Hakodate, Japan | 1934 | Urban fire caused by chimney collapse | 1,500[a,b] |
| 5 | Mecca, Saudi Arabia | 1990 | Collapse of pedestrian tunnel | 1,426[b] |
| 6 | Baghdad | 2005 | Bridge collapse due to stampede | 1,199[b] |
| 7 | Shanghai | 1871 | Theatre fire | 900[a] |
| 8 | Vienna | 1881 | Theatre fire | 850[a] |
| 9 | St Petersburg | 1836 | Fire at circus | 800[a] |
| 10 | Antoung, China | 1937 | Cinema fire | 658[a] |

Note: Excludes structural disasters instigated by natural phenomena.
Sources: [a] Ash (2001); [b] CRED (2011); [c] Smith (2001: 319).

altogether in a modern world characterized by crowded urban living and working. It is instructive to note that the Great Fire of London in 1666, which destroyed most of the city, claimed only an estimated five or six lives since escaping low burning buildings was straightforward. Urbanization is today most pronounced in the countries of the Global South where safety standards are usually as under-developed as the economy, and it is here where the chief threats lie.

## Industrial accidents

Most clearly associated with modern living is industrialization, which is itself associated with far more hazardous forms of employment and production than pre-industrial economic activity. Table 9.3 illustrates that, like structural disasters, major industrial disasters can be prevented. Most of the disasters listed occurred in countries in the early stages of industrialization and economic development.

The world's worst ever industrial accident occurred at Bhopal, India on 3 December 1984. During the production of the pesticide *Carbaryl* the plant, run by the US-based multi-national corporation *Union Carbide*, accidentally released 40 tonnes of the highly toxic chemical methyl-isocyanate (MIC) used in the production process. At least 2,500 people living near the plant were killed and around 180,000 other people have since suffered from a range of long-term health effects and birth defects. As an intermediate chemical, MIC did not feature on the world's foremost safety inventory of the time, UNEP's International Register of Potentially Toxic Chemicals, and Indian authorities were unaware that it was being stored. Investigations also proved that safety standards at the plant were weak and that previous fatal accidents had occurred.

According to Dudley, at a 1986 'Chemistry After Bhopal' conference organized by the chemical industry a spokesman likened the disaster to the sinking of the

**Table 9.3** The world's worst industrial disasters

| | Place | Date | Type | No. killed |
|---|---|---|---|---|
| 1 | Bhopal, India | 1984 | Chemical leak | 2,500 |
| 2 | Hineiko, China | 1942 | Mining disaster (explosion) | 1,549 |
| 3 | Courriereres, France | 1906 | Mining disaster (explosion) | 1,099 |
| 4 | Jesse, Nigeria | 1998 | Oil pipeline fire | 1,082 |
| 5 | Chelyabinsk, USSR | 1989 | Gas pipeline explosion | 607 |
| 6 | Oppau, Germany | 1921 | Chemical plant explosion | 600 |
| 7 | Texas, USA | 1947 | Ship carrying fertilizer exploded in port | 561 |
| 8 | Cubatao, Brazil | 1984 | Petroleum plant fire | 508 |
| 9 | Lagunillas, Venezuela | 1939 | Oil refinery fire | 500 |
| 10 | Mexico City | 1984 | Petroleum gas plant explosion | 452 |

Note: Excludes disasters instigated by natural phenomena, military strikes or military accidents. Examples of naturual phenomena: lightning strikes caused explosions of arsenals in Rhodes, Greece in 1856 and in Brescia, Italy in 1769 claiming around 4,000 and 3,000 lives respectively. Dam bursts are also excluded. Notable examples of military accidents include: the explosion at an ammunition dump in Lucknow, China in 1935 which killed 2,000; the explosion of the ammunition ship *Mont Blanc* after collision near Halifax, Canada in 1917 which killed 1,963, and the explosion of ammunition trucks in Cali, Colombia in 1956 which killed 2,700.

Sources: Ash (2001: 215); CRED (2011).

*Titanic* (Dudley 1987: x). In the same way that the world's most infamous transport disaster prompted an evaluation of safety standards but not the abolition of passenger sea travel, industrial chemical production should not be restricted on the back of one major disaster, it was claimed. Whether Bhopal was a freakish one-off, however, is disputed. The disaster prompted a rise in pressure group activity and academic research into chemical safety in the developing world which suggested a reversal of the *Titanic* analogy was more appropriate. Bhopal, rather, represented the tip of the iceberg with many less visible disasters lying submerged from public and political view. Twenty years on from Bhopal the International Labour Organization (ILO) suggested that the Indian government had reported 231 work-related fatal accidents when the true figure was nearer 40,000 (ILO 2005).

Whereas disasters in LDCs can escape public glare and political response, far less deadly accidents can produce significant responses when they occur in the developed world. The 1976 leak at a chemical plant in the Milan suburb of Seveso was a watershed for European chemical safety legislation and its impact continues to resonate despite claiming only one immediate casualty. A cloud of trichlorophenol (TCP) and dioxin TCDD formed around the plant as a result of the leak, although no acknowledgement of this was made to nearby villages for four days. Within three weeks animals and crops had died, thirty people were hospitalized and one person had died, whilst long-term, a significant increase in birth defects was recorded (Pocchiari, Silaro and Zapponi 1987). The disaster had profound political effects. The plant was owned by a Swiss company, prompting fears that they had exploited laxer safety standards in Italy. A so-called 'Seveso Directive' was drafted by the European Community (82/501/EEC) tightening safety standards and making it obligatory to notify a local population of any such accident. A similar shock to the European system occurred in 2010 when a spill of caustic waste at an alumina plant at Ajka, Hungary led to toxic chemicals burning nine people to death and turning a stretch of the Danube across several countries red making graphically apparent the physical and political interconnectedness of the EU.

The two most significant nuclear accidents of the twentieth century occurred in the two superpowers of that age whose unprecedented international political influences were built on that very power source. In 1979 at the Three Mile Island nuclear power plant in Pennsylvania a technical malfunction caused a release of radioactive gas from one of the reactors. There were no confirmed casualties from this accident but it attracted huge publicity which was seized upon by anti-nuclear protestors and no new nuclear power plants have been built in the USA since. The 1986 Chernobyl disaster in the former USSR was the worst ever nuclear power plant disaster and, in line with the added 'fear factor' associated with this form of energy production, stands as the most notorious industrial disaster to date. Lax safety standards are generally held as the key reason for an explosion and fire which destroyed one of the plant's four power reactors and released huge amounts of solid and gaseous radioactive material into the surrounding area. Thirty-two plant and emergency staff were killed in the immediate aftermath of the explosion and in the proceeding weeks some of this material was deposited over a large swathe of Northern Europe prompting an unknown number of long-term deaths. In 2011 nuclear safety was again put in the spotlight with the Fukushima Daiichi nuclear power station disaster, prompted by the devastating tsunami that struck Japan. Three workers were killed and thousands of residents moved out of the region and, whilst levels of public radiation exposure were officially reported as not being dangerous, many fear that significant longer-term health defects will come to emerge.

As with transport disasters and most human security threats, however, large-scale and/or high-profile disasters represent only a small, highly visible, fraction of the full picture. The vast majority of accidents in the workplace are individual or small scale. The International Labour Organization (ILO) have estimated that around a third of a million people a year in the world are killed in occupational accidents (including traffic accidents whilst working) (ILO 2011). If deaths when commuting to or from work and by illness caused at work are included the figure rises to over 1.2 million (ILO 2005).

## Personal injury

In addition to those encountered whilst travelling, working and congregating in public buildings, people increasingly face risks to their lives at home. Electrical appliances and cooking facilities characteristic of modern living present another component of 'everyday danger' confronting an ever-increasing proportion of the world's population. For example, the WHO estimate that over 300,000 people – mainly children playing – drown every year (WHO 2011). Table 9.4 lists the most prominent causes of accidental death across all of the categories and it is clear that

**Table 9.4** The top causes of accidental death, 2008

| Form of accident | Deaths |
| --- | --- |
| Road traffic injuries | 1,208,691 |
| Falls | 510,349 |
| Drowning | 305,929 |
| Poisoning | 252,459 |
| Fires | 195,227 |
| Others[a] | 1,145,981 |

Note

[a] 'Others' includes exposure to animate and inanimate mechanical forces (including firearms); exposure to electric current, radiation and extreme ambient temperature and pressure and to forces of nature; contact with heat and hot substances; and contact with venomous plants and animals (McGee 2003).

Source: WHO (2011).

many of these result from personal, domestic activities such as fires caused by deep fat fryers and children drowning in ponds. Again, domestic safety legislation has served to improve safety in the home but there is an observable tendency to accept the possibility of such 'mundane' ways to die.

## The collateral damage of industrialization? The rise of accidental threats

Deaths by accident are very much a feature of the modern world. There have, of course, always been accidental deaths but this form of threat to human life is closely associated with technological development and has risen in accord with industrialization and the onset of modernity. In fact it is possible to argue that accidents, in terms of their perception as such, did not exist for most of human history. The pre-industrial advance of science was significant in providing a means for comprehending unfortunate acts as something that could be explained and hence avoided. Green argues that: 'Before 1650, an accident was merely a happening or an event, and there appears to have been no space in European discourse for the concept of an event that was neither motivated nor predictable' (Green 1997: 196).

People are killed today in a variety of non-technological accidents, such as by drowning, but most accidental deaths are an unfortunate by-product of technological development. Health and safety legislation in developed countries has succeeded in reducing the potential hazards associated with transport, industrial production and the use of public buildings but, at the same time, people continue to travel more than ever and the industrial production and transportation of potentially hazardous substances continues to increase.

Smith posits that 1984 was a watershed year for technological disasters (Smith 2001: 322). Table 9.3 confirms this. As well the Bhopal disaster, that year also saw a petroleum fire in Cubatao, Brazil, kill 508 people and a petroleum gas explosion in Mexico City claim 540 lives. In total, more people were killed in major incidents that year than in all technological disasters of the previous forty years. In particular, the three prominent disasters were in LDCs avidly pursuing industrial development. This served to demonstrate that, as with natural disasters, there was a socio-economic dimension to industrial accidents. The vast majority of such deaths prior to 1984 had been attributable to small-scale accidents in the developed world, giving credence to the notion that these were an unfortunate but inevitable form of collateral damage offset by the overall social gains to be had from sustained economic growth and mass consumerism. The scale of the problem in industrializing LDCs or 'emerging markets' now far outstrips that in the Global North. Between 1998 and 2001, in contrast to stable or falling figures in the developed world, work fatalities in China rose from 73,500 to 90,500 and in Latin America from 29,500 to 39,500 (ILO/WHO 2005).

The 1984 disasters also illustrated that technological accidents had become an international political economy issue in another dimension. It became clear on investigation that safety standards at Union Carbide's Bhopal plant were far more lax than at their home plant in West Virginia. The disaster gave ammunition to pressure groups and commentators concerned that globalization was a 'race to the bottom' in which MNCs would escape domestic safety constraints and seek out low-wage, low-safety sites for their operations (see Box 9.1).

---

### Box 9.1 Warren Anderson

Warren Anderson was the Chairman of Union Carbide at the time of the Bhopal disaster in 1984. It is alleged that Anderson was directly involved in cost-cutting exercises and was fully aware of the safety short-comings at the Bhopal plant. On flying to India from the USA after the disaster he was arrested for 'culpable homicide' but freed on bail. He returned to the USA and has never faced justice even though he is still subject to an extradition request by the Indian government. He is officially recognized by Interpol as an international fugitive and is even an absconder from justice within the USA, where he has failed to appear in court on civil charges for compensation from the disaster. The fact that he has been regularly tracked down by the press (including the British newspaper the *Mirror*) and pressure groups (particularly Greenpeace) at large homes in Florida and New York marks him out as an unusual sort of fugitive. The US and Indian governments do not appear to have tried particularly hard to bring him to justice. Union Carbide and the Indian government reached an out-of-court settlement over the disaster in 1989 in which $470 million, well below the original claim, was to be paid to victims and their families. The Indian government, mindful of the importance of economic links with the USA, tried to reduce the charges against Anderson to the non-extraditable offence of negligence but this was rejected by the Indian courts and he hence remains 'on the run' from justice.

An added transboundary and global dimension to workplace accidents comes from the disproportionate number of victims that come from migrant labour. Whilst confirmed figures are not available reports have suggested a shocking death toll in the United Arab Emirates, a country with the highest proportion of migrant workers in the world. It has been suggested that two construction workers per week die in Abu Dhabi and that 880 Indians and Pakistanis working on Dubai's rapidly emerging skyline were killed on the job in 2004 (Sonmez, Apostopoulos, Tran and Dentrope 2011). Even in the country with what are regularly suggested to be the world's highest living standards and most liberal immigration policies, Norway, migrant workers are nearly three times as likely to suffer an accident at work than the working population as a whole (Langeland 2009).

## Risky businesses: the idea of risk society

The inherent risks of modern living prompted sociologists in the 1990s to construct a new framework for thinking both about societies and accidents, encapsulated in the term 'risk society'. This idea posits that modern (or postmodern) society has gone beyond thinking of accidents as avoidable and accepts them as an inevitability. Hence insecurity becomes a part of life. Most of the conveniences and benefits of modern living come with some associated side-effects. The huge toll of fatalities on the road is largely tolerated by societies because of the gains to be had from personal mobility. The most rigorous health and safety legislation could not make working in a modern petrochemical plant or offshore oil-platform entirely safe. The workers know this but accept the risk in exchange for monetary reward in excess of what they might be expected to receive in a safer occupation.

The gamble of taking on some degree of risk in order to achieve greater reward than attainable by safe behaviour is, of course, simple to understand in terms of individual behaviour and is as old as history. What characterizes today's 'risk society' as different from previous generations, however, is the social dimension of risk taking. Individuals can choose to play it safe by avoiding hazardous forms of transport or employment but may have to accept the possibility of a radiation leak from their local nuclear power plant. Such an individual would probably gain a pay-off from cheaper electricity but would be a largely involuntary participant in the deal and more vulnerable as well as wealthy, whether they like it or not.

From the perspective of society at large, avoiding all risk can be costly and even increase insecurity. Leiss and Chociolko make this case in appealing for greater appreciation that the benefits to be had from developing new pharmaceuticals or pesticides outweigh the costs, even when this is calculated in human lives. 'We ask individuals and groups to abandon all unreasonably risk-averse stances and to recognize that our well-being as a society depends upon continuous risk-taking activity'(Leiss and Chociolko 1994: 16).

The perception of the social dimension of risk, then, is crucial in determining the political demands societies make of their authorities, beyond even the 'real' risk. Proponents of nuclear energy have long been irritated by the fact that the public in developed countries have demanded far greater restraints on their activities than other power stations with worse accident rates. A irony of the backlash against

225

nuclear energy after the 2011 Fukushima disaster is that it could lead to a revival of electricity powered by coal, an industry which has a far worse accident rate. In this case, of course, the calculation is complicated by 'fear of the unknown' born not only of ignorance but of a genuine lack of clarity as to the hazard presented by nuclear radiation. A more clear-cut instance of rationality being distorted comes from contrasting public attitudes and government policy on transport safety. Travelling by rail is demonstrably far safer than travel by road. In the EU, if judged in terms of deaths per hour of travel, you are fourteen times more likely to die in a road accident than a train crash (ETSC 2003). The sporadic horror of train disasters compared to the steady background drip of car crashes compels governments to illogically favour the former in transport safety expenditure.

The leading exponent of the risk society paradigm, Ulrich Beck, has also advanced the thesis that risk society is increasingly a global social phenomenon.

> The new dangers destroy the pillars of the conventional calculus of security: damages can scarcely still be attributed to definite perpetrators, so that the polluter-pays principle loses acuity: damages can no longer be compensated financially – it makes no sense to insure oneself against the worst-case ramifications of the global spiral of threat.
>
> (Beck 1999: 142)

## Securing those at risk in the world: international policy on accidents

In the 1996 volume *The Long Road to Recovery: Community Responses to Industrial Disaster*, which was the culmination of a four-year United Nations University project investigating a number of disasters, James Mitchell argued that: 'it is difficult to argue that there has been much progress in converting these surprises into routing hazards' (Mitchell 1996: ch. 9, section 1). Amongst the chief policy recommendations of the book is for an international clearing house of industrial hazard information to be established to improve the learning process (Mitchell 1996: ch. 9, 'Recommendations'). This is a particularly dismal conclusion since such a proposal has been on the global political agenda since the 1920s when debated by the International Labour Organization (ILO).

## *The ILO and industrial accidents*

The ILO was founded in 1919 as part of the League of Nations system, absorbing the work of the International Association for Labour Legislation which had been set up in 1901. The ILO's 1929 *Prevention of Industrial Accidents Recommendation (R31)* incorporated a resolution of the previous year's International Labour Conference (ILC) that information be collated systematically on accidents and their causes. Numerous ILO Conventions dealing with worker safety have been drafted and signed in the proceeding decades, culminating in the 1993 Prevention of Major

Industrial Accidents Convention (C174). Amongst the key requirements placed on ratifying states of this Convention are:

- *Article 4*: the formulation, through consultation with stakeholders, of state safety policies.
- *Article 16*: the dissemination of information on safety measures on how to deal with an accident and prompt warning in the event of an accident.
- *Article 17*: siting hazardous installations away from residential areas.
- *Article 22*: ensuring the prior informed consent of importing authorities before exporting substances or technologies to other states prohibited for safety reasons in your own state.

These provisions are in accord with received wisdom on industrial safety and the domestic legislation of most industrialized countries but many are ambiguous and the Convention, as a whole, is surprisingly short for a legal document on such a broad, technical issue. A further limitation comes from the fact that it is also written into the agreement that the provisions do not apply to the nuclear industry, to military installations, or to offsite transportation (except pipelines). Despite all of this, nineteen years after the Convention had been signed, only sixteen countries had ratified it (it entered into force in 1997 after the second ratification).[2] This is, in part, due to the snail's pace of international legislation but it can also be seen that most governments do not take much interest in international safety policy. The ratification rate for older ILO safety conventions is little better. The 1985 Occupational Health Services Convention (C161), which requires that a state's occupational health services advise employers and workers on safety, by 2012 had been ratified by only 30 of the ILO's 185 member-states. This is particularly telling since, whilst many developed states can cite the fact that they have more thorough domestic legislation as a basis for not ratifying the Accidents Convention, the ILO consider that few non-ratifiers to C161 do have equivalent existing laws (Takala 1999: 4).

In order to improve ratification and increase the general awareness of occupational hazards, the ILO in 1999 launched the 'In Focus Programmes on Safety and Health at Work and the Environment' (known as 'SafeWork'), headed by Takala. SafeWork are unequivocal in their belief that injuries and deaths are not an inevitable side-effect of modern work. 'If all ILO member states used the best accident prevention strategies and practices that are already in place and easily available, some 300,000 deaths (out of the total of 360,000) . . . could be prevented' (Takala 2002: 6).

## *Chemical safety policy*

The obvious hazard inherent in trading chemicals across borders has prompted the most extensive of all global regimes in the industrial safety sphere. Two similar regimes, developed in the 1980s and implemented in the 1990s around the principle of 'Prior Informed Consent', bear testimony to Beck's assertion in support of his Risk Society thesis that: 'In contrast to material poverty. . . . the pauperization of the Third World through hazard is contagious for the wealthy' (Beck 1992: 44). The 1998 Rotterdam Convention[3] and 1989 Basel Convention[4] initiated effective international regulatory systems compelling the exporters of, respectively, chemicals or hazardous wastes to notify state authorities in the importing country if the material is restricted in the country of origin. These agreements provide some safeguard against the exploitative dumping of dangerous materials in countries poorly equipped to deal with them but also help wealthy countries feel surer that such dangerous substances will not revisit them in foodstuffs or pollution in the 'circle of poison' effect described in Chapter 6.

Global regulation with regard to the use and production of, rather than trade in, hazardous chemicals is predictably less rigorous but has developed over time. The WHO have had a role in developing international labelling guidelines for pesticides as far back as 1953 (Hough 1998: 55–7). A plethora of international standards in this area were brought together in 2002 under the Globally Harmonized System of Classification and Labelling of Chemicals (GHS) co-managed by three IGOs. The OECD are responsible for managing the development of health and environmental hazard information for developing a classification scheme. It has set up an expert advisory group towards this end. The United Nations Committee of Experts on the Transportation of Dangerous Goods (UNCEDTDG) have the task of determining criteria for classifying the physical hazards of chemicals (for example their flammability). The ILO have assumed responsibility for the overall coordination of the system, acting as its secretariat, and have also set up a working group containing governmental and worker representatives charged with the task of producing the means of communicating the classification scheme. As well as labelling standards this includes data sheets for workers involved in chemical transport and guidance information for governments on how to implement the scheme. The system began the process of ratification in 2003 and by 2011 had been implemented by sixty-seven states. It should be noted, though, that harmonized global standards are becoming more popular as much because they can facilitate trade by levelling the 'playing field' as because they enhance human security.

The Seveso disaster was the catalyst for a series of EC initiatives on industrial safety culminating in the creation of the EU Major Accident Reporting System (MARS) which was fleshed out in the 'Seveso II' Directive of 1996 (96/82/EC). MARS is an extensive database of accidents administered by the Major Accidents Hazards Bureau within the European Commission's Joint Research Centre in Ispra, Italy. MARS has proved so effective that it has fostered cooperation well beyond the EU's borders in what could be considered an instance of 'spillover-spillover'. The Organisation for Economic Co-operation and Development (OECD) utilize the system to facilitate information exchange on chemical spills and the UN's Economic Commission for Europe (UN/ECE) use it as the centrepoint of a regime based on their Convention on the Transboundary Effects of Industrial Accidents. The UN/ECE Convention, which came into force in 2000, links the EU states with other European states including Russia and features a notification system whereby the parties commit themselves to giving full and prompt information to neighbouring countries in the event of an accident.

## *Nuclear power politics*

As has been demonstrated, safety standards for the production of nuclear energy and the transportation of its constituent elements and by-products tend not to be included in general international policy on accident prevention. Instead, the responsibility for this lies with the International Atomic Energy Agency (IAEA), an IGO set up by the UN in 1957 to coordinate policy on both military and civilian uses of nuclear power. The IAEA has an International Nuclear Safety Advisory Group which has coordinated the establishment of a range of 'Safety Principles' and a 'Codes of Practice on the International Transboundary Movement of Radioactive Waste'. Prompted by the Chernobyl disaster and the end of Cold War secrecy, the IAEA codified their most extensive legal instrument to date in the 1990s with the Convention on Nuclear Safety, which came into force in 1996. The Convention covers a range of issues including the siting and construction of power plants and emergency preparation. However, despite the implied strengthening of IAEA standards with the use of the term 'convention' in place of 'principles' and 'codes of practice', this is not a robust piece of legislation. In the IAEA's own words: 'The Convention is an incentive instrument. It is not designed to ensure fulfilment of obligations by Parties through control and sanction' (IAEA 2003).

The high perception of risk attached to the production of nuclear power has made this a contentious issue of domestic politics in many countries but has also promoted a most literal form of spillover, inducing political cooperation between states. The Chernobyl disaster, more than Soviet–Western rapprochement, was the spur for the EC to launch the TACIS programme (Technical Assistance to the Commonwealth of Independent States) in 1991 which gives grants to the successor states of the Soviet Union[5] and has a strong focus on the modernization of the nuclear industry.

On the other side of the coin, concerns over the potential risk from nuclear accidents in other countries has also served to sour relations between closely integrated countries. Chernobyl was also a key factor in instigating independence movements in the Ukraine, where the plant was based, and in nearby Belarus. In both of these Slavic Soviet Socialist Republics anti-Russian nationalism was less of a spur for secession than the feeling of being treated as the USSR's industrial wasteland. Hence many of the Ukraine's large Russian minority voted for independence and Belarus has sought to maintain as strong as possible links with Russia since gaining independence.

Further west, the desire of former USSR satellite states to integrate themselves into the European Union's integration project has brought nuclear safety questions to the fore. The Austrian government, backed by public opinion, threatened to veto the Czech Republic's accession to the EU unless it halted the development of its Temelin nuclear power station located near the Austrian border. The EU, satisfied by an International Atomic Energy Agency (IAEA) review in 2001 and a 2000 Austro-Czech bilateral agreement on safety (The Melk Protocol), did not make closing the new plant a condition of membership but the issue remained contentious in Austrian civil society and party politics. The EU collectively in 2002 called upon Lithuania to close its Soviet-built nuclear plant, Ignalina, as a condition of membership, and in doing so agreed to provide substantial aid to assist in the project and compensate for the funding of alternative sources of energy production.

Even within the established ranks of the EU, government policies on nuclear power differ substantially and cause friction amongst the most integrated states on Earth. The avowedly non-nuclear Republic of Ireland's government has long complained about the UK's Sellafield nuclear power station, located on the Irish Sea coast and in 2001 attempted to take legal action against the expansion of the plant. The case was dismissed by the International Tribunal for the Law of the Sea but the issue continued to be a source of diplomatic tension between the two states. Similarly, the Finnish government's declaration of its plans to expand its reliance on nuclear power in 2002 drew criticism from a number of its fellow EU member-states, many of whom had begun to phase out this source of energy production. The 2011 Fukushima leak caused a backlash against nuclear energy just as its stock was rising due to its relative attractiveness *vis-à-vis* fossil fuels in terms of mitigating climate change. Japan and Germany were at the forefront of countries reversing future reliance on nuclear power.

## Road safety

A WHO role in road safety, alongside their more traditional work on disease and sanitation, has gradually emerged since the turn of the millennium. A Five Year Strategy on Road Traffic Injury Prevention was launched in 2001 aiming to universalize proven accident-reducing practices such as alcohol limits for drivers, the use of seat belts and particular forms of speed controls and road design. A WHO Steering Committee on Road Safety has met since 2002 and, in collaboration with other UN agencies, pressure groups such as the Global Road Safety Partnership (GRSP) and the French government in the wake of their national initiative, released the World Report on Road Traffic Injury Prevention on World Health Day in 2004. Working with the Steering Group, the government of Oman, inspired by orthopaedic surgeon Dr Wahid Al-Kharusi, drafted a series of UN General Assembly resolutions from 2003 to 2005 prompting the first UN Global Road Safety Week held in 2007. The culmination of this raised international political awareness was the launch of the UN Decade of Action for Road Safety in 2011.

## Maritime safety

International maritime safety standards centre on the Safety of Life at Sea (SOLAS) Conventions, initiated in 1914 in the wake of the *Titanic* disaster. Measures declared mandatory for all ships on the high seas included reduced speed limits after the sighting of ice and lifeboat training for all crew members. In 1960 an updated version of SOLAS was adopted by the UN's Intergovernmental Maritime Consultancy Organization, which later became the International Maritime Organization (IMO). The IMO, based in London, is today the focal point for global maritime safety standards, such as the Global Maritime Distress and Safety System, which from 1998 has ensured that any ship in distress can receive assistance even if it does not have a radio. As Table 9.1 indicates, safety on international waters has improved with most disasters now occurring domestically in overcrowded ferries in the Global South.

## Air travel safety

Global flight safety standards are much more embryonic than those covering sea travel. The International Civil Aviation Organization (ICAO), the relevant UN agency, has generally played a technical rather than regulatory role with safety standards left to governments. In response to rising accident figures in the Global South, however, the ICAO worked with the airline industry in devising the Global Aviation Safety Roadmap, launched in 2006, which seeks to harmonize national and regional safety standards up to Global North standards and share good practice.

## Personal injury

From the 1990s the WHO have also taken on board the task of highlighting and coordinating global action on reducing personal injuries. In 2002 a first ever World Congress on Drowning was hosted in Amsterdam and highlighted the need to work towards eliminating an estimated 80 per cent of deaths which are avoidable (mainly children) through better education on the causes of drowning and the use of life jackets and resuscitation techniques (World Congress on Drowning 2002).

## Conclusions

Accidents are the most atypical of global security concerns and yet represent a much bigger threat to most people's lives than those most typical of security concerns: war and terrorism. Most of you reading this are hundreds of times more likely to die in an accident than be killed by a soldier or terrorist. Security 'wideners' and even some human security advocates, whilst acknowledging that diseases, crime, environmental change and natural disasters can sometimes be matters of security, are reluctant to grant this status to accidents and human-made disasters. This reluctance seems to boil down to two objections: (1) there is no military or power politics dimension; (2) they are not deliberate 'attacks' on countries or people.

Security wideners ignore accidents because there is no real scope for sending in troops to fight anyone or help clear up in the aftermath. However, such a line of argument makes sense only if you are to assume that security is a synonym for 'involves the military' rather than a description of what you are striving to provide for your people in political life. A further barrier to the 'securitization' of disasters for some is the absence of direct and deliberate human causation. Even MacFarlane and Foong Khong, whilst purporting to advocate human security, opine that natural disasters and accidents: 'fail the "organized harm" test – tsunami waves, traffic accidents, the spread of viruses and crop failure are usually not organized by individuals to do their victims in' (MacFarlane and Foong Khong 2006: 275). For most human security advocates, though, there is a fatal fatalism in assuming that only direct and deliberate threats to life can be deemed worthy of security status. Securing people against such accidents is, again, a political task accepted by industrialized governments from as far back as the late nineteenth century when 'social security' policies began to evolve in response to changing economic and social conditions. Accidents, hence, are actually no more unavoidable than other social systemic problems like war and crime and people can be secured against them, at least to some degree. The human agency argument is flawed on two levels. First, there is human agency in most accidents. Human failings, whether at the state, corporate or individual level, account for most accidents and, hence, can be addressed in political actions. Second, must we deduce from this line of reasoning that anyone threatened or killed indirectly is not insecure? Are the 'collateral killings' of war or insurgency then not military or terrorist victims? Securing people against accidents has long been recognized as a task of responsible democratic government and, whilst that remains, there is compelling logic that globalization has now shifted some responsibilities to a wider level.

If there is a 'responsibility to protect' those imperilled by political violence why should there not be for those imperilled by their government's or host government's political negligence? Indeed it could be argued that the international community should feel a greater sense of responsibility when it comes to industrial accidents since they are more functionally connected to these events in enjoying the fruits of this hard labour. The contemporary deaths of Chinese miners or Indian construction workers recruited to build skyscrapers for global finance firms and hotels in the Gulf States should trouble Western consumers and governments as much as notorious domestic disasters did in the nineteenth and twentieth centuries.

This process, though, has a long way to go. Global standards on the safety aspects of business and employment are limp when set against comparable standards for facilitating the trade in the produce of this process. The ILO and the IAEA do not have the same sort of authority in compelling states to protect workers and citizens living near areas of industrial production that the World Trade Organization has in compelling them to allow goods into their countries. Hence we see one reason why many political activists have come to view economic globalization as a dangerous exercise in unfettered Liberalism, guided only by the profit motives of the Global North. It is indeed telling that, whereas the idea of freeing up the movement of products, services and money is well established as a global norm, the notion of a free movement of the workers producing such common goods is barely conceivable. As Davergne says of accidents: the 'global jury of states is assigning no blame, no ethical responsibility, dismissing these deaths as mere accidents in the quest for global prosperity' (Dauvergne 2005: 44).

However, 'unfettered Liberalism' is not the political system which has emerged from the political evolution of states which have industrialized and modernized and there is no reason to believe that it will be for the global polity. The industrialization of Western European and North American states prompted the emergence of policies to protect those put at risk by these social changes based both on compassion and pragmatism. An ideological consensus emerged in the late nineteenth century in support of the notion of state welfarism. The dangers associated with industrial employment and the economic uncertainties of trade prompted the emergence of interventionist Liberalism in place of its previous unfettered free-market version, paternal Conservatism and the birth of Socialism. The development of welfare systems in Western Europe, and to a lesser extent in the USA, arose from a blend of altruistic human security concerns and internal state security. Germany, under the arch-Conservative Bismarck, pioneered the idea of state protection for workers, prompted mainly by the pragmatic realism that reform from above was the best means of preventing revolution from below. Bismarck's aim was not so much human security as state security: maintaining the unity of his newly formed country which was witnessing some of the earliest manifestations of Socialist thought.

In addition, the precedent for freeing up trade between countries on a regional scale is that a levelling of an uneven playing field is a necessary precursor to achieving this. The issue may not arise for countries of a similar level of economic development, like the European Free Trade Association (EFTA) or the European Economic Community in its early years. The logic of spillover later dictated, however, that the EC embrace a social dimension alongside the 'Single Market' when it took on board the relatively poor states of Ireland, Portugal, Spain and Greece. States with poor safety standards are either: (1) (from an economic pers-pective) giving themselves an unfair competitive advantage; or (2) (from a social perspective) being exploited. Hence even the North American Free Trade Associ-ation (NAFTA), set up very much on an economic rationale without the idealism of the European integration project, featured from the start the 'North American Agreement on Labor Cooperation' (NAALC). NAALC, centred on an industrial dispute resolution mechanism incorporating occupational safety, came into force alongside the main NAFTA agreement in 1994 to overcome the problem of Mexico's comparative advantage/disadvantage compared to its wealthier partners to the North.

With the inexorable rise of a coherent global economic system global society is now, albeit slowly, awakening to this need for worker safety standards. Incidents of workers or residents near industrial plants in LDCs being killed are no longer unfortunate problems unconnected with the relatively safe lives of people in the Global North. Developed world consumers are functionally connected to these systemic failures as never before and increasingly aware of this fact. The rise in the Global North of 'fair trade' products, in which the consumer pays a premium for goods imported from developing countries on the premise that the workers have not been exploited, and the 'anti-globalization' social movement bear testimony to this fact. What is needed, though, is not the abandonment of globalization but a more rounded notion of globalization which balances profits with responsibilities as is broadly the norm in most developed democracies.

Such changes are slowly occurring. As with most of the areas of security considered in this book, the globalization of democracy and human rights offers hope for improving personal safety from accidents since more and more people are able to demand action from their governments. Studies have shown, for example, that the unionization of workforces increases human security in that countries, such as China, without independent trade unions tend to have higher numbers of accidents (Abrams 2001; Cheng 2003).[6] In addition, recent evidence points towards the development of a 'union effect' on safety at the global level. In 1997 work initiated by the WTO towards establishing ISO (International Organization for Standardization) standards for health and safety management, alongside other 'technical standards' by which to harmonize the global trading environment, was abandoned in the face of intensive global lobbying led by the International Confederation of Free Trade Unions (ICFTU). The ICFTU campaigned, principally over the internet, for global standard setting to be informed more by human safety than an economic rationale and so be coordinated by the ILO with its union affiliations. Evidence is now beginning to emerge of a globalization of a safety culture. Whilst progress has been limited on the C174 and C161 conventions, ratifications for subsequent ILO conventions on occupational safety and health (OSH) have notably improved since most countries committed themselves to a 'national preventative safety and health culture' and the notion of a 'right to a safe and healthy working environment' at the Seoul Declaration on Safety and Health at Work (ILO 2011: 155, 187). International guidance has been disseminated more effectively in a networking of the 'good safety is good business' message. As evidence of progress the number of global work fatalities has reduced in recent years. Having risen from just under to just over 350,000 per year from the late 1990s to early 2000s, the figure recorded for 2008 was 320,580. Securing people at work, at home, travelling or at leisure is for governments and societies, though, more than charity or even duty. A more secure and healthy workforce and society is more productive and contented. Some 4 per cent of global GDP is estimated to be lost to accidents and around this amount was trimmed off the Japanese GDP by the single Fukushima disaster (ILO 2011). State welfarism was introduced to the world in the nineteenth century by the arch-Conservative German Chancellor Bismarck in order to undercut rising support for Socialist alternatives to the economic uncertainties of capitalism. Exploiting workers and short-changing citizens is only profitable for so long when such people can be shown that there are alternatives. Disillusioned and angry workers have been a factor in nearly all revolutions. Health and safety is the dull stuff of politics and business but it is, nonetheless, 'life and death' both for members of society and for governments and has long been recognized as such in industrialized democracies.

Such evidence of progress cannot disguise the fact that the WTO far outstrips the ILO in global influence but it indicates that globalization is not entirely driven by corporate profit and that a future, more evolved form of the process may see a world in which human security is enhanced alongside the spoils of increased trade.

## Key points

- Most human-made accidents (transport, structural, industrial or personal) are avoidable and, therefore, political matters.
- Most accidental deaths are linked to modern, industrialized living and are, to some extent, tolerated as inevitable.
- Developed countries have evolved the capacity to contain accidents to some extent and less developed countries now bear the greatest burden of such deaths.

- Global policy on accidents has been subsumed by the rise of Economic Liberalism but demand for global safety standards, like those in developed countries, is growing through recognition that this is a global and not just a domestic matter.

## Notes

1     The death rate from aircraft accidents in the 1990s was 1,128 per year and fell to 794 per year in the 2000s. The figure in 2010 was 828.
2     The ratifiers are: Sweden (1994), Armenia (1996), Netherlands (1997), Colombia (1997), Estonia (2000), Brazil (2001), Saudi Arabia (2001), Albania (2003), Zimbabwe (2003), Belgium (2004), Lebanon (2005), India 2008, Luxembourg 2008, Bosnia-Herzegovina 2010, Slovenia 2010, Ukraine 2011.
3     The Rotterdam Convention on the Prior Informed Consent Procedure for Certain Hazardous Pesticides and Chemicals in International Trade. For an analysis of this Convention see Hough (2000).
4     The Basel Convention on the Control of Transboundary Movements of Hazardous Wastes and their Disposal.
5     Latvia, Lithuania and Estonia are not included in TACIS. One non-former Soviet state, Mongolia, is included.
6     Around 4,000 workers per year in China die in mining accidents alone (Cheng 2003).

## Recommended reading

Abrams, A. (2001) 'A Short History of Occupational Health', *Journal of Public Health Policy*, 22(1): 34–80.
Beck, U. (1999) *World Risk Society*, Cambridge: Polity.
Dauvergne, P. (2005) 'Dying of Consumption: Accidents or Sacrifices of Global Morality', *Global Environmental Politics*, 5(3): 35–47.
Green, J. (1997) *Risk and Misfortune: The Social Construction of Accidents*, London: UCL Press.
Mitchell, J. (ed.) (1996) *The Long Road to Recovery: Community Responses to Industrial Disaster*, Tokyo, New York, and Paris: UN University Press, http://www.unu.edu/unupress/unupbooks/uu21le/uu21le00.htm.
Smith, K. and Petley, D. (2009) *Environmental Hazards: Assessing Risk and Reducing Disaster*, London and New York: Routledge.

## Useful web links

International Atomic Energy Agency, 'Convention on Nuclear Safety': http://www.iaea.or.at/worldatom/Documents/Legal/nukesafety.shtml
International Labour Organization: http://www.ilo.org/public/english/new/index.htm

# Criminal threats to security

No one country can effectively fight transnational organized crime within or outside its borders. Therefore, I submit, countries must relinquish some of their procedural or substantive sovereignty in order for the purpose for which sovereignty exists in the first place to remain intact.

Ronald Noble, Secretary-General of Interpol (Noble 2003)

## Introduction

Crime has always represented a threat to the security of ordinary people in all countries and, occasionally, to state institutions also. In recent years, however, this threat has changed in nature through utilizing the opportunities presented by globalization, undermining the capacity of governments to protect both their citizens and themselves. The use of legitimate sovereign force to uphold domestic law and order in the name of state and human security is universal and has a long history. Indeed, in many ways, this is the chief explanation for the gradual spread of sovereign rule from the mid-seventeenth century. In some countries state security has long been as much a domestic political issue as an international one. In Italy during the Cold War, for example, the domestic threat posed by political violence (most notably the Red Brigade) and criminal violence (most notably the mafia) dominated state security policy to much the same extent as the Soviet threat preoccupying the rest of Western Europe. This fact manifests itself in the existence and prominence in Italy of the paramilitary police force the *Carabinieri*, in contrast to its relatively modest military capabilities. This situation, though, has become more common as more countries have turned to paramilitary policing in recent years as a blurring of the distinction between internal and external security has prompted a commensurate blurring of the traditional roles of the military and police. In the USA, for example, the number of Special Weapons and Tactics (SWAT) police operations rose from 3,000 per year in the 1980s to around 40,000 per year in the 2000s (Kraska 2005).

Statistics are inevitably sketchy when dealing with an issue which is illegal, transnational and something many governments would prefer to downplay, but crime has undoubtedly grown worldwide since the 1990s. The IMF estimates that the amount of criminally acquired money in the world grew from $85 billion to $5,000 billion between 1988 and 1998 (Kendall 1998: 264). This trend has continued and the global black market now accounts for over $2 trillion per year or 6 per cent of global GDP (UNODC 2011a). The true figure, though, is higher still since the UNODC do not take full account of tax evasion. A breakdown of the cost of some of the key forms of contemporary transnational crime is given in Table 10.1.

Most pertinent to the consideration of security is the fact that nearly half a million people per year are murdered (UNODC 2011b) and one in five of all people fall victim to serious contact crime (robbery, sexual crimes or assaults) (Newman 2002: ch. 1). One of the most comprehensive and reliable studies of international crime, by the Council of Europe, showed that the number of convictions for completed homicide rose from 1.5 per 100,000 people in 1990 to 2.9 in 1996 (European Council 1999: Table 3.B.1.2). It is in the Americas and Africa, though,

**Table 10.1** The ten costliest forms of transnational crime

|  |  | Annual economic cost (US$) | Annual human cost |
|---|---|---|---|
| 1 | Corruption | 1.6 trillion[g] | |
| 2 | Cyber crime | 1 trillion[f] | |
| 3 | Drug trafficking | 400 billion[a] | 200,000 deaths[a] |
| 4 | Counterfeits | 250 billion[b] | |
| 5 | Environmental crime (oil, wildlife, timber, fish) | 33.6 billion[b] | |
| 6 | Human trafficking | 31.6 billion[b] | 27 million victims[e] |
| 7 | Stolen goods | 20 billion[c] | |
| 8 | Maritime piracy | 9.5 billion[d] | 11 deaths, 1,000 hostages |
| 9 | Human organ trafficking | 0.9 billion[b] | 7,000 victims[b] |
| 10 | Arms trafficking | 0.6 billion[b] | 99,000 deaths[h] |
| | Total | 2.1 trillion (excluding tax evasion) of which 1.6 trillion is laundered[a] | 450,000 homicides |

Sources: [a] UNODC (2011a); [b] Global Financial Integrity (2011); [c] Baker (2005); [d] IMO (2011); [e] USA (2011); [f] UK FCO (2011); [g] BBC (2009); [h] Author's estimate extrapolated from 1/4 of small arms trade is illegal (UN 2006) Small Arms Review and small arms account for 3/4 of the world's 526,000 violent killings (Geneva Declaration 2011).

**Table 10.2** The top ten homicide rates by country, 2010

|  |  | Homicides per 100,000 |
|---|---|---|
| 1 | Honduras | 82.1 |
| 2 | El Salvador | 66 |
| 3 | Ivory Coast | 56.9 |
| 4 | Jamaica | 52.1 |
| 5 | Belize | 41.7 |
| 6 | Guatemala | 41.4 |
| 7 | US Virgin Islands | 39.2 |
| 8 | St Kitts & Nevis | 38.2 |
| 9 | Zambia | 38 |
| 10 | Uganda | 36.3 |
| | Global Average | 6.9 |

Source: UNODC (2011b).

where life-threatening crime is most prevalent (see Table 10.2). The availability of firearms appears to be a major factor in explaining international variation in homicide rates. Nearly three-quarters of all homicides in the Americas are committed by firearms, a rate over three times that of Europe (UNODC 2011b).

Colombia epitomizes the security threats posed by crime. As well as providing a major human security threat to ordinary Colombian and foreign citizens, criminal organizations (in tandem with violent political organizations) have seriously undermined the capacity of the government to rule the country. Foreign troops have been called in to fight drugs barons whilst a large tract of Colombian territory was, for a number of years, conceded to 'narco-terrorists'. Colombia is an extreme case but in many countries throughout the world governments are increasingly threatened or undermined by armed groups terrifying their citizens, damaging their economy and corrupting their institutions (see Box 10.1).

## Box 10.1 Pablo Escobar

The technologically advanced and international military operation mounted to assassinate Colombian drugs magnate Pablo Escobar in 1993 illustrates how crime had entered into the realms of 'national security' in the post-Cold War years. Escobar was finally killed after US special troops the Delta Force and various crime-fighters from the USA were brought in to help by an exasperated and under-pressure Colombian government. His cover was blown when a telephone call was traced by surveillance equipment bringing to an end one of the most lucrative and destructive criminal careers in history.

Escobar was born in 1949 during the decade-long Colombian civil war. He followed a typical criminal career path starting with schoolboy scams before becoming involved in the thriving cocaine industry in the 1970s. By the end of the 1980s he was head of a cartel controlling over half of the cocaine entering the USA from South America and was estimated to be amongst the ten richest people in the world. Although a thoroughly ruthless gangster, Escobar successfully courted popular support amongst poor Colombians by playing the role of a contemporary 'Robin Hood'. He funded various public schemes and social programmes and even gained a seat in the Colombian parliament. With growing US pressure being mounted on Colombian authorities from the late 1980s to extradite him, as part of their war on drugs, Escobar focused his attentions on getting Colombia's extradition treaty with the USA closed down. A campaign of terror to secure himself within Colombia saw him authorize the bombing of a passenger plane in 1989 in the hope of killing Presidential candidate Cesar Gaviria. Gaviria was not on the plane but 110 other, unconnected people including two Americans were. This triggered the US into action and led eventually to Escobar's downfall. The trade in cocaine, of course, has yet to be curtailed (Bowden 2001).

## Global crime in historical context

Despite its recent rise to prominence and traditionally marginal role in international relations global crime has a long history.

### *Narcotic drugs*

The use, production and sale of narcotic drugs can be traced back to ancient history. Opiates were common in Ancient Greece (their use is referred to by Homer), marijuana was in use in China over two millennia ago and coca was as much an integral part of life in the Inca civilization as it is in some parts of Andean South America today. The trading of opiates occurred within Asia for many centuries and from the mid-eighteenth century extended into Europe. This was at the time an entirely legal form of commerce since the use of opiates was not distinguished from the use of medicinal drugs or foodstuffs and was common amongst societal elites. When Imperial China did take steps to restrict the legality of opium in the mid-nineteenth century Great Britain twice took up arms against them (the Opium Wars of 1839–42 and 1856–8) in order to protect their flow of imports from China and exports to China from their colony, India.

The shift of positions of Western governments from fighting wars *for* drugs to the contemporary fighting of wars *against* drugs began in the latter part of the nineteenth century. By this time the use of opiates in Western Europe and the USA had begun to spread beyond that of literary and political elite social circles and come to be associated with working class sloth and crime, prompting moves towards domestic prohibition. An international conference in Shanghai in 1909 initiated attempts to control the trade in opiates, which became codified in the 1912 International Opium Convention. The League of Nations made reference to the problem of narcotics in its charter and in 1920 established the Advisory Committee on Traffic in Opium and Other Dangerous Drugs (Bentham 1998: 90–2).

### *Piracy*

The menace caused to international commerce by the actions of pirates has, of course, a long and well-documented history and illustrates that threats to security from armed non-state actors are not a new phenomenon. Piracy is recorded as being of concern as early as the fourth century AD in the China Seas and gradually spread and grew through the centuries becoming particularly rife in the Mediterranean from the sixteenth to eighteenth century (Chalk 2000: 57).

The motivation for pirates to conduct robberies at sea rather than on land was that it made it harder for states to act against them. As such, piracy represents a classic concern of international law which, traditionally, is focused on tackling problems which do not fall under the direct jurisdiction of states. A series of international conventions were signed from the nineteenth century outlawing robbery on the high seas, culminating in the 1958 Geneva Convention which permits any state to try the perpetrators of such crimes regardless of the nationality of the criminal. The success of these conventions has produced an unusual twist for international relations with the uncharacteristic effectiveness of international law enforcement diverting the criminals to take on domestic law enforcers instead. Modern-day pirates tend not to operate on the high seas, where they run the risk of encountering the full might of great naval powers, and prefer to challenge the sovereign authorities of less powerful states in ransacking ships in territorial seas, in anchorage or in the harbour (Chalk 2000: 57–60).

## Slavery

International action against the age-old practice of slavery represents the first manifestation of human rights in international relations, with states acting to outlaw a crime through moral outrage rather than for economic reasons or for the safety of their citizens. The rise of outrage in nineteenth-century Western Europe at the barbarism of using forced human labour, and of profiting from the trade in human cargo, translated itself into the diplomacy of the *Concert of Europe*. The 1815 Congress of Vienna saw the great powers of Europe acknowledge an obligation to make the international trade in slaves contrary to international law. A similar agreement was made part of the Treaty of Ghent between the USA and Great Britain in the same year. This obligation became official at the 1885 Treaty of Berlin and was codified in the 1890 Brussels Convention, producing the world's first piece of human rights legislation. Great Britain, on a number of occasions, took the step of enforcing this law by intercepting Arab slave ships off the coast of East Africa and freeing the captives (Robertson 2000: 14). As discussed elsewhere in this volume, humanitarian interventions of this kind are still rare and highly contentious today. The act of slavery itself was made illegal under International Law by the 1926 Slavery Convention which put slavers in the same category as pirates, subject to the jurisdiction of any state regardless of where the crime took place.

## Webs of deceit: the rise in prominence of transnational crime

Although it is clear that crime on an international scale or with international repercussions is by no means a new phenomenon, the 1990s witnessed a significant rise in the scale of and political attention given to transnational organized crime. The ending of the Cold War and the onset of greater economic globalization can, in many ways, be seen to have created the conditions for a growing 'global underworld'.

The end of the Cold War can be understood to have facilitated the rise in significance of and priority given to crime in three main ways:

## The rise of 'failed states'

Since the 1990s the term 'failed states' has come to be attributed to those countries where a single government could not be said to be in effective political control within its own borders beyond what could be understood as any sort of period of transition or temporary civil strife. In effect, such territories can be seen to be in a permanent state of insurgency or general lawlessness. The preponderance of failed states increased after the ending of the Cold War partly because many such countries lost the patronage of either superpower in a New World Order where they ceased to hold such a strong military security attraction.

The classic case of the failed state is that of Afghanistan. Invaded by the USSR in 1979 Afghanistan became the focal point of the Second Cold War, with the USA providing substantial financial and military backing to the *mujaheddin* resistance fighters. The thawing of relations between the USA and USSR saw Soviet Premier Gorbachev announce the withdrawal of troops from the bloody and intractable conflict in 1988. This ended the proxy war between the two superpowers but did not end the conflict in Afghanistan, where rival factions continued to fight out a civil war in the power vacuum created by the sudden disinterest of the world's two most powerful states. The political legacy of this for the USA in terms of the rise of anti-American terrorist groups from the mujaheddin is well documented, but Afghanistan also rose again as a crucial haven for the global heroin industry. Ironically it was the toppling of the Taliban by the US-led invasion of 2001 that served to increase lawlessness in the country, and a resurgence in the export of opiates to the West, since that government had begun to clamp down on narcotics production.

Somalia represents another quintessential failed state, with much of the country existing in turmoil since the collapse of the Soviet-backed Barre government in 1991. Against this backdrop we can easily see how gangs of pirates have been able to thrive off the coast and become a scourge of international cargo and tourist liners travelling through the region. The pirates themselves have even cited the lack of sovereign authority as a justification for their actions in seizing control of their country's waters from international criminals.

> We don't consider ourselves pirates. We consider pirates those who illegally fish in our seas and dump in our seas and carry weapons in our seas. Think of us like a Coast Guard.
>
> (Ali 2008)

Failed states are significant in international relations because they stand in contradiction to conventional notions of the sovereign state system. Sovereignty is traditionally viewed as the cement that holds together the state system and maintains international order. The crucial component of the multi-faceted concept of sovereignty, enshrined in International Law in the 1933 Montevideo Convention on the Rights and Duties of States, is that a sovereign state has a government in 'effective control'. The rise in cases where countries cannot be said to have a sovereign government in effective control – such in Afghanistan, Somalia or Colombia – is, of course, a recipe for increased lawlessness in the world.

## An end to 'turning a blind eye' to international crime

On the other side of the coin to the failed states argument it is, of course, naive to suppose that transnational crime, and narcotics trading in particular, did not occur during the Cold War years. As well as increasing in incidence in the 1990s, narcotics trading was able to be given greater priority by governments with the shadow of the Cold War no longer obscuring other political issues. It is incontrovertible that the superpowers were prepared to tolerate corrupt governments being involved with or even directing criminal operations if they were in charge of important military allies or client states.

The clearest illustration of a U-turn in tolerating crooked regimes can be seen with the US invasion of Panama in the dying days of the Cold War in 1989. One of the principal reasons for the breakdown in relations between the two countries, which led to the overthrow of the Panamanian government, was the refusal of President Noriega to yield to US demands to act to curb the flow of cocaine passing through his country to US cities. Noriega's connections to the drugs underworld were well known to the Americans throughout the 1980s, as a military general until 1987 and as the President thereafter. At that time this was not viewed in such a negative light since he had aided the USA in anti-leftist operations in Central America (Tatham and McCleary 1992). The USA's security for the most part of the 1980s was construed almost entirely in terms of the Communist threat, which Noriega stood as a bulwark against, rather than in the threat posed by cocaine addiction and related crime in US cities. By 1989 this was beginning to change.

Similarly, the Soviet Union, whilst no supporter of narcotics, supported the fiercely conservative Communist regime of Eric Honneker in East Germany despite surely being aware of the leader's personal involvement in importing and selling cocaine. The Soviets also helped supply Colombian revolutionaries FARC, despite their well-known links to local cocaine cartels. International crime, like human rights, was not prioritized during the Cold War when state security was seen to trump human security.

## The rise of mafiocracies

One of the most prominent features of the post-Cold War political landscape has been the process of transition of many former Communist countries towards the Western model state with a partially free market economy and democratic political system. Welcomed by most Western governments and analysts as reducing the likelihood of military conflict in the world and even signalling 'the end of history' (Fukuyama 1992), this wave of democratization can also, however, be construed as having brought with it new security threats to the world.

Transition from a one-party state to a multi-party democracy, and from a centrally planned economy to a more diverse mixed economy with private industries and shareholders, is a very difficult process. Poverty and social upheaval are always favourable conditions in which crime can thrive and even the successful transition states have witnessed increased problems with black marketeers and illegal traders of various kinds. EU states have helped alleviate this for those joining the Union by providing policing advice and training to their eastern neighbours through aid and EU accession preparations.

It is the former Communist countries further east which have found most difficulty in making the transition to capitalism and democracy and where crime has become most prevalent and of greatest concern to the rest of the world. Rapid, wholesale privatization programmes in countries without experienced businesspeople, shareholders and private bankers inevitably run the risk of leaving key industries in the hands of black marketeers and inscrutable individuals. Godson and Williams use the term *mafiocracies* to encapsulate the problem of criminal syndicates buying into crucial aspects of state apparatus and winning political influence (Godson and Williams 2000: 113). The ownership of most of Russia's economy is by a small group of 'oligarchs', able to act as a cartel and exercise leverage over members of the Duma (parliament) protected by law from criminal prosecution.

Between a quarter and a third of Russia's economy is black and the murder rate has rocketed since the fall of Communism. Criminal gangs or *mafiya* are a prominent feature of Russian life, with extortion rackets rife in most cities. These syndicates are generally far from new and can be traced back to the Communist era. Additional recruits, though, came from newly redundant military and security personnel as some of the post-Cold War peace dividend turned to filthy lucre. Their influence has also extended into operations in many parts of Europe and elsewhere in the world.

Perhaps the clearest illustration of a new security threat emerging in international politics with the ending of the Cold War, and souring the toasts being made to global peace, is the rise in black market trading in weapon-grade nuclear material. Nearly 700 incidences of such operations were documented in the 1990s, principally focused in the successor states of the Soviet Union (Williams and Woessner 2000). Here, President Yeltsin had assumed control from Gorbachev of a country shorn not only of fourteen of its fifteen republics and six colonies but also a large chunk of its huge nuclear arsenal.

A further illustration of how post-communist transition can serve as a catalyst for international crime at the same time as enhancing wider state security is provided by Kosovo. The Yugoslav successor state, fought for and sustained by Western compassion and interest, has become a haven for criminality whilst its sovereignty slowly evolves. The 2005 UN Drug Report identified Kosovan organized crime groups as the key controllers of heroin traffickers into Western Europe and the 2007 Report additionally noted that they were becoming important players in the transport of cocaine from South America to Western Europe (UNODC 2005, 2007). The rise of criminal gangs in the former Soviet Union and their diffusion into the Western world thus encapsulates the dark side of three generally positive developments in international relations in the 1990s: the fall of the Iron Curtain, democratization and globalization.

Globalization, denoting the increased level of cross-border economic activity and increasingly global political framing of such change, can be seen to have influenced the rise in prominence of global crime in a number of ways.

## *The increased volume of traded goods*

The opportunities for trading in legal commodities are much greater than ever before in terms of costs, speed and the existence of global regulations favouring free trade over state protectionism. Such opportunities are also, however, present for the trading in illegal commodities. It is easier and cheaper for criminals to operate internationally and the sheer volume of traded goods makes it difficult for state authorities to detect the movement of drugs, arms shipments and other illicit cargoes.

Drugs traffickers have come to make effective use of that very symbol of globalization, the internet, to boost their operations. Gangs are known to have used encrypted websites to communicate and share information on their activities whilst employing information technology experts as hackers to alter information held on customs databases and create phantom websites to put state officials off the scent of the real sites. A simple illustration of how modern technological aids to commerce can serve murkier purposes also comes with evidence that Australian drug traffickers have brazenly used the web service offered by legitimate couriers allowing customers to track the location of the goods they are having delivered (International Narcotics Control Board 2002: 2).

## *The growth of cross-border financial transactions*

Ever-increasing cross-border financial flows can also present opportunities to international criminals as much as to international businessmen. Large-scale criminal activity is usually accompanied by money laundering as crime groups seek to protect their ill-gotten gains from state authorities by moving the money around or investing it in legitimate businesses. This process is becoming increasingly globalized as criminal organizations learn to exploit the inadequacies of the sovereign state system by moving money from country to country. Investing the proceeds of crime into legitimate businesses in a state other than where the crime took place illustrates the nature of criminal globalization's challenge to the state system. A crucial aspect of a crime may not be construed as criminal in the country where it occurs and may even be considered to be a beneficial overseas investment.

The globalization of 'white-collar crime' is another price that governments and individuals have paid for reaping some of the benefits of financial liberalization. Many governments – such as the USA and UK – consciously began taking a more 'hands off' approach to banking and financial services from the 1990s in order to accrue inward flows of investment. Whilst this bore many fruits for a while, such a voluntary relaxation of sovereign controls came to appear more questionable from 2008 when a global recession unfolded as a consequence of shoddy banking practices. Some bankers exploited the laxer regulatory environment, others went further and blatantly broke laws safe in the conviction that they would never be caught. A rival contender to Escobar as the world's 'greatest' ever criminal thus emerged in US financier Bernie Madoff, sentenced in 2009 for 150 years in prison for fraud to the tune of $65 billion.

## *Urbanization*

The global trend towards urban living is a factor behind the rise of crime since city dwellers are statistically far more violent and lawless than their rural counterparts. The homicide rate in the urban municipalities of Brazil, for example, is over three times that of the rural municipalities (Small Arms Survey 2007: 230–1). Around one-sixth of the world live in urban slums, the majority of which are in the Global South (UN-Habitat 2003). Deprived urban living is closely associated with the development of criminal gangs and this is a growing phenomenon in many megacities in both the Global North and South. Urban gang culture is nothing new but appears to be globalizing not only via migration routes but through the global media. Hence the notorious Los Angeles *MS-13* have, in recent years, become the biggest gang, and significant societal and governmental menace, in Honduras and El Salvador, two countries with amongst the world's highest homicide rates (see Table 10.2) (Hagedorn 2005).

## *The growth of 'global crime'*

A key factor in the globalization of crime is the increased tendency for organized criminal groups to follow the lead of transnational corporations and set up operations in a number of other countries. Cheaper international travel costs favour criminals as much as they do other profit-seeking individuals. Godson and Williams describe how transnational criminal organizations can come to utilize a *home state* from where they direct operations, a *host state* where they carry out crimes or sell their produce, a *transportation state* where criminal activities will seek to ensure an unhindered passage of goods to the host state and a *service state* in countries where favourably secretive banking laws allow for profits to be secured (Godson and Williams 2000: 115). Hence, a genuinely transnational operation can be established where, for example, a Colombian-based narcotics gang could secure access to markets in the USA by bribing Mexican officials to permit the transit of the drugs and then invest the proceeds in a Cayman Islands offshore bank account. Over 40,000 Mexicans were killed between 2007 and 2012 in the context of internecine criminal wars based on the transit of South American narcotics into North America (BBC 2011).

## *The growth of global criminal alliances*

At the 1994 United Nations Conference on Internationally Organized Crime, UN Secretary-General Boutros-Ghali referred to an 'empire of criminals' to highlight the problem of globally operating criminal gangs but also to illustrate the fact that many of these organized gangs were cooperating with other, like-minded groups to extend the reach of their operations. There is a long history of criminal gangs extending their influence into other countries but this, traditionally, had been in line with patterns of migration. Hence the mafia's influence in the USA from the 1930s followed large-scale Italian migration and, to a far lesser extent, Jamaican *yardies* and Hong Kong *triads* extended operations to the UK from the 1980s.

The 1990s, however, witnessed the increased formation of strategic alliances between transnational criminal organizations exploiting changing political rather than demographic circumstances. Phil Williams, the world authority on transnational crime, illustrates this development clearly:

> Colombian–Sicilian networks brought together Colombian cocaine suppliers with Sicilian groups possessing local knowledge, well-established heroin distribution networks, extensive bribery and corruption networks, and a fully fledged capability for money laundering. Italian and Russian criminal networks have also forged cooperative relationships, while Colombian and Russian criminals have been meeting in various Caribbean islands to engage in guns-for-drugs deals.
>
> (Williams 2001: 75–6)

> International criminal cooperation can sometimes even thrive where societal and governmental cooperation is absent. Serb and Albanian gangsters, for example, are known to have worked together extensively in human trafficking operations in the Balkans.
>
> (Williams 2006: 198)

## Criminal exploitation of political integration

Globalization not only provides criminals with the opportunities to widen their operations it can also sometimes be seen to create new opportunities for crime. Political integration is a by-product of an increasingly interdependent world where states recognize the limitations on independent action in the global economy and work towards 'pooling' their sovereignty by creating new, wider economic and political communities with nearby states. By far the most extensive case of such political integration is in Europe with the European Union (where the desire to create a *security community* must also be seen as a crucial spur). The EU is very much a leap of faith since no comparable project has been attempted before and, as a result, merging together the economic activities of twenty-seven states has had some unintended side-effects.

Organized crime groups, for example, are known to have exploited the complexity of the EU's costly and highly bureaucratic Common Agricultural Policy (CAP). The payment of subsidies to olive producers inadvertently has helped finance the mafia who have long had an 'influence' on that industry in Sicily. The opening up of borders between the member-states of the EU since the late 1980s has provided a further boost to the mafia by making the service of giving safe passage across the Adriatic to illegal immigrants from East Europe to Southern Italy attractive since migrants can more easily head north to wealthier parts of the EU.

The EU has responded to such developments through the establishment of a Justice and Home Affairs 'pillar' to accompany measures furthering economic integration and greater police cooperation but smuggling of illegal immigrants and contraband across weak spots on its vast borders remains a pressing concern.

## The global consumption of criminal enterprise

A key reason for global crime is the existence of a global market for such products and services. The use of special UK and US military forces from the 1990s to take on South American drugs cartels marked a recognition of the state securitization of international crime but the ever-increasing flow of cocaine into those countries also showed the limitations of such an approach. At the same time as the American and British governments have been dispatching troops to Colombia the Colombian government have been dispatching diplomats and politicians to London and Washington to appeal for action to clamp down on the markets for the drugs. Rudimentary criminology recognizes that controlling crime is about tackling the demand as well as the supply side of the activities but such strategies are difficult to implement in the traditional practices of international security politics so focused on externalizing threats. Again there is a tendency to see global problems as solely emanating from the global 'badlands' when much of the problem actually lies closer to home. The consumers of drugs, cheap pirated goods and sex worker services perpetuate these areas of global crime and these people generally reside in wealthy and apparently respectable countries.

## Global policemen? The rise of international political action on crime

### Interpol

Established in 1923, Interpol is undoubtedly the best known global institutional response to the problem of transnational crime. Its membership is impressively universal with 190 member-states. Each member-state is represented by delegates at the organization's headquarters at Lyon, France, and each hosts a National Crime Bureau (NCB) which serve as the nodes in an information network to aid state police forces and promote cooperation amongst them. The 190 NCBs are linked by a computerized database which contains pooled information resources on known criminals and stolen goods, such as cars, to aid in the detection of transnational criminals and speed up the process of their extradition (although the process of extradition is still a bilateral matter between the governments concerned). In addition to this chief function of facilitating the exchange of information, Interpol also seeks to promote greater regional cooperation between police forces (as, for example with the Mercosur countries: Brazil, Argentina, Paraguay and Uruguay) and act as a 'value-added service provider' giving advice to governments on how to develop extradition agreements and to state police forces on updating their information technology resources. Interpol as an intergovernmental organization has a conventional decision-making structure. Each member-state is represented by a government-appointed delegate at an annual General Assembly, which votes by simple majority on the adoption of new procedures. The General Assembly also elects an Executive Committee of thirteen member-state delegates, which meets three times a year and prepares the agenda for the General Assemblies, as well as managing the implementation of decisions. Day-to-day administration is carried out by a permanent secretariat at Lyon headed by the Secretary-General, elected for a five-year term of office by two-thirds majority of the General Assembly (Interpol 2012).

Despite proclaiming amongst its objectives that it aims to act 'in the spirit of the Universal Declaration of Human Rights' (Interpol Constitution Article 2) Interpol has always sought to play a non-political role. Article 3 of its Constitution makes this clear: 'It is strictly forbidden for the organisation to undertake any intervention or activities of a political, military, religious or racial character'. This somewhat contradicts the previous article since racial and religious persecution are amongst the crimes renounced in the Univeral Declaration on Human Rights but it would, of course, be impossible for an organization of this nature to maintain its broad membership without such a precondition.

Another limitation to the work of Interpol is its modest budget, derived from member-state contributions calculated on the basis of population and GDP. This point was clearly expressed by Secretary-General Ronald Noble: 'we have a multi-billion dollar problem being tackled by an organization running on just 30 million euros' (Interpol 2002). Sheptycki, with provocative irony, has argued that where Interpol has grown it has evolved like a series of protection rackets. As a largely informal arrangement, without an explicit treaty or fixed budget, Interpol inevitably 'chases the money' and focuses on illicit trade cases referred to it by state police in wealthy countries, rather than tackling global crime in the global interest. Hence issues uncomfortable for any particular state, such as the corruption of government officials or the dumping of toxic waste, rarely occupy the time of Interpol officers on temporary secondment from national jobs (Sheptycki 2003). Interpol is clearly a valuable resource to police forces around the world in arresting transnational criminals but, in its present guise, can only be a limited player in the development of global policies to arrest the rise of transnational crime. '[W]hat is needed is an agreed calculus by which to allocate policing resources in order for them to be efficiently and effectively targeted on criminal activities that cause social harm' (Sheptycki 2003: 53).

## The World Customs Organization

A similar body to Interpol, the WCO aims to facilitate cooperation between customs officials and coordinate national customs procedures in order to combat illicit trades. Based in Brussels the organization is also impressively universal with 177 member-states and has been in operation since the 1950s but, like Interpol, is limited in what it can do in the face of increasingly sophisticated global criminals. By the WCO's own admission, 'efficient and effective performance is not spread evenly among all Customs administrations, or in all regions of the world' (WCO 2006).

## Europol

The rise in cross-border crime in the European Union, referred to earlier in this chapter, prompted the organization in the early 1990s to instigate an Interpol-style institution of its own to coordinate the work of its member-state police forces.

Europol was agreed upon at the 1992 Treaty on European Union (Maastricht Treaty), in line with the creation of a 'Justice and Home Affairs' dimension to the EU's political integration process, and came into being in January 1994. Like Interpol, Europol has a central database, The Europol Computer Systems (TECS), serving a system of offices in the member-states. Still in the early stages of evolution Europol has already outgrown its global 'parent'. Its budget for 2011 was 84 million euros, more than double the amount it ran on ten years previously. In addition to a permanent secretariat in the Hague, Europol employs 137 'Europol Liaison Officers' (ELOs) in the 27 member-states, principally made up of experienced police and customs officers (Europol 2012b).

The birth and subsequent growth of Europol represents a classic case of *spillover*, a concept associated with the Neo-Functionalist theory of political integration and often applied to the development of the European Union. The crux of the concept is that political cooperation in one area inevitably leads to the need and desire to cooperate in other functionally related areas. The chief spur to the creation of Europol was concern at the increased opportunities for the transboundary movement of narcotics within the EU in the light of the relaxing of border controls between the member-states. There were two dimensions to this problem. Drugs originating from within the EU could exploit a wider market and drugs from outside of the EU could also exploit this wider market if successfully smuggled into one of the member-states (exploiting a weak spot in a now very large border). The first of these two dimensions of the problem was exacerbated by the fact that one EU member-state, The Netherlands, had notably more liberal state laws with regard to the use of cannabis than its neighbours, opening up the possibility of an unregulated flow of that drug out of its borders.

Hence the first manifestation of Europol in 1994 was the creation of the Europol Drugs Unit. Other units have subsequently been created and Europol's role has expanded rapidly. Article 30 of the 1997 Amsterdam Treaty, a follow-up legal package seeking to expand upon the developments agreed upon at Maastricht, authorized the extension of Europol authority and it now has the sort of political clout not possessed by Interpol. At the 1999 European Council Summit in Tampere, Finland, it was agreed that member-states should be obliged to initiate investigations in a case if requested to do so by Europol.

A further way in which Europol has moved beyond the role of facilitating the exchange of information between police forces is in the promotion of judicial cooperation. The European Judicial Network was set up in 1998 as an information exchange service for lawyers in the member-states. In 2001 this development was augmented by the creation of Eurojust, a sister organization to Europol, made up of representatives of the legal professions, such as magistrates and prosecution services. Again this is spillover in practice with the drive to improve the detection of transboundary crime being accompanied by a desire to achieve a commensurate improvement in the capacity to arrest transboundary criminals.

The 2008 Lisbon Treaty brought Europol fully into the EU political system with the possibility of unilateral national vetoes ending and its decisions now made on the basis of qualified majority voting. Given its budgetary and political growth we can thus expect the informational, legal and political roles of the EU in the fighting of crime to continue to evolve.

## *United Nations*

As with the European Union, the role of the UN with regard to transnational crime originated in efforts to coordinate action against the trade in narcotics before evolving into activities dealing with other realms of global criminal activity. The UN took over the management of the League of Nations' work on tackling the narcotics trade, as it did with many functional agencies established by its forerunner. The League's well-documented failures with regard to military security should not obscure its pioneering work in developing global responses to other great threats to humanity. The League's Committee on the Traffic in Opium and Other Dangerous Drugs was transformed into the Commission on Narcotic Drugs (CND) but the UN soon expanded its role and the 1961 Single Convention on Narcotic Drugs created a sister organization to the CND, the International Narcotics Control Board (INCB). This signalled an attempt by the UN to deepen the global response to an increasingly politically contentious issue, but the further creation of various groups and programmes over the next three decades served to confuse the picture and prompt a rationalization, in line with other structural changes to the UN, at the close of the Cold War.

A special session of the UN General Assembly in 1990 recognized the growing threat posed by narcotics and instigated the creation of a single programme to replace the 'alphabet soup' of small UN groups that had developed in this policy area. The UN International Drug Control Programme (UNDCP) started operations in 1991 to coordinate UN policy, with the CND and INCB taken under its wings as committees. A further rationalization of UN operations occurred in 1997 when the UNDCP married its operations to a new body, the UN Centre for International Crime Prevention (CICP) as subsections of the UN Office for Drugs and Crime (UNODC). This step marked a recognition by the UN of the growing significance of a range of transnational criminal operations first evident in the sponsorship of a major conference in Naples in 1994 attended by government ministers from 136 states.

The CICP did not appear from nowhere but it represented a greatly souped-up version of its predecessor the UN Crime Prevention and Criminal Justice Division (CPCJD). The CICP is very much the junior partner within the UNODC, with a permanent staff of 15 compared to over 300 in the UNDCP. It is, however, assisted by a separate 40-man body, the Commission on Crime Prevention and Criminal Justice (CCPCJ), which is a subsidiary of the Economic and Social Council, the UN's chief steering mechanism for developing global policy on non-military issues. The CCPCJ cooperates with pressure groups, academics and politicians in organizing congresses which produce draft resolutions which direct the CICP in its work of defining 'internationally recognized principles for criminal justice'.

The culmination of the work of these congresses, and a Global Action Plan initiated by the 1994 Naples Conference, was the UN International Convention Against Transnational Organized Crime which was adopted by the General Assembly in November 2000 and entered into force in 2003. Article 1 of the Convention succinctly describes its purpose as 'to promote cooperation to prevent and combat transnational organized crime more effectively' (UN 2000: 1). Subsequent articles of the Convention deal with a wide range of issues relating to transnational organized crime. These are summarized in the Table 10.3.

**Table 10.3** UN Convention on Transnational Organized Crime

| | |
|---|---|
| Articles 2–4 | Definitions and scope of the convention |
| Article 5 | Criminalizing the participation in an organized crime group |
| Articles 8–10 | Corruption |
| Articles 11 and 12 | Punishment |
| Articles 13 and 14 | International cooperation on confiscation |
| Article 15 | Jurisdiction |
| Articles 16 and 17 | Extradition |
| Articles 18–22 | Mutual legal assistance and investigative cooperation |
| Article 23 | Criminalizing the obstruction of justice |
| Article 24 | Witness protection |
| Article 25 | Victim protection |
| Article 26 | Encouraging public notification of crime |
| Article 27 | Law enforcement cooperation |
| Article 28 | Sharing information |
| Article 29 | Law enforcement training programmes (initiation or improvement) |
| Article 30 | Assistance to LDCs in implementing the convention |
| Article 31 | Prevention of organized crime at the domestic level |
| Articles 32–41 | Implementation |
| Protocols: | 1 Trafficking in persons |
| | 2 Smuggling of migrants |
| | 3 Illegal trading in firearms |

A 'Conference of the Parties' has met regularly since 2003 to oversee the implementation and development of the Convention. The Convention is a step forward in terms of providing the basis for greater international harmonization in tackling money laundering and corruption but, as with most intergovernmental arrangements of this kind, there are no enforcement measures beyond peer pressure. The compulsory sharing of information amongst parties, for example, is cited as a necessary next step by the UNODC (UNODC 2010).

## Conclusions

The UN Convention marks a watershed in global policy on crime but, at the same time, represents only a tiny first step towards effectively tackling the problem. Transnational crime, more starkly than any of the issues of global security politics, illustrates the limitations of the Westphalian system of sovereign states in protecting citizens' lives and livelihoods. Lives lost to wars, disasters, disease, poverty and organized discrimination will almost certainly be far fewer in the present century than the last and there is at least some scope for optimism that environmental Armageddon can be averted. These are problems that would be best addressed by a more globalized polity but could be significantly reduced in their significance by greater political will within an intergovernmental framework. Global crime, in contrast, is a security problem that is getting worse and does not look likely to recede in the face merely of greater cooperation between sovereign states. Criminals used to exploit the lack of holism in domestic law enforcement by operating across (US) state boundaries or even (UK) county borders until such inappropriate de-centralization was addressed politically. That situation has now arisen globally.

> States have become almost outmoded organizations: in effect, we are attempting to deal with a twenty-first century phenomenon using structures, mechanisms and instruments that are still rooted in eighteenth- and nineteenth-century concepts and organizational forms.
>
> (Godson and Williams 1998: 324)

## Key points

- Internationally operating criminal groups are not new but have become an increased threat to both human and state security by utilizing the opportunities offered by globalization and post-Cold War socio-political change.
- International political action to combat transnational crime has increased in recent years but remains insufficient in tackling a problem now beyond control by conventional inter-state politics.

## Recommended reading

Glenny, M. (2011) *Dark Market: CyberThieves, CyberCops and You,* London: Bodley Head.

Godson, R. and Williams, P. (2000) 'Strengthening Cooperation against Transsovereign Crime', in Cusimano, M. (ed.) *Beyond Sovereignty: Issues for a Global Agenda*, Boston: St Martins: 111–46.

Madsen, F. (2009) *Transnational Organized Crime (Global Institutions)* Abingdon: Routledge.

UNODC (2010) *The Globalization of Crime: A Transnational Organized Crime Threat Assessment.*

Williams, P. (2001) 'Transnational Criminal Networks', in Arquilla and Ronfeldt (eds) *Networks and Netwars: The Future of Terror, Crime and Militancy*, Santa Monica: RAND: 61–97.

## Useful web links

Europol: http://www.europol.net/

Interpol: http://www.interpol.int/

United Nations Convention Against Transnational Organized Crime: http://www.unodc.org/unodc/en/treaties/CTOC/

United Nations Crime and Justice Information Network: http://www.uncjin.org/

United Nations Office on Drugs and Crime: http://www.unodc.org/

# Towards global security?

We are accustomed to regard the world as neatly divided into compartments called states. ... But this vision of the world divided into isolated compartments is not a true reflection of facts as they exist in a large portion of the earth today.

(Woolf 1916: 216–17)

## Thinking global: integration theories and global politics

Understanding global security necessitates ridding oneself of the preconceptions rooted in the traditional and still dominant political culture that the security under consideration must be that of states, as determined by states. In an age when people's fates were inextricably linked to that of their governments, and the only significant cross-border interactions were military, diplomatic and economic exchanges between governments, this preconception was largely appropriate. This age, however, has now passed into history and the assumption that an individual's life is solely determined by their government is anachronistic. People in the twentieth century were dependent on their governments like no time before and like they will never be again. The diplomatic manoeuvrings of elected or self-appointed leaders did much to dictate the fate of a large proportion of the world's population in the age of total war. Many millions died, many millions of others were saved by their governments from death at the hands of other governments. Many of those same people were more directly still at the mercy of their governments, who could determine whether or not to murder them in order to enhance their own security.

War and politicide persist and the fates of many of the world's people continue to be determined by politics 'from above' but this is far from the full picture. Strokes of fate from outside of the traditional political world, like plagues, pestilence and disasters, determine, to a far greater extent, whether people live or die in today's world. They also determined the fate of most people in yesterday's world, although this was obscured by governmental preoccupation with human threats they knew how to deal with. This is no longer so, on both counts. External human threats have diminished and the capacity for governments to safeguard their people against non-human foes is also in decline.

No life-threatening strokes of fate in today's world are, in fact, from outside of the realm of politics, even if they are outside the control of individual governments. Governments can imperil their own people without dragging them into wars against their interest or victimizing them for their own interests by failing to address, in concert with their fellow governments, global sources of human insecurity. Environmental degradation, transnational crime and infectious disease simply cannot be properly legislated against by a government acting in isolation. The September 11th 2001 al-Qa'ida strikes on the USA proved that military defence comes into this category as well. Life-threatening poverty and vulnerability to disease and disaster can be insured against by some governments, but this can be to the detriment of the security of other state's citizens. Economic cushioning, such as agricultural protectionism and exploitative market expansion, can come at the cost of the lives of those squeezed out. Optimizing global security is only possible by looking at the bigger picture.

## *Political integration*

Recognition of the inadequacy of state and state-to-state politics in assuring the security of the world's people came early in the era of total war. The folly and horror of the First World War prompted a number of polemical works advocating world government in place of the sovereign system of states. British Socialists John Hobson and Leonard Woolf wrote books advocating world government as a means of retreating from endemic war and imperialism (Hobson 1915; Woolf 1916). Woolf was a firm advocate of the League of Nations, which emerged after the First World War, whereas Hobson was highly dismissive of the organization as little more than a victors' club for a war of which he did not approve. Woolf was more positive, considering the League to be furthering the trend established in nineteenth-century international affairs, before the build-up to world war, of international organizations assuming the political stewardship of certain functions from governments (see Box 11.1).

Woolf and Hobson thus represented pioneers of two differing strands of political integration theory which were further developed, and partially applied, after the Second World War. Woolf's work was a source of inspiration for Mitrany and the Functionalists, who favoured a gradualist, bottom-up approach towards world government in which ordinary people would rationally come to switch their loyalties from their states to international non-governmental bodies (Mitrany 1975). Hobson's route to world government was more direct and 'top down': the immediate creation of supranational agencies assuming control from governments of certain, clearly defined political areas. World Federalism of this sort gained momentum with the failure of the League of Nations and the even greater horrors that unfolded in the Second World War. The British and Indian premiers, Churchill and Nehru, both advocated this as a recipe for world peace and the scientist Einstein, fearful in particular of the impact of atomic weapons on international relations, added his support. Advocacy for World Federalism receded as the Cold War reactivated the

### Box 11.1 Leonard Woolf

This prominent literary and political writer formed part of the celebrated 'Bloomsbury Group' of intellectuals which included student friends from his days at Cambridge, including the philosopher Bertrand Russell, economist John Maynard Keynes and the feminist novelist Virginia Stephens, whom he later married.

Woolf resigned from a position in the Ceylon Civil Service due to his distaste of colonialism and was a conscientious objector during the First World War. The ideas which underpinned his most notable political work, *International Government*, were used by the British government in the talks leading up to the creation of the League of Nations, for whom Woolf later worked in a number of capacities.

'national interest' and economic recovery provided more 'optimism' amongst states that sovereignty had not died alongside the millions of casualties of the Second World War. Churchill even backtracked on earlier support for Western European Federalism, leaving this venture to recent allies and adversaries across the English Channel.

Federalism has yet to happen in Western Europe, despite profound political integration for over half a century, with Churchill's successors leading resistance to the sheer mention of the 'F' word in EU policy. Federalist ventures for a United Arab Republic linking Egypt, Libya and Yemen and a Federation of the West Indies collapsed altogether within a few years of their inauguration in 1958. It has been apparent since then that there is little prospect of a surrender/pooling (depending on your political perspective) of government sovereignty to a global federal authority. The European integration experiment, in fact, recognized from the start that governmental and public support for a United States of Europe had quickly evaporated as the shadow of the Second World War lifted and the European Communities (EC) were modelled on a modified version of Functionalist theory. Monnet, Spaak, Spinelli and the other founding fathers of the EC set about achieving a United Europe in a gradualist manner, starting with the European Coal and Steel Community in 1951 selected deliberately to act as a catalyst for political 'spillover' into other sectors. Mitrany had little time for the EC, seeing it as a 'top-down' plan which would simply replace a number of states with one bigger one, rather than fundamentally change international relations.

Neo-Functionalism was devised and embraced for the EC experiment for pragmatic rather than idealistic reasons. It was a half-way house between Functionalism and Federalism inspired by the fact that both theories appeared hopelessly utopian by the 1950s. Federalism on a limited regional scale had failed to get off the ground and the functional international organizations which inspired Functionalism remained limited in influence and still controlled by governments. By the 1990s the continuation of integration without any real likelihood of a United States of Europe emerging from it, despite a revival of the direct approach to its achievement, prompted a new theoretical approach to explain what was happening. The Consociationalist theory of European integration contended that the states of the now restyled European Union would continue to merge economically and politically, not inspired by any holy grail of an idealized end-state but through pragmatic, economic necessity (Taylor 1991). Hence, from this perspective, the launch of a single EU currency did not mark the beginning of the end of sovereign member-states so much as the practical realization by the governments that this would speed up business and that, apart from the German mark, the national currencies were increasingly irrelevant on the global stage.

Neo-Functionalism and Consociationalism are theories very much designed to fit the European experience but they have some currency when looking at the bigger picture. Consociationalism has global application to the development of the WTO and the numerous international regimes of common rules to which governments increasingly voluntarily commit themselves in order to ease the complications of dealing with modern economic interdependence. The United Nations does not have an equivalent of the European Commission to cultivate global integration from 'above', as Neo-Functionalists describe and advocate, but many

## Box 11.2 The specialized agencies of the United Nations

- FAO (Food and Agriculture Organization of the UN)
  Works to improve agricultural productivity and food security.

- IAEA (International Atomic Energy Agency)
  Works for the safe and peaceful uses of atomic energy.

- ICAO (International Civil Aviation Organization)
  Sets international standards for the safety, security and efficiency of air transport.

- IFAD (International Fund for Agricultural Development)
  Mobilizes financial resources to raise food production in developing countries.

- ILO (International Labour Organization)
  Formulates policies and programmes to improve working conditions and sets international labour standards.

- IMF (International Monetary Fund)
  Facilitates international monetary cooperation and financial stability.

- IMO (International Maritime Organization)
  Works to improve international shipping safety and reduce marine pollution.

- ITU (International Telecommunication Union)
  Fosters international cooperation to improve telecommunications and coordinates usage of radio and TV frequencies.

- UNESCO (UN Educational, Scientific and Cultural Organization)
  Promotes education for all and scientific and cultural cooperation.

- UNIDO (UN Industrial Development Organization)
  Promotes the industrial advancement of developing countries through technical assistance.

- UNWTO (UN World Tourism Organization)
  Serves as a global forum for tourism policy issues.

- UPU (Universal Postal Union)
  Establishes international regulations for postal services.

- WHO (World Health Organization)
  Coordinates programmes aimed at solving international health problems.

- WIPO (World Intellectual Property Organization)
  Promotes the international protection of intellectual property.

- World Bank Group
  Provides loans and technical assistance to developing countries to reduce poverty and advance economic growth.

- WMO (World Meteorological Organization)
  Promotes research on the Earth's climate and facilitates the global exchange of meteorological data.

initiatives from within its system have served to push forward the natural progress of spillover. Cases in point include: the work of the International Law Commission in advancing human rights law and establishing the International Criminal Court, the Human Development Reports of the UNDP and the work of Secretary-General Annan culminating in the 2004 High Level Panel on Threats, Challenges and Change and 2005 Report 'In Larger Freedom' (Annan 2004). UN decision-making remains intergovernmental but, there is no doubt, that the myriad programmes and specialized agencies under its umbrella are more than the sum of their formal governmental parts (see Box 11.2).

Some governments have also attempted to sow the seeds of global governance within the United Nations system, guided by human security. The governments of Canada and Norway, the leading members of the Human Security Network, and particularly Japan, have been most prominent in this regard. The UN Commission on Human Security was established in 2001 comprising twelve prominent international statesmen and thinkers co-chaired by Indian economist Amartya Sen and Japanese academic and former UN High Commissioner for Refugees Sadako Ogata. The Commission held five official meetings culminating in the production of their final report *Human Security Now*, after which it was succeeded by an eight-person Advisory Board chaired by Ogata. The report makes ten key recommendations (see Table 11.1) and calls for multilateral, multi-layered governance in order to:

> build a protective infrastructure that shields all people's lives from critical and pervasive threats. That infrastructure includes institutions at every level of society: police systems, environmental regulations, health care networks, educational systems, safety nets and workfare programmes, vaccination campaigns and early warning systems for crises or conflict.
> (Commission on Human Security 2003: 132)

Best suited to the promotion of human security, however, are pressure groups because of their transnational character, closeness to local populations, willingness

**Table 11.1** Key recommendations of the Commission on Human Security

1  Protecting people in violent conflict
2  Protecting people from the proliferation of arms
3  Supporting the security of people on the move
4  Establishing human security transition funds for post-conflict situations
5  Encouraging fair trade and markets to benefit the extreme poor
6  Working to provide minimum living standards everywhere
7  According higher priority to ensuring universal access to basic health care
8  Developing an efficient and equitable global system for patent rights
9  Empowering all people with universal basic education
10 Clarifying the need for a global human identity while respecting the freedom of individuals to have diverse identities and affiliations

to confront the political status quo and capacity for coalition-building (Michael 2002: 2). The Norwegian government has recognized this and worked extensively in international affairs with conflict resolution groups such as International Alert and developmental organizations such as the Aga Khan Foundation. Over 1,000 European humanitarian and development-focused pressure groups brought together in 2003 under the umbrella of the Confederation for Cooperation of Relief and Development (CONCORD) have made human security the cornerstone of their campaigns, which have featured extensive lobbying of governments holding the EU presidency and notably succeeded in getting an increase in foreign aid pledges from the member-states in 2005. Similarly, human security was the theme of the 2003 Annual Conference of the 'World Association of NGOs' held in Bangkok and many pressure groups have individually indicated their support for the concept. In 2007 a campaign for the Establishment of a United Nations Parliamentary Assembly was launched by NGOs such as the World Federalist Movement, former UN Secretary-General Boutros-Ghali and several hundred national parliamentarians seeking to democratize the UN and ensure it is formally structured in order to meet human rather than state interests.

## Acting global: global solutions to global problems

### A *state utilitarianist path to enhanced global security*

Although contemporary international political practice marks a recognition of the fact that human and state security both rest on more than the preservation of sovereignty by force, it is clear from examining the issues of global security that this has not gone far enough. The 'cosmopolitan ethics' of Pluralist International Relations scholars like Beitz and Liberal philosophers like Rawls found satisfaction in the late twentieth-century codification of international human rights law and deepening economic interdependence, as they confirmed that the individual was emerging as an entity in international politics from under the shell of the sometimes clumsy protection of the state (Beitz 1979; Rawls 1971).

When, in the 1990s, the changed international political environment facilitated the further advance of global justice and interdependence it became apparent, however, that this alone was not the solution to all of the world's ills. Despite major medical and technological advances in the second half of the twentieth century, which had seen world life expectancy grow at unprecedented rates and the health gap between North and South reduce, it was clear by the end of the century that economic globalization was not enough to continue this improvement and even part of the problem. What was needed, however, was not the abandonment of globalization, increasingly advocated by a growing global social movement, so much as 'globalisation with a human spin' (Lee, Buse and Fustukian 2002: 279). Similarly it was not so much globalization as partial globalization, the globalization of the value of economic gain without the commensurate globalization of the value of human security, that was at the root of other global ailments becoming more apparent at the end of the millennium.

Frankman described the emerging global polity of the 1990s as 'hard democracy', a limited form of democratic representation dished out by political elites without properly empowering the stakeholders (Frankman 1997: 324). The term had originally been coined to describe the semi-democratization of some South American states in the 1980s by military dictatorships, driven by populist expediency rather than a genuine desire to free their citizens. Delving further back into history in trying to characterize the global political system at the start of the twenty-first century, a number of writers have contended that Bull's cautionary 'new medievalism' has come to pass (Bull 1977: 254; Mathews 1997; Held, McGrew, Goldblatt and Perraton 1998: 85). This perspective argues that the complex overlap of competing jurisdictions and multiple levels of authority that increasingly mark the contemporary system resembles European politics before Westphalian order was imposed.

A restoration of Westphalian order today, however, would not address the problems of global security. A measure of good governance is that it enhances human security and it is clear that neither the state nor the partially globalized world order can claim to be achieving this, or be able to achieve this. Falk claims that there are three damnable indictments against 'inhumane' global governance: the 'global apartheid' of poverty, the persistence of the 'avoidable harm' of discrimination and 'eco-imperialism' (Falk 1995: 47–78). Rawls's widely applied test of justice for a political system contends that inequality in the distribution of social goods can be considered fair if the least advantaged nonetheless gain increased social goods over time (Rawls 1971). The onset of political globalization from the mid-twentieth century has broadly been just according to these criteria since, in spite of the growing disparity between rich and poor, the quality of life has improved for most people in nearly all countries. Across-the-board increases in life expectancy, and more latterly and indicatively of Human Development Index (HDI) scores, support this. A recent drop-off in HDI of some states, however, largely due to chronic underdevelopment and disease, suggests that global governance is beginning to fail the Rawls test. Some sixteen sub-Saharan African states experienced a decline in HDI between 1990 and 2007 (UNDP 2008). This is very much against the norm. Only four African states, ravaged by internal conflict, 'went backwards' in the 1980s and only one state registered a lower HDI by the end of the 1990s than in the mid-1970s (UNDP 2003). The overall, long-term trend is still upwards but a significant enough number of exceptions to the 'rule' have emerged to be put down to chance or purely internal factors.

Keohane, a less radical Liberal than Falk or Mitrany, suggests that there is now compelling evidence for five tasks to be assumed control of by a global level of governance.

1    Limiting the resort by states to large-scale violence.
2    Limiting the resort by states to exporting 'negative externalities' which arise from interdependence, such as pollution and protectionist 'beggar thy neighbour' economic policies.
3    The establishment of coordinated standards and language in global commerce. This would doubtless be controversial and initially costly but once agreed upon becomes efficient and in the interests of all.

4    A global facility for dealing with global 'system disruptions', such as economic depression.

5    A means of guaranteeing the protection of people against the worst forms of abuse by their states (Keohane 2002: 248–9).

In a similar vein, Wendt, a non-Liberal notable for projecting his Neo-Realist instincts through a Social Constructivist filter, has made a state-utilitarian case for the inevitability of a world state within the next two centuries. Since the international system has gradually evolved from anarchy to a 'system of states' and then a 'world society', through the self-interest of states seeking to tame international war, he posits that further progress towards a world state is both inevitable and in the interests of even powerful states.

> [I]f the choice is between a world of growing threats as a result of refusing to recognize others versus a world in which their desires for recognition are satisfied, it seems clear which decision rational Great Powers should take.
>
> (Wendt 2003: 529–30)

Wendt and Keohane's prescriptions represent a more limited model of global governance than that generally advocated by World Federalists or Functionalists. They have some parallels with the Consociationalist approach to European integration, in that the suggested abrogations of state powers can largely be construed as being in the states' own interests since they are a means to the end of solving problems beyond their control. From such a state-utilitarian base more ambitious schemes proposed to aid global governance could eventually develop as state interests come to be redefined and non-state opinions become more influential. Some proposals for future global governance, going beyond the state-utilitarianism of Consociationalism, have attracted significant levels of government support, even if they are still some distance from realization. The idea of a global 'Tobin Tax', named after the Nobel prize winning economist, has gained the official advocacy of many governments including those in Brazil, France and Germany and gained momentum since the onset of the 2008 recession. The tax would be a levy on cross-border currency speculation, the proceeds of which would be transferred to alleviate poverty and other global problems. Whilst the cynic could argue that this is still utilitarianism since transnational currency speculators are an economic threat to some states, the championing of another globally redistributive levy applied to international air travel by many developing countries and some developed world statesmen is even more obviously in the global rather than national interest.

   Appropriate divisions of political responsibility vary over time as societies change and this needs to be acknowledged by responsible politicians if their aim is to serve their constituents' interests. The principle of subsidiarity underpins federal systems of government and has come to be a measure of the appropriate division of the responsibilities in the EU's part-federal political system. Subsidiarity is the guideline that decisions should be taken at the most appropriate level of governance for the satisfaction of the political goals at stake. Under this principle decisions should be taken as closely to the local level as possible, with higher levels of authority only utilized when this is necessary and preferable. The logic of this premise can be seen outside of constitutional legal frameworks in a general political trend. The observable simultaneous decentralization and regional convergence of many democratic political systems in recent years serves to show that contemporary states are increasingly both too big and too small to satisfy the demands of their people in a number of policy areas. Governments are becoming aware of this but they are also, of course, sufficiently informed by the logic of self-preservation to resist the transfer of authority beyond that which serves their own interest.

In line with this trend towards regionalization there is a political logic that certain aspects of governance should be undertaken at the global level, since they simply cannot be satisfactorily carried out at even the regional inter-state level. The new medievalism problem, which has occurred as a result of the natural 'drift' towards multi-level governance, would also be resolved by a clear demarcation of responsibilities, in place of the ad hoc development of patchy international and global governance. The application of subsidiarity to global governance would not merely be about the sanctioning of ever-greater authority to remote institutions, of the form which has provoked a prominent 'anti-globalization' social movement. The de-centralization of certain international political institutions and policies would also be a consequence, where it is clear that policies may be better formulated and implemented at the regional level. Howse and Nicolaidis, for example, argue that the principal target of anti-globalization activist anger, the World Trade Organization, would gain greater legitimacy if subsidiarity were applied to its operations. Through reform more of its decisions could be taken at the state or regional level and a clear process found for resolving clashes between its rules and international environmental law, thus disarming the most significant criticisms of its workings (Howse and Nicolaidis 2003). In military politics the difficulties in getting global solidarity for collective security could be offset by the unambiguous delegation of such responsibilities to regional bodies like NATO or ECOWAS, as is already happening in an ad hoc and controversial manner.

The partial nature of global governance has served to inhibit functional spillover from occurring naturally. Clear injustice in a political system holds back its progress towards a better system by reducing the inclination of the disadvantaged to participate in the global discourse necessary for engineering improvement (Habermas 2001). Apel, like Habermas a firm believer in the existence of universalist ethics, has rationalized this setback in the progression of cosmopolitanist moral governance. Apel contends that the natural equilibrium between human actions and ethics, which had seen human rights policy develop alongside the proliferation of greater transnational interactions, has eroded due to the dark side of globalization becoming more apparent in poverty and environmental degradation. The dominance of Economic Liberalism in the global political discourse has hindered the development of the natural human ethic of social responsibilty. Apel considers that for a more rounded 'planetary macro ethics' to emerge from the shadow cast by Economic Liberalism a global 'communications community' needs to develop, in which the private sphere of human values is able to take its place alongside the public sphere of profit-based rationality inherent in trading rules (Apel 1991). Hence the dark side of globalization necessitates permitting the full emergence of the light side, rather than a retreat from globalism.

[T]he process characterized so far should only be considered a phenomenon of first-order globalization. It is a challenge to the philosophical reflection and thereby to a mobilization of moral responsibility for the establishment of a novel order of human interaction that could be called second-order globalization.

(Apel 2000: 138)

Global ethics exist, and have gradually become more established, as evidenced by the development of human rights law, but they are undermined by the lop-sided nature of recent global political developments driven by economic gain (which, of course, has a light side as well as a dark side). Plenty of evidence shows that social responsibility is not absent in the political world so much as stifled by the focus on the freeing-up of trade at the highest levels of governance. A survey of international organizations by Social Policy specialists led by Deacon in the late 1990s concluded that: '[t]he old world of unreconstructed fundamentalist liberalism associated with the IMF is on the wane within the global discourse' (Deacon, Hulse and Stubbs 1997: 200). The reform of the World Bank, from being an advocate of 'unreconstructed liberalism' into a more socially oriented set of institutions, is the clearest example of such normative change. The World Bank now routinely considers the environmental or social cost of any development project, as well as its economic viability, before granting it its seal of approval. This metamorphosis occurred through the development of a different epistemic community working within the system of organizations making up the 'bank' in response to pressure group criticism and necessitated by having to deal with the difficult socio-economic transition of former communist countries in East Europe (Deacon, Hulse and Stubbs 1997: 198). Similar change has occurred in the UNDP as the normative shift from advocating 'pure' economic growth to more human-centred development has occurred amongst experts in the field. At the same time, international organizations clearly dedicated to welfare and social reform, such as the ILO, UNICEF and the office of the UN High Commissioner for Refugees (UNHCR), continue to propagate the ethos of co-responsibility in their work. As highlighted throughout this volume human-focused approaches have come to evolve in the politics of all the issues of global security. An emergent global discourse has promoted the normative change that has seen principles like a right to health and a responsibility to protect and concrete aims such as the Millennium Development Goals become established on the international stage not directly equitable with national interests.

Global values of justice and co-responsibility are also evident in global discourse outside of the mainstream political sphere. Global sports bodies, for example, did more than inter-state politics to ostracize apartheid-era South Africa by banning them from prestigious competitions such as the Olympic games. Football's ruling body, the International Federation of Association Football (FIFA), has intervened in cases where minority nationals appear to have been discriminated against in the selection of 'national' sides. The spirit of 'fair play' underpinning these stances represents a good gauge of global morality since no hegemon or self-interest is behind the development of such rules. Where unrestrained human dialogue occurs a code of ethics follows. Global political dialogue has, however, become somewhat skewed of late and the resultant ethics have become distorted.

Globalization opens up both opportunities and problems in the same way that industrialization and the transition from Communism to Liberalism, has in many states of the world. Twentieth-century Liberals in Europe recognized that Economic Liberalism alone was not sufficient to maximize individual freedom, prosperity and security in domestic politics and arrived at a consensus with Social Democrats and Conservatives on the need for a state role to help facilitate this. Hence today health and safety standards, welfarism and the notion of 'social security' are accepted as integral to the governance of most developed democracies. Similarly 'ecocentricism' has often triumphed over 'anthropocentricism' in the environmental legislation of states such as the USA, who appear to be driven only by the latter in global policy. Human co-responsibility and a respect for non-human life sometimes supersede economic and government self-interest in democratic domestic govern-ance because people demand that to be the case. As Sen's 'entitlements thesis' convincingly argues, the democratic peace argument for enhancing military security can be applied, with greater rigour, to non-military security issues like famines and diseases (Sen 1981). Democratic governments are compelled to be responsive to the needs of ordinary people whose security is imperilled, either directly or indirectly due to the pressure of the media or other concerned citizens, for reasons of their own self-preservation if nothing else. Ironically it is in the realm of military politics that the limitations of state egoism have been most clearly acknowledged by govern-ments in recent decades since dialogue and cooperation have proven to be the best means of breaking the security dilemma and the spiral of inter-state war once considered inevitable. Effective global governance, ultimately, serves national as well as human security. Hence advancing human security need not be driven just by human compassion but by the same hard-headed conservative logic that prompted Bismarck to pioneer the world's first state welfare policies: the recognition that reform from above can prevent revolution from below.

## Discovering universal values as a path to maximizing global security

Good global governance, that which enhances human security, requires the restoration of the natural equilibrium between human actions and the ethics which guide them. This necessitates positive action to 'identify' the missing norms, which are in the interests of all but obscured from view. Hence, this approach takes a step further from the Communitarianism of Liberal philosophers like Rawls and IR scholars like Keohane and Wendt in going beyond the identification of common interests.

> [A] genuine universalization principal of morality . . . must also be capable of preventing those factual forms of consensus that are reached at the cost of affected but absent parties.
>
> (Apel 2000: 152)

Showing that universal values are 'out there' is something that UNESCO has worked on since the 1980s when the organization's Universal Ethics Project initiated a process of identifying core universal values and principles. This process has seen the employment of both empirical and 'reflective' methodologies to find the ethics already out there, in addition to those which have as yet been unable to inform global policy and discourse. The culmination of this work was the 1999 Declaration of Human Duties and Responsibilities, whose drafters included the academic Richard Falk and prominent statesmen Bernard Kouchner[1] and Ruud Lubbers.[2] The reflective method permits one to 'derive ethical values and principles considered necessary in relation to the problems to be solved' (Kim 1999). Hence from the core empirical ethic of human survival other values can be deduced, since they contribute to the satisfaction of this. Examples include reciprocity, the prohibition of violence, truth-telling, justice and social responsibility. Hence the 1999 declaration reads as a charter for the advancement of human security. Amongst many articles, Articles 1 and 2 deal with the 'Right to Life and Human Security' and Articles 3 to 9 with 'Human Security and an Equitable International Order' (Kim 1999).

Similarly, attempts have been made to distil core values from the array of the world's religions, frequently cited as evidence of the relativism of human morality. The centenary 'Parliament of the World's Religions' in 1993 brought together representatives of 120 different faiths and produced a declaration drafted by Kung (a Swiss Catholic theologian). In the declaration two principles were espoused as universal: (1) every human should be treated humanely; (2) people should behave towards others as they would expect them to behave towards them. From this more precise moral guidelines can be deduced such as: non-violence and respect for life, solidarity and just economic order, tolerance and truthfulness and equal rights between men and women (Kung and Kuschel 1993; Kim 1999).

'Identifying' missing norms is distinct from the imposition of normative standards since inclusiveness is a prerequisite for allowing the normative dialogue to grow. Those who consider a political system to be fundamentally unjust will resist even the imposition of just norms. By identifying the common denominators of mutually beneficial living the functionalist imperative can be reactivated and good governance can evolve. Most democratic states needed some sort of push of this form, such as the codification of a constitution or a bill of rights, to assist in the evolution of gradually more just political systems. An important point here is to recognize that the 'creation' of normative ideas and principles today can affect future human behaviour. Even 'rational egoists' are less likely to overturn moral norms once they are established, unless for compelling tyrannical reasons, which will then be clearly understood as such (Keohane 2002: 259). If amoral action is against the norm it is less easily resorted to, even by the instinctively amoral actor. Reputation is important in international politics. Since the mid-twentieth century governments gradually have less frequently violated global human rights standards or resorted to unjust wars because of the implications for their standing in the world. Similarly, MNCs have begun to act in a more socially and environmentally responsive manner through fear of the effects of naming and shaming and a general recognition that the moral climate in which they operate is changing. Human rights and justice cannot be undone as quickly as they are evolving so long as they are understood as the rights of all humanity and justice for all.

## *Conclusions*

Throughout the world governments increasingly have come to recognize their own limitations and see the Canute-like futility of a sovereign resisting the waves of globalization. This is partly a pragmatic appreciation that the world is changing and they must adapt or die but it is also a response to pressure from their constituents who recognize that their welfare and security are better met by different forms of governance. Hence there is a rational actor script by which global governance could be seen to continue to grow in the future. At some point in the future, however, that script comes to an ending not as happy as it could be for the people of the world as their security comes into conflict with government security once any meaningful remnant of sovereignty is faced with a curtain call. 'Rational' governments may come to accept new versions of a social contract more weighted to the interests of their citizens but few are likely to 'do the decent thing' and allow themselves to be submerged by the waves if that is what is in their citizens' best interests. Identifying the best interests of human beings thus needs to be done directly, rather than indirectly through intermediaries acting on their behalf but also according to their own interests. To ensure that this happens there is compelling evidence that global spillover needs to be 'cultivated' as a means of getting over the 'national interest' barrier. The logic of Functionalism could then be reactivated and humanity be permitted to take up its rightful place at the centre of politics.

## Key points

- The present state system is inadequate for the satisfaction of human security.
- Political integration at the regional level marks a recognition of the limitations of the state in satisfying human needs and this logic is now applicable at the global level.
- The current growth in global governance is not meeting human security needs because it is skewed by the fact that economic liberalization is advancing at a greater rate than global policy formulated purely in the human interest.
- A restoration of the natural balance between human ethics and actions in global policy, by the promotion of more 'rounded' globalization, would enhance global solidarity and permit the advancement of human security.

## Notes

1   A founding member of the pressure group Médecins Sans Frontières, former health minister in the French government and head of the UN's civil administration in Kosovo.
2   Former Prime Minister of The Netherlands and the UN High Commissioner for Refugees.

## Recommended reading

Commission on Human Security (2003) *Human Security Now,* New York: CHS.

Keohane, R. (2002) *Power and Governance in a Partially Globalized World,* London and New York: Routledge.

Mitrany, D. (1975) *The Functional Theory of Politics,* London: Robertson.

Wendt, A. (2003) 'Why a World State is Inevitable', *European Journal of International Relations,* 9(4): 491–542.

Yunker, J. (2011) *The Idea of World Government from Ancient Times to the Twenty-First Century,* Abingdon and New York: Routledge.

## Useful web links

Annan, K. (2005) 'In Larger Freedom: Towards Development, Security and Human Rights for All', Report of the Secretary-General, New York: United Nations: http://www.un.org/largerfreedom/

Federal Union, 'World Federalism': http://www.federalunion.uklinux.net/world/

UNESCO: http://www.unesco.org/

# Glossary

**authoritarian:** non-democratic.

**bilateral:** involving two parties.

**bipolar:** dominated by two sides.

**client state:** a state sponsored by another (to, for example, fight a war).

**codify:** write down in law.

**conflate:** mix together two ideas.

**defoliant:** chemical used to strip leaves from trees and plants.

**diplomatic immunity:** the package of measures which gives official state representatives legal privileges in the country in which they are serving.

**diplomatic recognition:** the process whereby one government acknowledges the legal existence of another government so permitting them to function as a sovereign entity in international law.

**Eastern Bloc:** the USSR's East European satellite states during the Cold War: East Germany, Poland, Hungary, Czechoslovakia, Hungary, Romania and Bulgaria.

**emerging markets:** states successfully undergoing economic development.

**empirical:** based on factual evidence (such as data).

**endogenous:** from within (a country).

**epidemic:** localized disease outbreak above the norm.

**epidemiological:** related to the study of disease.

**epistemic community:** transnational group of experts on a given subject.

**epistemic consensus:** broad agreement amongst an epistemic community.

**epistemology:** how you come know something. The theory of establishing knowledge.

**ethnocentricism:** the tendency to consider one's own nationality as more significant or superior to others.

**First World:** collective term for the states of the developed, capitalist world during the Cold War.

**fossil fuels:** fuels produced from fossilized organic material (for example, oil, coal and natural gas).

**Fourth World:** the least developed of the less developed countries once referred to as the Third World.

**Global North:** the world's developed and most wealthy states (which are principally in the northern hemisphere).

**Global South:** the less developed countries (which are principally in the southern hemisphere).

**Grotian:** a liberal, internationalist world view espousing the importance of a rigorous and moral-based system of international law. Named after the seventeenth-century lawyer Hugo Grotius.

**gross domestic product (GDP):** the sum total from all economic activity in a given country.

**gun boat diplomacy:** the provocative display of military force (typically naval) intended to influence a target state without the resort to war.

**Hegelian dialectic:** historical process, associated with the writings of the philosopher Hegel, whereby an opposing thesis and counter-thesis (such as ideologies) clash until a new synthesized thesis emerges.

**hegemony:** the exercise, usually by a single state, of international dominance and leadership, particularly in economic relations.

**herbicides:** chemicals used to kill pest plants.

**holistic:** a systemic approach favoured on the basis that 'the whole is greater than the sum of its parts', making the understanding of the sub-units of a system insufficient.

**Idealist:** term applied to statesmen and academics of the 1920s and 1930s who advocated greater levels of international cooperation, epitomized by the creation of the League of Nations.

**integration:** the process whereby states merge some of their economic and political responsibilities into a wider political unit.

**interdependence:** the condition of inter-connectedness between actors in international politics which makes them reliant on each other.

**intergovernmental organization (IGO):** an international organization comprising government representatives of more than one country.

**international non-governmental organization (INGO):** an international organization comprised of private individuals rather than government representatives.

**international regime:** system of rules and policy-making procedures, either formal or informal, which influence the behaviour of actors in a particular international issue.

**Iron Curtain:** term applied to the tight border established by the USSR during the Cold War to isolate its allies in Eastern Europe from Western Europe.

**liquidity:** monetary reserves.

**multilateral:** involving more than two states.

**multipolar:** a political system with more than two dominant focuses of power.

**neo-imperialism:** the economic domination of a state by another without there being formal imperial control.

**New Right:** a strand of Conservative political thought favouring reduced state involvement in economic affairs. Rose to prominence in the 1980s in the Reagan and Thatcher administrations in the USA and UK, though its origins lie in Classical Liberalism of the nineteenth century.

**nihilistic:** extremely sceptical to the point of denying the existence of morality altogether.

**non-combatant immunity:** principle that civilians should not be targeted in warfare.

**non-state actor:** an organization with international political significance other than a state. A generic term for both INGOs and IGOs.

**normative:** moral-based.

**ontological:** inquiry into 'what there is' (ontology).

**overpopulation:** condition whereby a given state has a population in excess of its capacity to support them to an optimal level.

**pandemic:** widespread international outbreak of disease.

**paradigm:** general perspective on International Relations. A set of assumptions on how and why international political events occur in the way that they do.

**power capabilities:** resources and attributes of a state which serve to determine how influential it can be. Includes natural resources, geographical location, population and level of economic development.

**proxy war:** war in which the participants are largely sponsored from afar.

**realpolitik:** amoral, self-serving political practice by states.

**regime:** *see* 'international regime'.

**relativism:** the assumption that something (such as morality) has no objective meaning and exists only in terms of someone's interpretation of it.

**renewable resources:** natural resources which are inexhaustable, such as wind power.

**Risorgimento nationalism:** a form of nationalist ideology (originating in nineteenth-century Italy) which supports the principle of national self-determination for all nations, rather than just the advancement of one's own.

**satellite states:** a technically independent but effectively colonized state.

**secular:** description of a state where religion is separated from government.

**security community:** a group of states enjoying such good and close relations that they form a community in which war is unthinkable.

**social construct:** something which can be defined only in the subjective terms of the participants rather than by objective, empirical analysis.

**social contract:** the 'deal' in political theory whereby government legitimacy is maintained through the trade-off of them granting rights to their citizens in exchange for the imposition on them of certain duties.

**social movement:** broad societal movement seeking political change through mass activism rather than the party political process.

**sovereignty:** status of legal autonomy enjoyed by states so that their government has exclusive authority within its borders and enjoys the rights of membership of the international community.

**spillover:** the tendency for political integration in one area to provide the momentum for integration to occur in other, related areas.

**statecentricism:** analysis which is biased towards the roles and motivations of states over other actors in International Relations.

**statist:** focused on the state.

**structural adjustment:** the package of conditions accompanying a loan given to a state, such as by the IMF. Such conditions typically entail monetarily conservative measures such as public spending cuts.

**Structuralist:** perspective which considers that individual behaviour is largely determined by the system in which the individual operates (as, for example, the behaviour of actors in the international system). Most (but not exclusively) associated with the Marxist paradigm of International Relations.

**superpower:** term applied to the USA and USSR during the Cold War because of their dominance of international relations, which superseded that of the *great powers* in earlier eras.

**symbiosis:** the natural science process whereby two living organisms coexist for their mutual benefit. Used in political science to denote situations when apparently contradictory aims (such as sovereignty and political integration) can both be simultaneously enhanced.

**'the other':** that which is distinguishable from 'the self' in the construction of social identities, such as nationality.

**totalitarianism:** autocratic rule in which the citizen is totally subject to the state.

**total war:** war in which civilians are targeted as well as military and state targets.

**trade preferences:** preferential terms of trade (for example, lower tariff payments) granted to certain countries.

**transnational:** linking societies in different countries.

**unilateral:** one (state) alone.

**utilitarian:** driven by the aim of maximizing the utility of something. Term most used in International Relations in situations where governments cooperate to reap mutual material gains.

**value-free:** inquiry which is objective and not influenced by the inquirer's own opinions.

**Westphalian:** pertaining to the sovereign state system (named after the 1648 Treaty of Westphalia at which the concept of sovereignty is considered to have originated).

# Bibliography

Abbasi, K. (1999) 'The World Bank and World Health: Changing Sides', editorial, *British Medical Journal*, 318, 27 March: 365–9.

Abrams, A. (2001) 'A Short History of Occupational Health', *Journal of Public Health Policy*, 22(1): 34–80.

African Leadership Forum (1991) 'The Kampala Document: Towards a Conference on Security, Stability, Development and Cooperation in Africa', http://www.africaaction. org/african-initiatives/kampall.htm (accessed 23.7.03).

Ali, S. (2008) Interview by J. Gettlem, *New York Times*, 30 September.

American Anthropologist Association (1947) 'Statement on Human Rights', *American Anthropologist*, 49(4): 539–42.

—— (1999) *Declaration on Anthropology and Human Rights*, AAA Committee for Human Rights, http://www.aaanet.org/stmts/humanrts.htm (accessed 12.3.03).

Ammann, A. and Nogueira, S. (2002) 'Governments as Facilitators or Obstacles in the HIV Epidemic', *British Medical Journal*, 324, 26 January: 184–5.

Amnesty International (2000) *Crimes of Hate, Conspiracy and Silence: Torture and Ill Treatment Based on Sexual Identity*, London: Amnesty International Report.

Anderson, B. (1991) *Imagined Communities: Reflections on the Origin and Spread of Nationalism*, London: Verso.

Annan, K. (1999) 'Statement by the Secretary General', in Ingleton. J. (ed.) *Natural Disaster Management: A Presentation to Commemorate the International Decade for Natural Disaster Reduction (IDNDR)*, Leicester: Tudor Rose: v.

—— (2002) 'Video Message for the '7th International Day of Commemoration for Workers Dead or Injured at Work' (Workers Memorial Day), ILO Headquarters Geneva, 29 April.

—— (2004) 'A More Secure World: Our Shared Responsibility', *Report of the Secretary-General's High Level Panel on Threats, Challenges and Change*, New York: UN.

Apel, K.O. (1990) 'The Problem of a Universalistic Macroethics of Co-responsibility', in Griffioen, S. (ed.) *What Right Does Ethics Have? Public Philosophy in a Pluralistic Culture*, Amsterdam: Vrije Universiteit Press: 23–40.

—— (1991) 'A Planetary Macroethics for Humankind', in Deutsch, E. (ed.) *Culture and Modernity: East–West Philosophical Perspectives*, Hawaii: University of Hawaii Press: 251–78.

—— (2000) 'Globalization and the Need for Universal Ethics' *European Journal of Social Theory* 3(2): 137–55.

Arie, S. (2002) 'News Round Up', *British Medical Journal*, 325, 30 November: 1261.

Arnold, M. and Merrick, P. (2001) 'Development for Disaster Reduction: The Role of the World Bank', *Australian Journal of Emergency Management*, 16(4): 34–6.

Ash, R. (2001) *The Top 10 of Everything*, London: Dorling Kindersley.

Ashdown, P. (2001) 'We Need Missile Defence', *Guardian*, 19 June.

—— (2011) 'Humanitarian Emergency Response Review', UK Department for International Development, http://www.dfid.gov.uk/emergency-response-review (accessed 20.9.11)

Avery, M., Drake, M. and Lang, T. (1993) *Cracking the Codex: An Analysis of Who Sets World Food Standards*, London: National Food Alliance.

Ayoob, M. (1997) 'Defining Security: A Subaltern Realist Perspective', in Krause, K. and Williams, M. (eds) *Critical Security Studies*, Minneapolis: University of Minnesota Press: 121–46.

Baker, R. (2005) *Capitalism's Achilles Heel*, Hoboken: Wiley & Sons.

Bankoff, G. (2001) 'Rendering the World Unsafe: "Vulnerability" as Western Discourse', *Disasters*, 25(1): 19–35.

Baylis, J., Wirtz, J., Cohen, E. and Gray, C. (2002) *Strategy in the Contemporary World*, Oxford: Oxford University Press

BBC (2000) 'Drugs: A Global Business', World News, http://news.bbc.co.uk/1/hi/world/774301.stm (accessed 22.5.07)

—— (2004) 'Pulse of Africa', World Service, http://news.bbc.co.uk/1/shared/spl/hi/pop_ups/04/africa_the_pulse_of_africa/html/1.stm (accessed 12.6.05).

—— (2009) 'Corruption Costs $1.6tn, UN Says', http://news.bbc.co.uk/1/hi/business/8350239.stm (accessed 21.10.09)

—— (2011) 'Mexican Drug-Related Violence', http://www.bbc.co.uk/news/world-latin-america-10681249 (accessed 8.10.11)

Beck, U. (1992) *Risk Society: Towards a New Modernity* London, New Delhi and Thousand Oaks: Sage.

—— (1999) *World Risk Society*, Cambridge: Polity.

Becker, J. (2000) *Hungry Ghosts: Mao's Secret Famine*, New York: Free Press.

Beitz, C. (1979) *Political Theory and International Relations*, Princeton: Princeton University Press.

Benatar, S., Daar, A. and Singer, P. (2003) 'Global Health Ethics: The Rationale for Mutual Caring', *International Affairs*, 79(1): 107–38.

Benedict, R. (1934) *Patterns of Culture*, Boston: Houghton Mifflin.

Benjamin, D. (2000) 'Past Is Not Prologue: A Reunified Germany Is Big but Not the Bully That Some Had Feared', *Time Magazine Europe*, 156(15), 9 October, http://www.time.com/time/europe/magazine/2000/1009/benjamin.html (accessed 4.6.03).

Bentham, J. (1876) *Theory of Legislation,* translated from the French of Etienne Dumont by H. Hildreth, London: Trubner & Co.

Bentham, M. (1998) *The Politics of Drug Control*, Basingstoke: Macmillan.

Bernard, E. (1999) 'Tsunami', in Ingleton, J. (ed.) *Natural Disaster Management: A Presentation to Commemorate the International Decade for Natural Disaster Reduction (IDNDR)*, Leicester: Tudor Rose: 58–60.

Betts, R. (1997) 'Should Strategic Studies Survive?', *World Politics*, 50(1): 7–33.

Blaikie, M., Cannon, T., Davis, I. and Wisner, B. (1994) *At Risk: Natural Hazards, People's Vulnerability, and Disasters*, London and New York: Routledge.

Bloor, D. (1976) *Knowledge and Social Imagery*, London: Routledge & Paul Kegan

Booth, K. (1991) 'Security in Anarchy: Utopian Realism in Theory and Practice', *International Affairs*, 67(3): 527–45.

Bowden, M. (2001) *Killing Pablo: The Hunt for the Richest, Most Powerful Criminal in History*, London: Atlantic Books.

Britton, N. (2001) 'A New Emergency Management for the New Millennium?', *Australian Journal of Emergency Management*, 16(4): 44–54.

Brock, I., Geis, A. and Mueller, H. (eds) (2006) *Democratic Wars: Looking at the Dark Side of Democratic Peace*, Basingstoke and New York: Palgrave.

Brown, C. and Goodchild, S. (2000) 'Space Watch for Earth-bound Asteroids', *Independent on Sunday*, 31 December: 9.

Brugha, R. and Walt, G. (2001) 'A Global Health Fund: A Leap of Faith', *British Medical Journal*, 323, 21 July: 152–4.

Brundtland, G. (1999a) '2000–1 Budget Speech to WHA', March, A52/INF.DOC/2.

—— (1999b) Address to the Geneva Group-UN Directors 'Changes at WHO', Geneva, 2 March.

Buccini, J. (2000) Chair of the 'Fifth Session of the International Negotiating Committee for an Internationally Legal Binding Instrument for Implementing International Action on Certain Persistent Organic Pollutants', Johannesburg, 4–9 Dec 2000.

Bull, H. (1977) *The Anarchical Society: A Study of Order in World Politics*, London: Macmillan.

Bullock, J. and Adel, D. (1993) *Water Wars: Coming Conflicts in the Middle East*, London: St Dedmundsbury Press.

Burleigh, M. (1994) *Death and Deliverance: 'Euthanasia' in Germany 1900–1945*, Cambridge: Cambridge University Press.

Buse, K. and Walt, G. (2000) 'Global Public and Private Partnerships: part II. What are the Health Issues for Global Governance?', *Bulletin of the World Health Organization*, 78(5): 699–709.

Bush, G. (1991) *State of the Union Address*, Washington, DC, 29 January.

Buzan, B. (1991) *People, States and Fears: An Agenda for International Security Studies in the Post-Cold War Era*, 2nd edn, Boulder: Lynne Rienner.

—— (1993) 'Societal Security, State Security and Internationalization', in Waever, Buzan, Kelstrup and Lemaitre (eds) *Identity, Migration and the New Security Agenda in Europe*, London: Pinter.

Buzan, B. Waever, O. and de Wilde, J. (1998) *Security: A New Framework for Analysis*, Boulder and London: Lynne Rienner.

Canadian Department of Foreign Affairs and Trade (1999) 'Human Security: Safety for People in a Changing World', Concept Paper, 29 April, Ottawa.

Carlile, Lord, of Berriew (2007) 'The Definition of Terrorism', *Report by Independent Reviewer of Terrorism Legislation,* Presented to Parliament March 2007, London: UK Government.

Carson, R. (1962) *Silent Spring*, Harmondsworth: Penguin.

Castello-Cortes, I. and Feldman, M. (1996) *Guinness Book of World Records 1997*, London: Guinness.

Chalk, P. (2000) *Non-military Security and Global Order*, Basingstoke and London: Macmillan.

Chapman, J. (1992) 'The Future of Security Studies: Beyond Grand Strategy', *Survival*, 34(1): 109–31.

Chellaney, B. (2001) 'India Paying for Its Soft Response to Terror', *Hindustan Times*, 13 December, http://www.hindustantimes.com/ (accessed 18.4.02).

Cheng, A. (2003) 'Fatal Accidents Fall Slightly on Roads, at Work', *South China Morning Post*, 17 April, http://www.china-labour.org.hk/iso/article.adp?article_id=4190& category_name=Health%20and%20Safety (accessed 5.6.03).

Christopolos, I., Mitchell, J. and Liljelund, A. (2001) 'Re-framing Risk: The Changing Context of Disaster Mitigation and Preparedness', *Disasters*, 25(3): 185–98.

Chyba, C., Thomas, P. and Zahnle, K. (1993) 'The 1908 Tunguska Explosion: Atmospheric Disruption of a Stony Asteroid', *Nature*, 361: 40–4.

Clark, I. (2001) *The Post Cold War Order: The Spoils of Peace*, Oxford: Oxford University Press.

Clausewitz, C.V. (1976) *On War*, edited and translated by Howard, M. and Paret, P., Princeton: Princeton University Press.

Coch, N. (1995) *Geohazards: Natural and Human*, Englewood Cliffs: Prentice Hall.

Comfort, L. (2000) 'Disaster: Agent of Diplomacy or Change in International Affairs?', in *Cambridge Review of International Affairs*, 14(1), Autumn–Winter, special section, *Disaster Diplomacy*, edited by Kelman, I. and Koukis, T.: 214–94.

Comfort, I., Wisner, B., Cutter, S., Pulwarty, R., Hewitt, K., Oliver-Smith, A., Weiner, J., Fordham, M., Peacock, W. and Krimgeld, F. (1999) 'Re-framing Disaster Policy: The Global Evolution of Vulnerable Communities', *Environmental Hazards*, 1: 39–44, http://jishin.ucsur.pitt.edu/publications/Reframing.htm (accessed 12.2.02).

Commission on Human Security (2003) *Human Security Now*, New York: CHS.

Cornwell, R. (2002) 'The War of the Worlds', *The Independent Magazine*, 7 September: 6–11.

Council of Europe (1999) *European Sourcebook on Crime and Criminal Justice*, PC-S-ST (99) 8 DEF, Strasbourg.

CRED (2011) *International Disaster Database*, Centre for Research on the Epidemiology of Disasters: Brussels, http://www.emdat.be/ (accessed 20.9.11).

Cronin, A. (2009) *How Terrorism Ends*, Princeton: Princeton University Press.

Dalby, S. (2002) 'Security and Ecology in the Age of Globalization', *The Environmental Change and Security Project Report*, 8, Summer: 95–108.

Das, P. and Samarakera, U. (2008) 'What Next for UNAIDS', *The Lancet*, 372: 2099–2102.

Dauvergne, P. (2005) 'Dying of Consumption: Accidents or Sacrifices of Global Morality?', *Global Environmental Politics*, 5(3): 35–47.

Davis, M. (2001) *Late Victorian Holocausts: El Nino Famines and the Making of the Third World*, London and New York: Verso.

Davson-Galle, P. (1998) *The Possibility of Relative Truth*, Aldershot: Ashgate.

Deacon, B., Hulse, M. and Stubbs, P. (1997) *Global Social Policy: International Organizations and the Future of Welfare*, London: Sage.

Despouy, L. (2002) *Human Rights and Disabled Persons*, Human Rights Studies Series, No. 6, Centre for Human Rights: Geneva (United Nations publication, Sales No. E.92.XIV.4), http://www.un.org/esa/socdev/enable/dispaperdes0.htm#_ftnref1 (accessed 13.3.03).

Deudney, D. (1990) 'The Case against Linking Environmental Degradation and Security', *Millennium*, 19(3): 461–76.

Deutsch, K., Burrell, S., Kann, R., Lee, M., Lichterman, M., Lindgren, R., Lowenheim, F. and Van Wagenen, R. (1957) *Political Community and the North Atlantic Area*, Princeton: Princeton University Press.

Disaster Center (2003) 'The Most Deadly 100 Natural Disasters of the Twentieth Century', http://www.disastercenter.com/disaster/TOP100K.html (accessed 18.8.02).

Donnelly, J. (2007) *International Human Rights,* 3rd edn, Cambridge, MA: Westview.

Dorrington, R., Bradshaw, D. and Budlender, D. (2002) 'HIV/AIDS profile in the provinces of South Africa – Indicators for 2002', Centre for Actuarial Research, University of Cape Town.

Downer, A. (2002) 'Advancing The National Interest: Australia's Foreign Policy Challenge', 7 May, http://www.australianpolitics.com/news/2002/05/02–05–07a.shtml (accessed 23.7.03).

Dreze, J. and Sen, A. (1991) *Hunger and Public Action*, Oxford: Clarendon.

Drouard, A. (1998) 'Eugenics in France and Scandinavia: Two Case Studies', in Peel, R. (ed.) *Essays in the History of Eugenics*, London: Galton Institute: 173–207.

DTI (2003) 'Home Safety Network', London: UK Government Department of Trade and Industry, http://www.dti.gov.uk/homesafetynetwork/index.htm (accessed 12.5.03).

Dudley, N. (1987) *This Poisoned Earth: The Truth about Pesticides,* London: Piatkus.

Duffield, M. (2001) *Global Governance and the New Wars: The Merging of Development and Security*, London and New York: Zed Books.

Dyer, H. (2000) 'Environmental Security: The New Agenda', in Jones, C. and Kennedy-Pipe, C. (eds) *International Security in a Global Age: Securing the Twenty-First Century*, London and Portland: Frank Cass.

Easton, D. (1965) *A Framework for Political Analysis*, Englewood Cliffs: Prentice Hall.

*Ecologist* (1991) *FAO: Promoting World Hunger*, special edition, (21)2.

*Economist* (2001) 'Defence Folly', 8 September: 10.

—— (2002a) 'Stop Denying the Killer Bug', 23 February 23: 69.

—— (2002b) 'Economic Focus: A Voice for the Poor', 4 May: 93.

—— (2002c) 'Mother Nature's Biological Warfare', 10 August: 42.

Eisenhower, D. (1961) 'Farewell Address', Washington, DC, 17 January.

England, R. (2008) 'Is the Writing on the Wall for UNAIDS?', *British Medical Journal*, 336(7652): 1072.

Enloe, C. (1990) *Bananas, Beaches and Bases: Making Feminist Sense of International Politics,* Berkeley: University of California Press.

ETSC (2003) *Transport Safety Performance in the EU: A Statistical Overview*, Brussels: European Transport Safety Council.

Euro-Atlantic Disaster Relief Coordination Centre (2002) 'Brussels: NATO', http://www.nato.int/eadrcc/home.htm (accessed 25.2.02)

Eurobarometer (2011) Internal Security Special, *Eurobarometer*, 371 Wave EB 75.4 November 2011 Brussels.

Europol (2012a) *EU Terrorism Situation and Trend Report*, TEAT 2012, The Hague.

—— (2012b) 'Europol at a Glance', http://www.europol.eu.int/index.asp?page=ataglance&language= (accessed 19.6.12).

Falk, R. (1995) *On Humane Governance, Toward a New Global Politics*, Cambridge: Polity.

FAO (2002) 'FAO What It Is: What It Does', http://www.fao.org/UNFAO/e/wmain-e.htm (accessed 5.4.02).

FAO/WHO (1992) 'Final Report of the International Conference on Nutrition', Rome, 5–11 December.

Feis, H. (1970) *From Trust to Terror: The Onset of the Cold War 1945–1950*, New York: Norton.

Ferris, E. and Petz, D. (eds) (2011) *A Year of Living Dangerously: A Review of Natural Disasters in 2010*, London: Brookings Institute.

Fidler, D. (1999) *International Law and Infectious Diseases*, Oxford: Clarendon Press.

*Flight International Magazine* (2006) '2005 Airline Safety Review', 9–15 January.

Forster, A. and Wallace, W. (2001) 'What Is NATO for?', *Survival: The International Institute for Security Studies Quarterly*, 43(4): 107–22.

Frank, A.G. (1971) *Capitalism and Underdevelopment in Latin America*, Harmondsworth: Penguin.

Frankena, W. (1988) *Ethics*, 2nd edn, Englewood Cliffs: Prentice Hall.

Frankman, M. (1997) 'No Global War? A Role for Democratic Global Federalism', *Journal of World-Systems Research*, 3(2): 321–38.

Freedom House (2011) *Freedom in the World 2011,* Washington, DC.

Friborg, J. and Melbye, M. (2008) 'Cancer Patterns in Inuit Populations', *Lancet Oncology,* 9(9): 892–900.

Fukuyama, F. (1992) *The End of History and the Last Man*, London: Hamish Hamilton.

Gaddis, J. (1997) *We Now Know: Rethinking Cold War History*, Oxford: Clarendon.

Galtung, J. (1969) 'Violence, Peace and Peace Research', *Journal of Peace Research*, 6(3): 167–91.

Garrett, L. (2007) 'The Challenge of Global Health', *Foreign Affairs,* 86(1): 14–38.

Genocide Watch (2003) http://www.genocidewatch.org/ (accessed 23.10.03).

Gentili, A. (1933) *De Jure belli libri tres*, Washington: J.C. Rolfe.

Gillies, R. (2004) 'The Real Reasons MSF Left Afghanistan', *MSF Website* http://www.doctors withoutborders.org/publications/article.cfm?id=2068

Gittings, J. (2002) 'Growing Sex Imbalance Shocks China', *Guardian*, May 13.

Gleick, P. (1994) 'Water, War and Peace in the Middle East', *Environment*, 36(3): 6–42.

Glenny, M. (2006) 'Boom Time for Crime Gangs', *The World in 2007,* Economist.

Global Alliance for Vaccines and Immunization http://www.vaccinealliance.org/home/index.php (accessed 2.8.02).

Global Disaster Information Network (2002) http://www.gdin-international.org/whats_GDIN.html (accessed 27.2.02).

Global Financial Integrity (2011) *Transnational Crime in the Developing World,* Washington DC: GFI.

Global Fund to Fight AIDS, Tuberculosis and Malaria (2002) http://www.globalfundatm.org/TRP.html (accessed 2.8.02).

Global Security (2007) *World Military Guide*, http://www.globalsecurity.org/military/world/index.html (accessed 21.5.07).

Godlee, F. (1994) 'WHO in Retreat: Is it Losing Its Influence?', *British Medical Journal*, 30, 9 December: 1491–5.

—— (1995) 'The World Health Organisation. WHO's Special Programmes: Undermining from Above', *British Medical Journal*, 10, 21 January: 178–82.

Godson, R. and Williams, P. (1998) 'Strengthening Cooperation against Transsovereign Crime: A New Security Imperative', *Transnational Organized Crime*, 4(3–4): 321–55.

—— (2000) 'Strengthening Cooperation against Transsovereign Crime', in Cusimano, M. (ed.) *Beyond Sovereignty: Issues for a Global Agenda*, Boston: St Martins: 111–46.

Goklany, I. (2002) 'The Globalization of Human Well-being', *Policy Analysis*, 477, 22 August, http://www.cato.org/pubs/pas/pa-447es.html (accessed 12.4.03).

—— (2007) *Death and Death Rates Due to Extreme Weather Events*, London: International Policy Press

Goldammer, J. (1999) 'Wildfire', in Ingleton, J. (ed.) *Natural Disaster Management: A Presentation to Commemorate the International Decade for Natural Disaster Reduction (IDNDR)*, Leicester: Tudor Rose: 67–9.

Goldstein, J. (2011) *Winning the War on War: The Decline of Armed Conflict Worldwide*, New York: Dutton.

Grau, G. (ed.) (1995) *Hidden Holocaust: Gay and Lesbian Persecution in Germany 1937–45*, London: Cassell.

Green, J. (1997) *Risk and Misfortune: The Social Construction of Accidents*, London: UCL Press.

Greene, O. (2001) 'Environmental Issues', in Baylis and Smith, *The Globalization of World Politics: An Introduction to International Relations*, 2nd edn, Oxford and New York: Oxford University Press.

Grein, T., Kamara, K., Rodier, C., Plant, A., Bovier, P., Ryan, P., Ohyma, T. and Heymann, D. (2000) 'Rumors of Diseases in the Global Village: Outbreak Verification', *Emerging Infectious Diseases*, 16(2): 97–102.

Grotius, T (1853) *De Jure Belli ac Pacis*, Cambridge: Wheelwall.

Gurr, T., Marshall, M. and Khosla, D. (2001) *Peace and Conflict 2000: A Global Survey of Armed Conflicts, Self-determination Movements and Democracy,* College Park: University of Maryland, Center for International Development and Conflict Management (CIDCM).

Habermas, J. (2001) *The Postnational Constellation: Political Essays,* translated and edited by Pensky, M., Cambridge: Polity.

Hagedorn, J. (2005) 'The Global Impact of Gangs', *Journal of Contemporary Criminal Justice,* 21(2): 153–69.

Hagmann, M. (2001) 'Globalization How Healthy?', *Bulletin of the World Health Organization,* 79(9): 902–3.

Halliday, F. (1986) *The Making of the Second Cold War,* London: Verso.

—— (2001) *The World at 2000: Perils and Promises,* Basingstoke and New York: Palgrave.

—— (2002) *Two Hours That Shook the World. September 11, 2001: Causes and Consequences,* London: Saqi.

Hansen, L. (2000) 'The Little Mermaid's Secret Security Dilemma and the Absence of Gender in the Copenhagen School', *Millennium Journal of International Studies,* 29(2): 285–306.

Hardin, G. (1968) 'The Tragedy of the Commons', *Science,* 162: 1243–8.

—— (1996) 'Lifeboat Ethics: The Case against Helping the Poor', in Aitken, W. and LaFollette, H. (eds) *World Hunger and Morality,* New Jersey: Prentice Hall.

Harman, G. (1996) 'Moral Relativism', in Harman, G. and Thomson, J. (eds) *Moral Relativism and Moral Objectivity,* Cambridge, MA: Blackwell.

Hazlitt, H. (1973) *The Conquest of Poverty,* New Rochelle: Arlington House.

Held, D., McGrew, A., Goldblatt, D. and Perraton, J. (1998) *Global Transformations: Politics, Economic and Culture,* Cambridge: Polity.

Heymann, D. (2001) 'The Fall and Rise of Infectious Diseases', *Georgetown Journal of International Affairs,* 2(2): 7–14.

Hicks, J. (1992) 'DDT-Friend or Foe?', *Pesticide News, Journal of the Pesticides Trust,* 17 September: 14.

Hobson, J. (1915) *Towards International Government,* New York: Macmillan Company.

Homer-Dixon, T. (1994) 'Environmental Scarcities and Violent Conflict: Evidence from Cases', *International Security,* 19(1): 5–40.

Homer-Dixon, T. and Percival, V. (1996) *Environmental Scarcity and Violent Conflict: Briefing Book,* Population and Sustainable Development Project, American Association for the Advancement of Science and University of Toronto.

Hough, P. (1998) *The Global Politics of Pesticides: Forging Consensus from Conflicting Interests,* London: Earthscan.

—— (2000) 'Institutions for Controlling the Global Trade in Hazardous Chemicals: The 1998 Rotterdam Convention', *Global Environmental Change,* 10(2): 161–4.

Howard, R. (1995) *Human Rights and the Search for Community,* Oxford: Westview Press.

Howse, R. and Nicolaidis, R. (2003) 'Enhancing WTO Legitimacy: Constitutionalism or Global Subsidiarity?', *Governance,* 16(1): 73–94.

Hufbauer, G., Scott, J. and Elliott, K. (1990) *Economic Sanctions Reconsidered: History and Current Policy,* 2nd edn, Washington, DC: Institute for International Economics.

Hughes, B., Kuhn, R., Peterson, C., Rothman, D. and Solorzano, J. (2011) 'Improving Global Health: Forecasting the Next 50 Years', in B. Hughes (ed.) *Patterns of Potential Human Progress,* Boulder: Paradigm.

Human Rights Watch (2003) *Compounding Injustice: The Governments Failure to Redress Massacres in Gujarat,* 15(3) July, http://www.hrw.org/reports/2003/india0703/ (accessed 8.5.07).

Human Security Centre (2005) *Human Security Report*, http://www.humansecurityreport. info/component/option,com_frontpage/Itemid,1/ (accessed 13.7.06).

Human Security Network (1999) 'A Perspective on Human Security: Chairman's Summary', 1st Ministerial Meeting of the Human Security Network, Lysøen, Norway, 20 May.

Humphreys, D. (2006) *Logjam: Deforestation and the Crisis of Global Governance,* London: Earthscan.

Hunger Project (1985) *Ending Hunger: An Idea Whose Time Has Come,* New York: Praeger.

Huntington, S. (1993) 'The Clash of the Civilizations?', *Foreign Affairs,* 72(3): 22–49.

IAEA, Convention on Nuclear Safety (2012) http://www-ns.iaea.org/conventions/nuclear-safety.asp (accessed 13.6.12).

ICAO (2011) *Implementing the Global Aviation Safety Roadmap,* Quebec: International Civil Aviation Organization.

ICC (2012) http://www.icccpi.int/php/show.php?id=home&l=EN (accessed 5.2.12)

ICIDI (1980) *North-South: The Report of the International Commission on International Development Issues,* London: Pan Books.

IFRC (2001) *World Disasters Report 2001: Focus on Recovery,* Geneva: International Federation of Red Cross and Red Crescent Societies.

IISS (2010) *The Military Balance 2010*, edited by Hackett, J. (International Institute for Security Studies), London: Routledge.

ILO (2002) SafeWork, *Global Estimates of Fatalities 2002*, http://www.ilo.org/public/ english/protection/safework/accidis/globest_2002/reg_world.htm (accessed 16.2.03)

—— (2005) 'Decent Work, Safe Work', Report to the 27th World Congress on Safety and Health at Work, Orlando, 18–25 September, Geneva: International Labour Organization.

—— (2011) *Introductory Report: Global Trends and Challenges on Occupational Safety and Health at Work*, 19th World Congress on Safety and Health at Work, Istanbul 11–15 September, 155, 187.

ILO/WHO (2005) *World Day for Safety and Health at Work: A Background Paper,* Geneva: International Labour Organization.

IMO (2011) 'Piracy: Orchestrating the Response', background paper, http://www.imo.org/ About/Events/WorldMaritimeDay/2011/background/Pages/default.aspx

Ingleton, J. (ed.) (1999) *Natural Disaster Management: A Presentation to Commemorate the International Decade for Natural Disaster Reduction (IDNDR)*, Leicester: Tudor Rose.

Intergovernmental Oceanographic Commission (2001) 'Eighteenth Session of the International Co-ordination Group for the Tsunami Warning System in the Pacific', (ICG/ITSU-XVIII), Draft Press Kit, 8–11 October 2001, Cartagena, Colombia.

Intergovernmental Panel on Climate Change (2007), *Climate Change 2007: The Physical Science Basis. Summary for Policymakers,* Geneva: IPCC.

International Atomic Energy Agency (2003) 'Convention on Nuclear Safety', http://www.iaea. or.at/worldatom/Documents/Legal/nukesafety.shtml (accessed 11.7.03).

International Federation of University Women (IFUW) (1999) 'International Convention on the Elimination of All Forms of Discrimination Against Women', http://www.ifuw.org/ advocacy/ia_cedaw.htm (accessed 5.4.03).

International Narcotics Control Board (2002) 'Report of the International Narcotics Control Board for 2001', E/INCB/2002/1, New York: United Nations.

Interpol (2012) 'An Overview', http://www.interpol.int/ (accessed 6.9.12).

ISDR (2002a) 'ISDR Vision', http://www.unisdr.org/unisdr/aboutvision.htm (accessed 27.2.02).

—— (2002b) 'Living with Risk: A Global Review of Disaster Reduction Activities', Geneva: International Strategy for Disaster Reduction.

Jacobs, G. and Aeron-Thomas, A. (2000) 'A Review of Global Road Accident Fatalities', TRL Report 44, Transport Research Laboratory: Crawthorne, UK, http://www.transport-links.org/transport_links/filearea/publications/1_771_Pa3568.pdf (accessed 15.9.11).

Jeggle, T. (1999) 'The Goals and Aims of the Decade', in Ingleton, J. (ed.) *Natural Disaster Management: A Presentation to Commemorate the International Decade for Natural Disaster Reduction (IDNDR)*, Leicester: Tudor Rose.

Jendritsky, G. (1999) 'Extreme Temperatures', International Decade for Natural Disaster Reduction (IDNDR) Programme Forum Geneva, 5–9 July, http://www.unisdr.org/unisdr/forum/tempwmo.htm (accessed 13.2.02).

Jones, A. (2000) 'Gendercide and Genocide', *Journal of Genocide Research*, 22 June: 185–211.

Kagan, R. (2003) 'Americans are from Mars, Europeans are from Venus', *Sunday Times News Review*, 2 February: 1–2.

Kaiser, R. (1997) 'Chinese Leader Urges US to Seek "Common Ground"', *Washington Post*, 19 October: A1.

Kaldor, M. (2007) *New and Old Wars. Organized Violence in a Global Era,* Cambridge: Polity.

Kant, I. (1970) 'Perpetual Peace: A Philosophic Sketch', in Reiss, H. (ed.) *Kant's Political Writings*, 2nd edn, Cambridge: Cambridge University Press.

Kaplan, R. (1994) 'The Coming Anarchy', *The Atlantic Monthly*, 273: 44–76.

Kegley, C and Wittkopf, E (2006) *World Politics: Trend and Transformation*, 7th edn, New York: St Martin's/Worth.

Kendall, R. (1998) 'Responding to Transnational Crime', *Transnational Organized Crime*, 4(3–4): 269–75.

Kennan, G. (1984) 'Soviet-American Relations: The Politics of Discord and Collaboration', in Kegley, C. and Wittkopf, E. (eds) *The Global Agenda*, New York: Random House: 107–20.

Kennan, G. ('X') (1947) 'The Sources of Soviet Conduct', *Foreign Affairs*, 25(4): 566–82.

Keohane, R. (2002) *Power and Governance in a Partially Globalized World*, London and New York: Routledge.

Keohane, R. and Nye, J. (1977) *Power and Interdependence: World Politics in Transition*, Boston: Little, Brown.

Ker-Lindsay, J. (2000) 'Greek-Turkish Rapprochement: The Impact of Disaster Diplomacy?', *Cambridge Review of International Affairs*, 14(1), special section, *Disaster Diplomacy*, edited by Kelman, I. and Koukis, T.: 214–94.

Kevles, D. (1995) *In the Name of Eugenics:. Genetics and the Uses of Human Heredity*, Cambridge, MA, and London: Harvard University Press.

Kim, Y. (1999) 'A Common Framework for the Ethics of the 21st Century', Paris: UNESCO Division of Philosophy and Ethics.

Kitchin, C. (2001) 'Early Discoveries', part of feature 'Focus: Asteroids', *Astronomy Now*, 15(1): 54–5.

Koivusalo, M. and Ollila, E. (1997) *Making a Healthy World: Agencies, Actors & Policies in International Health*, London and New York: Zed Books.

Kolko, G. and J. (1972) *The Limits of Power: The World and United States Foreign Policy, 1945–1954*, New York: Harper & Row.

Korey, W. (2001) 'Revisiting the U.N.'s Genocide Convention', *Forward*, 10 August, http://www.forward.com/issues/2001/01.08.10/oped2.html (accessed 12.3.03).

Kortunov, S. (1998) 'Is the Cold War Really Over?', *International Affairs: A Russian Journal of World Policy, Diplomacy and International Relations*, 5: 141–54.

Kraska, P. (2005) 'Researching the Police-Military Blur: Lessons Learned', *Police Forum*, 14(3): 1–14.

Krug, E., Dahlberg, L., Mercy, J., Zwi, A. and Lozana, R. (eds) (2002) *World Report on Violence and Health*, Geneva: WHO.

Kung, H. and Kuschel, K-J. (1993) *A Global Ethic: The Declaration of the Parliament of the World's Religions*, New York: Continuum.

Kunkel, K., Pielke, R. and Changnon, S. (1999) 'Temporal Fluctuations in Weather and Climate Extremes That Cause Economic and Human Health Impacts: A Review', *Bulletin of the American Meteorological Society*, 80(6): 1077–98.

LaFeber, W. (1991) *America, Russia and the Cold War 1945–1990*, New York: McGraw-Hill.

*Lancet* (1995) 'Fortress WHO: Breaching the Ramparts for Health's Sake', 345(28).

Langeland, B. (2009), *Work Related Accidents and Risks Among Migrant Workers,* European Working Conditions Observatory, Norway, http://www.eurofound.europa.eu/ewco/2009/07/NO0907019I.htm (accessed 22.6.12).

Laqueur, W. (1990) 'Reflection on the Eradication of Terrorism', in Kegley, C. (ed.) *International Terrorism: Characteristics, Causes, Controls*, New York: St Martins Press: 207–12.

Laurance, J. (2006) 'Climate Change Blamed for Legionnaire's Disease Surge', *Independent,* 18 October: 4.

—— (2010) 'Deadly Animal Diseases Poised to Infect Humans', *The Independent,* 4 January.

Lee, K. Buse, K. and Fustukian, S. (2002) *Health Policy in a Globalising World*, Cambridge University Press.

Leiss, W. and Chociolko, C. (1994) *Risk and Responsibility*, London and Buffalo: McGill-Queen's University Press.

Lemkin, R. (1944) *Axis Rule in Occupied Europe: Laws of Occupation: Analysis of Government – Proposals for Redress*, Washington, DC: Carnegie Endowment for International Peace.

Levy, M. (1995) 'Time for a Third Wave of Environment and Security Scholarship?', *The Environmental Change and Security Project Report*, 1, Spring: 44–64.

Lewis, J. (2005) 'Statement to the US Senate Committee on Environment and Public Works', 18 May, http://epw.senate.gov/hearing_statements.cfm?id=237817 (accessed 8.5.07)

Libiszewski, S. (1995) 'Water Disputes in the Jordan Basin Region and Their Role in the Resolution of the Arab–Israeli Conflict', ENCOP Occasional Paper No. 13. Zurich/Berne: Centre for Security Policy and Conflict Research/Swiss Peace Foundation.

Lippmann, W. (1943) *US Foreign Policy*, London: Hamish Hamilton.

Lomberg, B. (2001) *The Sceptical Environmentalist*, Cambridge: Cambridge University Press.

Lopez, G. and Cortright, D. (2002) 'Smarting under Sanctions', *The World Today*, 58(3): 17–18.

Lopez, M. (1987) 'The Politics of Lands at Risk in a Philippine Frontier', in Little, P. and Horowitz, M. (eds) *Lands at Risk,* Boulder: Westview Press: 230–48.

Loretti, A. (2000) 'The Health Sector in Disaster Reduction and Emergency Management', keynote address for the session 'Managing and Preparing for Disasters', International Public Health Congress, Health 21 in Action, Istanbul, 8–12 October.

LSHTM (London School of Hygiene and Tropical Medicine) with Save the Children (2002) *New Products into Old Systems: The Initial Impact of the Global Alliance for Vaccines and Immunizations (GAVI) at Country Level*, London: Save the Children.

Lynn-Jones, S. and Miller, S. (1995) *Global Dangers: Changing Dimensions of International Security*, Cambridge and London: MIT Press.

McDonald, M. (2002) 'Human Security and the Construction of Security', *Global Society*, 16(3): 277–95.

McEwen, F. and Stephenson, G. (1979) *The Use and Significance of Pesticides in the Environment*, New York: John Wiley & Sons.

MacFarlane, N. and Foong Khong, Y. (2006) *Human Security and the UN: A Critical History*, Bloomington: Indiana University Press.

McGee, K. (2003) 'Unintentional injury', Department of Injuries and Violence Prevention, World Health Organization, email (21.2.03).

McMichael, A., Campbell-Lendrum, D. and Kovats, S. (2004) 'Global Climate Change', in Ezzati, M.J., Lopez, A., Rodgers, A. and Murray, C. (eds) *Comparative Quantification of Health Risks: Global and Regional Burden of Disease Due to Selected Major Risk Factors,* Geneva: World Health Organization.

McMurray, C. and Smith, R. (2001) *Diseases of Globalization: Socioeconomic Transition and Health,* London: Earthscan.

McNeill, W. (1989) *Plague and Peoples,* Toronto: Doubleday.

McSweeney, B. (1996) 'Identity and Security: Buzan and the Copenhagen School', *Review of International Studies,* 22(1): 81–93.

—— (1999) *Security, Identity and Interests: A Sociology of International Relations,* Cambridge: Cambridge University Press.

Mandelbaum, M. (1999) 'A Perfect Failure', *Foreign Affairs,* 78(5): 2–8.

Marsh, G. (1965) *Man and Nature* (reprint) Cambridge USA: Harvard University Press

Marshall, M. and Gurr, T. (2005) *Peace and Conflict 2005,* Washington, MA: Center for International Development and Conflict Management.

Martine, G. and Guzman, J. (2002) 'Population, Poverty, and Vulnerability: Mitigating the Effects of Natural Disasters', *Environmental Change and Security Project (ECSP) Report,* 8: 45–68.

Mathers, C. and Loncur, D. (2006) 'Projections of Global Mortality and Burden of Disease from 2002 to 2030', *PLoS Medicine,* 3(11): 2011–30.

Mathews, J. (1989) 'Redefining Security', *Foreign Affairs,* 68(2): 162–77.

—— (1997) 'Power Shift', *Foreign Affairs,* 76(1): 50–66.

Matin, N. and Taher, M. (2000) 'Disaster Mitigation in Bangladesh: Country Case Study of NGO Activities', Report for Research Project *NGO National Disaster Mitigation and Preparedness Projects: An Assessment of the Way Forward,* ESCOR Award No. R7231.

Matthew, R. and Zalidi, A. (2002) 'People, Scarcity and Violence in Pakistan', in Matthew, R., Halle, M., and Switzer, J., (eds) *Conserving the Peace: Resources, Livelihoods and Scarcity,* Geneva: International Institute for Sustainable Development: 57–98.

Mazza, P. (1998) 'The Invisible Hand: Is Global Warming Driving El Nino?', *Sierra Magazine,* 83, May/June, http://www.sierraclub.org/sierra/199805/elnino.asp (accessed 2.2.03).

Mearsheimer, J. (1990) 'Why We Will Soon Miss the Cold War', *The Atlantic Monthly* 226(2): 35–50.

Meddings, D. (2005) 'After the Emergency: Injury, Health Systems and Data Collection', World Health Organization. http://www.survivorconference.org/ppt/13_Meddings.ppt.

Michael, S. (2002) 'The Role of NGOs in Human Security', Working Paper No. 12, submitted to the UN Commission on Human Security.

Mitchell, J. (ed.) (1996) *The Long Road to Recovery: Community Responses to Industrial Disaster,* Tokyo, New York and Paris: UN University Press, http://www.unu.edu/unupress/unupbooks/uu21le/uu21le00.htm (accessed 12.2.03).

Mitrany, D. (1975) *The Functional Theory of Politics,* London: Robertson.

Morgenthau, H. (1972) *Politics Among Nations,* 5th edn, New York: A. Knopf.

—— (1982) 'Another "Great Debate:" The National Interest of the United States', in Vasquez, J. (ed.) *Classics of International Relations,* Englewood Cliffs: Prentice Hall: 37–41.

Mueller, J. (1989) *Retreat from Doomsday: The Obsolescence of Major War,* New York: Basic Books.

Murray, C., Lopez, A., Mathers, C. and Stein, C. (2001) 'Global Burden of Disease 2000 Project: Aims, Methods and Data', Global Programme on Evidence for Health Policy Discussion Paper No. 36. Geneva: World Health Organization.

Myers, N. (1993) *Ultimate Security: The Environmental Basis of Political Stability*, New York: W.W. Norton.

Nakajima, H. (1997) 'Global Disease Threats and Foreign Policy', *Brown Journal of World Affairs*, 4(1): 319–32.

Narrain, A. (2001–2) 'Human Rights and Sexual Minorities: Global and Local Contexts', *Law, Social Justice and Global Development*, electronic journal, http://elj.warwick.ac.uk/global/issue/2001–2/narrain.html (accessed 10.4.03).

National Intelligence Council (USA) (2000) 'The Global Infectious Disease Threat and Its Implications for the United States', NIE 99–17D, http://www.cia.gov/cia/publications/nie/report/nie99–17d.html (accessed 8.2.02).

Natsios, A. (1999) 'The Politics of Famine in North Korea', Special Report, Washington DC: US Institute of Peace, http://www.usip.org/oc/sr/sr99082/sr990802.html (accessed 2.4.02).

Neumann, P. (2007) 'Negotiating With Terrorists', *Foreign Affairs*, 86(1): 128–39.

Newman, G. (ed.) (1999) *Global Report on Crime and Justice*, United Nations Office for Drug Control and Crime Prevention New York: Oxford University Press.

NGDC (2002) 'Tsunami Event Database', National Geophysical Data Center, http://wist.ngdc.noaa.gov/nndc/servlet/gov.noaa.nndc.idb.ShowDatasetsServlet?dataset=101327&search_look=7&display_look=7 (accessed 16.9.02).

—— (2003) 'Natural Hazards Data', http://www.ngdc.noaa.gov/seg/hazard/hazards.shtml (accessed 20.6.03).

Noble, R. (2003) 'Interpol's Way: Thinking beyond Boundaries and Acting Across Borders Through Member Countries' Police Services', speech delivered at Tufts University, Boston, 1 March. http://www.interpol.int/Public/ICPO/speeches/SG20030301.asp (accessed 20.7.03).

Nordas, R. and Gleditsch, N. (2007) 'Climate Change and Conflict', *Political Geography*, 26(6): 627–38.

NRDC (National Resources Defense Council) (2006) 'Global Nuclear Stockpiles 1945–2006', *Bulletin of the Atomic Scientists*, 62(4): 64–7.

Nye, J. (1990) *Bound to Lead: the Changing Nature of American Power*, New York: Basic Books.

—— (2005) *Understanding International Conflicts: An Introduction to Theory and History*, London: Pearson.

Ó Gráda, C. (1999) *Black '47 and Beyond: The Great Irish Famine in History, Economy, and Memory,* Princeton: Princeton University Press.

Oneal, J. and Russett, B. (1997) 'The Classic Liberals Were Right: Democracy, Interdependence, and Conflict 1950–1985', *International Studies Quarterly*, 41(2): 267–94.

O'Neill, S. (2001) 'Secret Group that Exports Fanatical Brand of Terror', *Telegraph,* 27 September, http://www.telegraph.co.uk/news/main.jhtml?xml=/news/2001/09/27/whunt127.xml (accessed 2.7.03).

O'Reilly, A. (2003) 'A UN Convention on the Rights of Persons with Disabilities: The Next Steps', Paper presented at the General Assembly Meeting of Rehabilitation International Arab Region, 8–9 March 2003, Kingdom of Bahrain, http://www.rehab-international.org/un/steps.html (accessed 9.4.03).

Ottoson, D. (2007) *State Sponsored Homophobia: A World Survey of Laws Prohibiting Same Sex Activity Between Consenting Adults,* International Lesbian and Gay Association.

—— (2009) *Report on State-Sponsored Homophobia,* International Lesbian, Gay, Bisexual, Tran and Intersex Association (ILGA).

Oxfam (2002) *Cut the Cost: Patent Injustice: How World Trade Rules Threaten the Health of Poor People,* Oxford: Oxfam.

Paddock, W. and Paddock, P. (1967) *Famine 1975*, London: Weidenfeld & Nicolson.

Pape, R. (2005) 'Soft Balancing Against the United States', *International Security*, 30(1): 7–45.

Paris, R. (2001) 'Human Security: Paradigm Shift or Hot Air?', *International Security*, 26(2): 87–102.

Paul, T. (2005) 'Soft Balancing in the Age of US Primacy', *International Security,* 30(1): 46–71.

Peeters, M. (1996) 'WHO Prescribes Socialist Medicine', *Wall Street Journal*, 14 May.

Peiser, B. (2001) 'Impact Scares and How to Avoid Them', in 'Focus: Asteroids', *Astronomy Now*, 15(1): 64–5.

Peterson, P. and Sebenius, J. (1992) 'The Primacy of the Domestic Agenda', in Allison, G. and Treverton, G. (eds) *Rethinking America's Security: Beyond Cold War to New World Order*, New York: W.W. Norton: 57–93.

Pettman, J. (1996) *Worlding Women: A Feminist International Politics*, London: Routledge.

Pirages, D. and Runci, P. (2000) 'Ecological Interdependence and the Spread of Infectious Disease', in Cusimano, M. (ed.) *Beyond Sovereignty: Issues for a Global Agenda*, New York: St Martin: 177–93.

Pocchiari, F., Silaro, V. and Zapponi, G. (1987), *The Seveso Accident and Its Aftermath*, Berlin, Heidelberg and New York: Springer-Verlag.

Popper, K. (1966) *The Open Society and Its Enemies. Volume 2, The High Tide of Prophecy: Hegel, Marx and the Aftermath*, London: Routledge & Kegan Paul.

Potter, J. (1992) *The 'Sultana' Tragedy: America's Greatest Maritime Disaster*, Gretna, USA: Pelican.

Power, S. (2002) *A Problem From Hell: America and the Age of Genocide*, New York: Basic Books.

Prescott, E. (2003) 'SARS: A Warning', *Survival*, 45: 207–26.

Preston, S. (1975) 'The Changing Relationship between Mortality and Level of Economic Development', *Population Studies*, 29(2): 231–48.

Prevent Genocide (2003) 'Key Writings of Raphael Lemkin on Genocide', http://www.preventgenocide.org/lemkin/ (accessed 1.4.03).

Price-Smith, A. (2001) *The Health of Nations: Infectious Diseases, Environmental Change, and Their Effects on National Security and Development*, Cambridge, MA: MIT Press.

Prins, G. (2002) *The Heart of War: On Power, Conflict and Obligation in the Twenty-First Century*, London and New York: Routledge.

Putin, V. (2004) 'Terror in the Moscow Subway' *MOSnews*, http://www.mosnews.com/mn-files/subway.shtml (accessed 11.5.07).

Ramonet, L. (1998) 'The Politics of Hunger', *Le Monde*, 1 November, http://mondediplo.com/1998/11/01leader (accessed 3.4.02).

Ramsey, P. (1968) *The Just War: Force and Political Responsibility*, New York: Scribner's.

Rasmussen, M. (2001) 'Reflexive Security: NATO and International Risk Society', *Millennium Journal of International Studies*, 30(2): 285–309.

Rawls, J. (1971) *A Theory of Justice,* Cambridge, MA: Harvard University Press.

Rennie, D. (2002) 'How Soviet Sub Officer Saved the World from Nuclear Conflict', *Telegraph*, 14 October.

Reuveny, R. (2007) 'Climate Change-induced Migration and Violent Conflict', *Political Geography*, 26(6): 656–73.

—— (2008) 'Economic Growth, Environmental Scarcity and Conflict', *Global Environmental Politic*, 2(1): 83–110.

Reza, A., Mercy, J. and Krug, J. (2001) 'Epidemiology of Violent Deaths in the World', *Injury Prevention*, 7: 104–111.

Risse, T. (1995) 'Democratic Peace: Warlike Democracies? A Social Constructivist Interpretation of the Liberal Argument', *European Journal of International Relations*, 1(4): 489–515.

Robertson, G. (2000) *Crimes against Humanity: The Struggle for Global Justice,* 2nd edn, London: Penguin.

Roe, P. (2000) 'Misperception and Ethnic Conflict: Transylvania's Societal Security Dilemma', *Review of International Studies,* 28(1): 57–74.

Rogers, P. (2000) *Losing Control: Global Security in the Twenty-first Century,* London and Sterling: Pluto Press.

Rosaldo, R. (2000) 'Of Headhunters and Soldiers: Separating Cultural and Ethical Relativism', *Issues in Ethics,* 11(1), http://www.scu.edu/ethics/publications/iie/v11n1/relativism. html (accessed 1.5.03).

Rose, R. and Shiratori, R. (eds) (1986) *The Welfare State East and West,* New York: Oxford University Press.

Rosenau, J. (1980) *The Study of Global Interdependence,* London: Frances Pinter.

—— (1990) *Turbulence in World Politics: A Theory of Change and Continuity,* Princeton: Princeton University Press.

Rostow, W. (1960) *The Stages of Economic Growth,* Cambridge: Cambridge University Press.

Ruggie, J. (1998) *Constructing the World Polity: Essays on International Institutionalization,* London and New York: Routledge.

Rummel, R. (1994) *Death By Government,* New Brunswick: Transaction Publishers.

—— (2003) 'Freedom, Democracy, Peace; Power, Democide and War', http://www.hawaii. edu/powerkills/welcome.html (accessed 1.2.03).

Russett, B. and Oneal, J. (2001) *Triangulating Peace: Democracy, Interdependence and International Organizations,* New York: Norton.

Russett, B. and Starr, H. (1996) *World Politics: The Menu for Choice,* 5th edn, New York: Freeman.

Salehyan, J. (2008) 'From Climate Change to Conflict: No Consensus Yet', *Journal of Peace Research,* 43(3): 315–26.

Schabas, W. (2000) *Genocide in International Law: The Crime of Crimes,* Cambridge: Cambridge University Press.

—— (2001) *An Introduction to the International Criminal Court,* Cambridge: Cambridge University Press.

Schlesinger, A. (1967) 'The Origins of the Cold War', *Foreign Affairs,* 46(1): 22–52.

Schmid, A. (1983) *Political Terrorism: A Research Guide to Concepts, Theories, Data Bases and Literature,* Amsterdam: North Holland Publishing.

Schweller, R. (2001) 'The Problem of International Order Revisited', *International Security,* 26(1): 161–86.

Seale, P., Shellenberger, S. and Spence, J. (2006) 'Alcohol Problems in Alaska Natives: Lessons from the Inuit', *American Indian and Alaska Native Mental Health Research: The Journal of the National Center,* 13(1): 1–31.

Sen, A. (1981) *Poverty and Famines: An Essay on Entitlement and Deprivation,* Oxford: Clarendon Press.

—— (1999) 'Democracy as a Universal Value', *Journal of Democracy,* 10(3): 3–17.

Sharma, S. (2010) 'Assessing Diet and Lifestyle in the Canadian Arctic Inuit and Inuvialuit to Inform a Nutrition and Physical Activity Intervention Programme', *Journal of Human Nutrition and Dietetics,* 23, special supplement, 7 September: 5–17.

Sheptycki, J. (2003) 'Global Law Enforcement: A Protection Racket', in Edwards, A. and Gill, P. (eds) *Transnational Organized Crime: Perspectives on Global Security,* London and New York: Routledge: 42–58.

Simmons, I. (1996) *The Fortean Times Book of Life's Losers,* London: John Brown.

Simon, S. (2002) 'The ASEAN Regional Forum Views the Councils for Security Cooperation in the Asia Pacific: How Track II Assists Track I', *National Bureau of Asian Research*

*Analysis*, 13(4), http://www.nbr.org/publications/analysis/vol13no4/ARF%20views%20CSCAP.html (accessed 12.6.03).

Singer, P. (2001) 'Corporate Warriors: The Rise of the Privatized Military Industry and Its Ramifications for International Security', *International Security*, 26(3): 186–220.

Singh, J. (1998) 'Against Nuclear Apartheid', *Foreign Affairs*, 77(5): 41–52.

SIPRI (2011) *Yearbook 2011: Armaments, Disarmament and International Security*, Stockholm International Peace Research Institute.

Sleeman, J. (1930) *Thug or a Million Murders*, London: Sampson, Low, Marston & Co.

Small Arms Survey (2007) *Small Arms Survey 2007: Guns and the City*, Geneva: SAS.

Smith, A. and Flores, A. (2010) 'Disaster Politics: Why Earthquakes Rock Democracies Less', *Foreign Affairs*, 15 July.

Smith, D. (1994) 'Dynamics of Contemporary Conflict: Consequences for Development Strategies', in Græger, N. and Smith, D. (eds) *Environment, Poverty, Conflict*, Oslo: International Peace Research Institute (PRIO) Report 2/1994: 47–89.

Smith, K. (2001) *Environmental Hazards: Assessing Risk and Reducing Disaster*, 3rd edn, London and New York: Routledge.

Smith, R. (2002) 'A Time for Global Health', editorial, *British Medical Journal*, 325(13): 54–5.

Smith, R., Corvalan, C. and Kiellstrom, T. (1999) 'How Much Global Ill Health is Attributable to Environmental Factors?', *Journal of Epidemiology*, 10(5): 573–84.

Snyder, J. (2000) *From Voting to Violence: Democratization and Nationalist Conflict*, New York: Norton.

Somavia, J. (2000) *Decent Work, Safe Work*, Geneva: ILO Safework, http://www.ilo.org/public/english/protection/safework/decent.htm (accessed 13.2.03).

Sonmez, S., Apostopoulos, L., Tran, D. and Dentrope, S. (2011) 'Human Rights and Health Disparities for Migrant Workers', *Health & Human Rights*, 13(2): E.17–21.

Sopoanga, S. (2002) 'Statement by Tuvalu', Johannesburg: World Summit on Sustainable Development, 2 September.

Stanton, G. (2002) *Genocides, Politicides, and Other Mass Murder Since 1945, with Stages in 2002*, Genocide Watch, http://www.genocidewatch.org/genocidetable.htm (accessed 21.3.03).

Starr, J. (1991) 'Water Wars', *Foreign Policy*, 82, Spring: 17–36.

Stern, G. (2000) *The Structure of International Society*, 2nd edn, London: Pinter.

Stern, N. (2006) *Stern Report on the Economics of Climate Change*, UK Government http://www.hmtreasury.gov.uk/independent_reviews/stern_review_economics_climate_change/stern_review_report.cfm (accessed 9.12.07).

Stott, R. (1999) 'The World Bank: Friend or Foe to the Poor?', *British Medical Journal*, editorial, 318, 27 March: 822–3.

Sukhdev, P. (2008) *Economics of Ecosystems and Biodiversity*, Berlin: Helmholtz Association.

Swiss Re (2012) *Natural and Man-made Catastrophes in 2011*, Sigma Study 2/2012.

Takala, J. (1998) *Global Estimates of Fatal Occupational Accidents*, 16th International Conference of Labour Statisticians, ICLS/16/RD 8 Geneva: ILO.

—— (1999) *Introductory Report of the International Labour Office*, 15th World Congress on Occupational Safety and Health, 12–16 April.

—— (2002) *Introductory Report: Decent Work, Safe Work*, 16th World Congress on Safety and Health at Work, Vienna, 27 May.

Tatham, C. and McCleary, R. (1992) 'Just Cause? The 1989 US Invasion of Panama', in McCleary, R. (ed.) *Seeking Justice: Ethics and International Affairs*, Boulder and Oxford: Westview Press.

Taylor, P. (1991) 'The European Community and the State: Assumptions, Theories and Propositions', *Review of International Studies*, 17: 109–25.

Theodoulou, M. (2002) 'Europeans Wary over US Hostility to Tehran', *The Times*, 31 January: 17.

Thomas, C. (2000) *Global Governance, Development and Human Security*, London: Pluto Press.

Tickner, A. (1992) *Gender in International Relations*, New York: Columbia University Press.

—— (2001) *Gendering World Politics: Issues and Approaches in the Post-Cold War Era*, New York: Columbia University Press.

Tran, M. (1999) 'I'm Not Going to Start Third World War for You Jackson Told Clark', *The Guardian*, 2 August.

Trenberth, K. (1998) 'El Nino and Global Warming', *Journal of Marine Education*, 15(2): 12–18.

Twigg, J. (2001) 'Physician, Heal Thyself? The Politics of Disaster Mitigation', Benfield Greig Hazard Research Centre Working Paper, http://www.bghrc.com/DMU/Working Papers/BGHRCWorkingPaper1–2001.pdf (accessed 21.7.02).

UK FCO (2011) 'Cyber Crime', *Global Issues*, http://www.fco.gov.uk/en/global-issues/cyber-space/ (accessed 25.6.11).

UK Government (2003) 'DIY Accidents', Department of Trade and Industry, http://www.dti.gov.uk/homesafetynetwork/dy_stats.htm (accessed 4.6.03).

Ullman, R. (1983) 'Redefining Security', *International Security*, 8(1): 29–153

UNAIDS (2009) 'What UNAIDS Does', http://unaids.org/about/what.asp (accessed 25.2.09).

UNDP (1993) *Human Development Report: People's Participation*, Oxford: Oxford University Press.

—— (2002) *Human Development Report: Deepening Democracy in a Fragmented World*, Oxford: Oxford University Press.

—— (2003) *Human Development Report: Millennium Development Goals: A Compact Amongst Nations to End Human Poverty*, Oxford: Oxford University Press.

—— (2006) *Human Development Report: Beyond Scarcity*, Oxford: Oxford University Press.

—— (2011) *Human Development Report: Conflict, Security and Development*, Oxford: Oxford University Press.

UNEP (2000) *Assessing Human Vulnerability due to Environmental Change: Concepts, Issues, Methods and Case Studies*, Nairobi: UNEP.

—— (2002) *GEO 3: Global Environmental Outlook*, http://geo.unep-wcmc.org/geo3/ (accessed 3.10.02).

—— (2011) *Human Development Report: Sustainability and Equity: A Better Future for All*, Oxford: Oxford University Press.

UN-Habitat (2003) *The Challenge of Slums: Global Report on Human Settlements*, United Nations Human Settlements Programme, London: Earthscan.

UNICEF (2009) http://www.unicef.org/ (accessed 22.5.09).

United Nations (2000) 'United Nations Convention against Transnational Organized Crime', http://www.uncjin.org (accessed 2.5.02).

United Nations General Assembly (2006) 'Unity Against Terrorism: Recommendations for a Global Counter-Terrorism Strategy', 27 April A/60/825.

United Nations Security Council (2000) Resolution 1308, 17 July, S/RES 1308.

University of North Dakota, *Volcano World*, http://volcano.und.nodak.edu/vwdocs/volc_images/southeast_asia/indonesia/tambor.html (accessed 3.10.02).

UNODC (2005) *World Drug Report*, Vienna: UN Office for Drugs and Crime.

—— (2007) *World Drug Report*, Vienna: UN Office for Drugs and Crime.

—— (2010) *The Globalization of Crime: A Transnational Organized Crime Threat Assessment*, Vienna: UN Office for Drugs and Crime.

—— (2011a) *Overview of Global and Regional Drug Trends and Patterns*, Vienna: UN Office for Drugs and Crime.

—— (2011b) *Global Study on Homicide: Trends, Context Data*. Vienna: UN Office for Drugs and Crime.

Uppsala/PRIO (2010) *Armed Conflict Dataset* http://www.prio.no/Data/Armed-Conflict/UCDP-PRIO/ (accessed 4.3.12).

USA (1983) 'United States Code', Title 22 section 2656f(d), Washington, DC.

—— (1994) *National Security Strategy Document*, Washington, DC.

—— (2011) *Trafficking in Persons Report*, Washington, DC: State Department.

Uvin, P. (1994) *The International Organization of Hunger*, London and New York: Kegan Paul.

Wadlaw, G. (1982) *Political Terrorism: Theory, Tactics and Countermeasures*, New York: Cambridge University Press.

Waever, O., Buzan, B., Kelstrup, M. and Lemaitre, P. (1993) *Identity, Migration and the New Security Agenda in Europe*, London: Pinter.

Wallace, C. (2002) 'Chain Reaction', *Time*, 11 February: 18–20.

Wallerstein, I. (1979) *The Capitalist World Economy*, Cambridge: Cambridge University Press.

Walt, C. and Buse, K. (2000) 'Partnership and Fragmentation in International Health: Threat or Opportunity?', *Tropical Medicine & International Health*, 15(7): 467–71.

Walt, S. (1991) 'The Renaissance of Security Studies', *International Studies Quarterly*, 35(2): 211–39.

Waltz, K. (1959) *Man, the State and War*, New York: Columbia University Press.

—— (1979) *Theory of International Politics*, Reading: Addison-Wesley.

Walzer, M. (1978) *Just and Unjust Wars*, London: Allen Lane.

Warren, M. (1985) *Gendercide: The Implications of Sex Selection*, Totowa: Rowman & Littlefield

Watkins, K. (2002) *Rigged Rules and Double Standards: Trade Globalization and the Fight against Poverty*, Oxford: Oxfam.

WCO (2006) 'About Us', http://www.wcoomd.org/home_about_us.htm (accessed 22.11.06)

Weir, D. (1987) *The Bhopal Syndrome: Pesticides, Environment and Health*, London: Earthscan.

Weiss, R. (2002) 'War on Disease', *National Geographic*, February: 5–31.

Wendt, A. (2003) 'Why a World State Is Inevitable', *European Journal of International Relations*, 9(4): 491–542.

Werner, D. (2001) 'Whatever Happened to "Health for All?"', *New Internationalist*, 331, January/February: 22.

WFP (2002a) *Mission Statement*, Rome: World Food Programme.

—— (2002b) 'WFP in 2000: A Quick Glance', Rome: World Food Programme, http://www.wfp.org/aboutwfp/facts/2000.html (accessed 5.4.02).

—— (2002c) 'Introduction', Rome World Food Programme, http://www.wfp.org/aboutwfp/introduction/overview.html (accessed 5.4.02).

—— (2009) 'Hunger', World Food Programme, http://www.wfp.org/hunger/stats (accessed 28.6.09).

—— (2011) *WFP Management Plan 2012–2014. Executive Summary. Follow up Briefing*, 5 October, Rome: World Food Programme.

White House (USA) (1994) 'National Security Strategy of Engagement and Enlargement', Government Printing Office, Washington, DC, July.

White, M. (2001) 'Wars of the Twentieth Century', *Historical Atlas of the Twentieth Century*, http://users.erols.com/mwhite28/war-list.htm (accessed 6.6.03).

Whittow, J. (1984) *The Penguin Dictionary of Physical Geography*, London: Penguin.

WHO (1998) 'Fifty Years of the World Health Organization in the Western Pacific Region', Report of the Regional Director to the Regional Committee for the Western Pacific, http://www.wpro.who.int/public/policy/50TH/50_toc.htm (accessed 1.8.02).

—— (1999a) Executive Board, 103rd Session, 18 January EB103/9.

—— (1999b) *World Health Report,* part 1, 'Health and Development in the Twentieth Century', Geneva: WHO.

—— (2000a) *Transport, Environment and Health*, edited by Dora, C. and Phillip, M., Copenhagen: WHO Regional Office for Europe European Series no. 89.

—— (2000b) *World Health Report 2000*, Geneva: World Health Organization.

—— (2001) 'Small Arms and Global Health: WHO Contribution to the UN Conference on Illicit Trade in Small Arms and Light Weapons', 9–20 July. WHO/NMH/VIP/01.1 Geneva: WHO.

—— (2002a) 'Roll Back Malaria', http://www.who.int/rbm (accessed 12.9.02).

—— (2002b) *World Health Report 2002*, Geneva: World Health Organization.

—— (2002c) *World Report on Violence and Health*, Geneva: World Health Organization.

—— (2003) *Structure of the WHO* http://www.who.int/aboutwho/en/structure.htm (accessed 1.8.02).

—— (2004) *World Health Report 2004,* Geneva: WHO.

—— (2004) *World Report on Road Traffic Injury Prevention*, Geneva: World Health Organization.

—— (2009) *Global Burden of Disease 2008*, Geneva: World Health Organization.

—— (2010) *Report on the Burden of Health Care Associate Infections Worldwide,* Geneva: World Health Organization.

—— (2011) *Global Burden of Disease 2008*, Geneva: World Health Organization.

—— (2012a) *Global Health Expenditure Atlas,* Geneva: World Health Organization.

—— (2012b) About WHO, http://www.who.int/about/en/ (accessed 16/8/12).

*Who's Who in the Twentieth Century* (1999) Oxford: Oxford University Press.

Wight, M. (1978) *Power Politics*, eds Bull, H. and Holbraad, C., Leicester: Leicester University Press.

Wilkinson, P. (1986) 'Fighting the Hydra: International Terrorism and the Rule of Law' in N. O'Sullivan (ed.) *Terror, Ideology and Revolution*, vol. 1, Oxford: Wheatsheaf: 205–24.

—— (1990) 'Fighting the Hydra: Terrorism and the Rule of Law', in Kegley, C. (ed.) *International Terrorism: Characteristics, Causes, Controls*, New York: St Martins Press: 253–8.

—— (2011) *Terrorism versus Democracy: The Liberal State Response*, Abingdon: Routledge.

Williams, P. (2001) 'Transnational Criminal Networks', in Arquilla and Ronfeldt (eds) *Networks and Netwars: The Future of Terror, Crime and Militancy*, Santa Monica: RAND: 61–97.

—— (2006) 'Strategy for a New World: Combating Terrorism and Transnational Crime', in Baylis, J., Wirtz, J., Cohen, E. and Gray, C. (eds) *Strategy in the Contemporary World*, 2nd edn, Oxford: Oxford University Press: 192–208.

Williams, P. and Woessner, P. (2000) 'Gangs go Nuclear', *World Today*, December: 7–9.

Wilson, N. and Thomson, G. (2005) 'Deaths from International Terrorism compared with Road Crash Deaths in OECD Countries', *Injury Prevention,* 11: 332–3.

Wirtz, J. (2002) 'A New Agenda for Security and Strategy?', in Baylis, J., Wirtz, J., Cohen, E. and Gray, C. *Strategy in the Contemporary World: An Introduction to Strategic Studies*, Oxford: Oxford University Press: 309–27.

Wisner, B. (2000) 'Disasters: What the United Nations and Its World Can Do', *United Nations Chronicle (online edition)* 38(4), http://www.un.org/Pubs/chronicle/2000/issue4/0400p6.htm (accessed 13.8.02).

Wolf, A. (2007) 'Shared Waters: Conflict and Cooperation', *Annual Review of Environmental Resources*, 32: 241–269.

Woolf, L. (1916) *International Government*, New York: Brentano's.

World Bank (1991) *World Development Report*, Oxford: Oxford University Press.

—— (1993) *World Development Report: Investing in Health*, Washington, DC.
—— (2003) *World Development Indicators Database*, http://www.worldbank.org/data/databytopic/GNIPC.pdf (accessed 25.6.03).
—— (2011) *Conflict, Security and Development: World Development Report 2011*, http://wdr2011.worldbank.org/fulltext (accessed 4.1.12).
World Congress on Drowning (2002) http://www.drowning.nl/csi/drowning.nsf/index/home/$file/home.htm (accessed 29.4.03).
World Meteorological Organization/United Nations Environmental Programme (2006) *UNEP/WMO Scientific Assessment of Ozone Depletion: 2006*, Global Ozone Research and Monitoring Project, Report No. 50, Geneva: WMO.
Wyn Jones, R. (1999) *Security, Strategy and Critical Theory*, Chapter 4, Boulder: Lynne Rienner, http://www.ciaonet.org/book/wynjones/wynjones04.html (accessed 14.3.3).
Yuval-Davis, N. (1997) *Gender and Nation*, London: Sage.
Zakaria, F. (1997) 'The Rise of Illiberal Democracy', *Foreign Affairs*, 76(6): 22–43.

# Index

Abyssinia, Italian invasion of 28, 34, 108
acid rain 15
Afghanistan, heroin industry 243
Afghanistan, Soviet invasion of 26, 29, 243
Afghanistan War (2001–2) 37, 40, 41, 85
African National Congress (ANC) 77
Aga Khan Foundation 261
Agenda for Peace, UN 37
Agent Orange 151–152
AIDS/HIV 15, 16–17, 123, 172, 173, 187–188, 189–190
air safety 218, 231
Al Jazeira 40
alcohol 178, 179, 230
Alexander the Great 160
Al-Kharusi, Wahid 230
al-Qa'ida 41, 44, 48, 53, 68–69, 70, 74, 75, 79–80, 82, 84, 85, 86, 87, 256
American Anthropological Association (AAA) 142
Amnesty International 132, 134
Anarchist terror 71
Anderson, B. 117
Anderson, W. 224
animal liberationists 73

Annan, K. 15, 198, 260
Apel, K.O. 139, 144, 265, 266
appeasement as response to terrorism 77–79
Arab–Israeli dispute 26, 29, 36, 50, 160
Argentina, financial crisis 105
Aristide, President 110
Arkhipov, Commander 49
armed forces, size of 52
Armed Islamic Group (Algeria) 68
Armed Revolutionary Nuclei (ARN) 71
Armenian genocide 127–129
arms control 46–50
Arnold, M. 208
Aryan Nations 70
Ashdown, Paddy 49, 213–214
Association of South East Asian Nations (ASEAN) 54, 210
asteroids 205–206
Atta, Mohammed 78
Aub Gaith, Suleiman 68
Augustine, St. 38
Aum Supreme Truth 70
Australia, national interest 4
avalanches 203
Axworthy, L. 16
Ayoob, M. 8